A Small Town in Ukraine

BERNARD WASSERSTEIN

A Small Town in Ukraine

The place we came from,
the place we went back to

ALLEN LANE
an imprint of
PENGUIN BOOKS

ALLEN LANE

UK | USA | Canada | Ireland | Australia
India | New Zealand | South Africa

Allen Lane is part of the Penguin Random House group of companies
whose addresses can be found at global.penguinrandomhouse.com

First published 2023
001

Copyright © Bernard Wasserstein, 2023

The moral right of the author has been asserted

Set in 10.5/14pt Sabon LT Std
Typeset by Jouve (UK), Milton Keynes
Printed and bound in Great Britain by Clays Ltd, Elcograf S.p.A.

The authorized representative in the EEA is Penguin Random House Ireland,
Morrison Chambers, 32 Nassau Street, Dublin D02 YH68

A CIP catalogue record for this book is available from the British Library

HB ISBN: 978–0–241–60922–4
TPB ISBN: 978–0–241–63270–3

For Charlotte and Tomer

Contents

Preface		ix
Acknowledgements		xv
List of Maps		xvii
List of Illustrations		xix
A Note on Place Names		xxi
1	The arrest	1
2	The three fishes	13
3	'The most splendid times'	27
4	The rise of the shtetl	41
5	The emperor's Krakowiec	57
6	The burning shtetl	79
7	Krakowiec to Berlin	101
8	Berlin to Krakowiec	113
9	Under three regimes	131
10	'*You* have nothing to worry about. *You* are one of *my* Jews'	149
11	'A little place – you won't have heard of it'	175
12	One fish	187
13	Return to Krakowiec	207
	Postscript	219
	Sources	223
	Notes	247
	Index	279

Preface

Krakowiec (*Krah-KOV-yets*) – the place we came from, the place we went back to. I first heard of it from my mother in the mid-1950s when I was about nine years old. She told me Krakowiec was the town in Poland from which my father's family hailed.

Actually, the name rang a curious bell in my childhood memory. Two or three years earlier, a visitor from the past had come to our home. His name was Majus. No doubt he had a forename but my father, if he mentioned him at all, always referred to him *tout court* by his surname, without 'Mr' or any other handle. I had the impression he did not welcome his arrival.

Majus (his forename, I later learned, was Pinkas, or more familiarly Pincze) was one of the few Jews from Krakowiec who had survived the Second World War. He talked with my father about his experiences. Then and later, I asked what he had said but for a long time my father would not reply. Perhaps he wanted to shield a child from dark shadows. Or maybe the reason was that he didn't altogether approve of Majus (who was later found guilty of operating an illegal still for the production of moonshine in the basement of his house in London). At any event, I discovered nothing of what our visitor related. I had to make do with the puppet glove monkey that he gave me, a creature whose inside felt warm and soft but whose exterior glared at me with a menacing grimace.

My mother had never been to Krakowiec and knew very little of the place. What with her relative ignorance and my father's stern reticence, I grew up knowing almost nothing about it. Yet throughout my youth I dreamt of this almost unmentionable, and therefore all the more mysterious, almost mythic, ancestral hearth.

Where exactly was Krakowiec? It was so small that it did not rate an appearance in our home atlas. Even when, years later, I consulted the largest-scale maps available, the answer was unclear, since it appeared to be smack on the border between Poland and the Soviet Union.

Suddenly, in 1989, the Iron Curtain was raised. With the disintegration of the Soviet Union two years later, Krakowiec emerged, as from a cloud, just inside the newly independent republic of Ukraine. Not long afterwards, in the company of my brother, I visited the town for the first time. It was an eerie, eye-opening experience, described later in this book, that insinuated into my mind a compulsive ambition: I would compensate for a lifetime of unrelieved curiosity about our origins by finding out everything that could be ascertained about Krakowiec and its connections with my family.

Pardonable genealogical curiosity burgeoned into an obsession. I spent the next three decades digging ever deeper into what turned out to be an immense historical quarry. I visited archives and libraries on several continents, consulted experts and struggled to acquire new languages. I had spent my life as a professional historian but now I penetrated further into the past than I had ever previously ventured. In the course of my research I built up vast data banks of official records, newspaper dispatches, census materials, registers of births, marriages and deaths, electoral results, medical reports, maps and photographs, as well as meteorological, geological, ecological, ornithological, architectural, judicial, military, ecclesiastical and every other category of information I could find. Soon I had assembled a veritable encyclopaedia of statistics and documentation, illuminating every aspect of a place that had once seemed unknowable. But all that was just the beginning.

Like the inhuman pedant Edward Casaubon in George Eliot's *Middlemarch*, with his project for the 'key to all mythologies', I conceived a crazily impossible aspiration: I would assemble a biographical dictionary of every single person in recorded history who had ever lived in Krakowiec. This would be no telephone directory but the life story of each inhabitant, a kind of Namierite super-prosopography. Sir Lewis Namier was the Polish-born English historian whose monumental *History of Parliament*, continued after his death, contains lives of

MPs (21,420 *so far*) and surveys of their constituencies (2,831 *so far*). More than sixty years after his death, the publication has reached only the year 1832. Namier's name will reappear in the story I have to tell.

Of course, my enterprise, like Casaubon's and Namier's, could never be completed. Yet driven by some inner need, I pursued it until it now encompasses entries for over seventeen thousand persons. At its peak, Krakowiec had a population of around two thousand. What I accumulated was thus an appreciable proportion of the total number of residents over the past six centuries. This Who's Who of Krakowiec includes Poles, Jews, Ukrainians, Germans, Russians, an Armenian (though I don't know his name), a French landscape designer and an infant girl born out of wedlock, the daughter of a Hungarian soldier garrisoned in the town. Some of my entries are merely half-faded names carved on tombstones in Latin, Cyrillic or Hebrew letters. Others are life histories that can be reconstructed in minute detail. Among them are serfs, aristocrats, craftsmen, merchants, rabbis, Christian clerics of the Roman and Greek Catholic rites, an eighteenth-century music-master, a nineteenth-century lady of leisure and a twentieth-century mass murderer revered today as a national hero. Most were humble folk but there were also a few prominent persons whose names and deeds reverberate down to our time. All these ghost-like figures, by dint of a gradual accretion of evidence, slowly acquired something close to flesh and blood, at any rate in my mind, so that I felt I had come to know and form indissoluble bonds with many of the people of the town.

No doubt to the relief of my readers, I have consigned the greater part of this heap of data to the dark side of my electronic retrieval system. In what follows there remains only alluvial sediment, historical gold dust relevant to my narrative. Out of the thousands of individuals I have come to know, sometimes as if they were intimates, just a handful are briefly recalled to life here as actors or witnesses.

In this autobiography of the period before I was born, I tell the story of Krakowiec, more particularly that of the Jews of this typical east European shtetl (small town), and most of all that of my family and our relationship with the place. By peering through this keyhole, I want to observe and understand how some of the great forces that determined the history of our time could affect ordinary people.

A central character in this narrative bears my name, though he is not me. I never met my grandfather Bernhard (known as Berl) Wasserstein, so this book is in part an account of my search for him and for those fragments of him that I find in myself.

In the course of my scholarly training, I was taught to eschew the first person in writing, to strain for impersonal objectivity and to address the past, *sine ira et studio*, as from an Olympian height. But such constraints collapsed as I investigated the history of my own family and explored its twists and turns. Above all, I wanted to understand how they – we – I – reacted to those events, always in our own way.

My goal has been to balance a filiopietistic reverence for my forebears with the historian's duty to respect the rules of evidence. Yet in spite of all my assiduous data-gathering, there was one area – the most important – that I could barely penetrate: my grandfather's head. That is because he left little in the way of diaries, letters and so on – what the Dutch-Jewish historian of the Shoah Jacques Presser called 'ego-documents'. The English writer Craig Brown has expressed the difficulty well: 'The real life of anyone takes place largely in the mind, yet it is only the secondary, external stuff – people met, places visited, opinions expressed, and so forth – that is accessible to the biographer. Unless they are spoken or written down, an individual's thoughts evaporate into nothing. The subject's head is, you might say, a closed book.'[1]

Until recently I never had much time for the school of historians who simulate the ability to enter other people's inner life, as in 'What must have been the thoughts of Napoleon and Kutuzov as they contemplated their forces at Borodino . . .?' Yes, I admit Leo Tolstoy essayed exactly that in *War and Peace*, with triumphant results both for fiction and perhaps for an understanding of history. I have hardly dared to follow in his footsteps. There are no facts or quotations here that cannot be substantiated from the sources given at the back of the book. I have nevertheless felt driven, at certain points, to speculate about the interior workings of the mind of my grandfather and others. Where I have taken that imaginative leap, I have done my best to make it clear that I am doing so. Often this was on the basis of glimmers of human insight derived from interviews with elderly survivors of the events I describe. One may stand for many: my father, in several recorded conversations near the end of his life, finally shared with me early memories of his youth and of Krakowiec. These have been my most vital and inspiring sources for this book.

My purpose has not been to extract lessons from this slice of the past. Each of my readers may choose whether and how to do that. I want rather to explore Krakowiec, 'a little place, you won't have heard of it', as my father used to say, and its people, with my family at its – and my – heart.

Acknowledgements

I thank the staffs of all the libraries and archives in which I worked on this book, as well as all the people who shared their memories with me. Brandeis University; the universities of Glasgow and Chicago; the Oxford Centre for Hebrew and Jewish Studies; the National Humanities Center in North Carolina; the Wissenschaftskolleg zu Berlin; the Swedish Collegium for Advanced Studies, Uppsala; and the Center for Urban History of East-Central Europe, Lviv, all supported my research. I am also grateful for the assistance I received in all sorts of ways from Eliyana R. Adler, Guido Alfani, Olena Andronatiy, Gerhard Artl, Steven E. Aschheim, David Assaf, David Barchard, Yehuda Bauer, Isabel Benjamin, Susan Benjamin, Tomasz Blusiewicz, Frederick E. Brenk SJ, Samuel K. Cohn Jr., Ihor Derevjanyy, Willy Dreßen, Thomas Ertman, Celia Fassberg, Steven Fassberg, Julia Fein, Rachel Feinmark, Sheila Fitzpatrick, John P. Fox, Sylvia Fried, Sir Martin Gilbert, Steven C. Gold, Tibor Gold, Leah Goldman, Yuliya Goldshteyn, John A. S. Grenville, Tony Grenville, Patricia Grimsted, Jane Grossberg, Israel Guttman, Shirley Haasnoot (most especially), Stawell Heard, John Paul Himka, Marc Jansen, George Kantorowicz, Kamil Kiedos, Hillel Kieval, Logan Kleinwaks, Kinga Kosmala, Fayvish Kressel, Jan Ledóchowski, Madeline Levine, Steven Lovatt, John Löwenhardt, Noah Lucas, Eugen Lunio, David G. Marwell, Evan Mawdsley, Barbara Meyerowitz, Reuven Mohr, Sarah Panzer, John Partyka, Anna Paton, Antony Polonsky, James F. X. Pratt SJ, Shimon Redlich, Paul Salstrom, Jenneken Schouten, Bozena Shallcross, Denis Shamo, Hannah Shlomi, Dovid Silberman, Nancy Spiegel, Harold Strecker, Lydia Tasenkevich, Leah Teichthal,

Maria Vachko, David J. Wasserstein and Joshua Zimmerman. Finally, I thank Stuart Proffitt, Alice Skinner, Anna Wilson and their colleagues at Allen Lane/Penguin Books and my literary agents, David Higham Associates in London and Folio Literary Management in New York.

List of Maps

1. East Central Europe   xxii
2. Galicia under the Habsburgs, 1772–1918   26
3. Krakowiec and its environs   40
4. Krakowiec in the early twentieth century   54
5. War in Galicia, 1914–15   78
6. East Central Europe between the wars   100
7. Occupied Poland, 1939–45   130
8. Paths taken 1898–1944: Berl and Addi Wasserstein   172
9. Poland and Ukraine, 2022   206

List of Illustrations

Every effort has been made to contact all copyright holders. The publisher will be pleased to amend in future printings any errors or omissions brought to their attention.

1. Coat of arms of Krakowiec (public domain)
2. View of Krakowiec over the lake, 1847, by Maciej Bogusz Zygmunt Stęczyński (Stefanyk National Library, Lviv)
3. Ignacy Cetner in his pleasure garden (nineteenth-century caricature)
4. 'Hermit's hut' in Krakowiec palace garden, 1847, by Maciej Bogusz Zygmunt Stęczyński (Stefanyk National Library, Lviv)
5. Countess Anna Potocka (*née* Cetner), 1791, by Elizabeth Vigée-Le Brun (public domain, via Wikimedia Commons)
6. Krakowiec palace, 1834, drawing by Kajetan Kielisiński (Stefanyk National Library, Lviv)
7. Greek Catholic church of St Nicholas in Krakowiec, photograph *c.* 1900
8. Roman Catholic church of St James in Krakowiec, *c.* 1900
9. Market square in Krakowiec, *c.* 1915 (postcard)
10. Winter scene in Krakowiec between the wars
11. Synagogue in Krakowiec, early twentieth century
12. Hebrew school in Krakowiec, 1933

13. Refugees fleeing from Galicia, 1914 (Imperial War Museum)

14. Kampel family, Krakowiec, between the wars

15. Wasserstein family, Berlin, 1934

16. Addi Wasserstein, Zbąszyń, 1939

17. Addi Wasserstein, Rome, 1940

18. General Stanisław Maczek (Central Military Archives, Warsaw)

19. Father Włodzimierz Ledóchowski

20. General Ignacy Ledóchowski (Central Military Archives, Warsaw)

21. Soviet war memorial in Krakowiec, 2019

22. Roman Shukhevych

23. Mikola Mikhailovich Olanek

24. Ukrainian postage stamp honouring Shukhevych, 2007

25. Shukhevych monument in Krakowiec, 2019

26. Memorial tablet for Jews of Jaworów and Krakowiec, 2019

27. Old and new Greek Catholic churches, Krakowiec, 2019

28. Ukrainian war refugees passing through Krakovets to Poland, 2021 (Dan Kitwood / Getty Images)

A Note on Place Names

One of the bugbears of writing about the history of eastern Europe is that many places have had more than one name. For example, the city known today by its Ukrainian name of Lviv was called Lwów by the Poles who ruled it before 1772 and again in the interwar period. The Austrians who governed it from 1772 to 1918 called it Lemberg, as did its German occupiers between 1941 and 1944. In official documents during much of its history, the name appears in its Latin form, Leopolis. Similarly, Krakowiec to Poles was Krakovets to Ukrainians and Krakowitz to Jews. To simplify matters, I have generally used the Polish forms for the period up to the end of the Second World War. For the more recent period, however, it seems more appropriate to employ the Ukrainian names in common usage for places now within the borders of Ukraine. Of course, all rules have exceptions: in cases where there are well-established English names, such as Warsaw or Cracow, I have preferred those over their Polish equivalents.

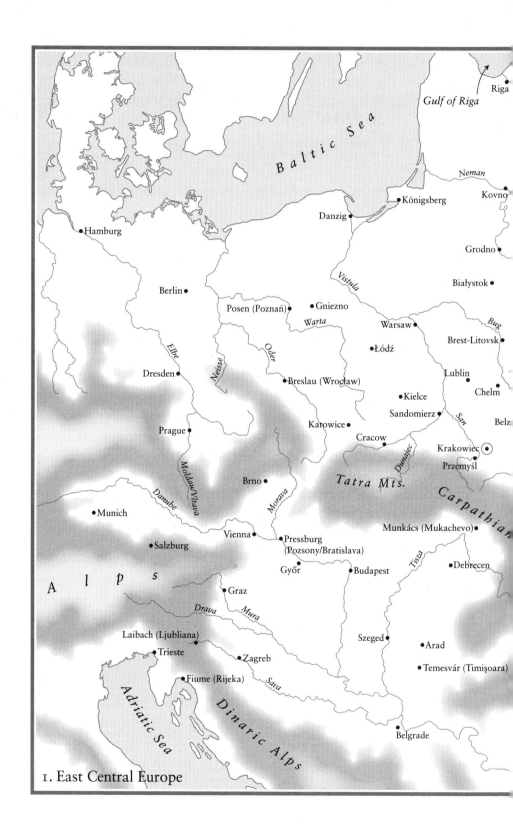

1. East Central Europe

I

The arrest

Berl Wasserstein was arrested one morning, though he had done nothing wrong. A respectable, middle-aged, middle-class businessman, he had always kept on the right side of the law. His ensuing ordeal was no less Kafkaesque than that of the protagonist of *The Trial*; but whereas Joseph K.'s was nightmarish fantasy, Berl's was implacable reality.

In the early hours of Friday 28 October 1938, policemen from the Berlin constabulary arrived at an apartment at 72 Neue Friedrichstrasse, awakened the sleeping occupants with loud knocking and asked for Bernhard (Berl) Wasserstein. They inspected his identity papers and handed him a letter from the Police President of Berlin informing him that he must leave the territory of the German Reich within twenty-four hours. Failure to comply would result in his forcible deportation. His son Abraham (known as Addi), a seventeen-year-old schoolboy, was handed a similar letter and told that he would have to go as well.[1] The two were given a few minutes to pack. They were allowed to take with them one small suitcase each, some food, and no more than ten marks in cash (worth about four US dollars at the time).

About eighteen thousand people, all Jews, were arrested all over Germany in the course of that night. None was accused of any crime. They were all told they must leave the country forthwith. Berl had been thinking of emigrating – but not like this.

Since the Nazi takeover of power in 1933, Jews in Germany had learned from experience that there was little to be gained by refusing to do as they were told by the authorities. Berl in any case was not the sort of person to argue with the police. He had spent his whole adult life building up a small manufacturing business on the basis of scrupulous honesty and avoidance of anything that might smack of sharp practice. In spite of ever-worsening Nazi lawlessness, he believed in the *Rechtsstaat* (the rule of law). He was a self-controlled man who knew how to keep his dignity, especially in front of his family. So he and Addi packed their bags and went along quietly.

Berl's wife, Czarna, and his daughter, Charlotte (Lotte), aged thirteen, looked on aghast. Czarna wept as her husband and son were escorted away, first to the local police station, then to the central police headquarters of Berlin. There was no violence, and the policemen behaved with exemplary formality. Although Adolf Hitler had held power for more than five years, the Berlin police, like much of the German capital's population, was not yet completely Nazified. So Berl and Addi, while bewildered and disoriented, were not in fear for their lives – yet.

There was a twisted logic to these events.

Berl's birthplace, Krakowiec, lay within the borders of the Austrian empire until 1918. Upon the fall of the Habsburg monarchy at the end of the First World War, and following a period of upheaval in the region that lasted until 1921, the town found itself in the reborn Republic of Poland. Former residents of the area consequently ceased being Austrians.[2] Berl, by then living in Germany, as well as his children born there, were henceforth Polish citizens.

The mass deportation order of 1938 was not the first manifestation in Germany of hostility to *Ostjuden* (Jewish immigrants from eastern Europe). They had been targets of xenophobic animosity for several decades. In 1885–86 ten thousand Jews had been expelled to Russian Poland on the orders of Otto von Bismarck in his capacity as Minister-President of the Prussian government. Although another twenty thousand gentiles had been deported at the same time, a significant motive behind the order was anti-Jewish and the measure was seen as the 'first tangible success' of the anti-Semitic movement.[3]

The aversion to *Ostjuden* was not limited to anti-Semites. German-born Jews, most of whom were themselves only one or two generations distant from newcomers from the east, feared that a further influx would endanger their own hard-won emancipation. They tended to look down on the immigrants as primitive, dirty and something of an embarrassment. Their presence complicated German Jews' efforts to present themselves as just another 'German tribe like the Saxons, Bavarians, or Wends' – as the philosopher and statesman Walther Rathenau termed them.[4] And *Ostjuden* themselves often laboured under something of an inferiority complex – exemplified, for example, by an article in Yiddish protesting, 'We have no reason to feel ashamed.'[5]

The Weimar Republic, established after the German Revolution of November 1918, was founded with a model democratic constitution and a veneer of liberal values. Yet from the outset nationalists were persuaded that Jews and leftists had 'stabbed Germany in the back', bringing about the downfall of the German empire and the country's defeat in the First World War. These extreme right-wingers sought vengeance through anti-Semitic agitation. *Ostjuden*, in particular, were denounced as carriers of bacilli, criminality and Bolshevism.

In the early post-war years many immigrants were rounded up in Jewish districts of Berlin and threatened with expulsion to their places of origin. Polish border officials often refused to admit them. As a result, several thousand '*fremdstämmige Ausländer*' (foreigners of alien stock), including women and children, were interned in former prisoner of war camps in various parts of Germany. There were complaints of poor hygienic conditions and ill-treatment of internees. Mathilde Wurm, a Jewish member of the Reichstag representing the USPD (the far-left Social Democrat party), denounced what she and others called 'concentration camps'.[6] They were eventually closed, partly on the ground of cost. Some of the inmates were deported, others allowed to remain in the country. But the position of *Ostjuden* in Germany remained fragile. Jewish applicants for naturalization, even under the Weimar regime, confronted almost insuperable obstacles and most *Ostjuden* remained Polish citizens.

Although by 1938 Berl Wasserstein had been living in Germany for nearly two decades, he had never attempted to take out German citizenship. As things turned out, it would have made little difference had he done so. From August 1933 the Nazi regime prohibited naturalization of *Ostjuden* altogether. Many of those who had previously been granted German citizenship were now denaturalized. Actually, Berl's legal position might have been even worse if he had been naturalized, since, upon revocation of German citizenship, he would have become stateless, as happened to many German Jews, whereas he still held a Polish passport.

Anti-Jewish oppression in the Third Reich quickened after the *Anschluss*, the annexation of Austria by Germany in March 1938. Hitler was accorded a hero's welcome when he arrived in Vienna to inaugurate the union of his native land with Germany. Cardinal Theodor Innitzer, later a critic of Nazism, ordered church bells to be rung in his honour. German anti-Semitic laws were extended to the 182,000 Jews of Austria, who became victims of vicious persecution. In the Austrian capital they were subjected to public humiliation. The elderly chief rabbi was among those ordered to clean the city's pavements with a toothbrush in front of jeering crowds. Jewish-owned businesses were seized. Jewish children were ejected from public schools. The concentration camp at Dachau, near Munich, saw an influx of new inmates. In consequence of all this, the many thousands of Jewish residents of Austria who held Polish nationality desperately sought refuge elsewhere.

A mass migration of Polish Jews from Austria to Poland suddenly seemed imminent. The Polish government reacted with dismay. Poland already held more than three million Jews, 10 per cent of its population. Anti-Jewish feeling was rampant and the government was, if anything, inclined to seek avenues for Jewish emigration rather than open the door to immigration. On 18 March, just six days after German troops marched into Austria, a bill was presented to the Polish parliament providing that Polish citizens who had lived abroad continuously for more than five years and who 'had given up all contact with the Polish state' could be deprived of their citizenship. Such persons would consequently no longer possess any automatic right to re-enter Poland. The bill passed through all its stages in the lower house and Senate within eleven days. A communiqué issued by the semi-official Iskra news agency explained that the purpose of the law was 'to make all Polish citizens residing abroad realise that the Polish state requires them to maintain an actively favourable attitude and not a passive and indifferent one towards it'.[7]

German officials viewed these Polish actions with concern. They feared that the Polish measure would saddle them with large numbers of Jews who could not be removed. On 9 April, Werner Best, head of the Foreigners Police Department of the Gestapo in Berlin, issued a circular ordering that Polish citizens seeking renewal of their residence papers must henceforth be granted no more than six months' permission to stay. Best's order did not mention the word 'Jew'; but to make his meaning clear, he specified that the order would not apply to *Volksdeutsche* (i.e. those regarded by the Nazis as 'Aryans', racial Germans) who were Polish citizens. Polish agricultural workers in Germany, very few of whom were Jews, would be similarly exempt.[8]

In the course of the summer of 1938 conditions for Jews throughout Germany worsened. In Berlin, houses, cafés and cinemas were raided in search of Jews to be sent to concentration camps. Jewish-owned shops were attacked and looted. 'It is no exaggeration,' wrote a British consul, 'to say that Jews have been hunted like rats in their homes.'[9]

On 15 October the Polish Minister of the Interior issued a regulation requiring the inspection by consular personnel of all Polish passports that had been issued abroad. Those considered valid would be stamped accordingly. Those without such an endorsement would become invalid for admission to Poland at midnight on 29 October. Once that happened, it would be impossible for the Germans to send home Polish Jews, of whom there were estimated to be as many as seventy or eighty thousand in the Reich. Long lines formed outside the Polish consulate in Vienna as Jews sought to validate their passports to enable them to return to Poland.

Polish policy-makers were plainly responding to the events in Austria, and the new measures were directly aimed at Jews. Although this was obvious to all, the Poles were somewhat embarrassed about the law's reception overseas. An official of the Foreign Ministry, in conversation with a British diplomat, 'denied that there was any connexion between events in Austria and the Polish Government's decision to proceed with this law which he described as only an instalment of a long overdue revision of the Polish nationality laws'. He admitted that the new edict 'might apply amongst others to persons of nominally Polish citizenship resident in Austria', but denied that it 'had any specific anti-Semitic significance'. In any case, he added reassuringly, 'it was intended to apply the new law, if and when it came into force, with moderation.'[10] In conversations with foreign diplomats, the

Foreign Ministry maintained that the object was to prevent mass expulsion of Polish Jews from Germany. The Poles' action, however, had the opposite effect.

On 26 October, just seventy-two hours before Polish citizens with unendorsed passports would lose the right to return to their country, the head of the German security police, Reinhard Heydrich, ordered the termination of all residence permits of Polish Jews in Germany.[11] His subordinate, Best, immediately issued a top priority instruction that all Polish Jews in possession of valid passports were to be arrested immediately, assigned for deportation, taken to the Polish frontier, and expelled. The operation, dubbed the 'Polenaktion', was to be completed by 29 October and the highest possible number, especially of adult males, was to be dispatched across the border before the deadline.[12]

A few days before the arrests, rumours began to spread that something sinister was afoot. Fearing the worst, some Polish Jews in Berlin went into hiding or took the train to Poland to beat the deadline for validation of their passports. Most, like Berl Wasserstein, awaited events, half-expecting, or at any rate hoping, that somehow things would work out.

According to a police report, about three thousand men were arrested in Berlin on 28 October.[13] Berl and Addi were taken with the others from the police headquarters to the Ostbahnhof station and put on trains heading for the Polish border. Up to seven hundred people were put on each train. Some were given pork sandwiches, a typical Nazi provocation directed at orthodox Jews like Berl, who had never in his life allowed pig-meat to touch his lips. The carriages were sealed and guarded. Passengers were not permitted to leave their compartments. Seven kilometres from the border, they were ordered off the train and told to walk forward. The Berlin police, with their punctilious decorum, had been replaced by other uniformed men with more brutal methods. By now it was dark. There was great confusion. People were screaming. Stragglers or those having difficulty with their luggage were beaten. When they arrived at the frontier village of Bentschen (Zbąszyń), Polish border guards admitted the first few but then forbade entry to the rest. Consequently a great mass of terrified people, including Berl and Addi, were stuck in darkness in no-man's-land, in open countryside. Fortunately the weather was mild.

Then it began to rain.

Although the Germans had forewarned the Poles, the expulsions came to them as an unwelcome surprise. The Polish government had made no preparations to deal with the arrival of thousands of deportees, perhaps not believing that the Germans would really carry out their threat.[14] The head of the Polish border police reported that armed units were massed in large numbers on the German side of the frontier. They stamped their feet and rattled their weapons as their commanders bellowed out orders, 'in order, it seemed to me [the Polish commandant stated], to ensure that we wouldn't try to send the expellees back.' At one point a group of several hundred Jews staged a sit-in on the German side of the frontier, refusing to set foot on Polish soil. 'As the [German] police and border guard units couldn't deal with that,' the Polish officer continued, 'German soldiers charged at them with fixed bayonets, punching and kicking. With blows from their bayonets and rifle-butts, they forced them over the frontier.'[15]

This description was corroborated by many journalistic and diplomatic accounts. The British ambassador in Warsaw reported:

> The worst conditions were at Zbaszyn on the main line from Berlin to Poznan. Here some 6,500 arrived, of whom a proportion were women and children. They had been compelled to detrain at the German frontier station and to proceed on foot across the frontier. Germans are alleged to have fired a machine-gun into the air, causing utter confusion and panic, so that families scattered and lost what few belongings they had been able to bring with them. The local Polish authorities showed goodwill, but had no accommodation and many of the Jews had, of course, no idea where to go, having had little connexion with Poland. After some delay the military authorities provided tents. I understand that 1,500 have now left for various destinations, but that 5,000 still remain, since the Polish authorities hope that the negotiations with Germany may result in their being allowed to return to their homes.[16]

Other diplomats sent similar dispatches. The American Embassy in Warsaw informed the State Department: 'At Zbaszyn, on the main railway line from Berlin to Warsaw, it has been learned that the refugees were handled very roughly and that as a result they arrived in Poland in great disorder. Many had lost what few belongings they had managed to bring with them including their travel documents. Many were hysterical, and it is said that a few died of fright and several cases of temporary insanity were reported.'[17]

Addi later recalled little of this journey or of the nightmarish scenes at the border. Perhaps his memory censored deeply disturbing events. Others who travelled the same route recorded the episode in horrifying detail and recounted their experiences to newspaper correspondents. Although the Nazi regime had steadily tightened the vice around Jews in Germany since 1933, this overnight, mass expulsion aroused worldwide censure.

The next day the German news agency issued an official explanation. This sought to shift the burden of responsibility on to Poland, claiming that the deportations had been precipitated by the Polish decision to recall passports for special endorsement. If this endorsement were refused, the statement pointed out candidly, the Polish Jews 'would become a permanent burden to Germany, and the German Government would no longer be able to avail themselves of the possibility, which is the legal right of all States, to expel them as undesirable aliens'.[18]

After a few hours the expellees were allowed to proceed to the Polish border town of Zbąszyń (*see map on p. 172*) but no further. In effect, they became prisoners in an improvised detention camp. At first, they took shelter in stinking cowsheds and stables 'that had previously been condemned [as unsuitable] for the use of horses', ten men to each horsebox.[19]

The camp at Zbąszyń has been called a 'special hell'.[20] So it felt to its denizens at the time, even if it pales by comparison with later horrors perpetrated by the Nazis and their accomplices. Some of the refugees, including Addi, were attacked and roughed up by local Polish youths. The episode left him with an enduring contempt for Poles. Years afterwards he recalled with fury the sight of Polish policemen manhandling Jewish women.

Jewish organizations mobilized immediately to help the deportees. At dawn on the first morning after their arrival at Zbąszyń, relief workers arrived to provide food and supplies. The Polish office of the

'Joint' (American Jewish Joint Distribution Committee) supplied money and logistical support. The internees were given blankets, medicine and books in German, Polish and Yiddish. 'The Polish Jews behaved like angels,' Addi later recalled.

Among those who came to organize relief was the historian Emanuel Ringelblum, later to find posthumous fame as chronicler of the Warsaw ghetto. In early December he recorded: 'Zbąszyń has become a symbol for the defencelessness of Polish Jews. Jews have been humiliated to the level of lepers, to fourth-class citizens, and as a result we are all affected by this terrible tragedy.'[21]

Another visitor was Wilhelm Alexandrowicz, a leader in Cracow of the Jewish socialist-autonomist party, the Bund. He stayed several months in Zbąszyń, organizing aid efforts. Addi used to discuss with him the competing claims of Bundism, Communism and Zionism. He remembered 'the look of disgust' on Alexandrowicz's face when they talked about the show trials in the Soviet Union. In accordance with Bundist doctrine, Alexandrowicz rejected the idea that the Jews' home was in Palestine. He insisted 'that his place was in the country where his forefathers had lived for a thousand years and that he and other Jews had the right to insist on their identity in that country'. Addi later reflected: 'He was wrong for the right reasons and the Zionists turned out to have been right, tragically so, for the wrong reasons.'[22] Alexandrowicz left a deep impression on the teenager. Many years later Addi wrote: 'He was an honourable man of whom I have often thought and whom I always seem to remember when I think of Polish Jewry.' He never saw him again. Alexandrowicz died in the ghetto of Tarnów, a small town between Cracow and Krakowiec, in 1942.

Some of the deportees were allowed by the Polish authorities to proceed to the interior of the country: unaccompanied minors who were sent to relatives or children's homes, old people requiring hospital treatment, or persons who could show visas for departure to foreign countries. But several thousand, including Berl and Addi, remained at Zbąszyń. The refugees soon outnumbered the permanent population of the town. Many were accommodated in a disused mill owned by a local Jew. Eventually some were able to rent rooms, or rather beds, from local residents. For the remainder of their joint stay, Berl and Addi shared such a rental, taking turns to sleep. All exits from the town into Polish territory were guarded by police who arrested those attempting to leave 'illegally'. Hygienic conditions were rudimentary. Food was strictly rationed: potato soup was a staple of the diet. During waking hours there was little to do. Some training courses and language classes were organized. Deportee soccer teams played against locals. When the weather grew warmer in the spring of 1939, people could swim in the nearby lake. Soon afterwards, however, the local authority announced that, 'for sanitary reasons', camp residents would be restricted to using the beach only at certain hours.[23] As the weeks of internment dragged into months, some of the expellees became severely depressed. A few committed suicide.

Among the deportees at Zbąszyń was the family of Herschel Grynszpan, a young Polish Jew who had been born in Hanover but was living in Paris as a *clandestin* (illegal immigrant) at the time of the deportations. In a state of extreme distress, outraged and anguished by the wrong done to his family, Herschel went to the German embassy in Paris on 7 November, obtained access to Counsellor Ernst vom Rath, and shot him. The diplomat died in hospital two days later.

The day following the attack, the State Secretary of the German Foreign Ministry, Ernst von Weizsäcker, met the Polish ambassador in Berlin. Weizsäcker remarked that he 'would not be surprised' if the assassination led 'to a very considerable increase in the severity of German measures against the Polish Jews'. The ambassador protested vigorously against the deportations. Weizsäcker countered that, as a result of the Polish government's actions, a 'clump of forty to fifty thousand stateless formerly Polish Jews would be left in the Germans' lap.'[24]

The Poles were unsympathetic to the Germans' predicament. Their Foreign Minister, Józef Beck, spoke darkly of retaliatory measures and officials considered counter-deportations. The Minister of the Interior issued instructions that German citizens (Jews only) and their families resident in Poland should be taken to the border and thrown out. The Foreign Ministry, however, objected that to single out Jews would appear racist. The German ambassador warned that any German-Jewish expellee who arrived in Germany would be sent straight to a concentration camp. A few people were deported from Poland but then driven back over the frontier by the Germans. In the end, the Poles decided counter-expulsions would serve no useful purpose. They turned instead to consider other forms of retaliation, including economic measures. Unwilling to escalate the issue, the Germans suspended the expulsions for the time being and declared themselves willing to open negotiations with the Poles.[25]

Meanwhile the murder of vom Rath was seized on by the Nazis as an intolerable provocation. On the night of 9–10 November mobs of Nazi thugs raided thousands of Jewish homes and Jewish-owned shops throughout Germany, plundering and smashing windows in what came to be called the Kristallnacht (night of broken glass). Synagogues all over the country were burned down. Brownshirts attacked Jews in the street. Hundreds were killed or injured. Twenty thousand people were arrested and thrown into prison or concentration camps. The government pretended that the violence was a spontaneous upsurge of popular indignation, sparked by the assassination in Paris; in reality, it was a state-sponsored pogrom, organized by the security apparatus and the Nazi party.

Kristallnacht opened the way to a new and even more barbarous stage of Nazi persecution of Jews. On 12 November Hermann Göring, the second most powerful man in the regime, presided over a meeting of senior Nazi officials. The purpose of the gathering was to give effect to an instruction from Hitler 'that the Jewish question be now, once and for all, coordinated and solved, one way or another'. The officials decided that all remaining Jewish property must now be 'Aryanized' so that 'the Jew would be eliminated from the German economy.' The German Jews would have to pay a collective fine of one billion Reichsmarks as an 'atonement penalty' for their 'abominable crimes'. Insurance companies would be barred from paying compensation to Jews for damage caused during the Kristallnacht. That would, after all, be 'insane', said Göring. Instead, such payments would be made to the government. Jewish-owned apartment buildings were to be requisitioned. New discriminatory measures against Jews were discussed, barring them from theatres, cinemas, circuses, public baths, parks, resorts and 'the German forest'. 'Non-Aryans' were to be segregated in schools and on trains. There was talk of forcing all Jews in German cities into ghettos. Heydrich said they should go further: the Jews should be 'kicked out of Germany'. In the meantime, those who remained should be marked out with a special 'insignia'. Finally, in the event of a war in the near future, 'it goes without saying,' Göring said, 'that we in Germany should first of all let it come to a showdown with the Jews.'[26]

Czarna Wasserstein and her daughter Lotte had remained at home because in the German capital, though not in the rest of the country, women were exempt from deportation. Probably the reason was logistical – the sheer numbers involved. No doubt the Nazis calculated that, with their menfolk gone, the women would in due course follow. The economic measures introduced by the Nazis after the Kristallnacht percolated down to their level. All Jewish-owned businesses were ordered to close, so Berl's livelihood was gone. Most remaining Jewish assets were confiscated. Czarna and Lotte were reduced to penury. A resourceful, resilient woman, Czarna somehow kept going and focused on caring for her daughter. But the outlook was grim.

Berl and Addi, trapped in Zbąszyń, could do nothing to help them. As weeks stretched into months, they contemplated their plight. They were being told to go back to Krakowiec, a place that Berl had left more than two decades before and that Addi hardly knew. Berl had no prospect of earning a living there. Addi would be unable to complete his education in a small town where there was no decent school and where, in any case, he did not know the language.

The Germans wanted to get rid of them. The Poles would not admit them. Neither Germany nor Poland seemed willing to recognize them as citizens, barely even as fellow human beings. But what was this place, Krakowiec, to which they were told on the one hand they must return and on the other that they must not enter?

2

The three fishes

Two axes and a flint knife-blade constitute the earliest surviving evidence of human habitation in Krakowiec, indications of the existence of prehistoric man in 'Red Ruthenia'.[1] The region acquired this name in later centuries, allegedly after the Turco-Mongol colour system for directions, in which 'red' meant 'south' – or alternatively alluding to reddish-brown deposits known to geologists as 'Krakowiec clays'.

Krakowiec is situated forty-three miles west of the regional capital Lwów, today known as Lviv, a little to the east of the San River (*see map on p. xxii*). Sitting amid swamps and sandy ground, it is surrounded by woods as well as good agricultural land, both arable, suitable for grain cultivation, and pasture, suitable for dairy farming.

The town skirts the western shore of the Krakowiec lake, sometimes called a pond, though it is larger than that suggests. In the course of history, its watery surroundings furnished Krakowiec with some protection against attack as well as providing an aquatic crown of sparkling beauty. On clear summer nights, the lake's surface glittered like quicksilver, reflecting the stars and the moon.

Just before harvest, local people would hunt for snails in the mud at the water's edge and, for want of much else, would eat them with bread. One nineteenth-century observer cautioned that this practice adversely affected residents' health, attributing to it their noticeably gaunt, pallid faces.[2] Snails being *trayf* (not kosher), Jews could not consume them. Whether, as a result, they had more healthy physiognomies our chronicler does not report.

Winters were harsh. Average night-time temperatures descended to minus 5°C (23°F). The lake and streams froze, melting only in late spring. If the winter was mild, skating children sometimes fell into the

water. In the rainy season flooding was frequent. The lake was encir-
cled by a profusion of bulrushes that grew to as high as eight feet.
Townspeople used to cut the watery reeds on the shoreline, dry them,
and use them to make baskets, fill mattresses and thatch the roofs of
their cottages. When the lake was frozen solid, hopeful anglers would
break holes in the ice and lower hooked lines. Great patience was
required for, as Izaak Walton noted, the carp, 'a very subtle fish and
hard to be caught', is reluctant to bite in the cold.[3]

The lake and neighbouring artificial ponds were noted for the suc-
culence of these carp, some of which grew to an impressive size.
Fishermen identified three types: common carp, often blackish-gold in
colour, a larger relative of the ornamental goldfish; mirror carp, with
shiny, irregular scales; and the rarer leather carp, with few or no scales
at all.[4] All three commanded high prices at the markets in Krakowiec
and Lwów. Christians customarily ate carp at their Christmas Eve feast,
as Poles do to this day. Jews ground it into balls, added meal, finely
chopped onions, root vegetables, seasoning, and (in this region) a pinch
of sugar, and served it on the Sabbath and holidays as *gefilte fish*.

Much of the area around the town was wooded with oak, birch,
beech and spruce, and, on higher ground, willow, hawthorn, poplar
and black alder. Deer, wild boar and wolves roamed the forest. A Fris-
ian traveller who visited the district in the late seventeenth century
described the southward vista towards Krakowiec: beech and linden
trees spread out in a forest, through which the town could be glimpsed
on the lowland; from the trees he heard the cooing of turtle-doves.[5]

Prickly stemmed wild teasels sprouted in the woods: their seeds
served as provender for moths and birds; their purple heads dried,
leaving hard combs that could be used to 'raise the nap' on wool. In
the dappled sunlight of open woodland, one might come across the
lilac bloom of the common teasel or the exquisite lady's slipper orchid,
with its golden, slipper-like sac, splotched in red on the inside. In late
spring, sandworts appeared near the water, their delicate white flowers
attracting butterflies (at least 1,700 varieties of Lepidoptera were
recorded in the region).[6]

The rich flora of the countryside provided material for many folk
remedies in use among the peasantry. In the sandy soil around the lake
was to be found the hairy, greyish-stemmed 'weedy cudweed', with tiny

yellow heads, said to be a cure for all kinds of ailments. The opium poppy, though unsuitable, owing to climatic conditions in the region, for use in the manufacture of morphine, was placed under the pillows of infants in the belief that it would help them go to sleep. The pretty, lavender-coloured germander was thought to protect against conception when worn by girls during lovemaking. And the common horsetail, found in meadows, was used to treat gonorrhoea.[7]

A rich variety of birdlife was attracted by the woods, marshes and orchards. Lapwings (peewits) and capercaillies (wood-grouse) were common. Wintering buzzards would flap their wings and drop into aggressive 'display stoops'. In the spring wild duck, warblers, and swallows would appear; occasionally also exotic-looking hoopoes, with their extraordinary, pinkish-brown, fan-shaped crests and long, rapier-like bills. On warm evenings the song of the nightingale might be heard. Storks were particularly beloved and householders would welcome them with scraps of food and wheels on the roof, on which they might build their huge nests. Sometimes storks sub-let accommodation within their dwellings to smaller birds such as sparrows or starlings. Herons and cormorants built nests on a little island in the lake. The ruff, a summer visitor from Africa, looking like a plump, over-dressed archduchess, seemed bizarrely out of place among the bogs and ponds. In the town, giant murders of scavenging crows would swirl in the air and swoop down in their hundreds, cawing harshly and opportunistically seizing and gobbling up infant ducklings or goslings.

On a sunny summer morning, man could feel at one with nature – as in the bucolic prose of the Ukrainian writer Ivan Franko, born in a village of the Lwów region:

A broad band of rye swayed slightly and rippled in the light, cool breeze. The rye was like gold. Its ripe ears bent under the weight of grain and pearly droplets of dew. The tall, slender ... yellow stems stood among the green leaves of bindweed, wormwood, milkweed, and other weeds creeping along the ground. Here and there, in the midst of this rustling golden and fragrant sea, one could occasionally spot the charming blue eye of a cornflower ... or the maidenly, blushing face of a wild poppy.[8]

15

Veritably *urbs in rure*, Krakowiec was formally a town; but its people thought of themselves as country folk.

Krakowiec (the name is said to derive from the harsh, croaking call of ravens, *kruki*) first appears in recorded history in 1423. In that year King Władisław II Jagiełło, Grand Duke of Lithuania and King of Poland, founder of the Jagiellonian dynasty and of the dynastic union of Poland and Lithuania, gave Krakowiec as a fief to a knight, Jan Pilkowicz of Łosie, a village south-west of Krakowiec. The grant included a smithy and a mill (the latter remained a prominent feature of the town until the twentieth century) as well as the neighbouring farmstead of Gnojnica. Jan undertook to collect an annual tax from local peasants and to provide one foot-soldier with a spear and four mounted cavalrymen with crossbows for each war expedition of the king.[9]

Just two years later, Jan sold the estate to Mikołaj and Stefan (Steczko) Wołoch of Tarnawa, a village south of Cracow. In a document ratifying the sale, the king recognized Krakowiec as a town (*oppidum*) and granted it Magdeburg privileges. These were a model form of legal rights often accorded to towns in the medieval period. The king authorized the holding of a fair once a year on 10 August, the feast day of Saint Wawrzyniec (Lawrence, an early Christian martyr). Ordinary markets could be held twice a week, on Sundays and Thursdays, 'for ever'. For eight years only, the town was granted freedom from certain taxes, including tolls and property transfer fees. The king also ordered that suspicious persons were not to be admitted to the town.[10]

The Wołochs did not remain lords of the estate for long. In 1435 it was accepted by a member of the Fredro family as security for a loan of 360 silver *grzywna* (silver coins). By the early sixteenth century the Fredros had become full owners of both Krakowiec and the neighbouring estates of Gnojnica and Przedborze. In fact, Franciszek Fredro, who received Krakowiec in a family share-out in 1509, identified so strongly with it that he adopted the surname Krakowiecki.[11]

The Fredros belonged to the elite of territorial magnates who ruled the roost in Red Ruthenia. The region formed part of what became the Polish-Lithuanian Commonwealth, founded as a federal union in

1569. The largest state in Europe, it was also notoriously one of the weakest, with next to no central government and power devolved mainly to the nobility (*szlachta*), who constituted between 5 and 8 per cent of the population.

Krakowiec had the legal status of a *miasto* or 'city' but it remained for long an overgrown village, with a population that never numbered much more than a couple of thousand. In the early days it was so small that it was sometimes called an *oppidulum*, a 'townlet', and treated as if it were a village.[12] There was nothing unusual about this: hundreds of other Lilliputian 'cities' existed in early modern Poland. Astride the road from Radymno to Jaworów and Lwów, Krakowiec functioned as a minor communications hub, a market town, and a district administrative centre. A toll on the bridge over the Szkło stream provided revenue to the owners, particularly from the ox trade.

The coat of arms of Krakowiec shows three fish, two facing to the left, one to the right. These might refer to the three types of carp in the Krakowiec lake. Another interpretation is that they recall the three lakes that had once surrounded the town, two of which subsequently dried up.[13] I prefer to imagine that they symbolize the three historic communities of the town: two, Roman Catholics and Greek Catholics, facing west (strictly, south-west, to Rome) and one, Jews, facing east (strictly, south-east, to Jerusalem). Politically too, Krakowiec sometimes looked west, forming part of the Przemyśl Voivodeship, and sometimes east, coming under the jurisdiction of Lwów.

Although the founders of Krakowiec were Poles from further west, most of the inhabitants of the surrounding countryside, as well as some townsfolk, were autochthonous Ruthenians. The Poles were Roman Catholics whereas the Ruthenians were Orthodox. But at the Synod of Brest in 1596 many Orthodox Ruthenians united conditionally with Rome: they recognized the supremacy of the Pope but retained the Old Slavonic liturgy, a separate hierarchy and a marriageable priesthood. Henceforth they were known as Uniates and later as Greek Catholics. The Uniate church became the central spiritual and cultural expression of the Ruthenians (later styling themselves Ukrainians) in what became known as eastern Galicia. They remained the majority of the population in the region until modern times, although, over the centuries, large numbers of Polish-speaking Roman Catholics settled there.

Other reverberations of discord within Christianity reached Krakowiec in the late sixteenth century. Stanisław Fredro (Krakowiecki), lord of Krakowiec at that time, was a follower of Faustus Socinus who had arrived in Poland as a refugee from Calvinist Switzerland in 1579. At Raków, north-east of Cracow, he established a heretical, anti-Trinitarian movement that won widespread support. Under Fredro's influence, the Krakowiec church was for a time controlled by Socinians.

Their dominance was overthrown, however, by Fredro's successor as owner of the Krakowiec estate, Count Aleksander Ostrogski. Born to a princely Ruthenian family, he owned vast lands, especially around Jarosław, and built a castle in Krakowiec in 1590. With his father, Konstantyn, Palatine of Kiev, he was a leading supporter of Orthodox Christianity and led resistance to the secession of the Uniates. His wife, Anna, however, was a pious Roman Catholic and, under her influence, two of their sons became Catholics. Alexander nevertheless remained stubbornly faithful to Orthodoxy. A hot-tempered man who, like many of the great magnates of the time, maintained a private army, he engaged in frequent battles with invading Tatars, fellow-noblemen and owners of neighbouring estates.

Ostrogski transferred the church in Krakowiec to the Orthodox rite, but upon his death in 1603 his widow restored it to the Catholics and bestowed the benefice on a priest faithful to Rome. This clergyman explained to the recently appointed bishop of Przemyśl, Maciej Pstrokoński, that the church urgently needed money for refurbishment and new appurtenances. The prelate immediately ordered one hundred florins to be made available. But an adviser pointed out that the bishop, who was on a tour of his new diocese, faced heavy travel expenses. As he had only about four hundred florins left, it would be prudent to put off the payment. The bishop reluctantly agreed but said he feared that he would soon regret taking this advice. According to his biographer, 'The event responded to his word, for on the following night a robber made off with the chest in which the money . . . was kept. When the bishop learned of this, he was not the least perturbed by what had happened. He said he was being punished by this theft for excessive parsimony in expenditure on pious purposes and ordered that the money promised for the support of the church be sent first thing once they reached home.'[14]

The first description of Krakowiec in Polish literature appeared in 1614 in 'The Krakowiec Guild', a poem by the demotic versifier and satirist known as 'Jan of Kijany' – a *nom de plume*: his real name is unknown:

> As long as I live I've never seen such a guild
> Anyone who saw such a thing would laugh until he died.
> It was founded in the city under the heretics
> Patched together in bits and pieces from cobblers, furriers, and tailors.
> (Now, even though they have a Catholic church in the city
> They all keep to their own faith, and they squabble with each other,
> As one of them remains Catholic, and the other is Orthodox,
> Or if a man is Catholic, he has an Orthodox wife.
> Or if he is Ruthenian, he has a Polish wife.)
> A carefree one can be found among the virtuous ones,
> But the children of different faiths can't concur.
> The father directs the children to the Orthodox church, and the
> mother forbids them to go.
> And so in one day the mum is celebrating, and the dad is fasting.
> People go to the Jews for the vodka and for piety.
> Because the Jews in the market square set a good example
> For people who, upon seeing them, follow their lead.
> And so the people get mixed up, they don't know what to believe,
> A holiday with a Jew, and with a Lutheran a supper.
> On the next day to an Orthodox priest, to the Orthodox church,
> for knish.
> And so no one knows what they are doing.[15]

'Jan' not only testifies to sectarian differences among Christians in Krakowiec; he also provides the first reference to a Jewish presence in the town. Unfortunately we do not know whether that represents historical reality or merely the poetaster's lively imagination and ready wit. A modern writer on food history has argued, on the somewhat flimsy basis of this text, that the well-known Ashkenazi-Jewish delicacy *knish* (a kind of savoury dumpling) originates in seventeenth-century Krakowiec.[16]

The earliest record of Jews in what came to be called Galicia dates from the early fourteenth century. Jews lived in Poland under the protection of the General Charter of Jewish Liberties (or Privilege of Kalisz), granted by Duke Bolesław the Pious in 1264. Originally applying only to the Voivodeship of Greater Poland, it was extended by King Kazimierz III the Great in 1334 to all the Jews of the kingdom. Their origins are uncertain: most probably came from German lands following the massacres of Jews during the Crusades and their expulsion from many German cities in the fifteenth and sixteenth centuries. Others arrived from Italy and Spain. In the main they were traders who settled in towns. As elsewhere in Christian Europe, Jews were a pariah people, subject to various legal restrictions, and their presence was dependent on the grace and favour of the monarch and/or great landowners. On the other hand, they enjoyed considerably more freedom than their co-religionists elsewhere in Europe: they were free men, could bear witness in court, conduct business (save where they came into conflict with guilds) and practise their religion without interference. They even enjoyed a degree of autonomy – though that has sometimes been exaggerated and was permitted mainly with a view to enabling them to distribute their tax burden. They were predominantly merchants and artisans, although some were leaseholders who ran smallholdings or salt mines.[17] Under the 'propination' laws, which granted the nobility a monopoly on alcohol production, Jews acquired leases to breweries, distilleries and taverns. They also often leased mills, another noble monopoly. Jews were frequently appointed factors or estate stewards by landowners who were preoccupied with political activities, social engagements or warfare. In 1620 an unnamed Jew is recorded as having leased an inn in Gnojnica, just west of Krakowiec.[18] By 1630, Jews in the Przemyśl district, of which Krakowiec at the time formed a part, constituted 3.5 per cent of the total population, and 14.1 per cent of town dwellers.

Ostrogski was not unusual among great Polish magnates in maintaining a private army that could be used to crush peasant revolts or engage in feuds with their enemies. As the statesman and political thinker Andrzej Maksymilian Fredro (related to the family who had once been lords of Krakowiec) wrote in 1660, the landowner was, in effect, absolute king in his lands.[19]

Unlike 'private towns', wholly owned by aristocratic magnates, Krakowiec, thanks to its royal charters, enjoyed a certain degree of independence. The great families who owned the neighbouring estate nevertheless wielded considerable influence. In Krakowiec, as elsewhere, they formed close commercial relationships with local Jews. Even though Jews there did not enjoy the *protekcja* (patronage) that sheltered Jews in some 'private towns', they could often look to the local lord for influential support when in legal or other difficulty. As we shall see, vestiges of such relations endured into modern times.

During the period of so-called 'neo-serfdom' in the late sixteenth and early seventeenth centuries, the Ruthenian peasantry found itself subjected to heightened exactions by Polish landowners. The serfs held small plots of land in return for which they were obliged to work a large number of days of unpaid labour (*corvée* or *robot*) on the lord's demesne. Such duties would consist of tilling, harvesting, threshing and transporting. They might also include, as at Krakowiec, maintenance of ponds and waterways, forestry and work in the master's brewery or distillery. Liquor might be purchased only in the lord's tavern. Peasants were forbidden to leave or marry without the lord's permission. They were subject to justice administered by the lord's court and could be sentenced to beating or imprisonment in his private jail. If one serf killed another, the murderer was subject to the death penalty. But if the murderer was a nobleman, then he had to pay a fine of one hundred marks, of which half would go to the dead man's lord and the other half to his survivors. If a lord killed his own serf, he went scot-free.[20]

Krakowiec suffered from the lawlessness of the nobility, who behaved with a pride in their independence that often spilled over into anarchy and violence. In 1631 the Krakowiec estate was purchased by Andrzej Łahodowski. His neighbours were terrified, as the Łahodowski family were reputed to be bloody killers. Some had even killed their own brothers. In 1650 Andrzej became involved in a conflict with Jan Sobieski, governor of the neighbouring town of Jaworów (he was later king of Poland and famous as the 'saviour of Europe' who beat off the Turkish siege of Vienna in 1683). The two came to blows and Łahodowski was forced to flee. He died three years later, pursued by civil and criminal lawsuits. Perhaps to atone for his sins, he left substantial property to the Krakowiec church. His will also established a parish school and provided a permanent endowment for a vicar, a violinist, an organist and a choirmaster for the church.

From 1648 to 1655 the region was in tumult as the result of a Ruthenian peasant uprising. The Cossack leader of the revolt, Khmelnytsky (known as 'Bogdan' or 'God-given'), allied with Crimean Tatars and inflicted a series of defeats on the Polish army. By 1649 he was in the first stages of establishing an independent state. Khmelnytsky's followers attacked Polish landowners, Roman Catholic priests and Jews. Many were seized and sold into slavery in Turkey. In his thrilling, kaleidoscopic novel *With Fire and Sword* (1884), the Polish novelist Henryk Sienkiewicz depicted unsparingly the savagery of these events, the drunken rampages of plunder and rapine, the frenzy of the mobs as they tore men, women and children limb from limb. The massacres of Jews ranked in scale and horror with those of the Crusades and the plague years, and were not to be surpassed until the twentieth century.[21]

These events, in different forms, later assumed mythic significance for Poles, Ukrainians and Jews. Transmuted by the literary alchemy of Sienkiewicz, the resistance of the Polish nobility to the revolt became a vital element in the construction of Polish nationalism. For Ukrainians, Khmelnytsky was fashioned into a romantic hero like Zapata or Robert the Bruce: statues and portraits of him are to be found today all over the country. Even the Soviet Union, viewing him as a model if primitive revolutionary, honoured this son of gentlefolk with the ultimate accolade: a postage stamp. Jews, however, recalled his name with shuddering horror, seeing him as a latter-day Amalek or Haman.

Krakowiec was one of the places where armed rebels gathered at the outset of the rebellion. The manor house on the estate was burnt down and the steward was killed. The attackers made off with massive loot. An infuriated Łahodowski accused the heads of the Krakowiec municipality of collusion in the violence.[22] That, at any rate, was his version of the matter. A source more sympathetic to the rebels recorded events differently: 'Of course, as frequently happens in civil war, the Ruthenians, who had rejoiced upon the arrival of the Cossacks, suffered deadly retribution at the hands of the Poles after their departure, especially in Rohatyn and Krakowiec, where priests, citizens, and Ruthenian residents were executed by order of the Polish lords.'[23]

Detestation of Jews was inspired partly by religious devotion. It was also social in origin, stirred in the minds of Ruthenians by images of Jews as agents of the Polish landowning class and as bloodsucking tavernkeepers, millers or tax farmers. Such activities brought them into more direct contact with the peasant population than the Polish magnates, and Jews consequently often bore the brunt of peasant economic resentments.

The end of the Khmelnytsky revolt brought no relief from bloodshed. The next century was punctuated by war after war, during which Cossack, Muscovite, Swedish, Turkish and other armies rampaged across the region. The civilians of Krakowiec, like those of other towns, suffered the consequences – Jews most of all.

In 1656 the Polish general Stefan Czarniecki, in a battle at Gołąb, north of Krakowiec, sustained a severe defeat at the hands of the Swedes but, by dint of clever manoeuvring of his forces and harassment of the enemy, compelled them to beat a retreat. Bivouacked in Krakowiec, he wrote to Queen Marie-Louise, the French-born wife of King John Casimir of Poland: he described how he had pursued a large body of Swedish troops, commanded by a Scotsman, General Robert Douglas, on to the ice-covered San River; the ice broke under their weight and three hundred Swedes were drowned.[24]

Twenty years later the area around Lwów was the arena for combat of the army of Jan Sobieski, by this time King of Poland, against Turkish and Tatar forces. A further series of disasters afflicted Krakowiec during the Great Northern War (1700–21), in which Charles XII of Sweden engaged in campaigns against the Danes, the Poles and the Russians. Another Cossack rebellion in 1702–24 led to renewed slaughter of Polish gentry, Roman Catholic priests and Jews. In September 1704 Charles XII's army passed through Krakowiec on its way to conquer Lwów. Two years later, Russian forces moved in and Peter the Great took up temporary residence at Jaworów, a few miles east of Krakowiec. Even after the Russian victory over Charles at Poltava in 1709, fighting continued among Polish factions.

In 1714 the lord of Krakowiec, Józef Cetner, received a *salveguarde* from King Augustus II, promising that royal troops would 'keep strict discipline and order', that they would not impose 'undue exactions' and that 'nobody, whoever it may be, shall be bodily harmed, nor his possessions, buildings, yards, harvest, livestock and harness [horse and cart], or anything else shall be disturbed or damaged.'[25] The order seems to have had only limited effect, to judge from the fact that another one had to be issued just two years later.[26] Alas, the king, known as 'Augustus the Strong', was unable to live up to his sobriquet. Both *salveguardes* remained dead letters. Much of Galicia was laid waste in further fighting and many towns suffered severe depredations. Twenty houses were destroyed on the market place of Krakowiec and a further thirty-two elsewhere in the town.[27] In 1721 the church was destroyed by fire. In spite of its considerable endowments, unsettled conditions long prevented reconstruction. Henceforth, for many years, the mass was celebrated in a barn.

During the War of the Polish Succession (1732–35) the region was overrun yet again, this time by Russian troops led by General Prince Ludwig Hessen-Homburg and a Scottish Jacobite soldier of fortune, General James Keith. Over the next generation Poland fell into increasing disarray until, in 1772, its neighbours fell on it like scavenging birds of prey. Prussia, Russia and Austria, by common agreement, each seized a portion of Polish territory. This was the first of the three partitions that within a quarter of a century eliminated Polish independence altogether.

Krakowiec fell within the area allocated to Austria that the Habsburg emperors henceforth called the Kingdom of Galicia and Lodomeria, an old, half-forgotten name. For the next 146 years

Galicia (later with somewhat altered borders) remained under Austrian sovereignty. It thereby gained a measure of stability, only occasionally interrupted by civil strife. For Krakowiec the partition ushered in an era of prosperity and construction that left a permanent mark on the town.

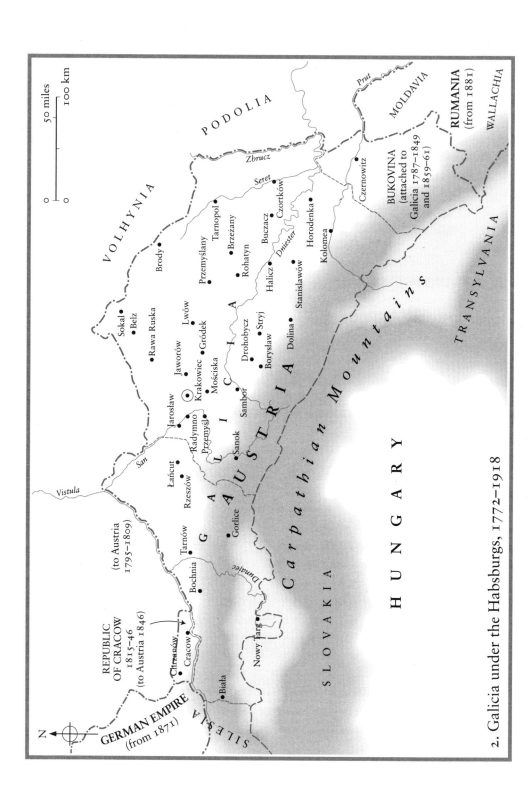

2. Galicia under the Habsburgs, 1772–1918

3

'The most splendid times'

In the age of reason, the final years of the first Polish Republic and the early period of Habsburg rule over Galicia, Krakowiec enjoyed an exceptional moment of economic growth and cultural efflorescence. The man chiefly responsible for this was the lord of the Krakowiec estate, Ignacy Cetner, a singular product of the Polish age of Enlightenment.

Born in 1728, Cetner was just three years old when his father died. In a funeral oration, the officiating priest addressed the bereaved child and predicted that he would be a 'morning star' that would rise, shedding 'a new light of honour in the Polish empyrean'.[1] He attended the Jesuit College in Lwów with his step-brother, Jan Sapieha, scion of one of the greatest noble families of the country, and with his cousin Ignacy Krasicki, later a celebrated belletrist, Enlightenment reformer, primate of the Polish church and lifelong friend. In March 1749 Cetner set out with Sapieha and a German tutor for a two-year-long grand tour, in the course of which they visited Austria, Italy, France, the Netherlands and Germany. As the heir to the Krakowiec estate and other lucrative properties, Cetner was assured of a comfortable income. Sophisticated, cosmopolitan and progressive, he was determined to make his mark in his troubled country.

Back in his homeland, Cetner embarked on a political career. Already commissioned as an officer in a fashionable regiment, he was elected a deputy for 'the Land of Halicz' (Galicia) to the Polish *Sejm* (parliament), though it seems he never spoke in the assembly. Something of an opportunist, he proved adept at accommodating himself to the rapidly shifting geopolitical conditions of his time. Like many of his peers who flaunted their patriotism, Cetner's first loyalty seems to have been neither to Poland, nor to Galicia, but to himself. By cultivating an *éminence grise* behind the Polish throne, he advanced in office and in 1763 secured appointment as voivode (governor) of Belz. He supported the election as king in the following year of Stanisław August Poniatowski, another former childhood companion. In 1767 he joined a special commission that replaced the *Sejm* and operated as a tool of Russian designs. A few months later, a revolt, known as the Confederation of Bar, broke out against the king. Patriotic noblemen, with French backing, opposed the interference in Polish politics of the Russian empress, Catherine II. Their supporters set up camp near Krakowiec, whereupon Cetner fled for a time to Hungary.

However, the first partition of Poland, in 1772, created a new political situation. The three partitioning powers acquired territory that altogether deprived Poland of half her population and a third of her land area (*see map on p. 26*). The Habsburgs, it has been said, acquired Galicia 'in a fit of absence of mind'.[2] Actually, there was more cunning statecraft behind this act of imperial aggrandizement than they pretended. The Austrian empress, Maria Theresa, is said to have wept out of pity for the Poles when the partition of their country was first proposed. Frederick the Great of Prussia, who participated in the carve-up, commented acidly: 'She wept as she took, and the more she wept, the more she took.'[3]

The Habsburgs were not greatly impressed by their new acquisition. Galicia was far from a jewel in the Habsburg crown. Maria Theresa's son and co-emperor, Joseph II, on his first visit to Galicia, in 1773, was horrified at the exploitation of serfs by Polish landowners. The Galician peasant, he declared, was 'an unfortunate who has nothing but a human face and physical life'.[4]

Although the largest, Galicia was also the poorest of the Austrian crownlands. Indeed, Galicia became a byword for rural misery:

If you could only see the peasants of Galicia, as I have, [wrote a traveller in the province] I doubt not but you would blush, as does your friend, to belong to the human species, upon seeing it as so susceptible to degradation. At the entrance to a village, as you head towards the inn, where the innkeeper is always a Jew, the roads are covered with dead-drunk men and women, sprawled snoring in the mud or dust. When you go inside the inn you fall back in face of the alcoholic vapours.[5]

Unusually, this writer, while charging that Jews were responsible for promoting drunkenness, praised them as the most industrious segment of the population: 'They are tailors, shoemakers, upholsterers, furriers, glaziers, goldsmiths, watchmakers, engravers . . . Everywhere in the countryside, even in the smallest hamlets, one finds them hardworking, energetic, industrious.' He contrasted their 'spiritual air' with the 'stupid physiognomy' of the Galician peasants who surrounded them: to compare the two, he maintained, was like comparing an orang-utan to a human.[6]

Under the Habsburgs, the Polish aristocracy and gentry in Galicia retained much of their social power. The landed magnates, formerly seen as champions of Polish independence, proved adept at transferring their allegiance to their new rulers.[7] Ignacy Cetner secured appointment as an imperial privy councillor, was admitted to the Austrian nobility and advanced rapidly in politics – though his new responsibilities did not prevent his serving for a time as a secret adviser to the Empress of Russia. In 1783 he reached the summit of his political career when the Austrian emperor Joseph II appointed him Grand Marshal of Galicia. Not all his friends approved of his opportunism. Krasicki diagnosed a certain 'moral arthritis' in him – 'a disease', noted the cleric, 'not so much unpleasant for those who suffer from it as for those who suffer *for* it'.[8]

The Habsburgs exacted a price for such transferred loyalty. Joseph, in particular, pushed for reform of the land system against the determined resistance of the great landowners. Maria Theresa and her officials delayed effective action, though a 'provisional serfdom *patent*' was issued in 1775 that sought to protect serfs against abuses. Upon the death of his mother and co-empress in 1780, Joseph assumed sole authority over the empire and the machinery of enlightened despotism moved into high gear. Shocked by the 'cabals, intrigues, and anarchy'[9] in Galicia, he resolved to take the province in hand and make it a testing-bed of reform. The nobility reluctantly acquiesced.

In 1782 Cetner signed an agreement with the senior municipal officials of Krakowiec. The agreement freed citizens of the town from the exacting duties of supplying labour to the lord for harvesting hay, fixing dykes and fences, periodic draining of fishponds, carrying beer to the palace, guard shifts and forestry. In return, every person in the town was to pay eighty złoty on St Martin's Day to Cetner and his successors and, in case of need, they were to provide guards for the lord's castle.[10] Cetner also issued a solemn statement granting to inhabitants of Krakowiec 'for ever' grazing rights on some manorial lands. The grant was restricted to 'Catholics only': presumably this formulation included Uniates, who had recently been dubbed 'Greek Catholics' by Maria Theresa. At the same time, Cetner permitted trees to be chopped and wood gathered in his forests 'once a week on Fridays, as an act of goodwill to the citizens of Krakowiec'.[11]

These concessions, however, applied only to townsfolk of Krakowiec. Joseph required that landowners go further. He abolished the traditional system of serfdom (*Leibeigenschaft*) that regulated the lives of the 84 per cent of peasants in the province who were in servile bondage. Peasants' liability for labour service, owed in return for use of a plot of land, hitherto six days a week, was limited to a maximum of three days and each peasant's obligation had to be laid out in writing in an inventory. Joseph baulked, however, at more far-reaching change. Manorial courts and prisons as well as corporal punishment of peasants at the whim of landlords endured until 1848. Peasants could submit formal complaints to the government against their lords but such pleas were dangerous: they could result in retributive punishment.

Cetner's political success was unfortunately not matched by financial acumen. In the early 1770s he was reckoned among the ten wealthiest men in Galicia, owning 240,000 morgen (about 143,000 hectares) of land. But his elevated political position required him to maintain a lavish lifestyle for which his income proved inadequate. In 1777 he bought the severely indebted city of Przemyśl, which thereby lost its autonomy and which he ruled as a great magnate. Yet within a few years he found himself heavily over-extended and obliged to surrender control of Przemyśl. By 1787 he had forfeited three quarters of his lands. Seeking new sources of revenue, he established a tobacco plantation and became involved in salt transactions with the emperor (salt was an important product of the Galician economy). For a time he was reduced to selling heraldic certificates to fellow noblemen. The basic problem was that he was a poor manager of his affairs, and his underlings took advantage of his benevolent disposition to plunder him mercilessly.

Overburdened by debts, Cetner declared bankruptcy in 1789. He entered into a 106-page-long 'compromise agreement' with over one hundred creditors. He owed them a total of 3,526,478 Polish florins and fifteen groschen. It is difficult to convert this in any meaningful way into modern values: suffice to say that it was a vast amount. Small creditors, including servants due unpaid wages, were paid in full. The rest had to be satisfied with part-payment. Cetner managed to retain a small amount of land, including the Krakowiec estate, in the form of life tenancies for himself and his daughter. Weeping, he bewailed his financial misfortunes, calling himself the most miserable citizen of Galicia. A contemporary punningly said of him that 'he had once been a cetnar (a hundredweight) but now he does not even weigh a pound.'[12] Yet even now he did not rein in his spending.

Cetner's continued profligacy was facilitated by his – and later his daughter's – connections with some of the wealthiest magnate families of Poland. He had made what appeared to be a brilliant marriage to the blue-blooded Ludwika Potocka, daughter of the voivode of Poznań. The union was not a happy one. Ludwika was 'an inveterate intriguer and busybody ... playing the patron to various shady characters'.[13] She was said to suffer 'strange mood-swings, whims, and humours'.[14] Ignacy gave her a free hand in politics. She took advantage of this to engage in plots and cabals. The couple's home life was tempestuous. Visitors reported that they were constantly arguing. Krasicki noted during one of his stays that Ludwika had been 'thus far quite amiable'. 'Lord grant that it may continue thus,' the man of God piously entreated.[15] Despairing of his wife, Ignacy doted on their only child, a daughter, Anna.

There was one other preoccupation, however, to which Cetner devoted much care and inordinate expense: Krakowiec. Around 1760 he built a substantial palace on the western edge of the town. It was approached by a majestic avenue, shaded on either side by rows of willow, ash and lime trees.[16] The avenue culminated in a *porte cochère*, opening into the courtyard. Designed by the French architect Pierre Ricaud de Tirregaille, the palace was a two-storey structure, with dormer windows set in the mansard roof. The building had fourteen rooms on the ground floor and more above. Two wings, at right angles on either side, enclosed a *cour d'honneur* and held a further twenty-five rooms. The main hall served as a drawing-room, ballroom and chapel.[17]

An inventory prepared after the death of Cetner's daughter in 1814 itemized the building's contents at that time and gives some idea of the family's reckless expenditure. The jewellery consisted of hundreds of pieces: necklaces, bracelets, and earrings of pearls, diamonds and emeralds; golden colliers, brooches, rings and medallions inlaid with every possible gem – onyx, lapis lazuli, garnet, sapphires, topaz, malachite, labradorite, carnelian, rubies, opals, turquoise, agate, coral, amber and so on. There were exquisite ornaments, birdcages, screens, lanterns, mirrors, candlesticks and porcelain, as well as silver jars, teapots, bowls, vases and cutlery. Much of the furniture was mahogany, including a Viennese grand piano. The contents of the princess's wardrobe included delicate oriental silks, furs and lace. The pictures in the palace were unfortunately not described in detail, but we know that they included a portrait of King Stanisław August as well as other portraits and landscapes.[18] Many of the most valuable volumes in the library were eventually bequeathed to the Jagiellonian University in Cracow.[19] Apart from books, the library held picture portfolios, old maps and a gallery of seventy-four copperplate engravings of monarchs and popes.

The geographer Ewaryst Andrzej Kuropatnicki, who visited Krakowiec 'during the most splendid times', recorded in his *Geography of Galicia*, published in 1786, that the hearts of visitors were filled with delight at all they saw. 'In Cetner's castle there were collections of paintings, portraits, engravings, books, old coins, seeds, snuff boxes, buttons, marbles, conches, birds and whatever can increase knowledge of the history of different countries and the natural world.'[20] This was a cabinet of curiosities on a grand scale.

Most magnificent of all was the landscape garden that Cetner laid out around his palace. When completed under his successors, it extended over thirty-five hectares (about eighty-six acres, more than double the area of the gardens at Buckingham Palace). It was bisected by a wide canal and surrounded by a promenade. On one side were orchards and meadows and on the other fishponds. At some distance from the palace were stables, greenhouses, hothouses famous for their pineapples, and an orangery. Fifty-nine varieties of tree were represented in the garden, including aspen, poplar, maple, birch, elm, horse chestnut, oak and acacia. Labyrinthine paths led through the trees to a typical eighteenth-century folly: a 'hermitage', 'built of wood with pretty arcades of birch and surrounded by varicoloured mosses' (*see plate 4*). It was inhabited by 'a hermit, the paid servant of the master, whose duty was to add a living comedy to the wooden one'.[21]

Another visitor was stirred to express delight in elevated verse:

> *You can pass sweet moments*
> *Near this hermit's hut.*
> *You can hear the murmur of the nearby stream*
>   *And a bird's sweet song.*
>   *The eye here drinks its fill of beauty,*
> *The heart beats with more feeling.*
> *The quiet wilderness assuages your troubles*
> *Because charm rules here sturdily.*
> *Here, in the all-encompassing tranquillity,*
> *We experience sensations*
> *Of pleasant memories*
>   *And of delight.*[22]

The garden was described as 'the largest and perhaps the most beautiful in Galicia ... The most wonderful thing about this garden is that its beauty owes nothing to nature; it is all a work of artifice which ... at the wave of a magic wand at the owner's will conjured up on a barren plain a real oasis ...' And so was created 'a magnificent garden indeed, with rare trees, plants imported from various regions, shrubs from overseas, and flowers from all countries and all climes, in which the voivode invested immense financial resources and the passionate fancies of his entire life'.[23] Cetner's sister sent him from Warsaw three cartloads of plants that a botanist had brought from England. These included cinnamon trees, carnations, nutmegs and other costly items. Kuropatnicki wrote that it was 'as if the whole of botany could be found there – could anything more be said about the exquisite taste of this magnate?'[24] All this did not sate Cetner's appetite for horticulture. He hired a celebrated French architect and landscape designer, Pierre-Denis Guibaut, to create another garden outside his town house in Lwów. This became a public park, the Cetnerówka, elements of which still exist today as part of Lviv University's botanical garden.

A discriminating patron of the arts, Cetner employed his own court painter and music master. He entertained on a grand scale. Guests flowed from all over to visit his palace and garden. One of his best friends was the celebrated poet Franciszek Karpiński, who shared his enthusiasm for landscape gardens and praised his sweetness of character.[25]

Another guest was his former schoolmate Krasicki, who had become a national figure. Known as the 'prince of poets' and hailed as a 'paladin of Polish classicism', Krasicki was the author of the first Polish novel.[26] Although a holder of high ecclesiastical office as Prince-Bishop of Warmia, he was fashionably anti-clerical. Krasicki was unimpressed by Cetner's extravagance. 'Much as I respect all these botanists,' he commented privately, 'I would prefer a cow to a flower.'[27] But he did not criticise his friend to his face. The two served together as senior officials of the royal tribunal in Lwów. They worked to make the body more efficient and limit its traditional 'feasts and revels', thereby provoking resistance and even physical onslaught at the hands of dissolute, disgruntled gentry.[28]

In 1787 Cetner paid for the construction in Krakowiec of an imposing Roman Catholic church, dedicated to St James the Apostle. Its design has been ascribed to Efraim Schröger (Szreger) who built several fine churches in Warsaw, but as he died in 1783 the attribution is doubtful.[29] Another authority credits the Italian-born Domenico Merlini, like Schröger a favourite of Stanisław August.[30] On grounds of style, this attribution too has been questioned.[31] Whoever may have been the architect, the church aroused admiration for the next 150 years as Krakowiec's finest public building. Facing on to the market place, it was a well-proportioned, classical, rectangular structure with a magnificent façade. A front relief featured Hope and Love, depicted as reclining women. The interior was decorated with pictures of the crucifixion, of a 'fat canon', 'a young knight' and the Virgin Mary with the Child, as well as a panegyric text devoted to one of Cetner's ancestors. The main altar, much older than the building itself, had been transferred there from an old Jesuit church in Przemyśl. Two smaller altars were specially made for the church.[32] Later it was further endowed by Cetner's daughter, Anna. She embellished the interior with wallpaper from a paper factory that she established in the neighbourhood.

One of the outstanding aristocratic women of her age, Anna married four husbands, all from great noble families. The first, Prince Józef Sanguszko, Grand Marshal of Lithuania, died in a hunting accident. Regarding the second, Prince Kazimierz Nestor Sapieha, Anna asked that her father pay off her groom's substantial debts. Ignacy, who was for the moment in strong financial shape, said that Sapieha would inherit nothing from him. He added that he would not hold any sort of party to mark the betrothal. 'Why all this fuss?' he said. The whole thing, he insisted, must be done quietly. All this according to an account by Krasicki's brother who happened to be present.[33] The wedding duly took place but Sapieha turned out to be a drunkard. Notwithstanding her religious devotion, Anna succeeded in obtaining a divorce decree in 1784. At her third marriage, in 1790, to Count Kajetan Potocki, the poet Feliks Radwański penned congratulatory verses that were privately printed.[34] She tired of Potocki and was unfaithful. That marriage too was dissolved. Finally and most magnificently, she married a Frenchman, Charles-Eugène de Lorraine. Last head of the Guise line, he bore several titles, including prince de Lambesc, duc d'Elbeuf, comte d'Armagnac, de Brionne et de Charny and more. He had distinguished himself as a soldier, notably on 12 July 1789 in the defence of the Tuileries against the mob. Exiled as a result of the revolution, he entered the Habsburg service, rose to the rank of lieutenant-general, and was appointed commander of Austrian forces in Galicia. With these formidable connections, the Cetners rose to the very top ranks of Polish society.

In 1791 Anna visited Rome where she commissioned three remarkable portraits. One was by Pietro Labruzzi, a fashionable Roman portraitist whose subjects included Pope Pius VII and King Stanisław August. Labruzzi often painted aristocratic visitors to Rome on the Grand Tour. His not very flattering picture shows a frumpish, heavily rouged and lipsticked Anna, with a profusion of curls and a faintly disapproving, simpering expression. The other two portraits were by prominent women painters of the day. Angelica Kauffman depicted Anna posing, with a rather awkward attempt at grace, in an arcadian setting reminiscent of the Krakowiec garden. Elisabeth-Louise Vigée-Le Brun, a former official court painter for Queen Marie-Antoinette, also painted Anna in Rome. Like Labruzzi, Vigée-Le Brun portrayed her against a romantic background, in this case a water-fall, probably inspired by the garden of the Villa d'Este in Tivoli, near Rome (*see plate 5*).[35] The artist later recalled: 'She came to me with her husband, and when he had left us, she observed with great *sang-froid*: "He is my third husband; but I think I shall take back the first one, who suits me better, although he is a drunkard."'[36] Perhaps Anna was joking – her first husband was dead by that time.

These were years of growth and prosperity for Krakowiec. Cetner's opulence brought considerable economic benefit. We know from population records that immigrants were attracted to the town, among them gardeners, carpenters, a master of music and such fig-ures as a 'dancing master', for whose services there had probably not been much call in earlier times.

We should not imagine, however, that life in Krakowiec in Cetner's time was a perpetual *fête galante* out of Watteau. Although the towns-folk profited from the lord's building works and expenditure, not much of Cetner's enlightenment percolated down to the local popula-tion. In spite of his establishment of an elementary school, most of the Christians of the town and the peasantry of the surrounding villages remained illiterate. Everyday social interactions, often coarse and oaf-ish, sometimes degenerated into violence. As in most such towns, brawls were common, often leading to court proceedings.

In 1783, for example, the municipal court heard a case involving Marcin Przyborz. His mother-in-law, the 'worthy widow Gawrońska', appeared before the magistrates, alleging that Marcin had come home 'deliriously drunk' one night and knocked her to the ground. The next day, she said, he ran up against her and tore open her coat. He also 'ripped open an eiderdown and the feathers blew away in the wind'. He pushed and hurt her grandson and 'did many other inexplicably bad things to the child'. He then stole some money from her to finance another drunken spree. The court decided Marcin should receive three lashes in public and pay a fine plus damages. The 'worthy widow', however, no doubt looking to the future with trepidation, urged clemency; whereupon the court decided that 'because the mother's mercy has been bestowed on her son-in-law, the state suspends the public punishment.' Marcin was warned, however, that 'if this happens again to the grandmother and the child, the decree will be enforced.'[37]

In another case a Mrs Jędrziowska lodged a complaint against Fedor Szowdrak:

It was a Sunday. I went to the town to sell some pork. I just wanted 23 groschen for it. Later on, in the evening, to my surprise, and I don't know why, Fedor Szowdrak attacked me, abusing me with foul expressions such as 'You beast!' He took the pork, threw it in the mud, and stamped on it so that it became worthless, except to be thrown to the dogs. Then he tore my dress as was witnessed by Michał Szamyło.

Nor did he stop at that. On the next day, Monday, I went back, not to sell the pork but to get it as evidence. Fedor Szowdrak assaulted me again, calling me names once again. I said [I'm going to report this] to the magistrate. He said: 'Oh yes, which ones?' To which I said, Mr Lambrani and Mr Daniel [Draczakiewicz]. He responded furiously that Lambrani was a nobody compared to himself. He was just as much of a magistrate and guildmaster . . .

Then he said: 'I'll throw you into the mud every Sunday and I'll kill you in the mud.' That was witnessed by Jan Halwaz.

When I was selling, he would take the plums I had brought to the market and would feed them to pigs during the season that was best for selling plums.

The court decided that as Fedor had been charged with abusive conduct several times, he should not only be fined but sentenced to corporal punishment. In this case too, however, the magistrates exercised leniency and let him off with a suspended sentence.[38]

Thefts were commonplace: of money, hay, grain from the mill, wood, a chunk of meat, a 'piece of canvas', a pipe, a hat, a horse, a pig, ducks, even a sparrow. The magistrates heard numerous cases of assault, often by men against women, particularly mothers-in-law, frequently accompanied by foul language. Weapons used included sticks and stones, a pitchfork, a shovel, a crowbar, an axe and a frying pan. Court-imposed penalties were generally light – perhaps because magistrates sometimes found themselves in the dock, accused of disorder or feuding.

The upheavals of the revolutionary period, the Kościuszko uprising of 1794, and the third partition in 1795, which extinguished what remained of Polish independence, affected Krakowiec only glancingly. In the 1790s elements of the Austrian Karaczay and Modena regiments were billeted there. With their bright red (Karaczay) and orange (Modena) uniforms, the cavalrymen enlivened the social life of the town. Soldierly roistering sometimes went too far: during celebration of the new year 1794, a young cadet of the Modena regiment fell into the town well: he was reported to have been 'submersus in aqua' and drowned.[39] Liaisons were formed with local women, resulting, in due course, in births. Perhaps fortunately for local maidenhood, the regiments were soon called away for service in the wars against the French.

In later times, the memory of the great days of Cetner acquired a legendary glow. The 'village poet' Wincenty Pol, in his celebrated narrative poem 'The Adventures of Benedict Winnicki' (1839), wrote:

> *Pan Cetner often stayed in Krakowiec*
> *But things were strange at that estate;*
> *A bit of French here and a bit of Polish there,*
> *Such was the fashion (as I understand it now).*
> *Things were not done in the typical gentry way:*
> *Pan Cetner did not want to have many courtiers,*
> *He did not go hunting, did not know anything,*
> *Was no good with horses, sat alone in his room,*
> *In slippers, with books. He fiddled with trinkets and hid bibelots.*
> *All he cultivated were Frenchmen and flowers.*
>
> *It was sad on the Krakowiec estate,*
> *As if a devout man was in a monastery,*
> *. . . .*

Cetner's herbaria were everywhere in the Krakowiec estate,
And the flowers had names in all languages,
Outside, under glass, under netting, under membrane,
In the ground and in the water. The only thing
That wasn't there was that charmed tree, which sang
As in a fairy tale
And had golden apples each night.
Oh, did Monsieur Jardinier do some work there!

At the table I often grew bored,
Because people praised the wit of some strangers,
And lands, and customs, and books, and faces,
And some famous French harlots . . .[40]

The satirical critique of Cetner as too Frenchified comes a little oddly from Pol, whose own mother was French. But he was a Polish patriot and in addition to being a poet was also a geographer who coined the term 'kresy' to denote 'a distant borderland living at its own pace'.[41] More specifically, the term came to be used for the eastern borderlands of the former Polish-Lithuanian Commonwealth, including eastern Galicia, which Pol maintained should form part of a restored, independent Poland. His portrait of a genial, cultivated, cosmopolitan Cetner may be linked to his larger political purpose of recalling – and calling back to life – an idyllic, multicultural Poland within its historic frontiers.

The last years of Cetner's life (he died in 1809) were darkened by political and personal misfortune.[42] According to one account, he found his only consolation in his garden, though 'sometimes the fear arose in him lest his creation perish with his death, lest wild weeds and grasses flourish on the clean garden paths. In such black moments, tormented by gout, walking through the garden while leaning on a servant's shoulder, he used to say, saddened by a sombre premonition, "When I am dead, the wolves will take over here."'[43]

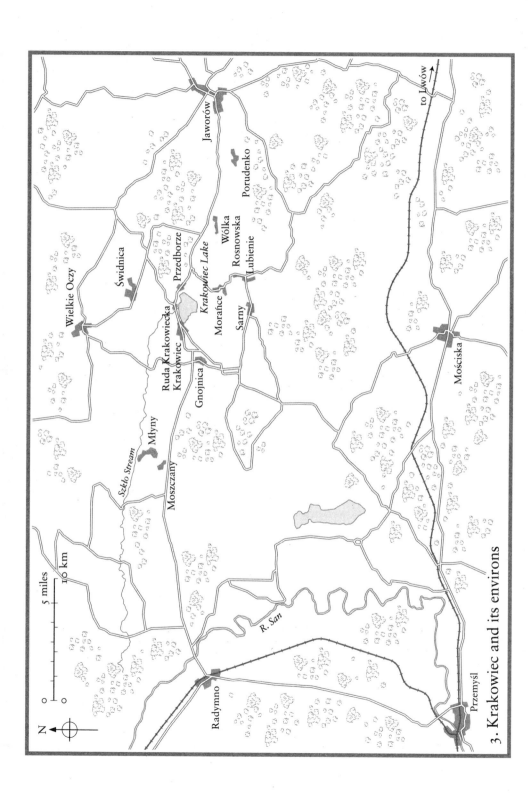

3. Krakowiec and its environs

4

The rise of the shtetl

In the course of the late eighteenth and early nineteenth centuries Krakowiec was transformed from what had originally been a Polish town into a predominantly Jewish one. The Jews' share of the population grew until they became the largest group and then an overall majority. The most commonly heard language in the street was Yiddish. The houses around the market square were, for the most part, inhabited by Jews. They owned all the stores. The rhythm of social and economic life was to a great extent determined by the Jewish calendar. From dusk on Friday until three stars appeared in the sky on Saturday evening, a Sabbath stillness prevailed in the centre of town. The shtetl, the characteristic settlement of Ashkenazi Jews, later the object of much mythologizing, nostalgia and sentimentality, attained its fullest flowering. Krakowiec conformed to this general pattern.

Since about 1580 Polish Jewry had enjoyed a measure of autonomy, exercised through a representative body known as the Council of Four Lands. Its main duty had been to allocate the distribution of taxes among communities. Until 1753 the *kahal* (Jewish community board) of Krakowiec, like those of many other small towns in the region, had fallen under the authority of the *kahal* of the nearby city of Przemyśl. This meant that Krakowiec Jews had no right to build a synagogue, appoint a rabbi or establish a burial ground without the permission of their big city brethren. Most importantly, the Przemyśl *kahal* had an absolute right to determine the share of taxes that each of the smaller surrounding communities must pay. These arrangements led to protests by the small communities and efforts to secure independent recognition. After a struggle lasting several decades and involving the local authorities, the bishop of Przemyśl and even the king, the small town communities finally succeeded in asserting their independence.[1] Henceforth the Krakowiec Jews were recognized as an independent body who negotiated their tax rate directly with the Council of Four Lands. Their victory turned out, however, to be empty, since the amount of tax levied on the Krakowiec community remained unchanged. Nor did Krakowiec ever secure direct representation on the council.

The new community organization, far from alleviating, in fact exacerbated the financial disarray into which the Jews – and Poland – had fallen. The acquisition of Jewish autonomy at the local level was soon followed by its loss at the national level. One of the first acts of Stanisław August, upon his election to the throne in 1764, was to order the abolition of the Council of Four Lands. The government decided to take over direct responsibility for the collection of Jewish taxes. In order to determine a basis for what was nominally a 'head tax', the king ordered a census of Jews. This found 750,000 Jews in the country, out of a total population that has been estimated at between eleven and twelve million.

In Krakowiec 301 Jews over the age of one year were counted. They occupied forty-eight out of the 246 houses in the town.[2] A further 144 Jews lived in surrounding villages with, in addition, nineteen infants, for whom no tax was payable. There may have been some under-counting to avoid tax, so that these must be regarded as minimum population figures. The capitation rate was two złoty each so that the community was liable for a tax of 890 złoty – quite a large sum, equivalent to the cost of about ten horses at that period. This was a big increase from the 410 złoty that the Krakowiec Jews had paid in each of the previous fifteen years.[3] Perhaps they could afford it since these were years that at last brought more settled conditions – and with civil peace came economic well-being, at least for some.

As in most *shtetlakh*, Jews now virtually monopolized trade in Krakowiec. Some acted as bankers both individually and collectively: they not only lent money but also received deposits and paid out interest. Their foremost client seems to have been the local Roman Catholic church. In 1771, for example, bequests to the church by Krakowiec residents for masses to be said for their souls after their deaths were deposited by the priest with the *kahal* who promised to pay 7 per cent interest each year.[4] This may be seen as an investment by the church or as a loan to help pay the Jews' greatly increased taxes. Perhaps it was both.

At a stroke, the annexation of Galicia in 1772 more than doubled the Jewish population of the Habsburg dominions. The Austrian government regarded this as anything but a blessing. Maria Theresa expressed 'horror and disgust' at the discovery that her new territory contained two hundred thousand Jews.[5] She considered the Jews 'a plague' who 'practise all sorts of dirty dealing which other, honourable men avoid'.[6]

An Austrian officer found Galician Jews 'indisputably the filthiest, most ignorant, superstitious, poverty-stricken, and yet most numerous of this unfortunate nation that is spread over the entire earth'. They were so uneducated that 'Mendelssohn was as foreign and unknown to them as Voltaire to the Laplanders.' (He was not much more impressed by the Poles: sloth and indolence were their chief characteristics, he observed, adding that they changed their clothes not more than once a fortnight.)[7] Yet as the reference to the enlightened philosopher Moses Mendelssohn attested, the writer did not regard all Jews as incorrigibly degenerate. His portrayal of the province was part of a broader tendency to regard Galicia as terribly backward but ripe for reform.

In 1781–82 Joseph II issued a series of 'toleration patents' (decrees) for Jews in various provinces of his empire. Galicia had to wait a little longer. A government report on the Lwów region in 1785 stated that 'The Jew is the most ready creditor and the Galician peasant is his natural debtor.'[8] Joseph's decrees for Galicia, issued in 1785 and 1789, were designed to alter this relationship, to achieve the modernization of his Jewish subjects, to limit Jewish communal autonomy and to integrate the Jews with the general population.

Jews were granted something close to equal rights, including the right to vote in local elections, provided they met stiff property criteria and other qualifications. They might even be raised to the nobility. Many, but not all, discriminatory laws, including the special Jewish head tax, were abolished. On the other hand, a new 'tolerance tax' was levied instead. The powers of rabbinic courts were limited. The use of

Hebrew and Yiddish was restricted: Jews were henceforth required to keep accounts in German or Polish; their children were to receive education in German. Jews were subjected, for the first time in the empire, to compulsory military service, though composition payments in lieu of service were later permitted. Henceforth Jews could become members of guilds and hold municipal office. They were required to hold family names. Generally, they selected or were issued with Germanic ones: for example, 'Laub' and 'Wasserstein'. Jews were not permitted to marry unless they had received at least two years of schooling (the much-maligned Jewish religious school, the *cheder*, did not count). For this reason and also because of the tax payable upon marriage, most Jews in Krakowiec, as elsewhere in the empire, celebrated only religious, not civil marriages throughout the nineteenth century. They were required to keep registers of births, marriages and deaths (*Matrikelbücher*). Most of these for Krakowiec survive, enabling historians to chart the demographic ups and downs of the community. These records were also to serve a more deadly purpose for German occupiers of Krakowiec, as of other towns in eastern Galicia, between 1941 and 1944.

An improvement in the social status of Jews was apparent in Krakowiec even before the first *Toleranzpatent* for Galicia was issued. In 1782 the minutes of the manorial court record a case in which a Jew, Oszor Chaimowicz, complained that he had been beaten up by a Christian townsman, Augustin Luba. Oszor's eye was nearly knocked out. Augustin was ordered to pay a fine as well as compensation to Oszor.[9] This is not the only occasion around this time on which we find Jews having successful recourse to the municipal or manorial court of Krakowiec in disputes with Christians. Such protection in a *Rechtsstaat* was an essential condition of Jewish integration into a modern society.

The Josephine reforms also had an economic side. Jews were permitted to buy land (for their own use), and even encouraged to do so. Anxious to wean Jews off supposedly unproductive and exploitative occupations such as peddling and tavern-keeping, the government ordered Jewish communities to finance the settlement of Jews on the land. The results were meagre. A government report in 1808 stated that between 1793 and 1805 the Krakowiec community had settled a total of just three Jews on land in the district. One of these was Aron Laub, probably an ancestor of mine, who appears to have arrived in Krakowiec in 1793.[10] Yet the 1789 edict seriously threatened Jewish economic survival, since it banned Jews from holding leaseholds of mills, inns and other properties. Jews who were not farmers were forbidden to live in the countryside. Only the death of the emperor in the following year prevented these prohibitions from being enforced.

Many of Joseph's other reforms were reversed under his successors, who took fright at the revolutionary upsurge that swept Europe in the course of the 1790s. At the local level too, a reaction set in. This affected the position of the Jews, who found that attempts to exercise their rights raised hackles among their neighbours. Sometime between 1809 and 1814 (we do not have an exact date) the Jews of Krakowiec submitted a petition to Princess Anna, daughter and heiress of Ignacy Cetner. They complained of discrimination against them by the Krakowiec municipality. Whereas Catholics could use common grazing land free of charge, Jews were being required to pay usage fees of four złoty per horse and two złoty per cow. The common, they pointed out, was dominical property (that is, it belonged to the lord of the manor, not the municipality). Moreover, Jews were being denied the right to take timber from the forest, whereas Anna's father's promise of free wood-gathering every Friday had been made without limitation according to religion. The Jews had other complaints as well. The mayor having refused to recognize their claims, they appealed to Anna for redress.[11] Unfortunately we do not know the outcome of the petition. But the document shows that Jews were not afraid to assert their recently gained rights, that in doing so they encountered resistance from other townsfolk, and that, in the time-honoured manner, they sought the protection of the local landowner.

The government's efforts to modernize Jewish life did not improve Austrian observers' opinions of Galician Jews. Visitors from elsewhere in the Habsburg domains were often repulsed by the sight of them. A traveller in 1809 wrote:

> In all Galicia one rarely sees well dressed Jews. They arouse abhorrence and disgust with their black coats on which one can make out years of mud, patched, torn, full of dirt, ... Arriving in a town where Jews

live . . ., you don't need any signposts or inquiries to find the Jewish streets. The bituminous stink, the filth, the shabbiness of the cottages, the windows done up with rags and paper, will soon enough indicate to the stranger: "Here lives the chosen people that alone deserves to reside in beautiful Galicia!"[12]

When the statesman Prince Klemens von Metternich visited the province in 1823, he wrote to his wife that he found it very beautiful – except 'what spoils the country is that Jews are met at every step; no one is to be seen but Jews: they swarm here.' He was deeply shocked by the poverty of the peasantry: 'The poor people here are excellently disposed, but they are so thoroughly miserable that it would be difficult to know how to preserve them from ruin.' When he fell ill in Lwów, his wife sent him oranges: 'I had tried every possible way to procure them here but in vain. *Hier blühen die Citronen nicht!* (Citruses don't flourish here!)' Presumably he had not visited Cetner's orangery – if it still existed. Metternich was enormously relieved when the time came to leave: 'I have never seen anything more striking than the change from Galicia to Moravia. The country is the same, and is as fine on one side as the other; but the first village on this side is the first which gives the idea of being inhabited by men. No rags, the houses neat and the inhabitants well clothed; no Jews; no squalor, misery, and death.'[13] Metternich had the reputation, to some extent justified, of being sympathetic towards Jews.[14] We may imagine, then, the attitudes of those who were less benevolently disposed.

Against this background of external opprobrium, Jews were engaged in fierce internecine conflict. In the late eighteenth and early nineteenth centuries, two overlapping struggles were waged for the soul of the Jew in Poland, especially Galicia. The first was between adherents of a self-proclaimed 'messiah', Jacob Frank, and mainstream Jews. Frank, who eventually converted to Christianity, attracted many erstwhile followers of an earlier 'redeemer', Sabbatai Tsvi, who had converted to Islam in 1666. In spite of the apostasies of their leaders, the Sabbateans and Frankists retained secret adherents among Jews in Poland and for a time their doctrines infiltrated to the heart of rabbinic Judaism.

The second struggle was between Hasidism and its enemies, *mis-nagdim* (literally 'opponents'). Hasidism glorified the 'rebbe' who was more than a mere rabbi: he was a *tsaddik* (holy man), a spiritual giant, imbued with esoteric insight and accorded unquestioned authority. Unlike Frankism, Hasidism did not challenge the basic tenets of Judaism as it was then understood in eastern Europe. It was a revivalist, enthusiastic movement that championed feeling, prayer, music and dance over scholarship and ritual. Hasidism spread widely, particularly in eastern Galicia, from the second half of the eighteenth century onwards. Its opponents included strict constructionists such as Eliyahu ben Shlomo Zalman, Gaon (a rabbinical title of honour) of Vilna, as well as proponents of the Jewish Enlightenment (*haskalah*), which spread east from Germany. Some historians have seen a connection between the two conflicts, tracing links between Frankists and early Hasidim.

Among the foremost Hasidic leaders was Rabbi Shalom Rokeach (1779–1855) of Belz. It was said of this first 'Belzer rebbe' that, after his marriage, he devoted 999 days and nights to uninterrupted study. On the thousandth night, so legend had it, the prophet Elijah came to him in the midst of a great storm and inducted him into the mysteries of the Kabbalah (mysticism). Belz, a small town sixty miles north of Krakowiec, had a Jewish majority. Here the rebbe built an imposing court to which his successors made further additions; it became the most impressive building in the town. Rendered uninhabitable by fire during Second World War, its blackened, burned-out shell still dominated Belz when I went there in 1993. The influence of Rokeach and his successors radiated from Belz until they became the most important Hasidic dynasty in Galicia. Pilgrims came from far away to visit the rebbe; they treasured crusts of bread that he tossed to the faithful from his *tish* (table). In later generations the rebbe's spiritual sway extended into Hungary and Ukraine and to emigrant communities far afield. Belzer Hasidim survive today in large numbers, living in isolated social bubbles in Jerusalem, New York, London and Antwerp.

Belzer Hasidim, like other Hasidic sects, exhibited certain distinctive characteristics. For example, it was said that 'a true Belz Hasid never walked slowly. He always rushed and was in a constant hurry, although he hardly ever had a reason [for doing so].'[15] This distinctive gait is still observable among Belzer Hasidim today. Rather than the customary wig, married women covered their shaven heads with a so-called 'Belz veil' and wore old-fashioned *jubkas* (shroud-like gowns). The men had unkempt beards, wound their *peyes* (sidelocks) round their ears, wore a *gartel* (belt) at all times, and shirts generally open at the collar. The Austrian government tried hard to dissuade Jews from wearing traditional clothing. But except among the assimilating professional class, barely represented in Krakowiec, Jewish males continued to wear a long black *kapote* (jacket) and *bekishe* (overcoat), and to cover their heads, generally with a black *yarmulka* (skullcap). This was the uniform of most Jews in Krakowiec in the nineteenth century.

Like other *tsaddikim*, the Belzer rebbe was reputed to have magical powers. Tales of the miracles wrought by the rebbe were recounted by the faithful. At his court, chamberlains would attempt to organize the throng of pilgrims on hierarchical lines. Amid much pushing and shoving, a visitor would present the rebbe with a *kvitl*, a piece of paper on which he had written his mother's name and his place of abode. The document would set out his problem and would be accompanied by a cash donation. The rebbe would push the money aside disdainfully (his assistant would pick it up and deposit it in the treasury) and then render the requisite guidance – albeit often in oracular, gnomic form. The rebbe's influence stretched even beyond the Jewish fold, since politicians seeking election to the Galician Diet, the Austrian parliament, and, in later years, the institutions of the second Polish Republic often sought his support.

The Czech-Jewish writer Jiří Langer visited the court of the third Belzer rebbe, Issachar Dov Rokeach, in 1913 and wrote a fascinating description of its life and atmosphere, which was little changed from the previous century. Although born to an assimilated Jewish family in Prague, Langer became an adherent of Hasidism, while at the same time participating in modernist literary circles (he was a friend of Kafka and taught him Hebrew). Langer's account of his stay in Belz is one of the very few reports on the life of a traditional Hasidic court that combines the empathy and spirituality of a believer with the perceptive eye of an outsider. He paints a vivid portrait both of the external details of Hasidic life and of its inner, ecstatic spirituality.

The rebbe was said to be so holy that he would not so much as glance at a woman, not even his wife – 'somewhat corpulent but still beautiful', as Langer described her.[16]

The Habsburgs did their utmost to combat Hasidism, which they regarded as an obstacle to their centralizing, rationalizing, modernizing legislation. In 1838 the police commissioner of Lwów, Leopold von Sacher-Masoch, listed twelve *tsaddikim* regarded as the chief exponents of Hasidism in Galicia. He called these men egoists, swindlers and drunkards, as well as idlers, hypocrites and beggars.[17] Yet Hasidism's popularity was by that time such that it could not be suppressed.

The Jews of Krakowiec were not indifferent to these religious controversies. One of the Hasidic leaders listed by Sacher-Masoch was Meir Julius (the name is a little uncertain) of Krakowiec. Unfortunately, nothing more is known of him. Many of the Jews in Krakowiec embraced Hasidism, the great majority following the Belzer rebbe. This was the most important spiritual influence on Krakowiec Jews down to the twentieth century. All of them, including my Laub and Wasserstein ancestors, were deeply affected by it.

We are fortunate in having a significant indicator of intellectual tendencies among Jews in Krakowiec in the late Habsburg period: lists of *prenumerantn*, pre-publication subscribers to Hebrew books published in the eighteenth and nineteenth centuries. These lists, which, helpfully for us, appeared in the books themselves, usually included, next to subscribers' names, the towns in which they lived. Berl Kagan, an indefatigable collator of these subscriptions, lists fourteen books subscribers for which lived in Krakowiec.[18] These subscriptions indicate that some Krakowiec Jews were keeping abreast of the religious scholarship of the age, in particular Kabbalah. Were they deeply engaged in the religious polemics that surrounded Sabbateanism, Frankism and Hasidism? We do not have information on the subscribers' motives or reactions. Should we regard their subscriptions as indicating a keen interest in mysticism or were these merely nineteenth-century versions of coffee-table books, a form of conspicuous intellectual consumption? Probably they were more than that. Most of the subscribers were humble folk, petty merchants or stallholders, but we should not underestimate their potential level of Jewish erudition.

What is perhaps most striking about the fourteen titles listed by Kagan is that none of them in any sense fell into the category of *haskalah* literature. We should not conclude from this that modernist Jewish intellectual currents did not reach Krakowiec. For one thing, the subscription method was particularly, albeit not exclusively, used by authors and publishers of religious works. Popular secular literature, including works by *maskilim* (followers of the Enlightenment) and Yiddish books, was more commonly distributed by wandering booksellers such as 'Mendele Moykher Sforim' (both *nom de plume* and a fictional character of the hugely popular writer S. Y. Abramovich). By the early twentieth century Yiddish and Hebrew newspapers and periodicals also began to penetrate the *shtetlakh*, carrying the messages of new political and social doctrines. These too gradually reached Krakowiec.

Initially, the Austrian government placed some hope in education as a means of combatting Hasidism. Special schools were founded to provide Jews with a modern education. These provoked fierce resistance from traditionalists and were soon abandoned. Krakowiec was too small for such a school to be established there. Jews in the town could, however, take advantage of the limited opportunities that began to be offered for general education.

In the eighteenth century no governmental provision at all had been made for the education of the great majority of the population. Ignacy Cetner established a 'Trivial Schule' (elementary school) in Krakowiec in 1788 with financial support from the Roman Catholic priest and the municipality, as well as a financial commitment from two local Jews.[19] In 1805 the government took over responsibility for the school's maintenance. But for a long time only a small proportion of local children attended. In 1852, of 195 children in Krakowiec 'able' to attend (i.e. of the right age and not mentally or physically handicapped), only fifty-four were enrolled as pupils and of those only forty-four actually attended.[20] Even after compulsory elementary schooling was formally initiated in 1869, it was laxly enforced. In 1873 the Polish conservatives who controlled Galicia reduced the required years of schooling from eight years to six. A majority of children of school age in Galicia in 1880 did not attend at all. As late as 1900, the census reported that 75 per cent of men and 83 per cent of women in the Jaworów district, which included Krakowiec, remained illiterate.[21] The rate was highest among Ruthenians, lowest among Jews.

Many Ruthenians in Krakowiec, especially peasants, did not receive any education at all. Jews had the highest level of participation but some Jewish parents, uneasy about the cross that hung prominently on the wall of the classroom, refused to send their children to the local school. On the other hand, all Jewish boys and many girls received rudimentary instruction in Hebrew and Jewish religion in the *cheder*.

A modest attempt to advance education in the district was the announcement in 1867 of a scholarship competition for students from Krakowiec attending gymnasiums (academic high schools) or universities. Open to all, regardless of faith or social status, the award was named after Agenor Gołuchowski, at the time governor of Galicia (he had no other known connection with the town; the reason for his benefaction to Krakowiec is unknown).[22] A handful of boys (no girls) from the town were as a result enabled to attend a gymnasium over the next few decades. I have traced six who did so up to 1914; of these, five were Poles and one a Ruthenian.

The miserable state of education in Krakowiec emerges from a newspaper report in 1897. At that time the local school could barely function, as the schoolhouse had burned down two years earlier. In the interim, the town council argued fruitlessly with higher authorities about how a new building should be paid for. A plan was prepared for a five-class school but the newspaper pronounced this 'a joke as already five rooms are too few for 311 pupils'. Meanwhile a doctor stated that temporary classrooms that were being used must be closed as they were 'not only meagre and damp but also dark and to the utmost degree unhealthy'.[23]

As that report indicated, poor public education walked hand in hand with poor public health. In the mid-nineteenth century, average life expectancy in Galicia was under thirty years for both men and women, one of the lowest rates in Europe. Krakowiec had no doctor and no hospital. Princess Anna had left a legacy to provide these for the town after her death in 1814. But as we shall see, legal disputes for a long time delayed these provisions of her will from taking effect.

In the absence of any medical provision, the town was hard hit by repeated epidemics, especially of cholera. Causing acute diarrhoea and massive dehydration, it often led to death within hours. At that period the nature of the disease and the critical role of contaminated water as a vector of infection were not properly understood. With its marshy surroundings, Krakowiec was peculiarly susceptible. Cholera arrived in Krakowiec in 1831 as part of a pandemic that affected much of Asia, Europe and the Americas. In his story *Boa Constrictor* (1878), Ivan Franko recorded its impact in Galicia: 'Entire villages died out, whole families disappeared from the face of the earth, melting away like wax over a flame ... Men, women, and mostly children fell like grass before a reaper's scythe, dying quietly in the corners and nooks of the huts.'[24]

Jewish dwellings in Krakowiec, concentrated around the central square, drew heavily on the well there, probably contributing to the Jews' disproportionately high infection rate. The Jewish ritual of washing the body after death may have further speeded transmission of the disease. There was no known cure or treatment. Some Jewish communities resorted to magical remedies such as the 'cholera wedding' in which two poor people (vagabonds, beggars, hunchbacks, the mentally ill or disabled) were married in the town cemetery to the accompaniment of uproarious celebration. According to one authority on mystical folklore, the coupling of such marginal people was intended to drive away demons that had supposedly caused the epidemic.[25] Others have interpreted the ritual as a kind of sacrificial offering. My great-aunt Hela (*née* Kampel) records in her autobiography an instance of such a wedding in Krakowiec in her youth. According to her, 'after this celebration the cholera suddenly stopped and the funerals became less and less.'[26]

In the plague year of 1831, we are for the first time given a cause of death in the official record: at least sixty-three Jewish deaths (some entries are unreadable) were attributed to cholera. Presumably the disease was indirectly responsible for many more. The total number of Jewish deaths in Krakowiec shot up from fourteen in 1830 to over a hundred in 1831. The dramatic effects of the plague were reflected in a different way in 1832 and 1833 when just five and six Jewish deaths respectively were recorded. Evidently the Jewish population had been so reduced that there were fewer people left to die.

Over the next half century, a high birth rate enabled the Jewish population to recover both absolutely and relatively so that Jews became a majority of the town's population. As remaining legal restrictions against them were eased, they came to play an active role in every aspect of social, political and economic life. Krakowiec became, in large measure, a Jewish town. In an age of ethnic mobilization, a reaction was perhaps inevitable. For the time being, the protective imperial umbrella shielded Jews from the resentments of their neighbours. If that were to disappear, they would be defenceless. Unsurprisingly, therefore, the Jews of Krakowiec, as elsewhere, became the most fervently loyal subjects of the Habsburg emperor.

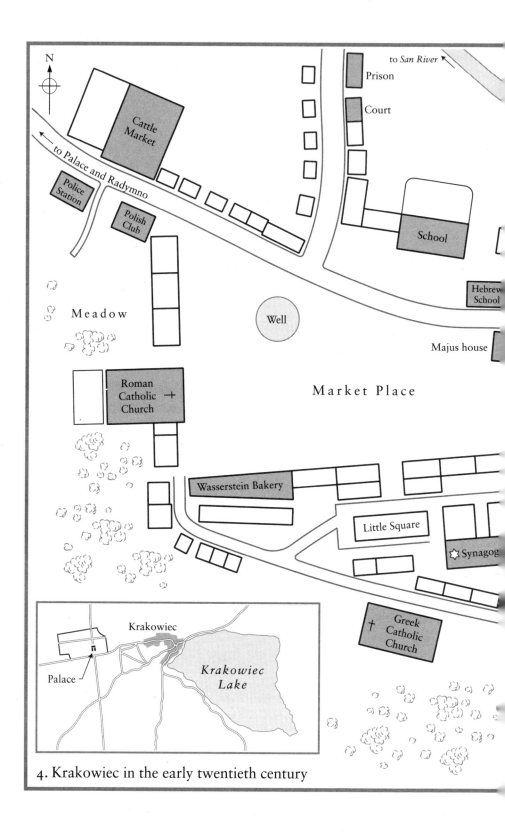

4. Krakowiec in the early twentieth century

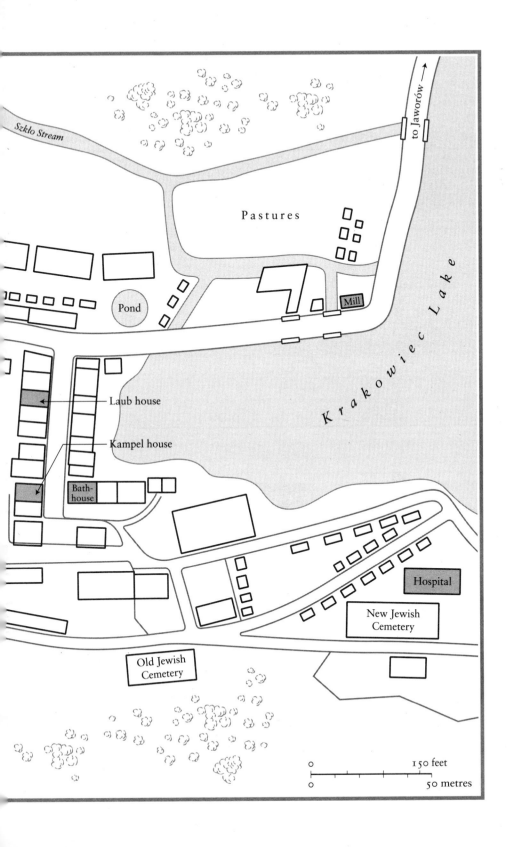

Szkło Stream

Pastures

to Jaworów →

Pond

Mill

Krakowiec Lake

Laub house

Kampel house

Bath-house

Hospital

New Jewish Cemetery

Old Jewish Cemetery

0 ——————— 150 feet

0 ——————— 50 metres

5

The emperor's Krakowiec

After the death of Princess Anna in 1814, the Krakowiec estate passed to her widower, Charles-Eugène, Prince of Lorraine, and then to the Potocki family. Count Leon Potocki, who took possession in 1829, conceived for a time the ambition of emulating Ignacy Cetner's greatest achievement. He employed a celebrated landscape designer, Joachim François Tascher. Of French or Swiss origin, he was said by some to be related to Napoleon's Empress Joséphine (*née* Tascher de la Pagerie). Joachim Tascher shared, if not kinship, Josephine's love of gardens, and greatly extended Cetner's at Krakowiec. He later performed 'garden miracles' on another of Potocki's estates, Livadia in Crimea (President Roosevelt stayed there during the Yalta conference of 1945). The Tsar was so delighted with Tascher's work that he engaged his services, decorated him, and granted him a lifelong pension.

With the purchase of Livadia in 1834, however, Potocki, one of the largest landowners in Poland, seems to have lost interest in Krakowiec. A year later the walls of the palace were reported to be cracking and the entire edifice was in danger of collapse. Shortly afterwards the central body of the building was demolished. All that remained were the two wings and the *porte cochère*, which featured 'two large statues depicting Sphinxes, with cupids sitting on them'.[1] In 1845 Potocki sold the estate together with surrounding farms to Prince Adam Lubomirski. The sale included the library, drawings, marbles, bronzes, kitchen equipment, glass and wine in the cellar.[2] But by that time little remained of Cetner's cabinet of curiosities. His pictures, books, coins, maps, ornaments, and other valuables were dispersed and, for the most part, disappeared.

An attempted national rising by Polish gentry in Galicia in 1846 was a fiasco. The revolt was snuffed out by the Austrian authorities who summoned peasants to rise up against their masters. In Lwów the *Kreishauptmann* (district captain) issued an order summoning 'all peasants with their scythes . . . to apprehend the rebels'.[3] Many heeded the call and turned viciously on their ancient enemies. They sacked manors and slaughtered noblemen. Like cats presenting mice tails to their masters, they offered the severed heads of landlords to Austrian officials. The violence was mainly concentrated in western Galicia. Mercifully, Krakowiec escaped it altogether. Yet there, as everywhere in Galicia, the peasantry's automatic deference to landowners was shattered. The historian Larry Wolff calls this event 'the defining and unforgettable moment of the province's history ever after'.[4]

The 'springtime of nations' in 1848 brought assertions of both Polish and Ruthenian national claims in Galicia. Barricades appeared briefly in Lwów. Having unleashed the tiger of peasant insubordination two years earlier, the government had little choice but to take the logical next step: abolition of most remaining vestiges of feudalism, including the detested labour duty. Jews became, in principle, equal citizens, though some restrictions persisted for another two decades. But the government set aside demands for broader political representation. Unlike elsewhere in Europe, the revolution in Galicia was not accompanied by anti-Jewish disturbances. In Krakowiec there is again no record of violence. The bombardment of Lwów by government forces in November marked the end of the revolution in Galicia. The next decade was one of 'neo-absolutism' in which the government reasserted its authority, though it could not turn the clock back on many of the reforms that had been enacted.

Adam Lubomirski did not take an active part in the events of 1846 or 1848. His passivity, however, inspired criticism:

> *We know Lubomirski - we know he has Krakowiec,*
> *And for sure a pretty wife and children*
> *But all that does not fill his docket with merit.*
> *To embellish a page of memories with your name,*
> *Should you not, Your Excellency, do something for your country?*
> *You have not in the past shown your virtues,*

And the brush has only just touched the canvas.
So if Your Excellency matches his virtues to those of his ancestors
Then will we say that Adam is one of us![5]

Unlike other members of the Lubomirski family, Prince Adam apparently failed, in the eyes of patriots, to rise to the occasion of these abortive attempts to recover Polish freedom.

During the sixty-eight-year reign of Emperor Franz Joseph from December 1848 to 1916 Habsburg policy was, above all, devoted to attempting to harmonize the often mutually antagonistic interests of the nationalities of the multi-national empire. Franz Joseph acquired great personal popularity. He was reputed to rise each day at 4.00 a.m. to 'labour for the people's welfare'.[6]

Galicia was treated by Austria essentially as a colony for the supply of raw materials. Polish aristocrats and some gentry retained large estates but tens of thousands of Ruthenian peasants farmed plots that inexorably diminished as land was subdivided generation after generation. Punsters called the Kingdom of Galicia and Lodomeria 'Golicia and Głodomeria' (kingdom of the naked and hungry).[7] The province was relatively under-developed. Per capita income was one tenth that of the rest of the empire. An estimated fifty-five thousand people a year died there of starvation in the late nineteenth century.[8] It has been argued that contemporary impressions of continuous rural immiseration may have been exaggerated.[9] Nevertheless, pressure on land and grinding poverty led to large-scale movement from the countryside to cities in Galicia and beyond.

The Prussian victory over Austria in 1866 shattered Habsburg pretensions to primacy among German rulers. The ensuing *Ausgleich* (compromise) of 1867, transforming the empire into a 'dual monarchy' of Austria and Hungary, also had consequences for Galicia. The government in Vienna felt compelled to devolve further autonomy to the region. Under this system the Polish landowning nobility consolidated its power. The electoral system, heavily weighted against Ruthenians, ensured continued Polish dominance. Polish replaced German as the primary language in the bureaucracy. Since the Poles in Galicia, unlike Russian Poland, enjoyed such considerable autonomy, the region came to be regarded as the hearth of Polish nationalism – a 'Polish Piedmont' that would be the foundation-stone of a unified nation-state, as in Italy in 1861.

The national movement was not universally hostile to Ruthenians. But Polish landowners, officials and members of the Galician Diet (provincial assembly) and the imperial parliament used their influence to conserve their dominance. Ruthenians, while chafing at the bit under Polish control, saw the imperial government as their protector and Franz Joseph as liberator of the peasants.

In Krakowiec as elsewhere the major landowners, although no longer feudal overlords, still held sway over the economy and society. In 1889 Prince Hieronym Lubomirski, who had inherited the Krakowiec estate from his father in 1873, sold it to Count Kazimierz Łubieński. The latter paid the colossal price of 400,000 gulden for the property (equivalent in 2022 purchasing power to nearly seven million dollars). Descended from an old noble family whose members had served Poland in high offices of church and state, Kazimierz had participated in the anti-Russian uprising of 1863.

Łubieński adapted the surviving portions of the palace to meet his needs. The right-hand wing became the family residence while the left-hand one accommodated guest rooms, estate offices and workshops. The remnants of Cetner's garden were poorly maintained. Exotic shrubs withered away; mature oaks were cut down for firewood. Soon little remained of it but a memory. Upon Kazimierz's death in Krakowiec in 1906, the estate was inherited by his widow, Jadwiga. She too could boast a patriotic pedigree, as a great-granddaughter of the statesman and poet Józef Wybicki, lyricist in 1797 of the 'Dąbrowski march'. This 'song of the Polish Legions' inspired nationalists throughout the nineteenth century in Poland and beyond, and was declared the national anthem of the second republic in the interwar years.

In the late nineteenth century, Galicia was increasingly recognized as a potential *Kriegsschauplatz* – a likely arena of combat between Russia and Austria. The dawning recognition in Vienna of this danger had come in 1849 when the Russians sent an army across Galicia to 'rescue' the Habsburg monarchy from revolution in Hungary. If the

Tsar could invade so easily as a friendly gesture, what might he not do as an enemy? For the Russians, Galicia was a potential gateway to Austria; for the Austrians, it was the launchpad for any invasion of Russia. As the Russians sponsored Slavic nationalisms in the Balkans, their relations with Austria deteriorated. Military planners on both sides therefore began to prepare contingency plans.

One consequence was the construction by the Austrians from 1872 onwards of immense fortifications at Przemyśl, which became the headquarters of the Austrian military garrison in the region. The San River was seen as a natural defence line. War games were staged each autumn in the area around Krakowiec, where field commanders would set up a temporary command post. The manoeuvres were often attended by the emperor who would survey the mock battlefield, appear on horseback to inspect his troops, and address them in German and Polish (Galician units were recruited mainly in the region itself).

During the manoeuvres of September 1889, Franz Joseph stayed with the Łubieńskis at the palace in Krakowiec. A triumphal arch was erected to welcome him and the clergy, gentry and officials of the district lined up to pay homage. Giving voice to the *kaisertreu* loyalty of the population, Alfred, Count Łubieński's twelve-year-old son, delivered a poem specially composed in honour of the visitor:

> *Forsooth, O lord, my boldness is great*
> *That I, a little man among your subjects,*
> *Should seek to dignify your kindness, your glory,*
> *Following the voice of my honest feelings.*
>
> *Though I have not become your soldier yet –*
> *My arm is, unfortunately, still too weak –*
> *I know that when this honour is bestowed upon me,*
> *I will find the strength, the valour, and the arms.*
>
> *This day, so splendid for my family,*
> *I shall treasure in my grateful memory . . .*[10]

Alfred did indeed later serve in the imperial army as a lieutenant in the 3rd Lancer Regiment. But at the age of twenty-five in 1902 he met a tragic end. His father wanted him to enter an arranged marriage. Alfred refused. A quarrel ensued. Alfred got on his high horse (literally) and galloped off in high dudgeon. About a hundred yards outside Krakowiec, he was thrown from his steed and killed. His tombstone can still be seen at the family mausoleum in the Krakowiec graveyard.

Among those who paid obeisance to the emperor in 1889 was the head of the Krakowiec Jewish community, carrying the *sifrei torah* (scrolls of the law), bedecked with velvet coverlets and silver bells and breastplates. The scene or something very like it was imported into fiction by the novelist Joseph Roth. Born in the Galician town of Brody in 1894, Roth was a backward-looking monarchist, who wrote with wry insight into the life of the region in the last decades of the empire. A striking passage in his masterpiece, *The Radetzky March*, depicts an encounter between a venerable Jewish notable, bearing a large, decorated Torah scroll, and the emperor, who deigns to offer his hand.[11] Unlike Joseph II and Metternich, who had been repelled at the very sight of Galician Jews, Franz Joseph developed a bond with his Jewish subjects that was sealed by such ceremonies. They affectionately Yiddishized his name as 'Froyim Yossel', acclaiming him as the father of their emancipation.

Well pleased with his reception in Krakowiec, the emperor presented a handsome monetary gift to the poor of the town and a separate sum to the Jewish community towards the restoration of the synagogue and nearby bathhouse. He sent a handwritten letter to Cavalry-General Prince Windisch-Graetz, expressing his satisfaction with the conduct of his troops during the manoeuvres.[12] To his intimate friend Frau Katharina Schratt he wrote that he was 'lodged very well in a one-storey castle. *Zacherl* powder not necessary' (*Zacherl* was a well-known brand of insecticide: presumably he meant that there were no bedbugs). But he delivered a snub to his hosts by declining to dine at the palace 'as, owing to lack of space, I have no kitchen of my own here.' Instead, he attended a 'very ample and animated dinner' with his officers in the nearby cavalry barracks.[13]

The next day the emperor proceeded from the palace to the centre of Krakowiec. There another triumphal arch had been constructed. In front of it, Rózia Pona, the little daughter of a Greek Catholic farmer, dressed 'in a Greek outfit and holding a flag, welcomed him with a beautiful and original demeanour'. A report on the ceremony in the *Gazeta Lwowska* provides saddening incidental information about the condition of the Krakowiec manor house at this time. Alas, following the demolitions undertaken by its previous owners, it hardly deserved to be called a palace anymore. It is not surprising that the emperor found fault with the available space. Of the central section of the building only the foundations remained. The two wings gave little indication of its former splendour. Cetner's fabulous park had been reduced to half its former size and was poorly maintained. The 'most beautiful ornament of the district' now was the lime-tree avenue leading from the manor to Krakowiec. Young couples were reported to repair there for what the paper delicately called 'rendezvous'.[14]

A couple of weeks later, the same paper presented grim news. Just ten days after the emperor's visit, hay in a barn belonging to Dmitri Pona, father of demure little Rózia, caught fire at five o'clock in the morning. The barn was situated next to the lime avenue. The fire destroyed the entire barn and its store of hay. When the conflagration was extinguished, a pair of shoes was found next to a charred corpse. It was presumed to be that of a soldier of an Uhlan (lancer) regiment who had come to Krakowiec for a 'rendezvous' with his lover.[15]

When the emperor next visited Krakowiec, for the manoeuvres of 1893, he was again welcomed with all possible honours. This time, however, the precaution was taken of mobilizing fire brigade units from Krakowiec, Jaworów and Wielkie Oczy.[16]

It is to this period that we owe the following anecdote. The Krakowiec garrison were very proud of the schnapps served in their mess, which acquired such a reputation, near and far, that it was called a veritable 'elixir of life' (*Lebenselixir*). One day a barmaid was serving drinks but accidentally missed out a newly arrived cavalry captain. Whereupon he said, '*Gnädige Frau, geben Sie mir auch so einen Lebensklystier*' (Dear lady, please give me an enema too).[17] Full appreciation of this rather primitive double entendre requires acquaintance with German but as the only recorded joke about Krakowiec, it is presented here for the reader's consideration.

Galicia was generally believed to suffer from acute rural overpopulation: nearly eight million people lived there in the first decade of the twentieth century. The Jews, about 11 per cent of the total, were heavily urbanized: in the largest city, Lwów, in 1900 they constituted 28 per cent of the population and in some smaller towns they were a majority. But a significant minority of Jews in eastern Galicia lived in villages – including several hamlets around Krakowiec. Whereas the great majority of Ruthenians and Poles earned their living from the land, Jews engaged mainly in trade, industry and handicrafts. An estimated 88 per cent of Galician trade in 1900 was, as the saying went, 'in Jewish hands'.[18] Although they were the main commercial element in small towns such as Krakowiec, most Jews, like the surrounding population, were poor, often desperately so.

These years saw massive emigration by both Jews and non-Jews. No fewer than two million people, including 350,000 Jews, left Galicia between 1880 and 1914. The largest numbers went to the United States but many moved to other parts of the empire, especially Vienna and Budapest, or to great European cities such as Berlin, Paris and London. A tiny rivulet flowed to Palestine. In spite of emigration, however, the Jewish population of Galicia rose from 687,000 in 1880 to 872,000 by 1910, mainly because of a high birth rate and declining death rate. The number of Jews in Krakowiec, however, was declining. From a high point of 1,003 in 1880, more than half the town's population (1,891), it fell to 668 by 1910. Jews were leaving the shtetl for new homes near and far. The main spur was economic: they sought enhanced opportunities in big cities, especially in the *goldene medine* – the United States.

Immigrants recorded at Ellis Island in New York between 1880 and 1914 included many from Krakowiec, both non-Jews and Jews. Among the latter, for example, was Reisel Nusskern, who landed in April 1899 with one of her two young daughters. She was listed as married but 'separated'. Travelling with her (at any rate, he was immediately in front of her in the line awaiting inspection by immigration officials) was Grzegorz Choma, aged twenty-seven, a Polish Roman Catholic labourer from Krakowiec. Alte Perl Wasserstein, aged thirty-five, arrived in 1901 to join her husband, Elias Gerstler, who was also from Krakowiec; she was detained for a time but then allowed to proceed. Rosa Krug first came to New York in 1900; in 1908 she returned with her small children, Chaje, Tomas and Willy, planning to join her husband, Moses. Debora Kahane, aged sixteen, disembarked in 1907 with three other teenage girls from Krakowiec, all intending to settle in New York. Abraham Wasserstein (not my father but another man of the same name), a self-employed junk dealer, later known as Abraham Stein, also arrived in 1907; he died in San Francisco in 1960.

In exile, Krakowiec Jews maintained contact with and affection for their home town. By 1899 they were numerous enough on the Lower East Side of New York to establish a *landsmanshaft*, the Krakovitser Kranken Untershtitsing Verein (society for the support of the sick). This was not only a benevolent and burial society but also a synagogue, with premises at 10 Avenue D in the East Village. It was never very large: in 1918 it reported forty-five members and soon after that the congregation dissolved. The burial society, however, remained in existence, eventually interring 140 members in its designated section of Mount Hebron cemetery in Flushing, Queens. The last such interment took place in 2008. The society was liquidated in 2016, by which time, presumably, all of its members had been buried.

Krakowiec around 1900 exhibited mixed signs of progress and decay. It enjoyed occasional moments of glory during the emperor's visits. The market still attracted crowds from surrounding villages. A handsome new school was built. The Jewish community began construction of a new 'Great' synagogue in the same central location near the market place as the smaller old one. It was a brick-built structure, cemented with a mixture of limestone and sand. In the traditional style, it had a *bimah* (raised platform) in the middle and a gallery for women above the entrance in the western wall. A small *bes midresh* (study and prayer hall) was later attached to the side of the building. It was an imposing structure, larger than the nearby Greek Catholic church although not so splendid as Cetner's great Roman Catholic edifice.

Yet in spite of all this, Krakowiec was going through a wretched phase. It was said to have 'the worst of reputations because of continuous denunciations to the courts ... Here as elsewhere the poorest of the poor are the village shopkeepers, to the relatively large number of forty, living out their miserable days.'[19] A conservationist reported that the tombs in the Krakowiec church were in a deplorable condition.[20] Unlike the previous quarter century of stable prices, the period

1890–1914 was one of high inflation in the surrounding area. Land prices and rents more than tripled.[21] In many ways Krakowiec gave the impression of being left behind by history.

One reason was that the railway never reached the town: plans for a line passing through Krakowiec were considered repeatedly but always foundered.[22] The main line between Przemyśl and Lwów, which opened in 1861, passed instead through Mościska, eleven miles to the south. A newspaper from Lwów consequently might take two days to reach Krakowiec, a distance of just forty-five miles.[23] Most residents rarely left the town in the course of their lives. Hardly any visitors came to the neighbourhood; one of the few who did so, a field botanist, complained that often, when he called at a village inn, all he would be offered was some dry bread and, if he was lucky, a sour cucumber or milk. Not surprisingly, he concluded that the area was hardly inviting to tourists.[24] For the Jews, however, there was perhaps a silver lining: the relative isolation of Krakowiec from major channels of commerce helped them to retain their dominant position in the local market.[25]

The comparatively mild rule of the Habsburgs permitted the expression of nationalist feeling among the Ruthenians of eastern Galicia. The first glimmerings of modern Ukrainian literature in the 1830s and 1840s provoked the chief of police in Lwów to write: 'We already have enough trouble with one nationality [the Poles] and these madmen want to resurrect the dead-and-buried Ruthenian nationality.'[26] But some Austrian officials welcomed the Ruthenian national awakening as a counterweight to Polish nationalism. The national bard of Ukraine and father of modern Ukrainian literature, Taras Shevchenko (1814–61), saw Russian domination as the primary obstacle to the freedom of his people. Shevchenko never visited Austrian Galicia. Because his works were banned in the Russian empire, however, Lwów became the main centre for their publication. The Shevchenko Scientific Society, founded in Lwów in 1873, played an important role in the development of Ukrainian cultural consciousness. By extension, Shevchenko also had a broader influence, since his work, though tainted by occasional anti-Semitic motifs, was admired by Yiddish writers such as Shalom Aleichem.

For Ruthenians, like Poles, Galicia came to be seen as a 'Piedmont', the hearth of their national project.

The chief resistance to Ruthenian nationalism came less from the government than from Polish nationalists who claimed that the Ruthenians were merely an 'artificial nation.' Unlike their co-religionists across the Russian frontier, who suffered severe persecution and forcible conversion to Orthodoxy until 1906, the Galician Uniates enjoyed full religious freedom under Austrian rule. But Poles, who considered themselves one of the 'historic' nations of Europe, despised the Ruthenians as uncultured boors.

The rivalry of Poles and Ruthenians was reflected in friction between their respective Roman and Greek Catholic churches. As in many regions of competing Christian sects, there were complaints of poaching. In May 1900, for example, the Greek Catholic priest in Krakowiec sent a letter of complaint to his bishop in Przemyśl listing the names of forty-four Greek Catholic village children who had allegedly been improperly baptised in the Latin rite by Father Jan Szczepek, the Roman Catholic parish priest in the town.[27]

Around the turn of the century Ruthenian nationalists in Galicia increasingly made common cause with their kinsmen under Russian rule. They began to call themselves 'Ukrainians'. An internal struggle among Ukrainians, between Russophile and Ukrainophile tendencies, resulted in victory for the latter. The nationalist movement began to envisage the creation of a state that would be independent of Russians, Habsburgs and Poles.

Krakowiec too was affected by these developments. A branch of the Ukrainian cultural organization Prosvita (Enlightenment), founded in 1868, was active in the town from 1893, enthusiastically promoted by the Greek Catholic priest, Seweryn Metella. Its adherents were mainly supporters of the Ukrainophile rather than the Russophile orientation. Prosvita encouraged reading – often out loud by those who were literate to those who were not – as well as agricultural innovation and efficiency. Books purchased for the Prosvita library in Krakowiec included a judicious mixture of those with some practical utility (for example, such titles as *Choice of Cement Roof*) and nationalistic histories (such as *From the Great Days*). By 1910 the society had 164 members in Krakowiec plus a few dozen others in surrounding villages where there were also reading rooms.[28] Such clubs, which often urged temperance on their members, were seen as competitors with Jewish-owned taverns and thus acquired an anti-Semitic tinge. Not to be outdone, a Polish 'popular education society' established Polish reading rooms: in 1906 there were two in Krakowiec holding a total of 201 volumes.[29]

National conflict reached Krakowiec in 1907 when a Ukrainian member of parliament arrived to address a public meeting. 'Several agitators were shouting slogans', according to a Lwów newspaper report. They demanded redistribution of land belonging to the nobility. 'Flags were prepared, to give the impression of a huge Ruthenian demonstration.' But the event was a flop because the Commissioner of Police turned up with three of his men, reinforced by 'a festively clad pack of vigilantes' and a couple of burly local yokels. Disappointed by lack of support among the local population, the MP left the meeting early.[30] This, at any rate, was how the occasion was depicted in the Polish nationalist *Słowo Polskie*, but perhaps its reporter deliberately played down the degree of enthusiasm for the Ukrainian cause.

Among notable Ukrainians in Krakowiec was Osip Shukhevych, one of the three judges of the Krakowiec court. He arrived in the town in 1904. Active in the Shevchenko Scientific Society, he also signed up as a member of the volunteer fire brigade, of which he was elected chief. In that office he changed the Polish eagle on the helmets of his men to the Ukrainian hawk. The story was told that he lived with his family in a house belonging to Dr Józef Gracko, a Pole, who had left to take up an appointment in Lwów. Gracko put the house up for sale but refused to allow Shukhevych to buy it, saying he would not sell it to a 'Russian' (presumably he meant a Ruthenian). Thereupon a Jew, one Sonnenthal, flautist in the local band, bought the house and promptly resold it to Shukhevych.[31] In 1907 Shukhevych's wife, Yevhenia, bore him a son, Roman, who was to play a significant role in Ukrainian history. Together with another Ukrainian judge, Osip organized support for nationalist candidates at elections to the Galician Diet. The contests in 1908 and 1912 were hard fought and hundreds attended election meetings in Krakowiec. Perhaps because of his political activity, Shukhevych was moved out of Krakowiec shortly afterwards.[32]

Polish hegemony in the province was bolstered by electoral malpractice. 'Galician elections' (the term was almost synonymous with fraud) were still conducted on a severely restricted franchise. Although universal, equal, direct and secret male suffrage was introduced in 1907 for elections to the imperial parliament in Vienna, reform of the franchise for the Galician Diet was repeatedly postponed. It therefore continued to be dominated by Poles up to the fall of the empire. In general, Ukrainian nationalism stayed within constitutional limits but the fervour of its adherents sharpened in these years. In 1908 the viceroy of Galicia, Count Andrzej Potocki, was assassinated in his office in Lwów by a Ukrainian student, Myroslav Sichynskyi. The assassin bellowed, 'You killed my people and for this I must punish you!'[33] The head of the Greek Catholic church, Metropolitan Andrey Sheptytsky, condemned the murder but other Ukrainian leaders were more ambivalent in their reactions. Polish–Ukrainian riots erupted in the city and tension was high throughout the province. Polish militants called for revenge while Ukrainian peasants sang 'Our Sichynskyi lives and Potocki rots.'[34]

In this atmosphere of growing Polish–Ukrainian dissension, Jews occupied an uncomfortable intermediate position. Although they had been emancipated as a result of the 1848 revolution, some restrictions were reintroduced in the 1850s. It was not until 1868 that full equality for Jews in Galicia took effect. The removal of all legal discrimination based on religion did not, however, lead to immediate and complete social equality. Over the next half century the Jews of Galicia became the 'whipping boys of the competing Christian nationalisms'.[35] 'The triangular intimacy and enmity of Poles, Jews and Ruthenians', writes Larry Wolff, 'became increasingly explosive in the context of the late nineteenth century Habsburg political scene.'[36] As in many other cases, so between Jews and non-Jews in Galicia, emancipation inflamed rather than healed relations. Two episodes in Krakowiec illustrate this.

The first was reported in a Vienna newspaper in 1869:

In the Krakowiec district a Jewish girl, Deborah, wanted to convert to Christianity. Her parents naturally set themselves against that intention but the girl was determined nonetheless not to abandon her plan. One morning the local priest succeeded in rushing the matter. Without consulting the girl's parents, he sent her to a safe place, namely the convent of Moszczan [Moszczany]. The nuns hid their little treasure and started instructing her with a view to preparing her for baptism in three or four days.

Meanwhile her parents found out where she was and summoned the Jews of the town for militia duty to save their child for Judaism. The coreligionists of the Jewish maiden went to the convent in Moszczan where they besieged the gates. A delegation presented itself to the prioress and . . . declared that before her flight Deborah had stolen all sorts of utensils from her parents' house. In small Galician towns, abductions of girls or conversions are often connected with pilfering of money or precious objects. The nuns, either because they took seriously the claims of the Jewish deputation or because they were afraid of a scandal, gave way and handed Deborah over to her coreligionists. They hastened back to Krakowiec with their booty and deposited her with one of her coreligionists.

But the priest of Krakowiec stood firm on his rights and strained every sinew to rescue Deborah. His efforts bore fruit . . . He managed to have her delivered to a pious sister in Krakowiec.

The Jews, however, also had their informants and spies: they girded up their loins and set forth on a holy war against that Christian house. A civil war would have broken out in Krakowiec over the maiden, had not the priest acted with great energy and circumspection. Naturally turning the matter to good account, he arrived on the spot accompanied by a military force. Within a few hours Deborah was delivered, under the protection of the gendarmerie, to the town hall of Krakowiec.

Her parents turned up there too and, amidst much sobbing and wailing, tried to dissuade their daughter from converting, but in vain. Deborah declared that she was adopting Christianity out of 'conviction'. The parents were at their wits' end and the priest himself was deeply moved by this confession story. He comforted the parents as best he could and then sent Deborah to Przemyśl to be baptized by the bishop.[37]

Unfortunately the newspaper did not give Deborah's full name, nor her age. But the incident shows how powerless Jews remained when confronted by the authority of the church, which could so easily call for armed support from the authorities.

The affair was of a piece with other abduction/conversion affairs of this period – most notoriously the kidnapping and baptism of six-year-old Edgardo Mortara by his nanny in Bologna in 1858.[38] That case became a worldwide *cause célèbre* but the Pope himself refused to relent and permit the boy to be returned to his Jewish family. He was educated for the priesthood and died in March 1940 in a monastery in Belgium. Perhaps fortunately so, for had he survived a little longer, he would have been a candidate for deportation to a death camp by the Nazis.

Did Deborah in a similar way end her life as a cloistered nun? Or worse? She might well still have been alive when the Germans arrived during the Second World War. Their brutality in Poland, even more than in Belgium, knew no bounds. No further press reports appeared on the case, so we do not know whether Deborah was eventually reconciled with her family or what became of her in later life. Evidently the writer of that newspaper account, so admiring of the priest's 'energy and circumspection', regarded its outcome, the baptism in Przemyśl, as a happy ending. Almost lost in all this was the little girl herself, shunted to and fro as a chattel, a symbol of possession, hardly a person, mere 'treasure' or 'booty'. We can only pity her and her family and speculate to what fate her conversion led. This episode was at least limited to the local area around Krakowiec. The second developed into a controversy on an empire-wide scale.

The Krakowiec hospital owed its existence to the endowment established by the will of Princess Anna, daughter of Ignacy Cetner, a year before her death in 1814. The will's complex provisions required that the lord of the Krakowiec estate support the annual costs of running the hospital, paying the salary of the doctor and providing medicines for patients.[39] Leon Potocki, however, simply refused to pay. Negotiations between the municipal authorities and his successor, Adam Lubomirski, proceeded very slowly. Eventually, in return for donating a new building plus a large sum in cash, Lubomirski freed himself and his successors from the obligation to provide annual support. The hospital finally opened in 1859. In 1870 the provincial government decided that the endowment would belong to the *gmina* (community) of Krakowiec but there were ongoing arguments about its management and related matters.[40]

In particular, a dispute arose between Krakowiec and surrounding towns. These demanded a voice in control of the hospital funds, complaining that the place was 'falling apart' due to maladministration.[41] Given the low quality of public health, the hospital played a crucial role in the district. In 1880 it had fifteen beds and in the course of the year tended 210 patients of whom the largest number were treated for typhus, *febris intermittens* and respiratory ailments.[42] In that year Oswald Bartmański, member of the Galician Diet for Jaworów and Krakowiec, took the matter in hand. Bartmański was described as a 'a stiff bureaucrat, who looked like a stick ... and always held his dignity like a glass in his hand.'[43] He presented a petition from the Krakowiec *gmina* to the assembly.[44] Neither the assembly nor the government proved able to settle the matter.[45] In the meantime, Bartmański died suddenly of a heart attack. The conflict remained unresolved for several years.

The imperial Ministry of the Interior eventually decided in favour of the citizens of Krakowiec but only at the expense of entanglement in further controversy. In 1891 an official decree of the Galician government set up a constitution for the hospital. This provided that it would tend 'the sick poor and their dependants of the Christian faith being subjects of the lordship of Krakowiec'. This formulation would have included residents of the town of Krakowiec as well as neighbouring villages such as Gnojnica and Ruda Krakowiecka – provided, of course, that they were Christians. The Jewish community of Krakowiec protested that they should not be excluded. The Ministry of the Interior agreed and accordingly set aside the restriction.

The matter was now taken up by an altogether more substantial figure. Count Jan Kanty Szeptycki, who took Bartmański's seat in the Galician Diet, was the head of a Polonized Ruthenian noble family and a large landowner. He occupied a number of important positions in Galician and Austrian society and government. His family played a major role in the modern history of the region. One of his sons, Stanisław, first an Austrian then a Polish military officer, became chief

1. Krakowiec coat of arms: the three fishes perhaps represent the three types of carp in the lake or the three historic communities of the town.

2. View of Krakowiec over the lake, 1847, by Maciej Bogusz Zygmunt Stęczyński, an artist noted for his landscape scenes of Galicia.

3. Ignacy Cetner, lord of Krakowiec, in his pleasure garden: a nineteenth-century caricature.

4. 'Hermit's hut' in Krakowiec palace garden, 1847, by Maciej Bogusz Zygmunt Stęczyński: it was inhabited by 'a hermit, the paid servant of the master, whose duty was to add a living comedy to the wooden one'.

5. The four-times-married Countess Anna Potocka (*née* Cetner) by Elizabeth Vigée-Le Brun: one of three portraits of Anna painted in Rome in 1791.

6. Krakowiec palace, 1834: a romanticized drawing by the folklorist Kajetan Kielisiński.

7. Greek Catholic church of St Nicholas in Krakowiec, photograph *c.* 1900: although Greek Catholics greatly outnumbered Roman Catholics, their church was much smaller and simpler.

8. Roman Catholic church of St James the Apostle in Krakowiec, pictured *c.* 1900. Built in 1787, this was the finest public building in the town. It was severely damaged in the Second World War. Later, the Soviets turned it into a plastics factory.

9. Postcard view of market square in Krakowiec, *c.* 1915: a charter of 1425 granted the town the right to hold markets twice a week, on Sundays and Thursdays, 'for ever'.

10. Winter scene in Krakowiec between the world wars.

11. 'Great' synagogue in Krakowiec, built around the turn of the twentieth century. After the war it was used as a cinema, then a bakery. Today, only the crumbling outer walls remain: weeds, shrubs and trees sprout up from the interior.

בית ספר עברי
בקראקוביץ
שנת תרצ"ג
מוכן א. 1933 ביהנוח

12. Hebrew school in Krakowiec, 1933, a modern establishment, distinct from the traditional *cheder*: note modern clothing and the presence of girls.

13. 'A melancholy picture of war': refugees fleeing from Galicia, 1914.

14. Lazar Kampel with his wife Sheindel-Rivka and their grandchildren, Krakowiec, 1930s. Lazar leased a mill from Countess Łubieńska. Lazar and his wife wear traditional attire, whereas the children are in modern dress.

15. Wasserstein family, Berlin, October 1934: Top row: (*l. to r.*) Czarna Wasserstein (*née* Laub), Berl Wasserstein, Hela Kampel. Front row: Addi and Lotte Wasserstein. This photo was taken at the time of Addi's bar mitzvah. Hela was on her way from Krakowiec to South Africa where she would marry Czarna's brother.

of the Polish General Staff in 1918. Another son took holy orders and, as head of the Greek Catholic church from 1901 to 1944, became the most respected figure among Ukrainians in the province. With Jan Kanty Szeptycki's support, the *gmina* of Krakowiec appealed against the Ministry's decision, arguing that Princess Anna's will had been intended to benefit *Unterthanen* (subjects) of Krakowiec, by which, they maintained, was meant only Christians. In any case, they pointed out that it had long been established practice in the hospital to exclude non-Christians.[46]

The case was heard before the Verwaltungsgerichtshof (Supreme Administrative Tribunal) in Vienna. This court, headed by Count Richard Belcredi, a former Austrian prime minister, specialized in issues involving minority rights. In a judgment issued in May 1894 it found that it was incorrect to assume that Jews could not be 'Unterthanen' in Galicia. Referring to Joseph II's Judenpatent of 1789, it declared that benefits from the endowment could not be made dependent on any religious test.[47] That was not, however, the end of the matter.

The Burmistrz (mayor) of Krakowiec, described as 'an Israelite' (I failed to discover his name), sought to implement the court decision but in vain.[48] The hospital administrators refused point-blank to give effect to the court's judgment. Appeals by the Jewish community to the district authority in Jaworów and the provincial government in Lwów were fruitless, as was a petition to the Galician Diet.[49] Meanwhile conditions in the hospital deteriorated: an inspector in 1896 found it 'very damp'. Jan Kanty Szeptycki proposed an ambitious plan for a new hospital 'in a beautiful and healthy location'.[50] The project foundered for want of cash or state support. Only the construction of a large, modern Jewish hospital in Lwów between 1898 and 1902 (a handsome building financed by a wealthy Jewish banker, politician and philanthropist, Maurycy Lazarus) reduced the pressure on Krakowiec Jews to pursue the matter further.

What this argument over access and funding disclosed was a new harshness, with an ethnic edge, to politics in Krakowiec, as in the region as a whole. In June 1897 *Gazeta Narodowa*, a 'democratic' Polish paper published in Lwów, commented on a report in the *Neue Freie*

Presse on the Jewish legal efforts to secure access for Jews to the hospital. 'What arrogance! Poor Galicia treats the Jews very well!'[51] The *Neue Freie Presse*, the leading liberal paper in Vienna, was known to be Jewish-owned. One of its foremost writers was Theodor Herzl, whose Zionist movement was about to convene its first congress in Basel.

Meanwhile, the rise of Roman Dmowski's populist Polish National Democrat party ('Endeks'), characterized by fierce anti-Semitism, threatened the Jews' traditional pro-Polish alignment in Galicia. In contrast, Ukrainian political parties, at this time generally liberal in orientation, were not hostile to Jews. Indeed, after 1905 Jewish-Ukrainian electoral coordination resulted in increased Jewish representation in municipalities and in the Galician Diet. But such cooperation among elites was more a matter of political tactics than shared outlooks. Ukrainian nationalism at grassroots level in rural eastern Galicia was beginning to take on an anti-Jewish colouring. Many villagers saw Jewish tradesmen, tavern-keepers, millers and estate managers as exploiters. A newspaper expressive of such views declared in 1879 that the Ukrainians in Galicia had 'two terrible enemies: one of them is the clever Jew, who sucks our blood and gnaws our flesh; the other is the haughty Pole, who is after both our body and soul.'[52]

Ivan Franko, the outstanding Ukrainian literary figure of his generation, condemned pogroms and wrote on the Jewish question with some insight and sympathetic understanding. He met Theodor Herzl and reviewed the Zionist leader's manifesto, *The Jewish State* (1896) favourably. On the other hand, Franko's stories and poems perpetuated unflattering stereotypes of the Galician Jew and he advocated restricting what he, in common with many others, regarded as the Jewish stranglehold over the Galician economy.[53]

In 1898 anti-Jewish riots broke out in western Galicia. Except in a few places such as Przemyśl, they did not spread to the eastern part of the province. The historian Daniel Unowsky explains that the animosity of Ruthenian peasants in eastern Galicia was directed more against Polish landowners than against Jews.[54] Absence of pogroms should not, however, be construed as absence of anti-Semitism. Hatred of Jews as bloodsuckers and purveyors of demon drink was surfacing in the countryside among both Poles and Ukrainians.

Tavern-keepers were particularly targeted: there were no fewer than seventeen thousand taverns in small towns and villages in Galicia in 1900. Eighty per cent of persons engaged in the production and sale of alcohol were Jews.[55] In Krakowiec there were calls for a 'Christian shop' that would reduce dependence on Jewish merchants alleged to be exploiting their monopoly of trade.[56] Among the urban population, newer forms of anti-Semitism were spreading, visible in newspapers, pamphlets and books published in Lwów in Ukrainian, Russian and Polish. Among these were works by Jakob Brafman, a convert from Judaism whose supposedly revelatory allegations concerning the Jewish community and the Talmud watered the soil for the conspiracy theorizing of the notorious forgery *The Protocols of the Elders of Zion.*[57]

Two Galician-born writers of this period furnish insights into Jews' relations with their neighbours in the waning years of Habsburg rule. In *The Emperor's Tomb*, Joseph Roth depicts the cordial, if patronizing, attitude of Galician Polish noblemen towards Jews, *their* Jews. Published in 1938 but set in the period just before the First World War, the novel recounts how Count Chojnicki helps a young Jewish student from his home province, whom he has not even heard play, secure entry to the music academy in Vienna. When the lad comes to thank him, he does so with an arrogant demeanour that almost belies the purpose of the visit. But Chojnicki is charmed: '"That is something!" he said after the boy had gone. "In our part of the world people don't even say thankyou; the opposite, rather. These Galician Jews, my Galician Jews, are proud folk! ... Everyone else becomes furious under persecution and servile when someone does them a good turn. Only my Polish Jews are unmoved by privilege or persecution" ... He said "my Polish Jews" in the same tone of voice as he had so often said to me: "my estates, my Van Goghs, my collection of musical instruments".'[58]

In a short story, 'The Bust of the Emperor', set in a small town in eastern Galicia, Roth describes the informal, but real power of the local landowner who was

more powerful than any of the administrative branches known to, and feared by, the peasants and the Jews, more powerful than the circuit judge ..., more so than the town mayor himself ... It seemed to the people of Lopatyny that 'Count' was not only a title of nobility but also quite a high position in local government. In practice they were not far wrong. Thanks to his generally accepted standing, Count Morstin was able to moderate taxes, relieve the sickly sons of Jews from military service, forward requests for favours, relieve punishments meted out to the innocent, reduce punishments which were unduly severe, obtain reductions in railway fares for poor people, secure just retribution for gendarmes, policemen and civil servants who had overstepped their position, obtain assistant masterships at the *Gymnasium* for teaching candidates, find jobs as tobacconists, deliverers of registered letters and telegraphists for time-expired NCOs and find 'bursaries' for the student sons of poor peasants and Jews.[59]

Roth is said to have called Galicia 'a paradise with minor flaws' ('ein Paradies mit kleinen Fehler').[60] Perhaps he was being ironical. Roth's writing is suffused with nostalgia for the lost world of his youth in a tolerant, multi-ethnic Habsburg empire, so it is more likely he meant it in earnest.

Less rose-coloured is the portrayal of that same world in the works of another, now almost forgotten novelist. Born in a shtetl near Lwów, Asher Barash spent the years before 1914 wandering around eastern Galicia, writing in Hebrew, Yiddish, Polish and German. His *Pictures from a Brewery*, first published in Hebrew in 1929, portrays a small town much like Krakowiec, situated next to a lake. A Jewish widow, Mrs Aberdam, runs a brewery that is leased from the local landowner, Count Molodecki. The Jews' homes are all clustered in the town centre 'like a tiny mite of cheese in a poor man's potato pancake'. In winter, residents, including the count's agent, skate across the lake: 'He was very good at it, gliding over the ice with the skill of a glazier drawing a diamond across glass.' When the ice melts, the count's servants drain the lake by opening the sluices of a canal. Then they pick up fish from the mud at the bottom. The brewery provides a steady income for the landlord, the leaseholder and the employees. But over time things take a turn for the worse. A fire destroys thirty of the one hundred Jewish houses in the town. An announcement is sent to a Lwów Jewish paper, appealing for aid. 'And everyone was full of wonder, for it was the first time that the name of their town had been printed in a newspaper.' The count falls heavily into debt. His new agent forbids Jews to skate on the lake. The brewery lease is not renewed and Mrs Aberdam and all her employees have to leave the premises. Even a letter from the Belzer rebbe fails to move the agent who sets his dogs on Mrs Aberdam. The novel ends with a terrible premonition of death by fire.[61]

N

Königsberg

Danzig

G E R M A N Y ✕

Masurian Lakes
(2–16 Sept. 1914 &
7–21 Feb. 1915)

Tannenberg
(26–30 Aug. 1914) ✕

Neman

← Eastern front line
on 31 Dec. 1914

← Eastern front line
on 30 Sept. 1915

100 miles

200 km

Niemirów

Warsaw

Bug

Vistula

Pinsk

Pripet

R U S S I A

P O L A N D

Chelm

Kielce

Kattowitz

Cracow

Gorlice/Tarnów
(2 May–22 June 1915) ✕

Gorlice

Tarnów

Jarosław

Krakowiec

Jaworów

Przemyśl
(siege Sept. 1914 –
Mar. 1915)

Brody

Lwów

Tarnopol

Dniester

Stanisławów

Munkács

Kolomea

A U S T R I A - H U N G A R Y

Danube

Budapest

Prut

R U M A N I A

5. War in Galicia, 1914–15

6

The burning shtetl

War in August 1914 dealt Krakowiec a sudden, direct, and shattering blow. In the front line from the outset, bombed, ravaged, repeatedly occupied and recaptured by contending forces, the town endured not four but seven years of unrelieved terror and carnage. The toll of bloodshed and destruction was monstrous. Nothing had prepared the townsfolk for such suffering. Many scattered never to return. As for the survivors, warfare inflicted psychic wounds, leaving a residue of vicious collective suspicions and hatreds. Ordinary human relationships collapsed into dog-eat-dog ruthlessness. The people of Krakowiec were plunged overnight into a dark realm. Their world would never be the same again.

As Austria-Hungary and its ally, Germany, came to blows with Russia, France and Great Britain, all the belligerent states looked over their shoulders, wary of the danger of subversion among their own citizens. Although the Austrian authorities regarded the local population in eastern Galicia as generally loyal, a report circulating in official circles in Vienna in August 1914 suggested that the supposed Austro-friendliness of the region's peoples had diminished over the previous decade.[1]

Poles were split in their sympathies. In Galicia most remained loyal to the Habsburgs, hoping to secure the liberation of their brethren in Russian-ruled Poland. Thousands volunteered for Józef Piłsudski's Polish Legion, which fought at the side of the Austrians. Only a minority heeded the call of the Endek leader, Dmowski, to cast their lot with the Russians.

Ukrainian political leaders in Galicia voiced support for the Austrians, with only a small Russophile minority dissenting. The authorities were nevertheless suspicious. In 1911 a senior Austrian military commander in eastern Galicia had reported that 'as matters now stand, the entire Ukrainian population must be considered unreliable.'[2] Upon the outbreak of war, the Austrians overreacted, arresting those regarded as enemy sympathizers. 'We fight on our own territory as in a hostile land,' the Austrian commander-in-chief, Franz Conrad von Hötzendorf, said.[3] Among those detained was a Ukrainian judge in Krakowiec who, with his colleague Osip Shukhevych, had participated in nationalist activity.

As war fever intensified, Austrian mistrust of Ukrainians led to persecution and atrocities against civilians. Thousands were executed. Suspects, including priests, were hanged in public, making 'tree branches top-heavy with horrific fruits', as a Polish observer noted.[4] Fourteen thousand Ukrainians, Austrian citizens, were interned in a camp at Thalerhof near Graz: one third of them died of typhus.[5] Some Ukrainians attacked Poles and Jews whom they suspected of denouncing them.

Of the three main population groups of Galicia, Jews alone were unambiguous in their attitude. Pro-Austrian, if only because of the ill-treatment of Jews by the Russian government, they responded to the outbreak of the war with strong affirmations of loyalty to Austria and to their beloved emperor. Such protestations availed them nothing. 'They know a lot and lie even more,' wrote an Austrian official. He considered that they might be useful but only under careful supervision.[6] As the conflict deepened, they were accused of treachery, malingering and war profiteering.[7]

The fighting quickly took a disastrous turn for the Austrians. The emperor's soldiers were shocked by what they saw as they marched through Galicia to meet the Russians. A subaltern wrote in mid-August: 'Dreadful filth, black, sticky, and it's drizzling. Marched through Rudki [Rudky, to the south of Krakowiec], the number of Jews, ghastly. Absolutely nothing except Jews.'[8]

The Russians tempted Conrad into an ill-judged push north into Russian Poland. After some initial, illusory success, he had to withdraw in the face of superior forces. The Russians advanced rapidly into Austrian territory and on 3 September captured Lwów. Then they struck west, aiming towards the great fortress of Przemyśl. Amid scenes of chaos and confusion, with roads and railways clogged by hordes of refugees and military supply traffic, the Austrians beat an improvised retreat.

Krakowiec was in the area of operations of forces under the command of Archduke Joseph Ferdinand, titular Grand Duke of Tuscany, known as 'the playboy archduke'. His Army Group of four infantry and two cavalry divisions formed part of the Imperial and Royal 4th Army, commanded by General of the Infantry Baron Moritz von Auffenberg, a former War Minister. It confronted the Russian 5th Army under General Pavel Wenzel von Plehve, a German officer in the Russian service.

Austrian attempts to break back towards Lwów were unavailing. Outnumbered and outgunned, commanded by officers too many of whom believed in the virtues of *Hurra-taktik* (senseless charges against the enemy by cheering infantry), they faced catastrophe.

On 11 September Conrad ordered a general withdrawal behind the San. He had already begun moving his headquarters from Przemyśl to west Galicia. A staff officer wrote that the roads were so blocked with ambulances and supply convoys that he could not travel by car but had to ride on horseback in pouring rain from Niemirów to the 'miserable hole of Krakowiec'.[9]

Austrian forces engaged the Russians in an intensive battle to protect the crossings over the Szklo stream, just north of Krakowiec, where Auffenberg set up his command post (*see map on p. 40*). On 13 September Conrad received a report that a Russian infantry division was advancing westwards from Krakowiec to Gnojnica. Auffenberg attempted to make a stand against the Russian cavalry at Krakowiec and Gnojnica. The rout of his forces was so dire that he had to pull back almost immediately as shells flew overhead. The Russians captured eight hundred Austrian soldiers in Krakowiec. A wretched fate awaited them as prisoners of war: one spent the next fourteen years in Siberia before being allowed to return home.[10]

In huge disorder and demoralization, the Austrians withdrew behind the San. 'The path is crowded with refugees,' Auffenberg recorded. 'Many Jews. The poor things imagine they can save their lives and their miserable possessions by running away. The whining and wailing is pitiful . . . A melancholy picture of war!'[11]

A Rumanian officer serving in the Austro-Hungarian army recorded what he saw at a village a few miles south of Krakowiec:

> We shared the road with an interminable file of refugees, mainly Jews. A girl described them as the 'second army' and told us that they had been on the road three weeks without the faintest notion as to where they were going. We had seen many of these Jews during the last few days, poor wretches who had left everything behind them except the few belongings on their backs, and, as a rule, a cow to share their wanderings. Just outside Starzava [a little south-east of Krakowiec] there was a camp for Jewish refugees, and what with their destitution and the rain, they presented a picture of truly piteous misery. Hundreds of dirty, ugly faces, drawn with hunger and terror, could be seen on all sides peering from drays and carts piled high with domestic utensils, furniture, poultry, women and children. The innocent faces of babies and here and there a slip of a girl were the only bright spots in that bleak landscape.[12]

The soldiers of the retreating army, who had not been fed for days, laid villages waste as they passed through: 'Hunger and an empty stomach prescribe a special code of morals,' the Rumanian observed philosophically.[13] In Krakowiec in mid-November all the shops were stripped bare, as armies passed through, plundering all the stocks.[14]

Over a million civilians, including half the Jewish population of Galicia, fled west. They were herded to distribution centres, including one in Upper Silesia at Oświęcim, later better known under its German name, Auschwitz. From there many set off under their own steam to Vienna. Others were packed off to camps in Moravia, in particular one at Nikolsburg (now Mikulov). Many Krakowiec Jews found temporary shelter there in overcrowded, filthy, disease-ridden barracks.[15] Among those who fled were my ancestors, members of the Wasserstein and Laub families.

The Austrians had started the war with 900,000 men under arms in Galicia. Within six weeks they lost at least a third of them, killed, wounded or taken prisoner. Winston Churchill later wrote of Conrad's soldiers that he 'broke their hearts and used them up in three weeks'.[16] The debacle marked the beginning of the end of Habsburg power in Europe. Several generals were dismissed. Others committed suicide. Auffenberg broke down, was removed to Vienna, and briefly imprisoned on a charge of financial irregularities. Conrad, who was most responsible for the fiasco, retained his post, bleeding new armies to death.

Krakowiec remained under Russian occupation for the next nine months. The area remained a theatre of military operations because of the Russian encirclement of Przemyśl. In an epic siege, the fortress held out against the Russians through the exceptionally bitter winter of 1914–15. Thousands of Austrian soldiers succumbed to frostbite. After eating nearly all their horses, as well as cats, dogs and mice, the defenders were finally starved out. The Austrian commander surrendered with his 123,000 men on 22 March 1915.[17] The city's fall was a further military disaster for the Austrians. When the aged Franz Joseph heard the news he burst into tears; his weeping subsided only after two days. A month later Tsar Nicholas II visited Przemyśl to inspect his new prize.

The savagery of the war on the Galician front caused massive devastation and human suffering. Homes were looted, villages destroyed, horses, cattle and foodstuffs plundered. In Horodenko, a small town to the south-east of Lwów, an official Austrian report described the entry of Russian forces: 'Music played as the Cossacks danced before the burning homes, and where a Jew, having remained inside, tried to save himself, he was thrown into the fire to the mocking laughter of the Ruthenian population in attendance.'[18] The San River, choking with the bodies of thousands of dead during the siege of Przemyśl, became a health hazard, spreading disease downstream.

The Polish novel *Austeria* ('The Inn', 1966) by Julian Stryjkowski (a Jew, born Pesach Stark in eastern Galicia in 1905) records, with tenderness, brutality and humour, the reactions of shtetl Jews to the imminent arrival of Cossacks. The invaders arrive like one of the ten plagues:

> The locusts descended suddenly. At noon it grew very dark, and a thick cloud moved in from the direction of the General Hospital. It was high in the sky and looked as if it were about to rain or even hail, until it blocked the sun. The noise did not resemble the roaring of the wind, because not a single leaf moved on the trees, not a speck of dust rose on

the road. Darkness fell on the earth slantwise, in clouds one after the other. The noise was so great that it drowned the voices of the cattle lowing in fright, the howling of the dogs and the shouts of the people. Shut the windows! Close the stable doors! Children were hurriedly brought indoors from the streets. Nobody could tell who was calling or screaming. The swarms of insects hit people in the face ... They made their way into the hall, the kitchen, the living rooms, the cow-shed, the milk pails. They piled up in layers, one on top of the other, a general mating occurring casually while food was being sought, at random, blindly, densely, on the move. The field, the rooftop, the road – everything seemed to crawl like one enormous leathery beast.

As rumours about the ebb and flow of battle reach the town, the terrified inhabitants, 'which means the Jews', are 'alternately packing and unpacking'. Eventually the invaders rape, pillage, kill, and set the town on fire, as the Jews flee or resign themselves to the mercy of their Creator.[19]

The conquering army promised the population of the occupied areas freedom and realization of their national aspirations. As with many military occupations before and since, such assurances proved of scant value. The Russian military administration was guided more by the object of annexing Galicia. The prime minister, Ivan Goremykin, called it the 'last diamond to the tsar's crown', though one of his predecessors, the liberal Sergei Witte, dissented, pointing out 'but it is full of Jews.'[20]

Accused of spying, sabotage, hoarding and price-gouging, Galician Jews were subjected by the occupiers to discriminatory decrees, maltreatment and atrocities. Jewish civil servants in Lwów and elsewhere were dismissed. Publications in Yiddish were prohibited. A pogrom by Cossacks in Lwów on 27 September 1914 left an estimated forty Jews killed.[21] In Przemyśl Cossacks attacked Jews with whips. The Russian military commander then ordered the entire remaining Jewish population to evacuate the city. As a result, crowds of refugees fled in all directions. Ukrainian peasants attacked the property of landowners and Jews. Further massacres were perpetrated in other towns in the region. The head of the Lwów district military administration accused Jews themselves of provoking the pogroms.[22] Tens of thousands of Jews were deported to as far away as Kamchatka in the Russian Far East.

Krakowiec suffered severely from the depredations of both sides. At some point the two sphinxes, remnants of Ignacy Cetner's grand palace, were carted off and never seen again. The entire contents of the palace (that is, of its remaining wings) were also looted. 'Only the bare walls of both outbuildings remained.'[23] As if the horrors of warfare were not enough, the region was struck by epidemics of typhoid, smallpox and cholera, which spread throughout the Austrian empire and reached Krakowiec in July 1915.[24]

The transformation of eastern Galicia into a battlefield and the flight of a large part of its population, particularly Jews, left the region eerily empty of civilians. A relief commission dispatched by the Rockefeller Foundation in the summer of 1915 reported that you could search Galicia in vain for a child less than ten years old.[25]

The Czech-Jewish playwright František Langer (brother of Jiří, the Belzer rebbe's guest two years earlier), who served as an army doctor in the Austro-Hungarian army, witnessed the exodus:

> The war swept through the Galician villages, churning them into mud or sending them up in flames. I saw the Jewish, Chassidic settlements, and the infinite misery, agony and despair of their inhabitants who had no idea why all this destruction and murder was going on and why, in particular, it should have fallen on their heads. They fled in desperation, on foot, with bundles on their backs, or pushed before them, on wheelbarrows, a few bed-clothes and cooking utensils. A few of them made better pace on carts pulled by emaciated horses, loaded up with children and some miserable possessions. Years later it was difficult for me to compare these heart-searing pictures of frenzied horror with that naive, almost childish state of bliss in which they had lived before this catastrophe.[26]

Not all onlookers, however, shared Langer's empathy with his kinsmen.

The sudden influx of these masses of Galician Jews to small towns in Hungary and Moravia as well as to Vienna incited a backlash on the part of the settled populations. Galician Jews suffered from a poor reputation among their co-religionists no less than among non-Jews: *Galitsyaner* were seen as semi-civilized, sharp-witted and cunning swindlers. The historian Jacob Katz, recalling his youth in a small village in Hungary, recounts: 'Even the Jews were taken aback by these figures, whose appearance was as bizarre as their language; the men had wild and unkempt beards and were dressed in threadbare caftans, and the women wore head coverings and dressed just as strangely.'[27] The negative stereotype endured even half a century later: Hannah Arendt, for example, expressed a view common among German Jews when she contemptuously dismissed Gideon Hausner, chief prosecutor at the trial of Adolf Eichmann in Jerusalem in 1961, as 'a typical Galician Jew, very unsympathetic'.[28]

Among those who fled their homes was Jiří Langer's former host, the third Belzer rebbe, Issachar Dov Rokeach. Unlike some rabbis who made patriotic speeches and enlisted as army chaplains, the Belzer *tsaddik* made no bones about his distaste for the war: when he passed a collection box for war contributions he burst out: 'Is that what we've got to do with our money – so still more people can be murdered?'[29] He retreated to Munkács in Sub-Carpathian Ruthenia, then in Hungary. The rebbe of that place shared the Belzer's profound belief in his own importance and deeply resented the arrival on his turf of a rival *tsaddik*. The two engaged in bitter polemics against each other for several years until the Belzer retired from this field of battle and returned to his mansion in Belz.

In April 1915 the tide of war on the eastern front turned, as large German formations reinforced the Austrians and launched a successful counter-attack against the Russians at Gorlice in the Carpathians. They broke through, scoring a decisive victory. Reliance on their ally was a humiliation for the Austrians but the Germans' help soon enabled them to regain control of eastern Galicia. On 3 June 1915 Bavarian troops recaptured Przemyśl, or what was left of it after nine months of artillery pounding, and the Austrians advanced rapidly against fierce opposition towards Lwów.

On 14 June Habsburg forces reached high land east of Gnojnica. Aerial reconnaissance spotted a long Russian supply line leaving Krakowiec for Jaworów. The *New York Times* reported: 'The Germans

have completed the refitting of their famous phalanx and have succeeded again in moving forward eastward from the San . . . The point
now reached by the Germans is at least fifteen miles from Jaworów,
somewhere west of Krakowiec. Fighting is of course continuous day
and night . . . The Germans are determined to force their way by the
sheer weight of their battering ram.'[30] The 39th Infantry Division of
the *Honvéd* (Hungarian army) moved forward but came under fire
from a Russian rearguard in swamps to the east of the Krakowiec
lake. After intense fighting north of the town, the Russians gave up
Krakowiec.[31]

Incensed by their military setback, the Russians found an easy
scapegoat in the Jews, alleging that they must be in collusion with the
enemy, or at any rate susceptible to enemy propaganda (the Germans
were, in fact, targeting Jews in the battle zone with pamphlets in Yiddish). As the Russians fell back, the chief of the general staff, General
Nikolai Yanushkevich, pursued a scorched earth policy, ordering mass
expulsion of all remaining Jews from areas near the front. Some were
sent towards the enemy lines; others into the interior of Russia. Most
had nowhere to go. Panic reigned.

The Russo-Jewish writer and ethnologist Shloyme Zanvel Rappoport (better known under his pen name, S. Ansky) was working at the
time with a relief mission just behind the Russian lines. He witnessed
the pillage and cruelty inflicted upon the Galician *shtetlakh* by the
retreating Russian forces. In Jaworów, he saw his 'first dismal tableau
of a routed army'. Local Jews told him that the Russian troops had
perpetrated 'a terrible pogrom, looting the entire town'. News came
that the Austrians had recaptured Krakowiec: 'The town commandant had bolted yesterday. All institutions were already gone. Since the
leftover supplies couldn't be taken along, the commissariat was dis-
tributing them to the passing soldiers and local Christians – Jews
didn't even dare approach. The recipients took as much as they
wanted, as much as they could lug. And yet tons of oats, dry crusts,
tin cans, and other food would remain and go up in smoke.'

That night, after a long search, Ansky and a companion found shelter in a nearby Jewish inn. Early the next morning they were woken
by noise outside.

I went to the window and saw lots of Jewish women dashing about, wailing and screaming, followed by half-naked children. We realized that something awful had happened. We threw on our clothes and hurried out. It seemed that around two a.m. troops had surrounded many Jewish homes and seized forty of the more prominent men as hostages. No one knew where they had been taken, and that was why their wives were rushing helter-skelter, looking for them . . .

The torrent of the retreating army, which had passed through since yesterday without a moment's interruption, was overflowing into the streets. Wagons and artillery, pedestrians and wounded men – pursued by the thunder of cannon.

The proprietor of the inn and her two daughters, who had been baking bread all night, fell to their knees before us, weeping and begging us to advise them whether to leave or stay. Could the last units, Cossacks, murder Jews, rape women? . . . What advice could we give?

When Ansky returned to the Russian divisional headquarters in Jaworów, he found that 'it was gone.' He barely managed to commandeer a car to take him back to Lwów, which was in chaos. The city was retaken by the Austrians a couple of days later.[32]

For some time still, the fighting ebbed and flowed over Krakowiec. On 17 September 1915, eve of the second Rosh Hashana (Jewish New Year) of the war, an observer recorded a scene on the road near the town. In the late evening a column of Austrian and Hungarian troops was moving along in disorder. Two pale Jewish girls and an old man were squeezed in among the soldiery and heavy equipment. One called out, 'Soldier sir, help us to get to Krakowiec before nightfall. It's erev Rosh Hashana!' . . .

Two hours later the Cossacks evacuated Krakowiec, but not before setting it ablaze. A young Austrian Jewish recruit entered the synagogue to confront a horrifying scene:

Whoever couldn't or wouldn't flee the burning shtetl, women, children, babies were lying in the vestibule all packed together. Screams, screeches, howls filled the air in the small space, inarticulate, unrestrained, limitless, as only the most horrific fear could produce. In the dim candlelight, he could barely make out shapes, just bundles of misery, twitching bodies, here and there emaciated arms holding up babies as if to curse them. In the inner chamber old men (there were no young ones) in white smocks, praying, crazy with fear, with loud cries, delirious pleas, curses, imprecations. The horrified western Jew could not understand what they were praying for in that small black space: it was the prayer for the dead.[33]

Deliverance from the Russians brought no respite for the Jews who were accused in the Polish press of having welcomed the Russian occupiers and of collaboration with the enemy.[34] The allegation, for which there was no factual basis, would have bloody consequences – and would find an echo a quarter of a century later with even more terrible results.

Soon the tide of war reversed again. A successful Russian offensive under General Aleksei Brusilov in June 1916 destroyed Archduke Joseph Ferdinand's 4th Army ('the most inglorious event in the *Ostfront*'s fighting record' according to a recent historian)[35] and drove back what remained of the Austro-Hungarian armies, threatening a Russian reoccupation of Lwów. Only the renewed support of their German allies saved the Habsburg forces from a total rout.

Some Jews, including many refugees from Russian-occupied areas to the east, still remained in the region, but their economic situation was dire. The American Jewish Joint Distribution Committee spent more than ten million dollars for relief of victims of the war throughout the world in 1916; but this colossal sum (equivalent to more than two hundred million dollars in 2022 purchasing power) was inevitably spread thin. Krakowiec received 700 crowns (equivalent at the time to about 86 US dollars).[36] Such aid was only a fraction of what was required.

The town had been devastated by the fighting. Several buildings, including the hospital, the government tax office and the Prosvita reading room, had suffered severe damage. Eighteen dwelling houses and thirty-six outbuildings had been totally destroyed and many more were in need of repair. The Austrian government offered compensation in 1917 to some of those who had suffered property losses. Among those who lodged claims was my great-grandmother Chana-Gittel Laub. The house on the market square where she lived with her husband Chaim-Yitzhak Laub and their nine children required large-scale reconstruction. The Austrian authorities awarded her a grant of 3,648 crowns (equivalent in this period of rapid depreciation of the currency to 57 US dollars) plus a loan of 20,340 crowns ($317).[37]

The outbreak of revolution in Russia in March 1917 and the Bolshevik seizure of power in November brought hope of an end to hostilities. But the disintegration of the Tsarist empire opened the door not to peace but to anarchy. In February 1918 Austria signed a peace treaty at Brest-Litovsk with the *Rada* (Council), a quasi-independent Ukrainian government that had been set up in Kiev. Ostensibly this marked the victory of the Central Powers in eastern Europe. The reality was different. Facing desperate food shortages in Vienna, the Austrians decided to yield territory in return for grain shipments. The district of Cholm (Chelm, to the north of Galicia and formerly under Russian rule) was promised to Ukraine. A secret annex to the deal provided that eastern Galicia would be combined with northern Bukovina to create a new 'Ruthenian crown land' of the Austrian empire. Krakowiec would have fallen within this new entity. Word of the arrangement leaked out, provoking fury among Polish nationalists, who had no intention of relinquishing any part of what they regarded as their historic patrimony.

Demonstrations and riots broke out against this 'fourth partition'. Polish army units mutinied. Dozens of protesters were killed. The *Rada* soon collapsed and the treaty disappeared into the diplomatic waste bin, but the damage had been done. Rather than securing the survival of the empire, the 'Bread Peace' paved the way to its demise. Austria-Hungary, it has been said, 'was destroyed by victory rather than by defeat'.[38]

The tottering Austrian government ordered refugees from the eastern war front to return to their homes. Those who did so found themselves confronted by utter ruination. In early 1918 hundreds of returnees were said to be dying each day in eastern Galicia.[39] In June an official report warned:

> The food shortages are leading the population to believe that distribution is unfair. Everyone complains that the central authorities in Galicia

are not conducting affairs properly. There is also bitterness here and there against the political administration who are said to be relying on far too many Jews as personnel in the supply administration, most of whom as a result have been exempted from military service.

These circumstances have led to looting of grocery stores and in connection with that to pogroms against Jews which also had their origins in the preference given to Jews in food distribution.

The authorities are also said not to have intervened with the necessary energy towards the pogroms, which in one case led to armed Jews resorting to self-defence.[40]

The Habsburg armies disintegrated as tens of thousands of servicemen deserted. The collapse of government left a dangerous power vacuum. Gangs of absconding soldiers emptied shops in Lwów and roamed the countryside, spreading mayhem. The historian Alexander Watson writes: 'People withdrew for protection into their own ethnic groups, and as communities nationalized, Jews in particular came to be regarded less as unwanted neighbours than as malign foreign objects with no right to belong.'[41]

On 1 November 1918 Ukrainian nationalists in Lwów seized the city hall and declared the establishment of a West Ukrainian People's Republic. Fighting broke out in the city between Ukrainian forces and smaller Polish army units. For the Poles this became a mythic battle of national liberation that they likened to the epic seventeenth-century struggle against Khmelnytsky. Leaders of the Jews in Galicia declared neutrality, thereby incurring charges of treachery from the Poles. When Poles loyal to the recently established national government in Warsaw, reinforced by troops from Przemyśl, succeeded in gaining control of Lwów by 22 November, the victorious soldiery was granted three days of freedom to plunder at will.

There followed a bloody, carnival-like pogrom in which at least seventy-three Jews were killed (an unpublished Polish government report put the number of dead at 150)[42] and 437 injured. Three synagogues were set on fire and a great deal of Jewish property looted. This was 'the most devastating pogrom in the period 1914–20 and indeed in known Polish history before World War II'.[43]

The Roman Catholic archbishop of Lwów, Józef Bilczewski,

condemned the violence, adding that 'he must leave the decision to what extent Jews had incurred some guilt themselves to the judgement of God and the courts of law.'[44] Bilczewski's delicately balanced comment barely concealed the predominant view of Poles and of the Polish Church, that the Jews had brought this upon themselves. With minor variations, this was to be the formulaic response of Polish churchmen and politicians after incidents of anti-Jewish violence throughout the interwar period.

In Przemyśl too, Polish troops had celebrated their capture of the city with a pogrom. The military commander there suppressed the disorder. He then issued a decree requiring the Jewish community, who had been accused of disloyalty, to pay a *cautionnement* (security deposit) of three million crowns within four days, failing which the money would be taken by force. The money was not paid. The order was eventually withdrawn after external pressure and negotiations; but the breach in communal relations was not easily erased.[45]

Reports of the Lwów pogrom and of massacres of Jews elsewhere in the region reverberated around the world and gravely damaged the reputation of the newly recreated Polish state. Polish politicians and diplomats grumbled that they were victims of a campaign of vilification by Jews.[46] The prime minister, Ignacy Paderewski, complained bitterly to US President Woodrow Wilson about anti-Polish propaganda in the United States, declaring that the violence was mainly a result of 'Jewish arrogance and agitation'.[47]

The Polish recapture of Lwów did not end the conflict in eastern Galicia. A full-scale Polish–Ukrainian war ensued. Galicia fell into semi-anarchy, as marauding bands looted, burned and killed. Jews found it ever harder to maintain neutrality: some opted for one side, some for the other. A few fought for the Ukrainians, persuaded by promises of full equality in an independent Ukraine. But it was an uneasy alliance. Vengeance for alleged treachery was wreaked against Jews by both sides. Among the perpetrators of pogroms were members of the 'Sich Riflemen', originally a 2,500-strong volunteer legion, recruited by the Austrians in 1914 from Ukrainians in eastern Galicia to fight against the Russians.

On 1 November 1918, simultaneously with the Ukrainian coup in Lwów, two units of *striltsy* (Ukrainian militiamen) from Jaworów, under the command of Vasyl Kvas, seized Krakowiec. In the course of their takeover, a member of the militia was killed. According to a Ukrainian account, one hundred inhabitants of the town and its environs rallied to the Ukrainian flag. The *striltsy* returned to Jaworów, leaving a force of civil and military policemen under the command of Andri Shakhinsky to maintain order in the town. They ordered the Jewish community to surrender horses and money without which they would take away ten young men. Some of the wealthier Jews complied (for which they were later accused of treachery by the Poles).[48] The hundred Ukrainian volunteers were sent to the front, along the railway line from Przemyśl to Lwów, to fight the Poles.[49] At the end of the month three hundred sledges, full of Polish legionnaires, passed through Krakowiec on their way to attack Jaworów, but they were beaten off by the Ukrainians. Heavy fighting ensued as the two sides battled for control of communications between Przemyśl and Lwów. It was not until March 1919 that a Polish force under Colonel Henryk Minkiewicz secured control of the Krakowiec area. The 'Blue Army', well-trained troops under General Józef Haller, were repatriated from France and augmented Minkiewicz's forces, allowing the Poles to gain the upper hand. By July they had consolidated their hold over the whole of eastern Galicia.

Meanwhile at the Peace Conference in Paris, diplomats fought a parallel battle of words. The Poles were infuriated at being required to sign a 'Minorities Treaty'. This was supposed to guarantee fair treatment of their Ukrainian, Jewish and German minorities, a third of the population of their republic. The treaty was imposed by the great powers as a condition of their recognition of Polish independence. Polish nationalists, however, regarded the treaty as a slur on their honour and an infringement of their regained sovereignty.

Eastern Galicia became an insoluble conundrum for the peacemakers, akin to that notorious bugbear of nineteenth-century diplomacy, the Schleswig-Holstein question. That was said to have occasioned the British prime minister Lord Palmerston's celebrated, though unverifiable, *bon mot*: 'The Schleswig-Holstein question is so complicated, only three men in Europe have ever understood it. One was

Prince Albert, who is dead. The second was a German professor who became mad. I am the third and I have forgotten all about it.'

Ukrainians based their claim to eastern Galicia primarily on demographic preponderance. They further asserted that the region was part of their 'historic Ukrainian land' and claimed to be defending themselves against a 'system of oppression residing in the mastery of the Polish . . . nobility'.[50] They accused the Poles of 'destroying our country, our fertile fields . . . ruining our villages, killing our peasants, for no other reason than their unwillingness to remain under Polish yoke.'[51]

The Poles countered Ukrainian demographic claims by asserting that the Jews, some 10 per cent of the population, should be counted as Poles (something no Polish nationalist in his right mind would have proposed under any other circumstance) and by suggesting that much of the Greek Catholic population was intermarried with Poles. In a meeting with the British prime minister, David Lloyd George, and other leaders of the powers, Paderewski explained that the national claims of Ruthenians in eastern Galicia were bogus: 'The people in Galicia pretend to be Ukrainians on account of the similarity of their language with the real Ukrainian people. These people are not Ukrainians.' Heatedly rejecting Lloyd George's suggestion that the Poles were 'more imperialists . . . than either England or France', Paderewski insisted that Poland had shown in the past that it was fit to govern 'primitive people . . . like the Ruthenians, even like the Ukrainians'.[52]

The historian Lewis Namier, who had spent much of his youth in eastern Galicia, advised the Foreign Office on questions relating to his native land. He later recalled a conversation around this time with a Polish diplomat who 'expounded to me the very extensive (and mutually contradictory) territorial claims of his country, and when I enquired on what principle they were based, he replied to me with rare frankness: "On the historical principle, corrected by the linguistic wherever it works in our favour." '[53] Namier was sympathetic to Ukrainian peasants' grievances against Polish landowners and opposed Polish rule in eastern Galicia, even though his parents in Poland were beaten up, their estate manager killed and their home ransacked by Ukrainian forces in 1919.[54]

The fate of eastern Galicia was closely tied to the fluctuating fortunes of the antagonists in the contemporaneous Russian civil war and to the interests of Britain and France. The Poles enjoyed the support of the French; the British tended to stress the right of self-determination based on majority status – not that this necessarily made them more pro-Ukrainian. Lloyd George declared frankly: 'The only Ukrainian I have ever seen in the flesh was upstairs. I haven't seen another ... and I am not sure that I want to see any more.'[55]

A. C. Coolidge, a Harvard professor and adviser to Wilson, proposed a solution whereby 'eastern Galicia should be left as an autonomous district in the hands of its present Ukrainian possessors, and Lemberg be ruled by a government half Pole and half Ukrainian, until the Peace Conference shall have determined the final boundaries.' This arrangement would have the advantage, he suggested, that 'in the meanwhile the forces of both can be used against the Bolshevists.'[56] The proposal was eminently reasonable and utterly unrealistic.

In March 1919 the Supreme Council of the Peace Conference asked its Commission on Polish affairs, headed by the French diplomat Jules Cambon, to recommend a 'minimum' eastern frontier for Poland. Here was the origin of the famous 'Curzon Line' (not so-called at the time) which played a decisive role in the later history of Poland, Ukraine – and Krakowiec. There were two versions of this line: 'A' and 'B'. The first, dated 8 December 1919, demarcated the eastern border of Poland, following the frontier of the third partition in 1795. *Stricto sensu*, therefore, it did not deal with eastern Galicia at all, since the region was by then part of Austria. But in June 1919 the commission proposed that the line continue southwards, dividing the districts of Jarosław and Przemyśl in the west from those of Jaworów and Mościska in the east. This would have placed Krakowiec, which lay within the Jaworów district, just outside Poland proper but in an area the future of which remained to be determined.[57] Line 'B', ran east of Lwów and therefore included Krakowiec in Poland. The commission pointed out that in the intermediate area between the lines (which included Krakowiec) Poles were in a clear minority, but the commissioners refrained from expressing a preference as to the future boundary.

The Curzon Line (or lines) was delineated more precisely on maps than it ever existed in the mind. The story is told of a Foreign Office official, Arthur Ransome (better known later as a children's writer, author of *Swallows and Amazons*), who visited the area in 1919, tasked with ascertaining the ethnicity of inhabitants. Engaging some peasants in a field one afternoon, he found that they were unwilling to identify themselves with any ethnic group. When pressed, they finally responded, 'We are *tutejszy* (local).' Ransome considered this a telling example of what Marx and Engels called 'the idiocy of rural life'.[58] But whatever label outsiders might wish to impose, *tutejszy* meant as much to many people in the region as any other category.

Following the commission's report, the conference decided that eastern Galicia should be assigned an autonomous position within Poland. A sceptical Namier warned: 'All the massacres in Macedonia will seem as nothing compared with those coming to Eastern Galicia.'[59] The Ukrainians appealed to the powers, claiming that they were victims of systematic terrorism by the Poles.[60] The British proposed granting Poland a fifteen-year mandate over eastern Galicia, after which the League of Nations would decide on the future of the region. This would have given the Poles effective control for the time being, without the sovereignty they craved. Ukrainian rights would supposedly have been safeguarded by the authority of the League. With some reason, the Ukrainians feared that the League would have little ability to enforce such a guarantee. The proposal was indignantly rejected by the Poles. Diplomatic wrangling dragged on for another year without any resolution.

In the summer of 1920 warfare returned to eastern Galicia. The Soviet 'Red Cavalry', commanded by Marshal Semyon Mikhailovich Budyonny, pushed back Polish forces and besieged Lwów. On 8 July at Tarnopol, Bolsheviks declared a Galician Soviet Socialist Republic. Wherever they went, Budyonny's troops, like the imperial Cossacks of yore, rampaged and spread terror, particularly among the Jewish population. Accompanying the Russian forces as a war correspondent was the young Jewish writer Isaac Babel. On 19 July 1920 he was with Budyonny and his Bolshevik commissar, Kliment Efremovich Voroshilov (later a Marshal of the Soviet Union and from 1953 to

1960 nominal head of the Soviet state), when they reached the neighbourhood of Krakowiec. Babel recorded the scene in his diary: 'Wounded men start coming in, bandages, bare stomachs, forbearing, unbearable heat, incessant gunfire from both sides, can't doze off. Budyonny and Voroshilov on the porch ... In front of us is Count Ledóchowski's mansion, a white building above the lake, not tall, not flamboyant, very noble ... At the medical assistants': a pitiful, handsome young Jew, he might well have been on the count's payroll, gray with worry ...'[61] The count referred to here was General Ignacy Ledóchowski, commander of the Polish 14th Artillery Brigade. He was married to Paulina, daughter of Jadwiga Łubieńska, owner of the Krakowiec estate. The 'mansion' might have been Ledóchowski's house at Wólka Rosnowska or (as the reference to the lake perhaps suggests) the Łubieński manor at Krakowiec where the Ledóchowskis often spent holidays and felt much at home.

A few weeks later the Poles won a decisive victory over the Bolsheviks near Warsaw in the so-called 'miracle of the Vistula'. For all the buccaneering of the Red Cavalry, this spelled the doom of the Soviet Republic of Galicia, which collapsed by 21 September. With their triumphs over the Ukrainians and the Soviet Russians, and with the support of their allies at the Peace Conference, the Poles finally succeeded in incorporating eastern Galicia in the new Polish state.

There was still much squabbling about the Curzon Line, with the Poles then and later complaining about the allegedly malign, Polonophobic influence of Namier. Recent research indicates that his role was much exaggerated.[62] In any case, as he later observed: 'States are not created or destroyed and frontiers redrawn or obliterated, by argument and majority votes; nations are freed, united, or broken by blood and iron, and not by a generous application of liberty and tomato-sauce.'[63] Commenting in mid-1919 on a British officer's endorsement of a report accusing Jews of welcoming Russian invaders of Poland, Namier (himself Jewish) wrote, 'it is but natural that the Jews should welcome them – in fact the Jews would welcome the Martians if these merely freed them from Polish insults and oppression.'[64] Whatever the role of Namier, the Polish victory was sealed in March 1921 by the Treaty of Riga in which Soviet Russia recognized

Polish sovereignty over eastern Galicia. Krakowiec now belonged to Poland.

The Bolsheviks nevertheless continued efforts to mobilize a Communist movement in the region. They sent trains loaded with bread to alleviate famine and helped finance rural Ukrainian cooperatives. One of their leading agitators was Iosip Krilyk, born in Krakowiec in 1898, who took the 'party name' Vasylkiv. He was the chief animator of a congress of the Communist Party of Eastern Galicia, which convened in October 1921 in a building adjacent to St George's Cathedral, the Greek Catholic mother church in Lwów. The assembly was raided by the police and Krilyk and others were arrested and charged with high treason. After a sensational fourteen-month trial, they were all acquitted. Krilyk and his followers continued their activity but he and his *Wasylkowcy* were eventually expelled from the Comintern as nationalist deviationists. Krilyk later fled from Poland to Soviet Ukraine. Like many comrades of his generation, his loyalty to the Soviet cause was rewarded with execution by an NKVD (secret police) firing squad.[65]

In March 1923 the Council of Ambassadors, representing the Allied Powers, finally endorsed Polish sovereignty over eastern Galicia. This international recognition, however, was conditional on Polish assurances that the region would enjoy a measure of autonomy. That undertaking, which would have given the Ukrainian majority a voice in their own government, was never honoured by the Poles. Unrest in the region persisted over the next several years, with sporadic banditry, demonstrations, riots, and incidents of incendiarism, sabotage, and politically inspired violence by Ukrainian nationalists.

According to a Ukrainian account, the Poles instituted a reign of terror against the Ukrainians, attacking their 'national and social life'. In Krakowiec the Polish police chief, Commandant Buczyński, was said to have 'destroyed anything that had the faintest indication of Ukrainian nationalism'.[66] Underground anti-Polish activity nevertheless persisted. Already in September 1921 a Ukrainian nationalist had tried to assassinate the Polish chief of state, Marshal Piłsudski, in Lwów. He emerged unscathed but the governor of the Lwów region, who was accompanying him, was injured. A series of further such incidents scarred Polish–Ukrainian relations in Galicia.

One outside observer who drew bleak conclusions from all this was the German-Jewish writer Alfred Döblin. Visiting Poland in 1924, he noted the fierce national antagonism in Lwów: 'Many Ukrainians disgorge a terrible, blind, numb hatred, an entirely animal hatred of Poles ... Hostility and violence lurk underground ... A primeval phantasmagoria survives here.'[67]

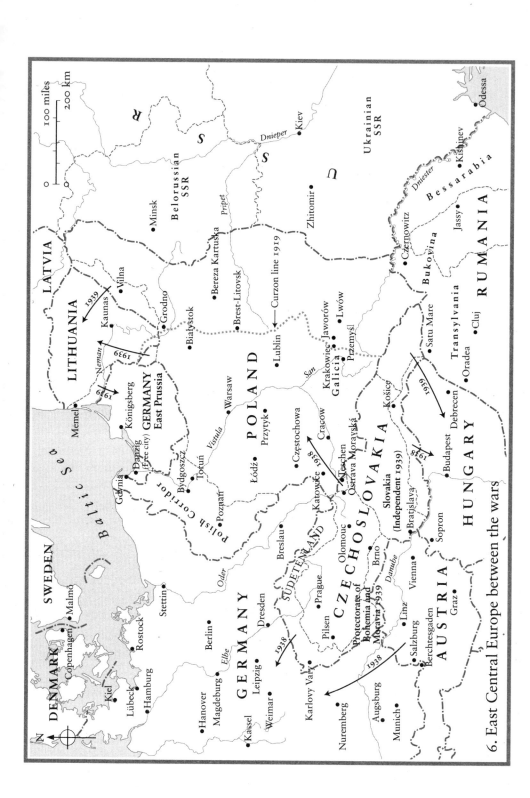

6. East Central Europe between the wars

7

Krakowiec to Berlin

Berl Wasserstein was born in Krakowiec on 5 April 1898. This was 13 Nisan in the Hebrew calendar. On the evening of the next day, therefore, his parents, Jacob and Hannah, had a double celebration: of his birth and of the *seder*, the festive meal marking the start of the eight days of Passover, the festival of freedom. For Jacob there was a further liberation: he would be released for the next week from the tyranny of work in his bakery, since the matzos (unleavened bread) for the festival had been baked in advance in a special oven that was free from any possible contamination by *chometz* (leavened bread).

The child's German, formal, legal name was Bernhard. His Hebrew name was Dov (meaning 'bear'), often rendered as Dov-Ber. But in the family he was usually addressed as Berl (-erl being a common domestic diminutive in German: Leopold Mozart, for example, addressed his little son as 'Wolferl').

Jacob Wasserstein was a small, thin man, with greying hair, a beard and spectacles. Like all the Jewish men of his generation in the shtetl, he dressed in traditional garb, with a black coat and black *yarmulka*. By the modest standard of Krakowiec, he was fairly prosperous. The family lived on the market place in a house which also accommodated his bakery.

Berl had two much older half-sisters, born to Jacob's first wife, who had died. Both were married and lived in the small towns of Radymno and Tarnów to the west of Krakowiec. Berl therefore grew up as, effectively, an only child.

Like most children in the town, Berl received only a minimal general education. Around the turn of the century the Jewish community applied to the fund established by the fabulously wealthy Baron

Maurice de Hirsch (dubbed 'Turkenhirsch', as he had made a vast fortune from investment in Ottoman railways) for support in establishing a Jewish school in Krakowiec. The application was rejected, apparently because the community was judged to be too small. Jewish children therefore attended the local 'Austrian' school, where they learned Polish. They were unlikely to learn much else there, since there were at most five teachers for over three hundred pupils. About half of Berl's classmates were Jewish. Of the remainder in 1908, 138 were Ruthenians and a small number Poles. Although the majority of the population of the district was Ruthenian, Berl did not pick up any Ukrainian – regarded as a coarse, peasant tongue by most Jews and Poles. The language of the home, as of the surrounding Jewish community, was Yiddish. Berl acquired Hebrew in the local *cheder* and from home study with his father of the *chumash* (Pentateuch) and other religious texts.

Conditions of daily life in Krakowiec during Berl's childhood were primitive. The town had no piped water supply or public sewage system. Water was drawn from the lake or from the wells, especially the one in the market square. Most houses were wooden, with tin or thatched roofs. The poorer ones did not have wooden floors, just clay or packed earth. Homes were lit by oil lamps or tallow candles. There was no electricity, no telephone, no motor vehicle, little connection with the outside world.

In the course of Berl's early years, Krakowiec was hit by a number of calamities. In 1903 there were serious fires in neighbouring villages and another in Krakowiec itself that left eighteen households without a roof over their heads. Arson was suspected.[1] In the same year there was an epidemic of scarlet fever. In 1910 disease led to massive death of pigs. Three years after that, horses suffered an outbreak of scabies. There were two attempted suicides, one of which, by a court official disappointed in love, was successful.[2] In 1902 a brawl between two townsmen, Fedek Krawiec and his relative Iwan Kowalyk, degenerated into an all-out battle: Iwan reached for his knife, jabbed Fedek twice, and split his stomach open, leaving him in a critical condition.[3]

Probably affecting Berl's family more directly was a mysterious episode in 1907. The death register for that year records that one Noe

Wasserstein, aged eleven, had been 'shot in the head'.[4] Was it an accident or homicide? An autopsy was ordered but unfortunately no further information has been found. The case is the more puzzling in that few if any Jews in the town owned guns. No newspaper report on the death appeared, so we may conclude that it was not a murder. Presumably Noe, just two years older than Berl, was related to him, though I have been unable to verify that. They would certainly have been known to each other in this small, tightly knit community. Whatever its cause, this event must have been an unsettling experience for the nine-year-old Berl.

When the First World War broke out, Berl was sixteen. Like most of the Jews in Krakowiec, his family moved away from what soon became the front. They stayed for a time in Nikolsburg in Moravia, where they sheltered with other refugees in large barracks. Conditions there were appalling: food and clothing were in short supply; heating was inadequate; infectious diseases were rife. The resident population of the town treated the refugees like prisoners. The local authorities argued with Jewish relief committees over who should pay for the upkeep of the refugees and where they should go.[5] Many moved on to Vienna, only to discover that conditions for them there were no better. Whether Berl and his parents were among them we do not know, though in December 1914 the 'Wasserstein family from Krakowiec' was sought in an announcement by a relative in the 'Missing Persons' column of a Vienna newspaper.[6]

Berl's movements over the next three years remain unclear. He was approaching the age where he would be liable for military service. Perhaps for this reason he left the Habsburg dominions, moving to neutral Holland and later to Germany. At any rate he did not join Conrad von Hötzendorf's killing (or suicide) machine.

In or about 1918 Berl married Czarna Laub. This may have been an arranged marriage. It appears, nevertheless, to have been a happy one. Berl was twenty, Czarna two years older. She too had been born in Krakowiec but for unknown reasons had left for Germany as a child before the war and had been brought up by relatives – perhaps in Bremen. Possibly it was there that she picked up the *Plattdeutsch* patois of north Germany. Her son later recalled her reading to him from the works of the nineteenth-century writer Fritz Reuter, written in that dialect.

Around 1920 the couple settled in Frankfurt am Main, where an elder sister of Czarna had lived for many years. The couple's first child, Addi (Abraham), was born in Frankfurt in 1921. A second, Lotte (Charlotte), was born in 1925. By this time Berl had moved with his family to the German capital, probably in pursuit of business opportunities.

For a time the family lived at 19 Grenadierstrasse, in the heart of Berlin's Jewish immigrant quarter, the *Scheunenviertel*. Every house in the street was reputed to contain a *shtibl* – a small prayer-room or conventicle, often Hasidic in orientation. The district teemed with street markets, kosher butchers and grocers, and shops selling Jewish books and ritual objects.[7] The immigrants from the east were not popular. In 1923 there had been anti-Jewish riots in the area. But in the relatively prosperous years of the middle and late twenties the trouble died down.

Later the family moved to a rented six-room apartment not far away, at 72 Neue-Friedrichstrasse, an old street in which several German literary figures had once lived. This was in a poorish district, again heavily Jewish. The apartment was in the typical style of Berlin apartment buildings. It had the 'Berliner Zimmer', with a small corner-window, that led into other rooms, including the 'Herrenzimmer' or salon, which served as both dining- and sitting-room. Heating was by an old-fashioned, tile-covered stove in the corner of the room, that used bricks of brown coal. Here Berl and Czarna adopted a contemporary, middle-class mode of existence, very different from what they had known in Krakowiec. Modern home appliances were purchased: a fridge and gas cooker, both unknown in the shtetl, and eventually a radio. The apartment walls were papered in the Berlin style of the time. Addi was quite surprised in later life when he went abroad and found that in other countries interior walls were often painted rather than papered. There was one housemaid, Lucy, a peasant girl, but by 1935, when Jews were forbidden to employ 'Aryan' domestics, she had to leave.

Berl had bourgeois aspirations and, but for the arrival of Nazism, might have become moderately prosperous. He worked from an office attached to his flat, reached by a separate entrance from the outside landing. His business, *Bernhard Wasserstein Regenmäntel Fabrikation*, was based on a special process that he had developed for bonding rubber with textiles. The result was a heavy and rather unwieldy material used in raincoat manufacture, which nevertheless found a market. Such processes were hazardous: in Paris the production of *caoutchoucs* (rubber raincoats), involving the use of dangerous chemicals, was said to result often in 'severe burns, lung ailments, and even asphyxiation'.[8] Berl subcontracted to a number of people working for him in their own workshops. He would supply them with textile materials that they waterproofed using his technique. Several agents sold the finished goods to retail stores.

In 1927 Berl became a property-owner. Together with a consortium of relatives, he purchased two blocks of flats in a working-class district of Berlin. These buildings, registered in the names of his wife and other relatives, comprised altogether several dozen apartments, and provided a rental income of forty thousand Reichsmarks per annum. That was equivalent in 1933 to around $10,000 (at least $200,000 in 2022 value) – a sizable sum; but from that would have to be subtracted costs of mortgages, taxes and maintenance, as well as the income shares of the partner-owners. This regular stream of money enabled Berl to ride out the great depression and the hardships of the early Nazi years.

When Berl Wasserstein departed Krakowiec, he left behind many of the superficial aspects of shtetl life. Like most Jews who moved away from the traditional setting, he no longer wore traditional garb or looked to the Belzer rebbe for answers to grave questions of personal destiny. Unlike his father he did not wear a beard. His wife did not wear a *sheitel* (wig) nor the 'Belz veil' that had been customary for the previous generation of married women in the old country. He never spoke to his son about his religious beliefs. Like his father, he seems to have taken them for granted. He maintained a sentimental regard for the old ways. In outward behaviour he was a traditional Jew, eating only kosher food and observing the Sabbath.

Berl brought up his children in the modern orthodox spirit. He sent Addi to the Realgymnasium of the Adass Jisroel community, which was unyielding in its adherence to the 613 commandments and at the same time rigorous in its standards of general education. This was the only Jewish school in Germany whose leaving certificate was recognized as equivalent to that of a gymnasium. As was the custom among observant Jews in Germany, Addi had to wear a cap whenever he was out of doors and a *yarmulka* while eating, praying or studying *limudei kodesh* (religious subjects). Otherwise he did not have to wear any head-covering so long as he was indoors. That is presumably why a photograph taken in 1934, around the time of his barmitzvah, shows Addi bareheaded (*see plate 15*).

Czarna shared her husband's adherence to a strict but modernized religious orthodoxy. She travelled in a car on the Sabbath only once in her life – when Addi, who was eight or nine years old, suddenly fell ill with appendicitis. She had to take him by taxi to the Jewish hospital in a far-away section of the city. Jewish law permits travel on the Sabbath in cases of medical emergency. But once Addi was safely installed in the hospital, she had to trudge all the way home on foot.

Once, Addi asked his father whether the world had really been created in six days. On another occasion he mentioned that he had noticed that there was a great change in the Hebrew style between the first and second chapters of Genesis and asked whether this might not indicate multiple authorship. Evidently he had heard vaguely about what was called 'Biblical criticism' – vehemently rejected by orthodox Jews. The questions were discussed without great heat. Such issues did not disturb Berl's deeply rooted faith.

Sometimes Berl attended services at the nearby Heidereutergasse Synagogue, the oldest (built in 1714) and most beautiful Jewish place of worship in Berlin. This was orthodox, very German in spirit and in its rigorous decorum. At other times he would go to a *shtibl* on Grenadierstrasse, frequented mainly by *Ostjuden*. The atmosphere there was quite different, informal and noisy, with congregants swaying to and fro as they raced through the prayers and frequently joking or exchanging gossip during the service. A *shtibl* had no rabbi; it had no need of one, since the members of the congregation could all perform the functions of *baal koreh* (reader from the Torah) themselves. The rights to such synagogal honours were auctioned in the community and the winner would either perform the role himself or designate another man to do so. Berl probably felt more at home in the *shtibl*, among his own sort of people, than in the Heidereutergasse where the congregation consisted more of 'the sort of people he was becoming' (as Addi later put it). The formulation is significant: Berl wanted to remain true to the faith of his fathers, yet at the same time leave behind the world of the shtetl and leap into modernity.

Berl's outlook, nevertheless, was far removed from the modernist Weimar culture that surrounded him. Although he lived in the heart of the German capital in its wildest period of Jazz Age hedonistic excess, he had nothing to do with all that. He took no interest in the avant-garde movements of the time, to a large extent nurtured by Jewish writers, artists and thinkers. The *Neue Sachlichkeit* ('new objectivism'), championed by many wealthy Jewish collectors, gained no foothold in his aesthetic consciousness. On his apartment walls he hung *Schinken*, large pictures of a type common in Berlin: still lifes of flowers and landscapes. Yet even those constituted a significant gesture towards modernity. In Krakowiec the only picture displayed in a Jewish house would have been the *mizrach* (literally 'east'), a plaque or painting, often of Jerusalem, hung on the eastern wall to indicate the direction of prayer.

In Berlin, the language of the home was German, not Yiddish. Berl and Czarna spoke German not only to their children but to each other, even though they had grown up in Krakowiec speaking Yiddish. This practice, not uncommon among *Ostjuden* in Germany at the time, reflected their view that German was the language of an advanced culture and of modern civilization. When the parents wanted to say something to each other that would not be understood by the children, they would speak Polish. Czarna's was fluent; Berl's halting – strange given that she had left Poland as a young girl whereas he had received all of his schooling in Krakowiec in Polish. Perhaps there was an element of wilful forgetfulness involved, as sometimes happens among emigrants. Yiddish was reserved for relatives and friends, most of whom were *Ostjuden*, generally quite humble people. They often met Czarna's brother Samuel ('Beinish'), who, like them, had moved from Krakowiec to Holland, then to Frankfurt, and finally to Berlin. Otherwise, they remained quite socially isolated. Berl had exactly one non-Jewish friend.

It has been observed of emigrant communities that the aspect of life they retain longest from their place of origin is diet. Czarna and Berl were a good example of this. Czarna's culinary offerings were wholly imported from Krakowiec. She had an unvarying meal system which consisted of seven menus, one for each day of the week. The Thursday dish, a thick brown 'Einbrennsuppe' (roux soup) with noodles and beans, gave the family particular pleasure. Sunday in the summer was the day for cold borscht. Like most orthodox homes, the household had four sets of dishes, one for meat, one for milk, and duplicate sets for the Passover.

On Friday evening, candles in heavy silver sticks would be kindled and the Sabbath would be welcomed with the ceremonial *kiddush*. Berl would always cut pieces from the two *challah* (braided white) loaves and distribute them to the family. In eastern Europe it had been common for the head of the family to tear the *challah* into pieces, but this was regarded in Germany as uncouth and Berl wanted to be a *German* Jew. Still, affection for the old ways would often rise to the surface and he would hum or sing the traditional Hasidic *nigunim* (melodies) that he had learned at his father's table in Krakowiec. This was when he was most relaxed.

Yet Berl seems, the rest of the time, to have been rather 'buttoned-up'. He always wore a dark suit, never a sports jacket. He was never seen without a tie. He did not play cards or bet. Unlike ultra-orthodox Jews, he would occasionally go to the cinema and the theatre, albeit not on the Sabbath. On Sundays he would sometimes meet a friend in a nearby café. Otherwise he had few recreations. He did not drink – except once a week at lunchtime on the Sabbath, when he allowed himself a glass of schnapps. As with most parents in that milieu and generation, his relationship with his children was formal and distant. He never spoke to them about his childhood or his business.

Although he had not had much schooling, Berl respected education and valued it not merely as the gateway to success but as the mark of a civilized man. He read widely. His twelve bookcases contained a library of some three thousand volumes, encompassing the German classics, rabbinic literature and books on German and Jewish history. A prized possession was a complete leather-bound, folio 'Vilna *shas*', the best edition of the Talmud.

Berl did not get involved in politics. As a non-citizen he could not, in any case, vote in German elections. He was very far from the revolutionary enthusiasm that led some *Ostjuden* towards the far left. His sympathies were more with the progressive centre, represented in particular by the liberal Deutsche Demokratische Partei. This enjoyed strong support among German Jews, so much so, indeed, that it became tainted in the eyes of some as an overly Jewish party. He kept up with current events, reading newspapers such as the *Frankfurter Zeitung* and the *Berliner Tageblatt*, both Jewish-owned and cautiously liberal in outlook – at any rate until 1933, after which they were squeezed into compliance with the Nazi *Weltanschauung*. He also read the *Jüdische Rundschau*, the main Jewish weekly, edited by the moderate Zionist Robert Weltsch.

The only memorable political remark that Berl ever made in the presence of his son was on Monday 30 January 1933, the day Hitler assumed power as Chancellor. Berl was talking to his brother-in-law Beinish. They had just heard the news. Berl commented, 'This is very good.' Beinish said, 'What nonsense are you talking?' The answer was: 'Well, you see, now that he is there, in six months he'll make himself so ridiculous that it'll all be over.' Beinish said, 'No, you're wrong!' Alas, Addi's recollection of this, Berl's only recorded political utterance, was a little vague. Perhaps, Addi suggested, it was the other way round and Beinish was the optimist and Berl the pessimist. Such are the limitations of oral history. Whoever expressed it, this was an unexceptional, widely held view of Hitler's prospects at the moment of the Nazi *Machtergreifung* (seizure of power).

Berl's family felt the weight of discrimination and persecution only gradually. This was partly because the Nazis introduced their anti-Jewish measures only step by step, perhaps also because Berlin was a city where the left was strong and because they lived in a heavily Jewish district. In 1932, when Addi was ten, he had witnessed a brief gun battle in the street between Nazis and Communists. But for quite some time after 1933 Nazi rule did not directly impinge on his life. Whereas some Jewish children were thrown out of public schools, he already attended an all-Jewish school. He continued to participate in Jewish youth movements such as the Labour Zionist Habonim and the further-left Zionist Hashomer Hatsair (the only avowedly Marxist organization still permitted to function in Germany). Plainclothes policemen used to sit at the back of the room at meetings of both organizations, observing without interfering.

One of the first manifestations of the Nazis' anti-Semitic policy was the announcement of a nationwide boycott of Jewish retail businesses on 1 April 1933. The *Jüdische Rundschau* carried the famous headline on 4 April, 'Tragt ihn mit Stolz, den gelben Fleck!' ('Wear the yellow star with pride!'). This was long before Jews were compelled to wear the yellow star, and Weltsch no doubt intended the phrase metaphorically rather than prophetically. The boycott was only spottily observed and was abandoned after just one day. In spite of its failure, it aroused worldwide attention and condemnation. Even in such a remote and insignificant place as Krakowiec, a protest demonstration took place, addressed by community leaders and the town's rabbi, Meir Klüger.[9] Berl was not directly affected by the boycott as his business was wholesale, not retail, and anyway most of his subcontractors, agents and clients were Jewish. As time went on, however, further Nazi measures began to affect his business.

Some Jews left Germany immediately: an estimated 38,000 (out of a total of around half a million) emigrated in 1933. Tens of thousands more departed over the next five years. The main countries of refuge were France, Austria, and Czechoslovakia, as well as Britain, Palestine and the United States. After the racist 'Nuremberg laws' were enacted in 1935, pressure for emigration increased. But the more desperately Jews tried to leave, the more they found barriers raised against them. Moreover, other countries in Europe, notably Poland, asserted with increasing vehemence that they too were 'over-populated' with Jews and sought ways to get rid of them.

By the mid-1930s Berl and Czarna were seriously considering departure. But quite apart from the difficulty of obtaining immigration visas, there was the problem of Berl's business and properties. These could be sold only at a huge loss and in any case capital could not be exported. They risked losing everything and finding themselves in a new country penniless.

The family's search for a refuge nevertheless became more serious as Nazi anti-Jewish persecution intensified. There was talk of moving to the United States but they had no prospect of qualifying for admission in the near future. The USA still operated the 'national origin' quota system for immigration, enacted in the early 1920s to ward off undesirables such as east European Jews. The quota for Polish citizens was much smaller than the one for Germans. As a result Berl and his family would have to wait many years before they could hope to reach the head of the queue.

After 1933 many German Jews emigrated to Palestine, then ruled by Britain under a mandate granted by the League of Nations. Most of the emigrants went there not out of ideological conviction (the Zionist movement was weak in Germany) but simply because the territory at that time had a relatively open-door policy to Jews. Moreover, thanks to the so-called *ha'avara* (transfer) agreement between the German government and the Zionist Organization, Palestine was the only country to which German Jews could legally transfer at least part of their capital. In 1935 no fewer than 61,854 Jewish immigrants, mostly from Poland and Germany, reached Palestine (the entire Jewish population there at the time was just 300,000). This, however, proved to be the high-water mark of *aliya* (immigration to the Holy Land) under the mandate. In the following year Palestine abruptly became a much less attractive or feasible destination. A nationwide revolt by Arabs in Palestine erupted. It lasted for three years, costing large numbers of British, Jewish and Arab lives and disrupting the economy. Confronted with a serious military and political challenge, the mandatory government bent to Arab nationalist demands and began to move away from its pro-Zionist policy. From the autumn of 1936 Jewish immigration was strictly limited.

As conditions for Jews in Germany worsened, possible salvation beckoned from South Africa. Two of Czarna's brothers from Krakowiec had emigrated there in the 1920s. They had prospered in Johannesburg and urged Czarna and Berl to move there with the children. In 1935 Czarna visited South Africa to scout possibilities. It was a bold venture in a period when overseas tourism was unusual. She had never set foot outside Europe. In fact, since the family never went away on holiday, she had barely travelled at all beyond Poland, Holland and Germany. She stayed in Johannesburg for several weeks and was able to admire the beauty of the country and notice the considerable affluence in which many of its white inhabitants, including her brothers, lived. This was more than a decade before the introduction of apartheid with its oppressive and demeaning restrictions; but there was a 'colour bar' and white domination was firmly entrenched. Czarna returned to Berlin and declared that she couldn't imagine living in a country where black people were not allowed to walk on the same pavement as whites. It was a fateful decision.

The South African option in any case soon receded from view. In 1937 the government enacted an Aliens Act, setting new restrictions on immigration to the Union. The prime minister, J. B. M. Hertzog, told parliament bluntly that the object of the law was to limit the influx of Jews. J. G. Strijdom, whose opposition National Party branch in Transvaal prohibited Jewish membership, jeered at Hertzog's candid admission. The government's legislation was, in fact, a surrender to pressure from anti-Semites.[10]

One possible destination that Berl and Czarna did not consider was their birthplace. Until October 1938 their Polish passports gave them the automatic right to return there. On the other hand, German financial controls prevented Berl from extracting his capital. Most importantly, he did not *want* to return to Krakowiec. It represented, after all, much of what he had spent his whole adult life trying to escape. To go back would be a confession of failure, a return to a primitive life form that he was determined to overcome.

On 15 April 1938 Berl and his family celebrated their last Passover *seder* in Berlin. A guest was an acquaintance originally from Krakowiec who had gone to live in Vienna. The *Anschluss* of Austria to Germany a month earlier had induced him, like thousands of other Polish Jews, to leave in a hurry. En route to exile, he had arrived temporarily in Berlin. Such encounters no doubt helped to enlighten Berl as to the potential danger that he too might face. Still, he could hardly dare to imagine that he would soon be ordered out of his home, forcibly separated from his wife and daughter, and told to return to Krakowiec.

The knock on the door on 28 October came as a stunning shock.

8

Berlin to Krakowiec

How had Krakowiec fared in the course of the quarter century since Berl Wasserstein had left?

The town recovered only very slowly and patchily from the horrors of the Great War and its aftermath. The first Polish census, conducted in 1921, registered a drastic demographic decline, both Jewish and non-Jewish: there were now only 529 Jews out of a population of 1,389. Both the Jewish and the general population had dropped by more than a fifth since 1910. It is hardly surprising that many people who had fled the region since 1914, among them Berl, decided not to return to their homes. Those who did go back often found that their homes were occupied by new residents who refused to vacate them. During the next decade the Jewish population declined more rapidly. The main reason was migration to larger cities such as Lwów and to other countries such as Germany, the United States and Palestine. By 1931 there were just 340 Jews left in Krakowiec out of a total of 1,706 residents. Half a century earlier Jews had been a majority of the population. Now they were the smallest of the three groups. The age profile had shifted: most of those who had departed were young; those who remained were disproportionately the elderly. These tendencies were reflected in local school statistics. In 1926, out of 111 children in the first three elementary classes, just forty-two (38 per cent) were Jewish.[1] In spite of their depleted numbers, however, Jews played a significant part in municipal politics. Fifteen out of the thirty-two councillors elected in 1927 were Jews.[2]

There were still no paved roads or pavements, though a wooden walkway led from the market square to the courthouse. Visitors from out of town, like young Addi Wasserstein, when he came from Berlin to stay with his grandparents, had to travel the last leg of the journey from the railway station in Lwów or Radymno by bumpy horse and cart along rutted country roads. A limited electrical supply was generated by a turbine at the mill, owned by Countess Łubieńska but leased to a Jew, Lazar Kampel. The town boasted two motor vehicles: a car belonging to the countess and a motorcycle with side-car that was the pride and joy of Dr Henryk Berger. A Viennese Jew, he was the only doctor in the town (why he moved to this out-of-the-way place is a mystery). One Jew in the town owned a radio. As late as 1939 the telephone directory listed just a handful of subscribers in the district (Krakowiec numbers 1 to 13), only four of whom were private citizens: General Ledóchowski, Dr Berger, the Roman Catholic parish priest, Adolf Łabno, and a Jewish merchant, Naftali Majus.

The socio-economic make-up of the region remained overwhelmingly rural. According to the 1931 census, 89 per cent of the Ukrainian (Greek Catholic) and 69 per cent of the Polish (Roman Catholic) population in Eastern Galicia derived their living from agriculture. By contrast only 10 per cent of Jews did so; 76 per cent of Jews worked in trade, crafts or industry; more Jews in absolute numbers were engaged in trade than Poles and Ukrainians combined. All but one or two of the merchants in Krakowiec were Jews.

Most Jews worshipped regularly in the synagogue, though a few attended only on the high holy days, Rosh Hashana and Yom Kippur. The synagogue could not accommodate everyone so the overflow, including Jacob Wasserstein, would pray in the adjacent *bes midresh*. Some of the more strictly observant held services in a separate *kloyzl* (small prayer room). As was the case throughout Europe, women attended much more rarely, restricted to the gallery of the synagogue; none went to the *kloyzl*.

The summer of 1928 was very hot, with temperatures as high as 51°C (126°F) reported in parts of the country. At midnight on 16–17 July a fire broke out in Krakowiec. Like the anecdote about Mrs O'Leary's cow and the Great Chicago Fire of 1871, the origin of this fire became the subject of much speculation and theorizing. In Krakowiec it was rumoured that it had been kindled deliberately by a Jewish woman who had set her own shop alight with a view to claiming the insurance. Once the blaze had started, it was difficult to stop its spread to the jumble of wooden houses around the square and on adjoining streets.

Fires were common occurrences in Krakowiec (serious outbreaks had occurred in 1786, 1801, 1806, 1874, 1895 and 1903), but this one was of historic proportions. Almost the whole of the central, mainly Jewish-inhabited, area of the town went up in flames. The town's volunteer fire brigade, manned largely by Ukrainians, could not cope: its equipment consisted of a horse, a cart and some buckets for carrying water from the well or the lake. Help was rushed in from Jarosław and a motorized fire unit was summoned from Lwów. By the time the last embers were extinguished, at 5.00 a.m. the next morning, twenty-six houses and shops had been consumed. Total damage was estimated at 600,000 złoty (about $55,000 at the 1928 conversion rate, equivalent to around $880,000 in 2022 value). A hundred Jewish families were left homeless.[3] A collection on behalf of victims attracted more than fifty contributors but the total sum raised was just 500 złoty ($45).[4] A photograph published a few months later in the New York Yiddish daily *Forverts* (unfortunately the quality is too poor to allow reproduction here) shows an assembly of Jews standing around forlornly among the ruins, supposedly discussing plans for reconstruction.[5]

As may be seen in that and other photos, by this time many Jewish men no longer wore traditional Jewish costume. Only a few older, Hasidic men wore *peyes* (side-curls). Increasingly women sought out modern fashions in clothing. Arranged marriages were no longer the norm. Jewish-owned shops were closed on the Sabbath but some *maskilim,* rather than studying sacred texts, might read a Lwów newspaper, the Yiddish *Lemberger Togblat* or the Polish *Chwila*, or a secular book in the afternoon. Young men were shaving their beards; a few even discarded their *yarmulkas*. But the traditional rites of passage, male circumcision, religious marriage and burial, were universally observed. The generation of my great-grandfathers Jacob Wasserstein and Chaim Yitzhak Laub still adhered to the old norms but their children were very different: they spoke Polish rather than Yiddish among themselves, frequented dances and ski resorts, listened to gramophone records and were indistinguishable in appearance from young people in Lwów, Cracow or Warsaw.

Jacob's house in Krakowiec was one of those burned down in the great fire. Afterwards he built himself a fine, new, detached house of two storeys in red brick. The house was on a little rise just off the market square. For a time this was the only two-storey dwelling in Krakowiec.

Czarna's father, Chaim-Yitzhak Laub, was stocky and powerfully built, of medium height. By the time my father knew him, in the late 1920s, his beard had turned white. Evidently he was respected by Jews of the town as a religious authority, since it was he who 'examined' the candidate for appointment as rabbi of Krakowiec, Meshulam Klüger. The last rabbi in its history, he was the son of the previous incumbent, Meir Klüger. Chaim-Yitzhak owned an egg-exporting business but, as often happened in Jewish families in the shtetl, the running of the business was left to his wife, Chana-Gittel. The man of the house meanwhile immersed himself in study of the Talmud.

Chana-Gittel bought her supply of eggs from peasants, mainly Ukrainians. They came each Thursday with their horses and carts from villages round and about to bring their produce to the market. The square would be packed. The peasants brought sour cream, butter and vegetables; in exchange they bought supplies of oil, salt and textiles from Jewish merchants, who owned the stores surrounding the square. There was very little business on any other day – none at all on Saturday or on Friday afternoon in winter (because of the early arrival of the Sabbath when darkness set in). Sometimes payment would be in cash, sometimes by barter. Market day was also a time for romantic assignations: an opportunity for girls to meet boys from other places. They might take refreshment at one of the many taverns, all Jewish-owned, near the centre of town. More enterprisingly, they might take a stroll along what remained of the famous lime avenue leading to the Łubieński manor house.

Addi, who first visited Krakowiec in 1929, aged about seven, remembered that, after paying a peasant for eggs, Chana-Gittel would always give the seller a piece of candy. Addi took a lively interest in these transactions because, when handing out sweets to peasants, his grandmother would also give one to him. Broken eggs were kept for consumption at home. The rest were exported to Germany. In those days of large families and before the dangers of over-abundant cholesterol had been revealed, people bought and consumed eggs in vast quantities. Addi recalled that in Berlin one would ask for 'ein Schock Eier' – which meant sixty eggs.

In Krakowiec, eggs were big business. According to Austrian census records there were 31,179 *Haushühne* ('domestic chickens') in the Krakowiec district in 1900. If we assume, conservatively, that the average chicken laid two hundred eggs per year, this would imply an annual production of 6,235,800 eggs. They were exported from Galicia to Germany and even to England – or so I have been told. I was sceptical until I came across a report that in 1914 Britain imported nine million pounds worth of eggs from as far away as Russia – to be sold after a journey of three or four weeks as 'fresh eggs'.[6] Jonathan Lynn has written that eggs from Poland were even exported to South Africa. 'This was before refrigeration. It's a wonder the ship didn't explode.'[7] Maybe some other form of preservation was used. Lady Antonia Fraser, in her memoir of wartime childhood in Oxford, recalls that eggs were preserved in spirit in the cellar of her family home.[8] Fortunately, this minor historical puzzle has been resolved by an expert in nutrition, my friend Steven Gold of Michigan (a descendant of Krakowiec Jews), who informs me: 'Eggs which haven't been washed or refrigerated will keep at room temperature for several weeks. Once the protective "cuticle" has been washed off, or if they've been refrigerated and then allowed to "sweat" when taken out of the refrigerator for a while before use, the chance of influx of bacteria through the pores of the shell increases greatly. So I wouldn't be surprised at eggs transported by sea to distant lands being still "fresh". No form of "preservation" was needed.'

A Galician Jew whose family moved to Berlin in the 1920s reports on the German end of the operation:

> The eggs had first to be sorted by size and candled to determine freshness. This process involved holding the egg against a hole in an electric lampholder in a darkened room. If the light showed a darkened area, the egg was no longer fresh and, depending on the degree of darkness, the egg was either allocated for commercial use (by bakeries) or discarded as unfit for consumption. A skilled candler holding four eggs in each hand and rotating these rapidly before the hole in the lampholder

could candle a full crate of twenty-four dozen eggs in less than one hour.[9]

This little rivulet of international commerce was even enshrined in literature: Herr Ziemler, a character in Shmuel Yosef Agnon's *A Simple Story*, exported eggs wholesale from the fictional shtetl of Szybusz (based on the author's native town of Buczacz, south-east of Krakowiec) to Germany. 'Not that there were no eggs or chickens in Germany – yet you could not compare the taste of a German chicken or egg to one from Galicia.'[10]

In spite of the downward demographic curve, Jewish social and cultural life in Krakowiec between the wars was quite animated. In 1932 a group of Jews, headed by Dr Berger, applied for official permission to register a Tarbut (culture) society for the dissemination of Hebrew language, literature and enlightenment. Perhaps these were regarded as dangerous objectives, since the application was rejected by the local authority – ostensibly on the grounds that it did not bear the requisite 3 złoty stamp.[11] A Jewish library, Zionist in orientation, was, however, granted the necessary permission.

Zionism was a strong political force among Jews in eastern Galicia and this found reflection in Krakowiec. A modern Hebrew school, distinct from the traditional *cheder*, attracted students (*see plate 12*). Several Zionist youth groups were active, including the left-wing Hashomer Hatsair, the right-wing Betar and the orthodox Bnei Akiva. But in elections to the international Zionist Congresses of 1931 and 1935, the largest number of votes from the town went to the officially 'non-party' General Zionists, headed by Chaim Weizmann.[12]

In earlier times there had been a strong religious and sentimental interest in Palestine. Two of my great-great-grandfathers emigrated there around 1914 and died on holy soil, one in Jerusalem, the other in Safed. But at least until the 1920s many Krakowiec Jews, in common with the strictly orthodox elsewhere, opposed Zionism on principle as a sacrilegious, presumptuous attempt to anticipate the arrival of the messiah. As in many other things, this was partly a matter of generations. Older members of the community remained aloof; younger people displayed more support for it, as for other political movements such as socialism.

Gedaliah Wasserstein, a cousin of Berl, was a moving spirit in Zionist activity in Krakowiec in the 1930s. He was one of several enthusiasts in the town who applied for immigration to Palestine in the 1930s. But the number of available certificates was limited and they were distributed by the Zionist Organization according to a 'party key' that involved political considerations. In 1935 the Krakowiec Zionist group 'Akhva' (Brotherhood) sent a furious letter to the steering committee of the Zionist Organization in Lwów, complaining that repeated applications for a certificate by Gedaliah, their chairman for the previous eleven years, had been ignored: 'It is simply incomprehensible! ... This member has worked to this day in the Zionist arena with blood and faith ... All requests on his account fall into the abyss ... Is this justice? Must it be so? ... Truly, comrade Wasserstein ... was not aiming at a prize in return for his labours for the redemption of the Land of Israel. Only his devotion to Zionism drove him.' All the indignation was to no avail. The office in Lwów replied that, though 'we have entered the name of comrade Wasserstein in the list of candidates', there were about a hundred listed, all 'commendable, veteran Zionists', of whom perhaps one might be allocated a certificate. As matters turned out, three were successful. Gedaliah was among the disappointed ninety-seven.[13] The pressure for Jewish emigration from Poland in the middle and late 1930s, hardly less than from Germany, was so intense that he had no realistic hope of gaining a certificate. Gedaliah perished in the Shoah.

In the course of the interwar period, simmering national animosity between Poles and Ukrainians, bound up with agrarian discontents, rose increasingly to the surface. Peasant and landowner in Poland still lived in separate and mutually hostile mental universes. Of course, the possessing classes in all times and places tend to exhibit a mulish sense of entitlement. The Polish landed elite were not perhaps any worse in this respect than the Junkers of East Prussia, the Magyar magnates of Transylvania or the perpetrators of the Scottish Highland clearances. Even so, the obtuse selfishness of some landlords was utterly shameless. An observer in 1919 recorded characteristic Polish landowners' objections to proposals for land reform:

Discussion of the cutting up of the large estates for division among the peasants has brought forth several interesting points from the owners of large estates, both in Cracow and Warsaw. They state that the peasant in the first place is lazy and would not work his ground properly. This they prove with instances of peasants owning lands in the vicinity of their properties or of land that they have rented out to the peasant for periods of six years. Secondly agriculture demands a certain amount of intelligence and knowledge that the majority of peasants have not got. Beet growing was particularly instanced. Thirdly is the question of implements and fertilizers which the peasant cannot afford for a small tract of land. In answering the question as to the possibility of educating the peasant it was stated that the minute that a peasant could read and write he was through with farming.[14]

The agrarian depression of the 1930s hit Poland hard. In 1937, according to one contemporary expert, 42 per cent of the rural population, or over five million people of working age in the countryside, were 'superfluous', that is, either unemployed or partly employed.[15]

Unable to feed their families or livestock, peasant fury was aroused on a scale unknown since the great *jacquerie* of 1846. In 1937 peasants in the Krakowiec district joined a national strike. They demanded higher prices for their produce, land redistribution and better pay for agricultural labourers. In Jaworów more than two thousand peasants, armed with sticks and pitchforks, blockaded the market. The police opened fire. There were mass arrests.[16] The government considered the disturbances in Krakowiec serious enough to send in the army. A Ukrainian committee offered to negotiate. But the administration refused to talk and arrested the delegates. The army attacked the strikers. Their leaders were seized and sentenced to eighteen months' imprisonment.[17]

Meanwhile, Ukrainians protested indignantly against the failure of the Polish government to implement its commitment to provide some form of autonomy for them in eastern Galicia. They complained that, although they were a majority of the population, they were discriminated against in official appointments. For example, whereas under the Austrians they had played a role in the judiciary, under Polish rule they found senior posts closed to them. There were no longer any

Ukrainian judges in the Krakowiec court. They had other complaints too. A government-inspired squeeze on Ukrainian-language education led to a decline of 80 per cent in the number of Ukrainian elementary schools in eastern Galicia between 1921 and 1935.[18]

Such discrimination energized nationalist activity, cultural as well as political. In Krakowiec the Prosvita library resumed activity and by 1938 held a stock of 492 books.[19] The relationship of the organization with the Greek Catholic church, however, was becoming strained. On the one hand, local clergy played an active part in the work of the society and the church brotherhood met in the Prosvita reading room. On the other, the parish priest complained that young people were gathering there and reading anti-religious literature.[20]

Most Ukrainians supported the constitutionalist wing of the nationalist movement which coalesced in the Ukrainian National Democratic Alliance (UNDO), founded at a congress in Lwów in 1926. UNDO contested elections and secured seats in local and national assemblies. But it failed to dent the government's determination to fashion a national Polish state out of a population one third of whom were non-Poles.

As a result, some Ukrainians gravitated towards more extreme politics. The Organization of Ukrainian Nationalists (OUN) was formed in Vienna in 1929 by former members of Ukrainian fighting groups. OUN was 'right-wing oriented, authoritarian and revolutionary ... anti-Polish, anti-Russian, antisemitic, anti-democratic, and anti-Communist.'[21] It dreamed of creating an ethnically pure Ukrainian state. The last of its programmatic 'ten commandments' declared brazenly that it aimed 'to expand the strength, riches, and size of the Ukrainian State even by means of enslaving foreigners'.[22] OUN forged links with Ukrainian exile groups in Germany and the USA and, in the late 1930s, cultivated contacts with the Abwehr, the German secret intelligence service. The organization's greatest strength was in eastern Galicia, though its extreme vision at first found support only among a minority of the Ukrainian population.

Poles resorted to a variety of stratagems to counter Ukrainian nationalism. A Krakowiec branch of the Polish youth group Defenders of the Homeland was established in 1928. It focused on military training, physical education and patriotic activities. One of its objects was to win Ukrainians over to the Polish cause. For this purpose it organized joint summer camps in which Polish and Ukrainian children were brought together. A report on one such camp near Krakowiec in 1937 stated that the participants all used Polish 'but a bit broken'. Two thirds of the campers were Poles, enabling the Ukrainian minority (so the report continued) 'to get used to speaking Polish and purified it from Ruthenian influences'. Sometimes such efforts rebounded on the organizers. At another camp, where the majority of children were Ukrainians, an inspector reported that they 'did not fulfil their obligations because it became a meeting-place of a very anti-Polish character'.[23]

In the early 1930s OUN subversive activity, including sabotage and arson, prompted a determined campaign of 'pacification' by the Polish security forces. The villages around Krakowiec were among those affected. The 14th Polish Uhlan Regiment, a cavalry unit that had seen heroic service in the war against the Soviets of 1919–20, was deployed to destroy the OUN in eastern Galicia. Ukrainian parliamentarians and propagandists complained bitterly of rough treatment meted out by Polish troops. At Świdnica, a village a little to the north of Krakowiec, in October 1930, 150 Ukrainians were allegedly driven into the Prosvita reading room and beaten. The Polish soldiery, it was said, had destroyed the local dairy and cooperative store, plundering four hundred kilograms of butter and eighty hundredweight of oats. After similar scenes in Morańce, another village in the district, peasants complained that soldiers had looted grain and then sold it to Jewish dealers. On 10 October that year, the police chief in Krakowiec summoned the *wójts* (headmen) of nearby villages and warned them to keep the peace and ensure that their populations voted for government candidates in the forthcoming elections. In response to Ukrainian protests to the League of Nations, the Polish government declared that it had merely taken such measures as were required 'for the purpose of restoring order and tranquillity' after Ukrainian revolutionary attacks accompanied by 'a vast campaign of slander and propaganda against Poland'.[24]

One of the founders of the OUN was Roman Shukhevych. Born in Krakowiec in 1907, he belonged to a family of nationalist intelligentsia. His paternal grandfather, Volodymyr, was a distinguished

Ruthenian scholar and ethnographer, one of the founders of the Prosvita cultural organization. His uncle Stepan had been an officer in the Sich Riflemen during the First World War and a senior commander in the army of the West Ukrainian Republic during the Polish–Ukrainian war in 1918–19; later he became a well-known lawyer. We have already met Roman's father, Judge Osip Shukhevych, who had been a leading figure in the Krakowiec branch of Prosvita before his removal from the district by the Austrian authorities. In 1918 Osip participated in the abortive effort to establish a Ukrainian state in Lwów.

In 1926, at the age of nineteen, Roman was involved in the political killing of the Lwów school superintendent Stanisław Sobiński. Yet he did not look like a thug. His self-image seems to have been that of a Garibaldian guerrilla leader. A hagiographic Ukrainian nationalist account later described him at this stage in his life as something of a sophisticate: 'In Lviv society he was regarded as a lady's man, a fine piano player, always courteously smiling, modernly dressed, diligent in studies.' The same writer stressed 'his fervent religiosity, his faith in goodness and justice of God and Christianity, upholding the Ukrainian expression of Christianity'.[25] But the genial, devout man-about-town was at the same time a fanatical terrorist, involved in a series of murderous attacks. In 1934 he was one of a group who assassinated the Polish Minister of the Interior, Bronisław Pieracki, whom the killers accused of responsibility for repression of Ukrainian nationalists in Lwów. The assassination led the authorities to detain Ukrainian activists at a 'place of seclusion', Bereza Kartuska, in north-eastern Poland. This, the first concentration camp established on Polish soil, developed into a holding-pen for a broad range of political prisoners, including Germans suspected of Nazi activity and Communists, among whom were some Jews. At his trial Shukhevych, who refused to speak Polish before the court, was defended by his uncle Stepan. Found guilty, he was sentenced to four years imprisonment, later reduced by amnesty to two. Temporarily cowed by the government's forceful reaction, the Ukrainian nationalists eschewed further spectacular attacks for a while, concentrating instead on propaganda and building up their organization.

In 1938–39, however, there was further unrest. The OUN launched a renewed campaign of demonstrations and protests. Extreme elements perpetrated terrorist acts throughout eastern Galicia. A disturbing symptom of acrimonious group relationships at this time was a series of attacks on mixed Roman/Greek Catholic families. The government responded with intensified repression. In Krakowiec a Ukrainian doctor, Bogdan Danysh, was arrested and sent to Bereza Kartuska.[26] In the *Sejm* (parliament) a Ukrainian deputy charged that Ukrainian prisoners in the Krakowiec jail were being maltreated and forced to speak Polish by Polish warders. Allegedly, one prisoner had been beaten up by other inmates, acting on orders from the guards. He tried to complain – in Ukrainian. The guard refused to acknowledge the complaint, claiming that he did not understand Ukrainian and that his 'national feelings were offended and his mother tongue likewise, comparing the Ukrainian language to that of horses.'[27]

Both the Germans and the Soviets sought to exploit the growing Ukrainian–Polish antipathy. On 21 August 1939 the German consulate in Lwów reported that mass arrests and persecution had so inflamed Ukrainian nationalism that a revolutionary situation was brewing.[28]

Amid this heightened Polish–Ukrainian antagonism, Jews once again found themselves caught in the middle. This time the protective umbrella of Habsburg rule no longer offered shelter. Anti-Semitism, always an undercurrent in the region but hitherto generally kept within bounds, assumed dangerous proportions.

Hostility between Ukrainians and Jews had intensified in the wake of the assassination of Symon Petliura in Paris in 1926. Petliura had served as supreme commander of the army of the Ukrainian National Republic from 1918 to 1920, and during the later part of that period was also president of its civilian Directory. He was widely held responsible for pogroms perpetrated by his soldiers during the civil war, though his role was and is disputed. The assassin, Sholem Schwarzbard, a Jew who had lost members of his family in the pogroms, gave himself up to the Paris police on the spot. His trial became an international sensation. In spite of Schwarzbard's admission that he had fired the shot that killed Petliura, a jury found him not guilty. In a simultaneous civil suit the same jury awarded deliberately humiliating

damages of one franc each to Petliura's widow and brother. Schwarzbard became a heroic symbol of Jewish vengeance; Petliura was
apotheosized as a martyr of Ukrainian nationalism. The affair spurred
anti-Semitic feeling among Ukrainians.

Polish anti-Semitism too became more outspoken in this period.
Polish nationalists were irritated by Jewish efforts to persuade the
government to implement the provisions of the Minorities Treaty. In
fact, Jews made little use of their right under the treaty to appeal to
the League. Since the League had no effective power of enforcement,
they realized that such complaints would merely infuriate the Poles
without securing redress. The government's unilateral renunciation of
the treaty in 1934 indicated its unwillingness to yield on such issues.
Until his death in 1935 the commanding presence of Piłsudski, who
afforded some patronizing protection to Jews, damped down extreme
anti-Semitism. Under his successors, however, Jews were subjected to
increasing verbal and, in some cases, physical abuse. A pogrom in the
small town of Przytyk in 1936 was seen as an evil omen of worse to
come.

In Krakowiec there was no anti-Jewish violence but the atmosphere
was changing. A minor incident at the local school, probably just
before Easter 1925, illustrated the fragility of communal relations.
Four Jewish boys, all aged about eight, waited behind after class until
everyone else had gone. They then climbed up and took down the
cross that hung on the wall above the teacher's desk. They broke it
into pieces and hid the fragments. A non-Jewish girl, who had witnessed what they did, ran to the school principal and denounced
them. The police were called. The broken cross was found. The mis-
creants were arrested. Word circulated throughout the district that
Jews were desecrating the cross. Much emphasis was laid on the fact
that one of the evildoers was a son of the local *shochet* (kosher slaugh-
terer), as if to suggest that this was no mere childish prank but a
wilful, religiously motivated act of desecration. The boys were interrogated and asked who had put them up to the crime: the *shochet*?
the rabbi? The malefactors denied that any adult had been involved.
They were tried, found guilty, and sentenced to four days behind bars
plus exclusion from school – from *any* school in the entire country.
The offenders' Jewish classmates brought kosher food for them to the

jail, where the prisoners lowered baskets and raised the supplies.[29] It was a perilous moment. Throughout Europe, alleged acts of desecration by Jews, especially around Easter, had traditionally been the touchpaper for a pogrom. Fortunately this episode passed without any eruption of violence but it left an unpleasant aftertaste.

More disturbing was the undermining of the economic position of Jews. Since the start of the century there had been pressure, from the Roman Catholic priest among others, for the establishment of 'Christian stores' to compete with allegedly price-gouging Jewish-owned ones. In the late 1930s these efforts were strengthened by a boycott movement directed against Jewish shopkeepers. Supporting the movement, a local newspaper in 1938 published a list of Polish-owned enterprises in the district: among these were a mill, bakery, restaurant and general store.[30]

The boycotts, strikes, and growing atmosphere of rancour led Jews to despair. 'The Jewish shtetls of Galicia are dying,' locals told a visitor from New York in 1936. 'People are in their death agonies.'[31] 'Sinister black clouds are hovering over our heads', a Jewish journalist in Lwów wrote in March 1939.[32] That month an appeal from Jews in Krakowiec to the Krakovitser *landsmanshaft* in New York lamented: 'Poverty and hunger in Krakowiec have never been so terrible: "*mamash a khurbn*"!' ('really a catastrophe!')[33] Israel Silberman, a Krakowiec Jew who had emigrated to New York and struck it rich with his 'Paragon Paint and Varnish Corporation', sent remittances from time to time. But the 'check from Uncle Sam' on which many families depended to eke out their meagre incomes often failed to arrive.

The German–Polish negotiations concerning the refugees at Zbąszyń (among them Berl and Addi) that had been broken off after the Kristallnacht resumed only in January 1939. Poland was in the final stages of an election campaign and the government was concerned to demonstrate that it was as hawkish as its opponents when it came to barring entry to Jews. While the Poles and Germans argued about where the Zbąszyń Jews belonged, writers in the *Manchester Guardian* and elsewhere expressed unavailing outrage at their treatment. British diplomats were disinclined to interfere 'in a matter which legally concerns Germany and Poland alone'. As the Warsaw embassy pointed out, 'it might seem injudicious at the present juncture for us to give any encouragement to Polish hopes of "planting" Jews in Palestine.'[34] Polish newspapers and diplomats argued that it was unfair to give preference to Jews seeking to emigrate from Germany. After all, Poland was much more heavily 'over-populated' with Jews and 'any international action to help the Jews in Germany should also be extended to help the emigration of Jews from Poland.' A Polish official warned ominously that any discrimination against Poland in this regard 'would be an incitement to pogroms'.[35]

At one point a rumour spread in Zbąszyń that an arrangement was in the offing whereby Polish Jews who owned real estate in Germany would be able to exchange it for property owned by Germans in Poland – apparently agricultural land in the Polish corridor (the strip of Polish territory that separated East Prussia from the rest of Germany). Berl Wasserstein took no interest in this proposal. He didn't like Poland. He didn't know Polish. He was not interested in becoming a farmer.

On 24 January 1939, Germany and Poland reached agreement on the disposal of the Zbąszyń refugees. The Poles consented to admit them as well as wives, and children under eighteen years of age. They would not be allowed to settle permanently in Poland but would have to show that they were making active preparations to emigrate elsewhere. Before moving to Poland, they were to be permitted to return temporarily to Germany 'to wind up their affairs'. They would have to liquidate their assets there. Six per cent of the proceeds would be transferable to Poland. The remainder would, in effect, be confiscated by the German government. The departing Jews would be permitted to take with them to Poland their tools of trade, jewellery and household effects. The Germans did not want all the expellees to return at once: they were to be allowed back to Germany in batches of one thousand at a time. The whole process was to be completed by the end of July.

Berl managed to lodge (apparently in absentia) an application at the American consulate in Berlin for immigration to the United States. Israel Silberman supplied an affidavit guaranteeing financial support. But that was only one of the several necessary prerequisites for immigration. Even if Berl managed to qualify, the waiting list was still impossibly long: he could expect that it would take years. A little more realistically, he hoped, with the help of Czarna's relatives in Johannesburg, to secure a visa for South Africa. That country's obstacles to would-be Jewish immigrants rendered this too a doubtful prospect but, without any viable alternative, Berl clutched at this straw.

In April Berl, but not Addi, finally secured permission to return to Berlin for a limited period 'to wind up his affairs'. Although relieved to be reunited with his wife and daughter, Berl's position was desperate. There was not much by way of 'affairs' left to wind up. His business could not be revived or sold. Jewish-owned concerns had all been 'Aryanized'. Jews' bank accounts had been blocked and were controlled by the Gestapo. Any remaining funds could be withdrawn only by permission and in fixed monthly amounts. Berl succeeded in selling one of his two apartment buildings at a knockdown price to an 'Aryan' buyer but the purchase price was never paid.[36] Berl had no job: like more than 70 per cent of German Jews over the age of fourteen, he was now classified as 'self-employed without occupation'. No longer able to afford their rented apartment, Berl, Czarna and Lotte lodged with friends.

By the end of May Berl's permitted residence period in Berlin had expired. The family had to leave Germany immediately and there was only one place for them to go: Poland. Berl and Czarna decided to return to Krakowiec for what they hoped would be a short visit. They would be able to stay with family members there while they arranged for emigration from Europe. Both Chaim-Yitzhak Laub and Jacob Wasserstein had by now died but Berl's mother and Czarna's were still alive, as were many other relatives living in or around Krakowiec.

The decision to return to their birthplace was very much a last resort. But they had no other choice. Berl's two decades of effort to establish himself in Germany and build a new life for his family there had been wiped out almost overnight. The socio-political climate in Poland, as in every country in east-central Europe, was growing ever more hostile to Jews. Economic prospects, especially in a backwater like Krakowiec, were dismal. The most Berl could hope for was that Krakowiec would be a *Nachtasyl*, a night shelter, while they sought a permanent home on another continent.

In mid-June Addi was granted permission to return to Germany from Zbąszyń for a short period. He had to show evidence that he would emigrate elsewhere. For this purpose he had managed to acquire a visa to a Latin American country. Such documents were available at a price. They were not usable for entry to the states whose representatives in Poland sold them to desperate people. Addi could not, however, go with the family to Krakowiec, as he had been required, prior to leaving Zbąszyń, to sign an undertaking that he would not return to Poland.

Addi arrived in Berlin just as his parents were finalizing preparations to leave for Krakowiec. German regulations permitted them to ship out some books, clothing and personal effects but otherwise all their possessions would have to be abandoned. Customs officials came to the apartment to seal the containers before they were removed for transportation to Krakowiec. Addi went to the Ostbahnhof station to say a painful farewell to his parents and sister. It was unclear where, when, or even whether they would ever meet again. This was the only time he ever saw his father shed tears.

N

Baltic Sea

(LATVIA)

(LITHUANIA)
REICHSKOMMISSARIAT OSTLAND

Neman

• Konigsberg

• Vilna
✠ Ponary

Danzig•
EAST PRUSSIA
Stutthof ✠

• Rastenburg

SUWAŁKI

REICHSGAU
DANZIG-
WEST PRUSSIA   ZICHENAU
• Bromberg

BEZIRK BIAŁYSTOK

Posen •

✠ Treblinka
• Warsaw

Zbąszyń•
WARTHELAND
Chelmno•

Pripet

Oder

Łódź •

✠ Gross-Rosen
Breslau

• Częstochowa

GENERAL
GOUVERNEMENT
1939–45

Sobibor
✠
Lublin •
✠ Majdanek

REICHS-
KOMMISSARIAT
UKRAINE

UPPER SILESIA

Vistula   San

Bełżec
✠

Jarosław
Auschwitz ✠
Cracow ✠
• Bochnia
Płaszów ✠
• Zakopane
PROTECTORATE
OF BOHEMIA
AND MORAVIA

Krakowiec •

Przemyśl •

• Belz
• Jaworów
Lwów •
• Przemyślany
DISTRICT
OF GALICIA
(added to GG 1941)
Stanisławów •

SLOVAKIA
• Bratislava

GERMANY

Dniester

HUNGARY

RUMANIA

—— Polish frontier 1939	▬ ▬ ▬ Grossdeutschland frontier 1941
••••• Nazi-Soviet demarcation line 08 Sept. 1939	▨ German administrative districts 1941
▨ Polish territories annexed to the Reich in Sept. 1939	✠ Nazi concentration and death camps
■ General Government 1939–45	

0   100 miles
0   200 km

7. Occupied Poland, 1939–45

9

Under three regimes

Krakowiec was within the area of advance of General Gerd von Rundstedt's Army Group South, one of the five German armies that smashed into Poland on 1 September 1939, initiating the Second World War in Europe. General Wilhelm List's 14th Army attacked eastern Galicia from the west and south-west. The Poles were woefully outnumbered and ill-equipped. Their 750 armoured vehicles, many of them obsolete, were no match for the Germans' 3,600 modern tanks and other armour on the eastern front. The Luftwaffe was no less superior in the number and quality of its planes. Above all, the German armed forces displayed strategic mastery, coordinating air and land forces in a war of swift movement. They were aided in their advance by fine weather. (Writing to Addi from Krakowiec a month earlier, Czarna had requested that he order sunglasses for Lotte.[1]) The war diary of the German army noted cheerfully: 'We had an extraordinarily steady weather situation during the days from 1 to 14 September, summer warmth, an almost cloud-free sky and no precipitation worth mentioning.'[2] By 9 September the Poles were already retreating from Przemyśl towards Lwów. They made a brief stand at Jarosław but this soon collapsed. On 11 September elements of General Ewald von Kleist's 22nd Corps had crossed the San River near Jarosław and headed east, passing to the north of Krakowiec. Meanwhile the 18th Corps moved north from the Carpathians and advanced towards Lwów.

Colonel Stanisław Maczek commanded the Polish Tenth Mechanized Cavalry Brigade, the only armoured unit in the Polish army. It took up position along the San, just west of Krakowiec. In his memoirs, Maczek later rejected the charge that the Poles' defensive line on the San had been 'a fiction, a *fata morgana* . . . No, I cannot reconcile myself to that proposition! This principal line of defence on the San was by no means merely the fruit of our imagination.'[3] But his own chief of staff told a different story: 'We expected the river to be strongly held and fortified . . . But the river San, dried up by the drought, did not come up to our expectations at all. We saw no fortifications of any kind – even no trenches. The water level was such that a hen could have crossed the river with ease.'[4] This was at any rate an original excuse for military failure: the inadequacies of the river were thus held accountable for the Poles' defeat.

As a child before the First World War, Maczek had often spent summer holidays together with his three brothers (all killed in that war) on the estate of his uncle at Wielkie Oczy, close to Krakowiec. Consequently, he knew the area well. Noticing that the swamps around the Krakowiec lake were unusually dry, he decided to conceal forces there. He hoped to make a defensive stand in order to bar the Germans' route towards Lwów. Maczek set up his field headquarters in the Łubieński manor house to the west of Krakowiec. He watched from an observation point as German artillery launched shells on the town, one landing on the mill near the lake (*see map on p. 55*).

At 6.45 p.m. on 11 September, as darkness fell, a German reconnaissance unit reached Młyny, a village four miles west of Krakowiec. The unit consisted of one motorcycle company, two Panzer scout squads, one cavalry gun platoon and one anti-tank gun. Polish troops were known to be in the area and the Germans therefore halted for the night. Meanwhile Maczek's 10th Mounted Rifle Regiment took up position in Krakowiec and the 24th Lancer Regiment, also part of his brigade, was ordered to the nearby hamlet of Porudenko. The Poles set up machine-gun nests and anti-tank guns on roads around Krakowiec.

On 12 September the Germans and Poles fought a fierce battle in Krakowiec. By coincidence, this was twenty-five years to the day since the Russo-Austrian battle there in the First World War. The German attacking force, the 4th Light Infantry Division, was commanded by Generalmajor Dr Alfred Ritter von Hubicki. Born in Carpathian Ruthenia and a veteran of the Habsburg army in the First World War, Hubicki, almost as much as Maczek, was fighting on home ground.

German artillery pummelled the Poles who were hampered by defect-
ive equipment, shortage of fuel and minimal air cover.

Early that morning the Germans brought in additional troops. Cavalry Captain Ferdinand Bentele, in command of the 7th Armoured
Scout Troop of the Second Battalion, Reconnaissance Regiment 9, in
Hubicki's division, describes the moment the first German soldiers
entered Krakowiec:

> I was moving in the lead vehicle. The armored car carefully felt its way
> forward into the curve. My face pressed tightly against the optics. I was
> looking for enemy riflemen AT guns. But I couldn't find even a mouse.
>
> Krakowiec was all quiet ahead of us, as if it were peacetime. The
> morning sun was smiling on us and, despite that, we knew: danger was
> lurking for us everywhere. Perhaps it would be riflemen or a well-
> camouflaged AT gun. That meant, 'Keep your eyes peeled.'
>
> 'Move out!' I ordered the vehicle driver. The speed increased as we
> approached the entrance to the village. An abandoned truck was off to
> the left of the road. It had already concealed us from quite a distance.
> Just before we got to it, we turned off to the right. Then there was a
> buzzing. I searched for the cause but didn't see anything. Only the
> whistling of enemy machine guns and rifles could be heard . . .
>
> 'Back up!' . . . For the moment nothing stirred . . .
>
> I thought to myself, Who dares, wins! I decided to advance for the
> second time. We slowly rolled forward . . .
>
> At that moment, we received a tremendous blow. Our vehicle pitched
> to the left. It had been hit . . .
>
> We hobbled back to the rear . . . Finally we were safe. We quickly
> took a look outside to see what the matter was and saw that the left
> front tire had been hit. Red earth pressed through the shredded tire. We
> looked at one another. One meter higher and it would have been us . . .[5]

Relief and frustration turned to jubilation half an hour later when
Bentele found that the Polish anti-tank gun in the middle of the road
ahead of them had been knocked out and was lying overturned in the
roadside ditch.

The Germans encountered heavy Polish resistance at Gnojnica,
immediately to the west of Krakowiec. A Polish tank was caught in a
trap and destroyed. The Poles then fell back on Krakowiec itself.

German artillery shelled the town and Luftwaffe planes dropped bombs, wreaking extensive damage. Polish bombers joined the battle, although the Polish Bomber Brigade's few remaining aircraft were almost out of fuel.[6] In the ensuing dogfight, one Polish plane was shot down in flames. The Łubieński manor house, which had been captured by the Germans, was heavily damaged in a Polish counter-attack. Two German tanks were destroyed. The Roman Catholic church was hit by a shell. The roof and much of the interior were gutted and all that remained were the exterior walls. Among the works of art destroyed were a portrait of Princess Anna Lotaryńska (Cetner) and paintings of saints by the Krakowiec-born artist Thomas Antoni Lisiewicz. The last remnants of Ignacy Cetner's architectural legacy to the town were thereby almost obliterated. The hospital, the vicarage and some other houses were also destroyed.

Maczek consoled himself with the reflection that he had succeeded in defending Krakowiec 'for a certain time'. But in the evening an order came from above to withdraw. The Poles retreated in disarray in the direction of Jaworów. Maczek's journey to Lwów that night was 'a veritable nightmare' along a gutted road strewn with the debris of war and amid dread of ambush by the Germans.[7] All the villages on the way were burning and large numbers of dead horses littered the ditches, so that a nauseous stink hung in the air. By 14 September the German High Command's map of the front line showed Krakowiec well within the territory occupied by the German army.[8] For his role in this battle, Hubicki was awarded the Iron Cross (second class) four days later.

Krakowiec now fell under German military occupation. In the First World War the conduct of German soldiers towards civilians in the region had been regarded as relatively civilized by comparison with that of their Austro-Hungarian allies or of the Russians. Based on that folk memory, some residents discounted the dangers of German occupation. Such complacency was soon confounded.

Behind the German army a number of special SS units, Einsatzgruppen, were dispatched to kill Polish elites, Jews and others regarded as enemies of the Reich. Einsatzkommando I/I, commanded by Dr Ludwig Hahn, was attached to List's 14th Army and, after the German capture of Przemyśl on 16 September, was sent across the San towards Lwów. At least five hundred Jews in the area around Przemyśl were killed. Survivors fled in all directions. In one town a dozen Jews were burned to death in the synagogue and another sixty shot. Some German military commanders objected to the interference of the SS with their authority but no counter-action was taken and soldiers joined in the maltreatment of Jews.

Among the Jews who fled from Przemyśl were three young men, cousins of Berl Wasserstein. They set off on foot, hoping to take refuge with relatives in Krakowiec. On the way they met a Polish officer who had been separated from his unit. A German plane flew overhead. The officer took out his revolver and shot fruitlessly at the plane.[9]

In Jaworów the Jews got a foretaste of what was in store for them. Immediately after German troops arrived, assaults on Jews began. The synagogue was set on fire, and Jews were ordered to burn Torah scrolls. A large group of Jews was driven into the yard of the courthouse. There they were told to face the wall and to perform physical exercises. They were chased around the courtyard, forced to crawl on all fours and directed to clear a high jump, all the while under crushing blows. Among those who suffered these beatings was an aged doctor, Saul Jahr, who had formerly lived in Krakowiec. He later hanged himself 'so as not to be a burden on his wife'. Forty Jews were taken hostage and two (according to another account, seven) were shot dead.[10] Ukrainian militia volunteers joined German troops and security personnel in committing atrocities.

A German army propaganda organ reported that 'the further east we came, the more friendly was the population.' On the other hand, the publication noted regretfully that the region was besmirched by the presence of Jews. It added a bulletin, strangely datelined 'Amsterdam': 'It has become known from Lemberg that five Germans were fetched out of their homes on Senatorska Street and murdered. The bodies were covered in petroleum and burned!'[11] I have not found any corroboration of this report; possibly it was an invention, designed to provide a pretext for the Germans' own atrocities.

Fear reigned in Krakowiec. At one point Jewish men were rounded up in the market square. But they were soon released following the intercession of a Greek Catholic priest.[12] Life seemed to return to normal. People cautiously emerged from their homes and began going about their business. After a few days, Jews who had fled to surrounding villages returned.

Berl and his family made do as best they could. They probably stayed with his mother. Czarna's former family home, on the other side of the market square, had been destroyed in the battle. Berl's original notion that his stay in Krakowiec would be temporary had evaporated. He was on the waiting list for a visa to the United States and still hoped somehow to get there or to South Africa. But unable to leave the war zone, he was marooned in Krakowiec.

Lotte could not go to school because, as Berl explained in a postcard to Addi, there was none available for her: aged fourteen, she was too old for the elementary school in Krakowiec. Unable to communicate with most of the people around her, since she spoke only German, she spent much of her time with her cousin Regina, daughter of Samuel (Beinish) Laub who, like Berl, had been deported from Berlin to Zbąszyń and then, with his family, to Krakowiec.

One day, Regina was sitting with another cousin, Sonia Berg, outside Sonia's home, when a German soldier passed by. Suddenly Regina shivered with fright: she recognized him as an acquaintance from Berlin. He greeted her and they chatted for a while before he moved on. The soldier behaved as if they were old friends who happened to meet while on holiday. Regina was terrified.[13]

Another German soldier approached Pinkas Majus (the 'visitor from the past' who gave me a puppet monkey in the 1950s). The soldier, apparently a believing Christian, uttered a 'Christian blessing' and offered Majus some advice. He warned him to leave Krakowiec as soon as possible. He clearly meant that Jews would not be safe under Nazi rule.

A third soldier administered this lesson in a less benevolent way to Berl when he went to the marketplace with Lotte. German army vehicles and soldiers were standing around doing nothing in particular and the general mood seemed relaxed. The weather was beginning to turn autumnal, and Berl was wearing one of his fine 'Wasserstein' coats. By chance, he met a cousin who had just arrived in Krakowiec, one of the three who had trekked from Przemyśl. Berl said reassuringly there was no point in panicking as everything in Krakowiec seemed peaceful. Suddenly a soldier accosted him and said, 'That's a fine coat you've got there. Hand it over.' Berl dared to protest, earning a slap in the face. 'It's not yours. It belongs to Germany,' the soldier said as he hauled off his booty.[14] It was a further stage in Berl's education in the ethics of the new order.

Wilhelm Prüller, among German infantrymen advancing from Krakowiec, recorded on 15 September that, as they occupied another village, 'all the Jewish shops are forced open and the civilian population plunders them.' He grumbled that there was nothing left for the troops: 'You couldn't get chocolate or cigarettes anywhere.'[15] Prüller ended up, after the war, as proprietor of a small gift shop on the outskirts of Vienna where, presumably, he could help himself to as much confectionery and smokes as he liked.

Lwów was already half-abandoned and awaiting the final blow. That came suddenly from an unexpected quarter. At 3.00 a.m. on 17 September, the Polish Ambassador in Moscow was summoned to the Foreign Ministry and handed a note. This announced that, in view of 'the internal bankruptcy of the Polish state', the Soviet Union had ordered its forces to cross Poland's eastern border to protect its 'kindred Ukrainian and White Russian people'.[16] Simultaneously the Red Army began the occupation of Poland's eastern provinces in accordance with the secret protocols of the Hitler-Stalin pact that had been concluded nine days before the outbreak of war. The German and Soviet dictators now seized their agreed shares of Polish territory. The remnants of Polish forces fled south to Rumania. On 21 September German and Russian armies were face to face near Lwów, though the Poles still held the city. The next day, as the Germans withdrew towards the west, the Russians entered the city. Polish defenders were promised safe passage – ordinary soldiers to their homes, officers to go abroad. In fact, most of the officers were sent to prison camps; nearly all of them were subsequently executed by the NKVD.

On 23 September Nikita Khrushchev, dispatched by Stalin to supervise the Soviet takeover of eastern Poland (or, as the Soviets preferred to think of it, western Ukraine), appeared in a village near Lwów and berated NKVD generals for their inefficiency: 'You call this work?

You haven't carried out a single execution … What weasels you are!'[17] Three days later the Red Army arrived in Jaworów. A Ukrainian observer thought the soldiers looked 'like slaves, hungry, skinny, and sad'.[18] By 28 September Krakowiec too was under Soviet occupation. Within a month it had found itself under three different regimes.

The confusion and panic of the opening days of the war are vividly conveyed in the diary/memoir of Paulina Ledóchowska, daughter of Jadwiga Łubieńska, the aged proprietrix of the Krakowiec estate. Paulina lived with her husband Ignacy, a retired Polish army general, at Wólka Rosnowska, down the road from Krakowiec (his was the 'mansion' that had been admired by Isaac Babel in 1921). Paulina described how, as the front line moved ever closer, she and her husband heard with growing alarm the noise of the battle in the west. They decided to flee to what they imagined might be the greater safety of Lwów. 'All the servants said goodbye to us with tears because it seemed to them they would never see us again.' That night, as they arrived in Lwów, 'the whole sky was burning and above Lwów was a sea of fire.' They took refuge in an Ursuline convent where one of their daughters was cloistered.

Three days after they arrived, they were bewildered to hear 'the Russians are coming.' They were 'stunned' when the Red Army took over the city. General Ledóchowski was apprehensive as to the treatment he might enjoy at the hands of the Soviets – and with good reason, as the Soviets soon started rounding up Polish officers. Paulina also worried about the fate of her mother, who was still in Krakowiec. 'We lived in continuous fear and uncertainty,' she wrote. In early November they fled westwards in an old jalopy. When they reached the outskirts of Przemyśl, they found a throng of desperate people seeking to cross the San to the German side of the Soviet-German demarcation line. Russian guards would not let them through. Eventually they managed to get hold of the required exit permits. At the bridge over the San they watched as German guards brutally removed Jews from the line. The Jews' explanations and arguments availed them nothing. They were ordered back 'nach Russland!' Somehow the couple struggled through and reached Ledóchowski's ancestral home at Lipnica in western Galicia.[19]

By 26 September 1939 the bulk of the German army had withdrawn west of the San. The next day the last German units in the Krakowiec area crossed the river. Tattered remnants of the Polish armed forces took up positions briefly in Krakowiec over the next few days before scattering or being captured.[20] The precise dividing line between the Nazi and Soviet zones was finally established on 28 September. That day an order to the Einsatzgruppen called for all 'undesirable elements' to be cleared out of the area adjacent to the line. 'In the first place, the Jewish pop. of these border locales is – in as far as it is possible – to be pushed to the east, over the San.'[21] The next day Russian forces entered Krakowiec and advanced to the river. The German High Command in Poland announced that the separation of forces at the demarcation line was being completed with the greatest mutual understanding.[22]

The Jews of Krakowiec were luckier than they knew in finding themselves on the Russian side of the new frontier (*see map on p. 130*). The original boundary between German and Soviet spheres, agreed between the German and Soviet foreign ministers in the secret protocol to their non-aggression pact on 23 August 1939, spoke vaguely of a frontier 'approximately along the line of the rivers Narew, Vistula, and San', i.e. west of Lwów and of Krakowiec. But the German High Command situation map for 4.00 p.m. on 17 September showed a north/south line running *east* of Lwów – which would have thrown Krakowiec into the German occupation zone. Four days later, on the High Command map for 21 September, the line suddenly shifted west. In the area north of Przemyśl, it now ran along the western bank of the San, thus depositing Krakowiec in the Soviet sphere.[23] Przemyśl itself, straddling the San, was partitioned, with the left (west) bank allocated to the Germans, and the right, containing most of the old city, to the Soviets. There were further changes in the line over the next few days, though these did not affect Krakowiec. Behind these cartographic modifications lay Russo-German diplomatic exchanges in the course of which Stalin demanded the oil-producing region of Borysław-Drohobycz, south-west of Lwów, in return for concessions further north. As a sweetener, the Russians promised to export the region's entire annual production of oil to Germany and indeed did so – with the result that two years later German tanks could move back into the area fuelled by petroleum that the Soviets themselves had supplied.

Shortly before the Wehrmacht troops withdrew from Krakowiec, Regina Laub's German soldier acquaintance came to the house of her cousin Sonia. He warned her mother that when the Russians arrived girls would not be safe.[24] If judged by the earlier standard set by the Russians in the First World War or by the later behaviour of Red Army soldiers advancing into Germany in 1945, the warning was apt. But in the autumn of 1939 the Russian conquerors of Krakowiec conducted themselves towards women with relative decorum.

Having tasted German rule, albeit briefly, most Jews in the area evacuated by the Germans greeted Soviet occupation with relief, if only as the lesser evil. The joke went round that whereas the Nazis had condemned the Jews to death, under the Soviets the sentence was commuted to life imprisonment.[25] Not for the first time, Jews were accused of welcoming an invader. Their allegedly friendly attitude towards the Red Army was resented by many Poles, who regarded it as nothing short of treasonous.

Soviet policies in the newly occupied territory heightened Polish resentment. Poles were dismissed from official positions and replaced by Jews and (many more) Ukrainians. Jews were widely identified with the Soviet regime, though the reality was different: an analysis of chairmen and secretaries of the 828 town soviets in the Lwów district in December 1940 disclosed that these consisted of 1,553 Ukrainians, sixty-five Poles, eighteen Jews and three Russians.[26] Jews were similarly under-represented in other organs of the new administration. On the other hand, they were *over*-represented among those arrested during the Soviet occupation.[27] Still, what mattered was what people found it convenient to believe, not what was actually the case. As Jonathan Swift noted two centuries earlier, 'Falsehood flies, and truth comes limping after it.'

After spurious elections, orchestrated by Khrushchev, an assembly of Western Ukraine convened at Lwów on 26 October and requested incorporation in the Ukrainian Soviet Socialist Republic, which petition was granted a few days later. Stalin acclaimed the result: 'From the kingdom of darkness and boundless suffering which the nation of Western Ukraine bore for six hundred long years, we find ourselves in the fairy land of true happiness of the people and of true freedom.'[28]

A resident of Krakowiec recalled how the plebiscite was conducted there:

> The lies and the hypocrisy in their speeches were much too obvious. We were told that the Polish political system was based on exploitation, anarchy, and on the oppression of peasants and workers, and that the eastern part of Poland had belonged for centuries to Russia and must be returned to her, and other rubbish of that kind. We had to listen to this and we could not protest.
>
> Their role was to stupefy the weaker people with sweet promises and force them to vote. Those who were aware of their scheming were already behind iron bars.[29]

This, at any rate, was the view of a disgruntled Pole.

The apparatus of the Soviet state was soon extended to the annexed region. Ukrainians who had collaborated with the Nazis during the brief interlude of German occupation were punished. Meanwhile other Ukrainians, mainly *vostochniks*, 'easterners', replaced Poles in official positions. Polish army officers, policemen, officials, intellectuals and landowners were arrested. Non-Communist politicians of all nationalities as well as ex-Communists whose loyalty was suspect were sent to prison camps. Thousands of people were executed for 'counter-revolutionary activity', many of them without trial.

A social revolution was launched with the object of stamping out all feudal (i.e. mainly Polish) and bourgeois (i.e. mainly Jewish) socio-economic elements. Banks, mines, factories and railways were nationalized. A start was made to the reorganization of agriculture. Land belonging to large landowners and churches was expropriated and redistributed to poor peasants, collectives and state farms – though the process began haltingly. A 'Shevchenko kolkhoz' (collective farm) was established in Krakowiec in March 1941. In keeping with the civilizing mission of Communism, the new rulers initiated an educational programme to eliminate illiteracy; behind this enlightened endeavour was a wide-ranging policy of cultural Ukrainianization. In December 1939 the Soviet rouble suddenly replaced the Polish złoty, which became almost worthless. No more than 300 złoty could be exchanged – and that at an unfavourable rate. As a result many residents lost their life savings.[30]

A report in the Red Army newspaper *Krasnaya Zvezda* (Red Star) on 18 September 1940 summarized the population's reaction to all this: 'The workers of the Western Ukraine and Western Byelorussia, thanks to the fraternal assistance of the Soviet people and its Red Army, were for ever liberated from the class and national oppression of the Polish bourgeois. They acquired a new homeland for themselves – the land of happiness – the Soviet Union ... Warmed by the sunrays of Stalin's constitution, people are joyfully building a new life.'[31]

This was not quite how all the inhabitants, particularly Poles, viewed matters. The same Polish witness from Krakowiec quoted earlier, recalled, in an account given in exile a few years later:

> All the Polish homes were plunged into mourning because there was not one family where a father, a brother, or a son was not arrested. The organs of the NKVD were carrying out a purge. Every night our houses were visited by armed patrols which carried out thorough searches. On many occasions whole neighbourhoods were turned upside down and women and children were hurt.[32]

This was perhaps an exaggerated account of the Poles' tribulations, arising from outrage that they were no longer top dogs. But there is some evidence to support it. For example, a Polish teacher in Krakowiec, Leopold Chruszcz, was arrested 'for an allegedly crude attitude towards Ukrainian and Jewish children'. He was interrogated by the NKVD in the Krakowiec prison and severely beaten. Later he was sent to the notorious Brygidki prison in Lwów where large numbers of inmates were murdered.[33]

Many Ukrainians too became disaffected. In a letter to the Vatican, Metropolitan Andrey Sheptytsky, head of the Greek Catholic church, gave his view of the Soviet government: 'Everything that emanates from the authorities seems to have as its object to provoke, to ruin, to destroy, to cause misery; and with that an unbelievable disorder ... Every order is issued with a threat of death.' He added: 'A prodigious number of Jews are invading the entire economic life of the country and lending to the actions of the authorities a character of sordid avarice that one had been accustomed to seeing only among dishonest and sordid Jewish petty traders.' The church was being suppressed, atheism was rampant, and his people were suffering. The new regime, he said, could not be explained save as a product of 'mass diabolical possession'.[34]

In Krakowiec the NKVD set up quarters in a Jewish-owned house on the market square. Some local Jews as well as Soviet Jewish new-comers were among its personnel. Apart from Iosip Krilyk, there had been no known Communists in the town before the Russians arrived. But now they 'came out like mushrooms', as one Jewish resident put it.[35] A Ukrainian schoolteacher, Ivan Onufrik, was one such: but his avowal of Marxist beliefs did not save him from arrest and 'disap-pearance'. Dr Berger, the only Jew in town who had not habitually covered his head (save when he wore a top hat), is said to have 'spoken to the people' in favour of Communism.[36] Another local Jew, Nochim Majer Pompius, a poor tailor, became a so-called 'commissar' – though he hedged his bets by continuing to attend synagogue services regularly. Pompius attracted the contempt of almost all elements in the population. Most of the town's Jews, while thankful that they no longer had to endure Nazi rule, resented the new regime's anti-religious policies and its attacks on private business.

A few months after the Soviet occupation of Krakowiec, an official report on the town was prepared. It took the form of answers to a questionnaire apparently sent to many localities and designed to acquaint the new rulers with the chief assets of their newly acquired territories. The answers for Krakowiec, unsigned and undated save for the year 1940, provide informative data.[37] They record the presence of the mill, now with three workers, as well as of a school, a library and a kindergarten. More puzzlingly, the document lists a fifteen-bed hos-pital as well as a children's hospital and two clinics. The hospital had, in fact, been destroyed in the fighting in September 1939. Perhaps it had been restored by 1940? Or was the respondent simply listing fea-tures of the town as they had existed before the war? We do not know. There were thirty-seven electric streetlights but no paved streets and just half a kilometre of paved sidewalk. Various other aspects of the town are delineated accurately and no mention is made of any damage caused in 1939. However, the questionnaire provided no question on that subject and the anonymous respondent did not volunteer additional data. When dealing with Stalin's government it was prudent, that person presumably judged, to give straightforward answers to questions posed, without embellishments.

The most interesting – and in retrospect disturbing – information came in response to questions about the population of the town. This was given as 2,100. There was no breakdown by religion, a topic that hardly concerned the Soviets.[38] Instead, a different, but from the Jewish viewpoint potentially sinister, categorization was adopted: the report noted that 1,821 residents were 'workers and peasants.' That left 279 persons unaccounted for. In Soviet parlance of the period the only categories to which it was politically safe to belong (and even then there was no guarantee of security) were 'worker' and 'peasant.' In fact, most of the Ukrainian and much of the Polish population of Krakowiec would fall naturally into one of those groups. The only exceptions might be large Polish landowners, Roman Catholic or Uniate priests, and Polish officials and army officers. On the other hand, there were next to no Jews in the town who would fall naturally into either of the favoured categories. Most would instead be defined as 'unproductive' merchants – a distinctly uncomfortable definition for anybody in the Soviet Union under Stalin.

For a while, small traders were permitted to operate. Artisans, including bakers, tailors, craftsmen and so forth, could continue to work, though they were encouraged to form *artels* (cooperatives). But price controls, requisitions and lack of supplies drove most of them out of business. As trade declined, the weekly market withered and eventually died. In the summer, chairs were set up in the square on some evenings and Russian films were shown.

Shortages of food and fuel soon developed, leading to large-scale hoarding, barter, and black and 'grey' market activity. One traveller in the region in the autumn of 1939 recorded that 'speculation' was rampant in all its small towns.[39] A few months later another observer reported 'terrible hunger' and 'indescribable dearth' among Jews in Lwów. The exultation of *Simchas Torah* (the joyous autumnal festival), he wrote, had given way under Soviet occupation to the lamentations of *Tisha be-av* (the dismal midsummer fast commemorating the destruction of the second temple and other disasters of

Jewish history).[40] Smugglers operated across the demarcation line, four miles west of Krakowiec, trafficking in refugees, alcohol and foreign currency. Refugees played a prominent role in the 'parallel economy'. One way or another people survived.

How Berl Wasserstein managed to make ends meet during the twenty-one months of Soviet rule we do not know. Whatever was in those sealed cases that he had managed to transport from Berlin, he could not have been left with much ready cash. Possibly his wife's brothers in South Africa had been able to send some money during the short period between his arrival in Poland and the outbreak of war. After that, such transfers from overseas became more difficult, although they were not impossible.[41] Berl had neither the skill, nor probably the inclination, to take over his late father's bakery business. There was no other paid work for him, especially as he spoke neither Russian nor Ukrainian. Relatives in the town, themselves in dire straits, were in no position to help.

Jewish life in the shtetl was rapidly forced into the Soviet mould. The structure of the *kehillah*, the organized Jewish community, was dissolved. Without its taxable authority, rabbis and other communal functionaries could not receive salaries. Synagogues, *mikvaot* (ritual bathhouses) and cemeteries could barely be maintained. Worship and religious rites of passage such as circumcision, bar mitzvah, marriage and funeral services, though permitted, were discouraged. Religious education, save in the home, was prohibited. After 26 June 1940, when the Supreme Soviet decreed a seven-day working week, Sabbath observance became impossible for many workers. Jewish autonomous institutions and political parties were closed. Bundist and Zionist leaders were arrested. Jewish youth movements were dissolved, to be replaced by the Komsomol. Communication with the outside world, although not totally cut off (the postal service continued but was subject to censorship) became difficult and sometimes dangerous as a ground for suspicion of anti-Soviet sentiment.

At first the Soviets did not prevent the entry to their zone of Jews expelled by or seeking to escape from the Nazis. Although the frontier between the Nazi and Soviet zones was officially closed after 30 October 1939, clandestine border-crossing remained possible, though hazardous. Many people arrested for crossing illegally into the Soviet sector were sentenced to terms in the Gulag. An authorized channel for crossing opened in the spring of 1940, when the Germans and Soviets reached an exchange agreement whereby people on either side of the demarcation line who wished to cross might do so. In June special commissions in Lwów and elsewhere considered applications by residents of Soviet-occupied Poland to cross into the German zone. Some were granted such permission. The story goes that when a train carrying Jewish refugees eastwards arrived at the border station of Biała Podlaska, it met a train carrying Jews going in the opposite direction. The first group shouted to the second: 'You're insane! Where are you going?' The reply came: '*You're* insane, where are *you* going?'[42]

The Soviet secret police often regarded the very act of applying to leave as evidence of treachery and in some cases, instead of sending the applicants west, rounded them up and deported them east to labour camps. The deportees were thereby, as it turned out, saved from death at the hands of the Nazis – unless they were among the thousands who perished from cold, hunger or disease, or were executed by the Soviets. Many of those who did not apply to leave and refused to accept Soviet passports were also deported to the Soviet east.[43] At least four Jews from Krakowiec were among those granted 'visas' to go west – perhaps to join relatives or to flee the worsening economic conditions.[44] Thousands of Jews found refuge from the Nazis in the Soviet zone before the border was more or less sealed in mid-1940.

On 29 November 1939 the Supreme Soviet of the USSR conferred Soviet citizenship on permanent residents of the newly incorporated territory. In February and March 1940 the new citizens were issued with Soviet identity cards. But refugees from outside the occupation zone (presumably Berl and his family were regarded as among these) fell into a special category. They were given a choice: they could either apply to a joint Nazi-Soviet Commission for permission to return to Nazi-occupied Poland or they could apply for Soviet citizenship. This was, of course, a Hobson's choice; moreover, the decision had to be made without access to reliable information. A manifestation of Stalin's desire to ingratiate himself with Hitler was the failure of the

Soviet media to publicize Nazi atrocities against the Jews in Poland and elsewhere. Foreign newspapers were unobtainable. Allied broadcasts were not, at this stage in the war, devoting much attention to Nazi persecution of the Jews. The Lwów radio station broadcast a 'Yiddish hour' but little that was useful could be gleaned from this – even assuming a wireless set was available. Only against this background is it possible to understand the extraordinary fact that some Jewish refugees in the Soviet-occupied zone of Poland returned voluntarily to the Nazi-held area.

Berl would not accept Soviet citizenship, which he well realized might confine him and his family in the Soviet Union for the rest of their lives. Moreover, persons who acquired Soviet passports became liable to 'paragraph 11', which prohibited residence within one hundred kilometres from the frontier: Berl and his family would accordingly have been required to leave Krakowiec.[45] Those who neither moved west nor accepted Soviet citizenship rendered themselves liable to deportation by the Soviets to labour camps in the far eastern or northern territories of the USSR. Many of these deportees, particularly from border areas such as Krakowiec, were politically suspect elements such as former Polish officials, Zionists, Bundists or 'capitalists'. Successive waves of deportation, starting in February 1940, led to the removal by the Soviets of several hundred thousand people from former Polish territory.[46] A large percentage were Jews, mostly refugees. Not all of these were forced deportations: many people, particularly Jews whose economic position had been undermined by Soviet policies, readily agreed to move, attracted by the prospect of employment in the Soviet interior. And some who would have liked to go were refused the necessary permits. Those deported from Krakowiec included both Poles and Jews. When the deportations and evacuations to the east began, Pinkas Majus, who held a minor position in the local Soviet administration, suggested to Berl that he join those departing. Berl refused.

His decision seemed reasonable at the time. Soviet recruiting propaganda painted a bright picture of life in Central Asia, the Caucasus or other places to which the volunteers would be sent. But there were grounds for suspecting that the reality would be different. As it turned out, conditions in most cases were so appalling that many evacuees made their way back after a short time – often to face arrest upon their return.⁴⁷ After the upheavals the family had already endured, would it make sense for Berl and Czarna to abandon what was, at any rate for the time being, a roof over their heads in a place they knew, in order to move with Lotte to an uncertain future in a foreign country ruled by a bloodthirsty despot? Stranded in Krakowiec, without access to any solid news, they could not know what was coming. A German attack on the Soviet Union, while, of course, conceivable, could by no means be predicted with certainty in early 1941, even by experts. If the Nazis and Communists did come to blows, how could one foresee that such a war would entail the wholesale destruction of the Jewish communities in the German path? Germany and Russia had fought in these regions before; Jews had scattered and suffered but, for the most part, had survived. The wisest policy, surely, was to lie low, keep out of the way of commissars and, if they arrived, the Gestapo, and wait for better times. This was another fateful decision.

10

'You have nothing to worry about. You are one of my Jews'

When the German attack on the Soviet Union began, in the early hours of Sunday 22 June 1941, it was too late for Berl to change his mind. The Germans achieved strategic surprise and swiftly beat the Russians back on a broad front. As in 1939, eastern Galicia fell within the command zone of von Rundstedt's Army Group South. The Wehrmacht quickly overran the Russians' frontier defences. German planes bombed Jaworów. Przemyśl, which had withstood the epic 133-day siege in 1914–15, succumbed immediately. The Seventeenth Army under General Carl Heinrich von Stülpnagel crossed the San north of Przemyśl and advanced in a south-easterly direction towards Lwów. The Red Army's south-western front, commanded by General Mikhail Petrovich Kirponos, at whose side stood his political commissar, Khrushchev, attempted pincer counter-attacks on the advancing Panzers but could not hold them up.

Krakowiec was engulfed by the invading forces almost immediately. German troops occupied the town on 24 June. Wehrmacht military intelligence reported on the late afternoon of that day that, although the Soviets still had considerable forces in the forest north of Krakowiec, they no longer appeared capable of effective resistance. Their retreat from the town was so precipitate that they abandoned weapons and equipment on the road towards Jaworów.[1] A farmer in Krakowiec watched some Red Army soldiers fleeing in their underwear.[2] The Russians attempted to make a stand to the east of the town but were almost immediately driven back. Jaworów fell at dawn on 25 June. In the first four days of fighting around Krakowiec, 3,200 Russians were killed and two thousand captured. The Germans destroyed or seized large quantities of materiel and vehicles, including seven aircraft.³ Before they left, Soviet soldiers pillaged the stores. German troops helped themselves to whatever was left behind.

Just ahead of the Germans, a few Krakowiec Jews, including Dr Berger and Pinkas Majus, managed to escape.⁴ But the speed of the German advance prevented most from leaving. Ongoing military operations, the disintegrating Soviet local administration, crowded transportation facilities and general panic precluded flight by more than a small minority.

Most Jews in Krakowiec probably did not fully appreciate the acute danger in which they now found themselves. Even though some information had seeped across the demarcation line, the impression of Nazi rule was of sporadic violence rather than systematic annihilation of the Jewish population. Hitler's definitive order for the 'final solution' in any case still lay in the future: it was not issued until November 1941. The onslaught on the Jews nevertheless escalated immediately.

Special SS units of Einsatzgruppen, whose primary function was mass murder, once again moved behind the German army. The line of march towards Lwów of Einsatzgruppe B passed directly through Krakowiec. On 29 June, one of its sub-units, Sonderkommando 4b, headed by Hauptsturmführer Günther Herrmann, entered the town. His men spent the night there before continuing to join other units in Lwów.⁵ The Jews of Krakowiec were spared – for the time being.

As in September 1939, local Ukrainians generally welcomed the Nazis as liberators, this time from the Soviets.⁶ Prior to the German attack, Ukrainian nationalists had received some encouragement from the Nazis. Leaders of the movement sought German backing for the recreation of a Ukrainian state. Some of the more intelligent Nazi officials took the view that the Germans would find it easier to control occupied eastern Europe if they treated nationalities such as Ukrainians as allies rather than as *Untermenschen* fit only for slavery. Even Hitler toyed occasionally with the notion of 'Germanizing' the Ukrainians. He had been impressed by blond, blue-eyed Ukrainian children he had met and remarked that 'Himmler had confirmed his impression that these were descended from the Goths.'⁷

In June 1940 Hans Frank, head of the General Gouvernement (the German-occupied central area of Poland ruled from Cracow), had permitted Volodymyr Kubijovyc, a Ukrainian nationalist and intellectual, to establish a Ukrainian Central Committee. This body, which had strictly limited functions of social welfare and education, was secretly controlled by the extremist OUN. Meanwhile, the OUN had split into two factions: OUN-M, followers of Andrii Melnyk, and OUN-B, led by Stepan Bandera. The latter, more radical wing resorted to unbridled violence against Communists, Poles and Jews. An Abwehr officer, Theodor Oberländer, organized military training of Ukrainian militants. But the Germans had no intention of permitting genuine Ukrainian political autonomy. As Frank later put it in a government meeting, Ukrainians and Poles would ultimately have to be removed from the region. For the time being, their labour was 'needed for the war'. With 'a certain camouflaging of our final political intentions', German policy should play them off against each other, promoting Polish–Ukrainian antagonism in what he called a 'tilting game of ethno-political conflict'.[8]

An SS report in the early days of the German occupation of east Galicia noted approvingly that the Ukrainian population 'showed welcome activity against Jews in the first hours after the withdrawal of the Bolsheviks'.[9] Heydrich ordered the Einsatzgruppen on 29 June: 'The self-cleansing endeavours of anti-communist or anti-Jewish circles ... are not to be hindered. On the contrary, they should be actively instigated, but without leaving any trace, intensified where necessary, and guided onto the right path.'[10]

An OUN-B (Banderist) unit arrived in Krakowiec on 25 June. Its twenty-eight-year-old leader, Vasyl Kuk, later recalled: 'Along the way there were meetings with the population, talks about how people lived, exchanges of information. Finding out more about the Soviet reality, we were struck by the devastation inflicted by the Soviet occupiers in less than two years.'[11] Upon arrival, Kuk presented himself to the German military command post and asked for news about the German advance. There was some confusion about passwords and the Germans were suspicious. Kuk was handed over to an intelligence officer who would not disclose any information but questioned him about the level of support for his organization in the neighbourhood. Around the same time a unit of the rival OUN-M (Melnyk's followers) arrived in the area. They too were held up by the Germans and sent back for interrogation. The Ukrainians busied themselves with taking control of the administration in surrounding villages as well as propagandizing and training young men.

In the village of Młyny, near Krakowiec, a Jew was said to have shot a German soldier and his horse. The alleged assailant was not found but the Germans retaliated by killing 'two conscious [Ukrainian] nationalists'. Later 'the Jews' were said to have shot two further Germans. A Ukrainian nationalist leader reported: 'The Jews deliberately provoke . . . They say they find the situation intolerable so they want to destroy our people and our population . . . We are making a militia which will help to remove the Jews and protect the population.' The Greek Catholic priest in the village, Lev Sohor, helped recruit a militia, the first of many throughout Galicia.[12] An OUN report stated that 'the guys were enthusiastic. [They constitute] very good material.'[13] These Ukrainian militias killed thousands of Jews in pogroms and massacres throughout the region in the early weeks of the German occupation.

In several cities large numbers of political prisoners had been shot by the NKVD prior to the withdrawal of the Red Army.[14] A Norwegian volunteer, serving in an SS unit that entered Lwów with the Germans, described in gruesome detail how he had found the prisons full of corpses. Those prisoners who remained alive had been so starved, he claimed, that they had torn flesh from the bodies and eaten it.[15] Although the victims included Jews, the killings were ascribed by the Nazis to 'Jewish-Bolshevik terror'. In Jaworów thirty-two bodies of prisoners were found, all described in an Einsatzgruppe report as Ukrainians.[16] Such accounts were widely publicized and used to justify mass killing of Jews that had, in fact, begun before the discovery of the prison massacres.[17]

Mobs attacked Jews with whips, sticks and bricks. Women were humiliated, tortured, and raped. Children were beaten. Newsreels depicting these scenes elicited what police described as 'encouraging exclamations' in German cinemas.[18] The historian Christoph Mick notes that, according to a number of Wehrmacht reports, the violence was not instigated by the Germans 'but had erupted spontaneously'.[19] This enhanced Nazi leaders' elation. '*Ein Furioso!*', Joseph Goebbels, Minister for Public Enlightenment and Propaganda, enthused in his diary. Hitler was no less jubilant. He phoned Goebbels and told him it was 'the best newsreel that we had made so far'.[20] In Lwów and other places German Einsatzgruppen and police battalions, assisted by Ukrainian militiamen, executed hundreds of Jews. By the middle of July at least four thousand Jews had been killed in the city, plus another eight thousand elsewhere in the region. The Germans also shot at least forty-five prominent Polish professors, scientists, doctors and intellectuals in the city (some allegedly denounced by their own Ukrainian students), among them the noted writer-critic Tadeusz Boy-Żeleński.[21]

Roman Shukhevych commanded the Ukrainian Nachtigall ('Nightingale') battalion that entered Lwów with the Wehrmacht, under the political control of Theodor Oberländer. This battalion had been recruited by the Germans among supporters of the OUN in occupied Poland. In 1939–40 Shukhevych had been trained, together with other Ukrainian nationalists, at an Abwehr school at Zakopane in southern Poland. The line of march of Nachtigall took them from Radymno, through Shukhevych's birthplace, Krakowiec, to Jaworów, and thence to Lwów. Shukhevych allegedly found his brother's body among the victims of the prison massacres in Lwów. Nachtigall members were among those who participated in the pogrom in the city.[22]

In Lwów on 30 June 1941 followers of Bandera, under the leadership of Yaroslav Stetsko, declared the establishment of a Ukrainian state. Shukhevych was designated deputy minister of war in Stetsko's 'government'. Among its central aims was what Stetsko described as 'the destruction of the Jews'.[23] The Ukrainian nationalists hoped for the support of the Germans, to whom they promised close cooperation.

The Germans, however, soon squashed the enterprise. Bandera and Stetsko were arrested. Other OUN-B leaders were imprisoned or killed. The OUN militias were dissolved, though the organization maintained a continuing existence as an underground political body. The Nazis subsequently recruited from among the former militia members a four-thousand-strong Ukrainian auxiliary police force. They were generously paid, well fed, and acted as willing accessories in genocide. Over the next two years these 'Hiwis' (*Hilfswillige*, volunteers) played an important role in round-ups and massacres of Jews in eastern Galicia. Some served as guards in labour and concentration camps. As they marched, they sang 'Death to the *Lakhs* [Poles] and the Judeo-Muscovite commune.'[24]

In spite of the arrest of some of their leaders, Ukrainian nationalists continued to regard the Nazis as a lesser evil than the Communists and to hope for some sort of alliance with Hitler against Stalin. As for the Germans, a shortage of 'Aryan' manpower obliged them, notwithstanding their disdain for Ukrainian nationalism, to rely heavily on local auxiliaries. Positions in the administration vacated by Poles or Jews were therefore taken over by Ukrainians, many of them secret members of the OUN.

Metropolitan Sheptytsky had condemned OUN's terrorism in the 1930s. In December 1939, as we have seen, he had drawn on anti-Semitic terminology in his denunciation of the Soviet regime. He now supported the effort to establish a Ukrainian state and welcomed the arrival of the German army in Lwów 'as deliverer from the enemy'.[25] He nevertheless called on Stetsko to follow a 'wise and just' policy for the benefit of all citizens 'regardless of confession, nationality, or social class'.[26] Sheptytsky commanded enormous reverence among his flock and his attitude was therefore significant. Shocked by the violence of the German occupation, he came to believe that the Nazis were even worse than the Communists. He reported to the Vatican on crimes committed against Jews and sent a protest to Himmler. In 1942 he issued pastoral letters warning his flock against shedding innocent blood and calling on them to show murderers in their midst 'the disgust and disgrace they deserve'. Yet even his horror at the genocide of the Jews did not prevent the Metropolitan from extending his blessing in 1943 to the formation of the Waffen-SS Division 'Galizien', whose Ukrainian recruits fought for the Germans against the Red Army and pro-Soviet partisans in east Galicia and elsewhere.[27]

The Polish population was fearful of the Germans and broadly hostile towards the Jews. The commander of the underground Polish 'Home Army' (Armia Krajowa, AK) reported to the government-in-exile in September 1941: 'Please accept it as a fact that the overwhelming majority of the country is anti-Semitic.'[28] In eastern Galicia there was the added factor that Poles generally believed the Jews to have been guilty of collaboration with the Communists during the period of Soviet occupation.

The Germans were not greatly impressed by their newly occupied territories or their inhabitants. Some of their comments recalled those of Austrian officials at their first encounter with Galicia after 1772. Culture, noted one senior Wehrmacht commander, 'came to an end with Lemberg [Lwów].'[29] A German official in Ukraine remarked in 1942: 'Putting it precisely, we are surrounded here by negroes.'[30]

As elsewhere in the Nazi empire, the various organs of German authority – army, civil government and SS, jostled for power. On 16 July 1941 Hitler ordered that the Galician District was to be appended to the General Gouvernement. The main object of this decision was to cut off the region's Ukrainians from their kinsmen further east.

Frank, a pompous lawyer, sought to aggrandize all power in the General Gouvernement under his exclusive control. He was known derisively as 'king of Poland' and his domain as 'Frankreich'. Frank engaged in a bitter contest for supremacy with the SS, particularly with its chief in the east, Friedrich Wilhelm Krüger, who was said to have been sent there by Himmler to 'finish off' Frank. In his attitude towards Poles, who he said should be treated like 'plant lice', Frank at least purported to stand for some semblance of legal discipline.[31] As for Jews, he told an audience at the University of Berlin in November 1941: 'This merry little people (Völklein), which wallows in dirt and filth, has been gathered together by us in ghettos and [special] quarters and will probably not remain in the Government-General for very long.' These words were greeted with 'vigorous applause'.[32]

The first head of the Galicia District after its incorporation into the General Gouvernement was Dr Karl Lasch. His headquarters were in Lwów. He succumbed to political infighting when accused of corruptly receiving valuables, including Persian carpets and works of art, from Jews in return for protection. It probably did not help his case that his mistress, Brigitte Frank, was the wife of his boss – so, at any rate, Hans Frank believed. Lasch was dismissed in January 1942 and later shot – or, as Frank told his wife, committed suicide.[33]

Lasch's successor, Otto Gustav Freiherr von Wächter, was an Austrian nobleman, son of a former Minister of the Army who had served as Statthalter in Galicia under the Habsburgs. In 1934 Wächter had taken part in an abortive Nazi coup in Austria. After the outbreak of war he was appointed governor of Cracow. In early 1942 he moved with his staff to Lwów, where he remained until the end of the German occupation. At the regional level, Wächter bore heavy responsibility for the genocide of the Jews of Galicia, including those of Krakowiec.

The incorporation of Galicia into the General Gouvernement automatically entailed the extension to the territory of all laws promulgated by the occupation administration. Jews lost all civil rights. Every Jew was obliged to wear a white armlet with a blue star of David. If a Jew passed a German in the street, he was required to remove his hat on pain of death. Large numbers of Jews were conscripted for forced labour. In the autumn of 1941 the Germans established ghettos in Lwów and other towns.

Initially, life in Krakowiec nevertheless seemed to carry on almost as normal. Jewish restaurateurs cooked eggs for Germans who ate them appreciatively. But soon after the Germans arrived, Soviet prisoners-of-war were brought to the town. A typhus epidemic broke out and spread to the populace.

From the autumn of 1941 the Germans began the systematic eradication of Jews in eastern Galicia. At first this took the form of mass shootings, as at Stanisławów in October 1941. By the end of the year an estimated sixty thousand Jews had been killed in the region. In March 1942 a special killing centre opened at Bełżec. Jews were transported there from Lwów and other cities and murdered in gas chambers. Between the end of July and the end of September, 126,000 Jews were killed in Bełżec.[34]

Jews could not look to the surrounding civilian population for much in the way of succour. Even seeming sympathizers could turn out to be false friends. In an incident in 1942, described by the historian Nicholas Stargardt, the wife of a German SS-man living in a confiscated Polish manor house near Lwów was on her way home from shopping when she came across six almost naked children at the roadside. She took them to the house and gave them some food while waiting for her husband to come back. After a while, when he failed to return, she led them out into the nearby woodland, lined them up next to a ditch, and shot them all one by one in the back of the neck.[35] Not for nothing has wartime German civilian life in the region been described as 'an island of normality floating on an ocean of blood'.[36]

Escape was virtually impossible. A few Jews nevertheless made their getaway. A spectacular instance was that of the fourth Belzer rebbe, Aharon Rokeach. Unlike Krakowiec, Belz (not to be confused with Bełżec: *see map on p. 130*) had found itself in the German occupation zone of Poland in September 1939. Like his father in the previous war, the rebbe fled. He took refuge first in Przemyślany in the Soviet zone. In July 1941 that town too was occupied by the Nazis. Synagogues and Jewish homes were set on fire. Rokeach's eldest son was among those burned alive. 'By the grace of God, I have contributed a sacrifice', was the rebbe's response.[37] He fled again, this time to Bochnia, near Cracow. In 1943, leaving behind most of what remained of his family, he was spirited across the border into Hungary. At that time Hungary, though allied to Germany, had not yet joined in the mass murder of Jews. According to some accounts, the rebbe made his escape disguised in the uniform of an SS officer. From Budapest he succeeded, in January 1944, in emigrating to Palestine, thus avoiding the round-up and deportation to Auschwitz of hundreds of thousands of Jews from Hungary a few months later.

The episode was the stuff of fierce recriminations down to the present day. The tale of the Nazi uniform may be a fabrication by his enemies. The quasi-official narrative put out by his followers had it that he crossed the frontier masquerading as a captured Russian general. His beard and sidelocks were shaved and, for the first time in his life, he wore 'European' clothes. A Hungarian officer was bribed to drive him into Hungary on the pretext that he was a Soviet prisoner of war. In this authorized version, stress was laid on the allegedly 'miraculous' nature of his deliverance. Such accounts distort the nature of the guidance given to his followers prior to his departure from Budapest, omitting key passages in which he explained his imminent *aliya* (emigration to Palestine) as motivated by spiritual devotion to the Holy Land and assured his followers that they would be safe in God's hands. What is undeniable is that he abandoned the greater part of his flock to face an uncertain future, bereft of his spiritual leadership. That he found refuge in the Jewish 'National Home', whose builders he had always denigrated, was a cruel irony.[38]

*

In early 1942 the Germans ordered the creation in Krakowiec, as else-where, of a Judenrat (Jewish Council). The Judenräte were required to carry out orders from the Germans: these included satisfying German demands for forced labour as well as 'contributions' of money or goods. The head of the Krakowiec Judenrat was Chaim Sandhaus, a *cheder* teacher in the town. He was an unexceptional, middle-aged, married man. Why or by whom he was chosen we do not know.

On 29 May Jews were ordered to concentrate in a 'living area' in Krakowiec. It was akin to a ghetto, though it was not enclosed. A cur-few prohibited its residents from going outside after 6.00 p.m. They were warned that departure from their appointed dwellings would be punished by death. Any person who knowingly afforded a hiding-place to a Jew would likewise incur the death penalty.[39]

On 10 June forty-seven Jewish families from the small neighbouring town of Wielkie Oczy were ordered to move to Krakowiec. About a hundred men from these families fled into the woods. Ukrainian police-men, however, rounded them up and delivered them to Krakowiec.[40]

Judenräte were under orders to support the work of Jüdische Sozi-ale Selbsthilfe (JSS, Jewish Self-Help). This organization, headed by a former theatrical director, Michael Weichert, was the only Jewish institution, apart from the Judenräte, permitted to function in occu-pied Poland. Its unique status was not really intended to provide for the welfare of the Jewish population. Rather it served as a receptacle for relief funds dispatched from Jewish bodies in the United States through the International Red Cross, supposedly to benefit Polish Jews. The organization's leaders claimed that their purpose was to provide for the needs of the Jews. Perhaps they half-believed this themselves, though their German masters knew otherwise. In reality the outfit was little more than a protection racket, squeezing the last pittances out of its victims.[41]

Three prominent Krakowiec Jews, Gedaliah Wasserstein, Naftali Majus and Jacob Gottesmann, were appointed local representatives of the JSS.[42] The headquarters of the organization sent fifteen identity cards of 'employees' to the Krakowiec branch, together with an invoice demanding 16.50 złoty per person (15 zł. per card plus 1.50 zł. for postage). It asked that photos of the employees be returned for its records.[43] These identity cards, it was hoped, would afford their holders some protection from Nazi harassment. There is no evidence that it did so.

Meanwhile, the Germans proceeded towards their goal of the murder of the entire Jewish population. In mid-July the head of the SS in Galicia, Friedrich Katzmann, ordered local authorities to submit an exact count of Jews in each district, town and village. He also called for figures on the strength of the security personnel in each district, underlining the importance of supplying all this information in the strictest confidence 'in order to avoid arousing any unnecessary disquiet'.[44]

The count found 928 Jews in the Krakowiec district – 772 in the town itself, the remainder in surrounding villages.[45] The figure for the town included the 168 Jews who had been transferred from Wielkie Oczy the previous month.[46] The reduction in numbers since 1940 is probably accounted for by deportations and flight to the interior of the Soviet Union as well as recruitment to the Soviet armed forces. On 30 October, in compliance with an order from the Kreishauptmann, Sandhaus handed over the Jewish *Matrikelbücher*: six birth registers, two death registers and two marriage registers, plus indexes to each volume.[47] This seemingly routine bureaucratic procedure had a sinister purpose: it furnished the Germans with a population registry, providing precise details of most Jewish residents in the town, a preliminary to their identification, deportation and murder.

The German police chief in Krakowiec, Wolf (his forename is not known), acquired a peculiarly vicious reputation. In his early fifties, self-important and big-bellied, he held the rank of Hauptwachtmeister. Wolf commandeered the house of a Jewish family in Krakowiec. He acquired a twenty-two-year-old girlfriend in the town, the daughter of a pig farmer. Proclaiming that he would make Krakowiec 'Judenfrei', he liked to set his attack dog, a German shepherd, on Jews. He would shoot passers-by in the street for sport, saying that 'he didn't enjoy his lunch if he hadn't yet killed a Jew.'[48] Witnesses reported that on one occasion he shot ten-year-old children lying on the ground in front of him. On another, he shot an old woman in the back of the neck from his car.[49]

In November 1942 the Germans launched a killing spree in Krakowiec, murdering an unknown number of Jews. A few weeks later the remaining Jews of the town were ordered to assemble in the market place. They were told they would be sent to Jaworów. A Ukrainian woman who lived nearby was warned by Wolf or his deputy to keep her children indoors that day so that they would not get mixed up with the Jews.[50] In a 'selection' conducted before the removal of the Jews, old men were separated from the rest. Among those singled out was Rabbi Klüger who was ordered to 'dance' for the entertainment of the Germans – a common Nazi ritual of humiliation.[51] The Jews protested against being separated from Klüger: they said that where they went their rabbi would go too. The Germans relented and allowed him to join the exodus.[52] The remaining two dozen old-timers were shot dead at the local cemetery.

The whole of the rest of the Jewish population were removed to the recently established ghetto in Jaworów. Some went by horse and cart, others had to walk the thirteen miles. Those who could not make it were shot on the way.[53]

Conditions in the ghetto were appalling. Jews from Jaworów itself, as well as from the surrounding countryside, had been concentrated there. An SS report on 11 January 1943 stated that 4,164 Jews were detained in the ghetto.[54] This multitude was stuffed into eighty houses, about sixty persons to each, and forced to live hugger-mugger.

> Sanitary and hygienic conditions became unbearable ... Those for whom there was no room lay down on the ground, caught a cold and died ... Everybody who didn't have money, gold, or other things to sell was condemned to death by hunger. People swelled up from hunger and after two to three days died in terrible pain ... Every day in the morning a few children were found dead at the ghetto wall.[55]

A new enemy soon descended: typhus. The disease, which is carried by fleas, had been endemic in eastern Poland for many years and epidemic in Jaworów to such an extent that a large part of the population there had been vaccinated against it before 1939.[56] But whether because such vaccinations had ceased since then or because the vaccine had become ineffective, large numbers of prisoners in the ghetto became infected. Dead bodies were removed each day. In the six months of the ghetto's existence, 1,500 people died of typhus, spotted fever or starvation.[57] The remainder 'just waited for death'.[58]

On 16 April 1943, two days before Passover, the ghetto was liquidated. The Jews had prepared matzos (unleavened bread), 'so that at least they might celebrate the coming Passover with dignity', as a survivor recalled. It was a warm, sunny day.

> At 5.00 a.m. eighty Gestapo men from Lwów with the help of Jewish police from Lwów ... surrounded the ghetto ... On the sound of the bugle, Gestapo men and the OD [Ordnungspolizei] started the 'action'. They entered the ghetto and took the Jews by force from houses, hiding places, from nooks and corners, and assembled them on the square in front of the synagogue. The Jews awaited their fate tired, emaciated, deathly scared, and ragged with bundles containing only parts of their clothes which they managed to take. Those who couldn't go or who tried to escape were killed on the spot. The Jews were rounded up and assembled on the square until noon. They collected three thousand Jews.
>
> Then everybody was ordered to stand in line and pass by the Gestapo man who had an open suitcase next to him. Everybody had to place there all the possessions they had with them. Everybody was searched which, of course, was accompanied by beating. Then women and children were driven into the synagogue and men were divided into two groups: on the right side those who were young and in good health, and on the left the old and the weak. The segregation lasted about two hours ...
>
> [Meanwhile] in the morning ... the Gestapo had chosen about forty strong men. A Jewish policeman took all the spades he could find in the ghetto and these were given to those men who were sent in two vehicles to the Porudenko forest [a couple of miles from Jaworów].
>
> At about 5.00 p.m. five trucks came. They began to put women and children from the synagogue in the trucks – fifty people in each one. They put them in a standing position, then they ordered them to sit down while beating them terribly. While this was going on, the women and children still in the synagogue prayed, screamed and cried. The screaming was so loud that the Gestapo men came inside and silenced them by firing shots ... When they had finished with the women and children, they began to put old and weak men in cars and transport them to the forest ...

I was told later by Polish and Ukrainian acquaintances what happened in the forest. Women and children were taken out of the trucks. They were forced to take off all their clothes quickly and to get onto a plank placed above a trench. A Gestapo man shot them with a machine gun and the victims fell into the hole, often only wounded. One layer of people was covered with earth and then others were murdered. Loud lamentations and prayers could be heard. They screamed, bade farewell, prayed, and implored. After they were all murdered, they were buried in four graves, as I was told and which I saw myself: 2.5 metres deep, eight metres long, and four metres wide. The blood of the victims began to show through cracks that formed in the earth covering the bodies. The German police used Poles and Ukrainians for a whole week to cover up those graves better. But it was no use. The blood continued to seep through the ground. Finally, lime was brought and used to cover the graves and the blood stopped leaking out of the ground.[59]

To ensure that no Jews remained hidden in the ghetto, the houses there were set on fire. Any people who emerged from the flames were forced back and burned alive. Afterwards local people were ordered to go to the burnt-out remains of the ghetto to clean up.

More than four thousand inhabitants of the Jaworów ghetto were killed in this manner. About two hundred more, who had been retained for possible use as workers, were rounded up and shot in the forest by Wolf. Another 160 men were transferred to the Janowska labour camp near Lwów. Sixty survived for a time as workers in a labour battalion in Jaworów.

Nearly all the Jews of Krakowiec, including the aged mothers of Berl and Czarna and all their relatives in the town, were among those massacred.

Polish reactions to these scenes mingled horror and terror. One onlooker, a member of the Home Army resistance movement, wrote:

I saw with my own eyes on the road to Krakowiec how Germans were taking poor, miserable people, destitute and starving ... My sons started to cry and the older one, twelve-year-old Eugeniusz called out 'Ornek', waving his hands. Eugeniusz's mother screamed, 'I will never be able to give him bread or potatoes ever again.' Orn attended the same school as Eugeniusz; he was a classmate. Even I myself wept and began to swear that there is no God because if there were he would never allow this to happen. The Polish population was devastated, fearing they would be next.[60]

This humane response was unusual. The common view of the Polish population, as reported by the Home Army in Lwów, was: 'All condemn the bestiality and premeditation with which the Jews are being murdered, but generally it is said that the Jews are getting their historical punishment ... There is a subconscious satisfaction that there will be no more Jews in the Polish organism.'[61]

The destruction of the Jaworów ghetto left some residual matters outstanding. One such was discussed in a memorandum submitted by a German official in Jaworów to the Kreishauptmann on 4 May 1943:

Following the liquidation of the Jewish ghetto in Jaworów (a few days ago) there remain in the Jewish cottages in the ghetto a great deal of old, lice-ridden laundry and clothing. The laundry has by and by been stolen by the inhabitants of neighbouring villages. As a result there is great danger of the spread of spotted fever through lousy Jewish laundry in Jaworów and its surroundings where at the moment many Wehrmacht units from the East are stationed for leave or rest ... I therefore request that the Kreishauptmann order the municipality and the police to arrange that all Jewish laundry and clothing be collected together in one building and there be either well guarded or burned.[62]

The document repays close analysis on at least three counts: first, conditions in surrounding villages must have been pitiful in the extreme if the inhabitants judged those filthy rags worth stealing. Second, note the candid reference to the 'liquidation' of the ghetto. In this internal memorandum there is none of the obfuscation that clouded the public vocabulary of the Third Reich.[63] Third, the motive for the request is clear: concern for public health – not, however, that of the civilian population but that of German soldiers enjoying their R&R.

On 30 June 1943 SS Gruppenführer Friedrich Katzmann submitted a 'final report on the solution of the Jewish question in the District of Galicia'. This detailed the measures that had been employed in the killing of 434,329 Jews in Galicia. The report was illustrated with over a hundred photographs, though none of actual killings. Unlike the memorandum just quoted, it employed characteristic Nazi euphemisms such as 'Sonderbehandlung' (literally 'special handling') or 'Aussiedlungsaktion' ('evacuation') to denote murder. During the operation a vast haul of valuables of all kinds had been captured. Katzmann enumerated the precise numbers of coins, jewellery, gold rings, gold teeth, silverware, watches, cameras, postage stamps, fountain pens, pocket knives, furs and so on, as well as bank notes. He recounted how Jews had 'not only tried to escape' but 'concealed themselves in the most improbable places, drainage canals, chimneys, even sewage pits . . . They barricaded themselves in catacombs of passages, in cellars made into bunkers, in holes in the earth, in cunningly contrived hiding places, in attics and sheds, inside furniture &c.' Katzmann noted that the SS-men and Ukrainian police who rounded up Jews 'were continually exposed to serious physical and mental strain. Again and again they had to overcome the nausea threatening them when they were compelled to enter the dirty and pestilential Jewish holes.' Katzmann concluded: 'Despite the extraordinary burden heaped upon every single SS-police officer during these actions, the morale and spirit of the men were extraordinarily good and praiseworthy from the first to the last day. Only thanks to the sense of duty of every single leader and man have we succeeded in mastering this *plague* in so short a time.'[64]

Remnants of the Jewish population continued to be hounded and slaughtered in the course of the next year. Forty or so Jews, mainly young men, managed to escape from the Jaworów ghetto and take refuge in the forest. A handful were sheltered for a time by local people but this was a perilous recourse. *Judenbeherbergung*, harbouring Jews, was a crime punishable by death. It was impossible to know whom to rely on. Some placed trust in people who offered help in return for payment: but these often turned out to be so-called *szmalcownicy*, blackmailers who milked their victims dry and then turned them in. In eastern Galicia there was the additional problem that the Jews were caught up not only in the Nazi extermination but also in the turmoil of a developing civil war between Poles and Ukrainians.

An extraordinary record of survival in the forest has been left by Leon Scher, born in 1915, whose family owned a farm near Krakowiec.

In 1943 he was a prisoner with his wife in the Jaworów ghetto. At the time of the massacre in April, they and some others hid in a cellar behind a double wall. The house where they were hiding was one of the few in the ghetto that was not burned down, lest the building next door, occupied by gentiles, caught fire. After three nights the Jews emerged and fled to the woods where they saw mass graves. They then walked back to Leon's village. For a time they were sheltered on the farm of a boyhood friend of Leon, a Ukrainian. Leon started building an underground 'bunker' nearby as a refuge. But while he was working on it, he was discovered by two young boys out collecting mushrooms. Ukrainians came from the village with hacksaws and other equipment to 'find the Jews' but Leon and his group managed to evade capture. After some wandering and several adventures, he dug a new bunker in the forest. A Polish friend brought them food. Soon, however, he said he would have to leave the area as Ukrainians were attacking Poles. Before departing, he left Leon some supplies. Leon and his companions camouflaged the bunker with branches and settled in for the long haul. One night he ventured out with a cousin to look for water. Suddenly he heard some people talking in Yiddish. Five men emerged from hiding and said, 'Yidn, we are Jews too.' They turned out to be Jewish friends of Leon from Krakowiec. He agreed to take them into his bunker. They gave money to a Polish woman who lived in the forest. She bought food for them in Krakowiec. Leon and his companions would also go and steal food from cottages, preferably one where a woman lived alone. They would take along a fake gun to threaten the woman, say they were 'passing through', and help themselves to the contents of the larder. Once, Leon took a pig. They cut it up and it kept them going for some weeks. Miraculously, they made it through the winter of 1943–44. Outside the bunker, snow piled three or four feet high.[65]

Scher's testimony demonstrates the almost impossible odds of survival in the forest. The help he received in the initial stages from non-Jewish friends was crucial. Only vigorous young people could ride out life in the wild through a bitter winter. Above all, they were lucky to escape the attentions of Ukrainians who repeatedly came to track them down.

*

These hunters did not consist only of malignant individuals. In many instances they were organized formations. In March 1943 elements of the OUN formed the Ukrainian Insurgent Army (Ukrainska Povstanska Armiia, UPA), composed mainly of Banderists. Many were former members of the German-controlled Ukrainian auxiliary police who feared enlistment for compulsory labour service. The UPA's main objective was to prosecute a partisan war against the Soviets. According to a former UPA fighter, the organization's 'German allies – Hungarian and Rumanian troops – soon came to respect the fighting abilities of the UPA units, willingly supplying them with arms and ammunition, sometimes in exchange for foodstuffs, sometimes "to be left unmolested." '[66] Although the OUN issued a new, superficially liberal programme in April 1943, promising toleration of minorities, this appears to have been designed mainly for external consumption, in particular in the hope of gaining legitimacy in the eyes of the western powers. At the same time, the *Banderovtsy* behaved viciously towards Poles and the few remaining Jews in Volhynia and Galicia, burning down villages and killing thousands of civilians.

Roman Shukhevych, now known by the *nom de guerre* 'Taras Chuprynka' (after a Ukrainian poet and anti-Bolshevik fighter executed by the Soviet secret police in 1921), became 'Supreme Commander' of the UPA. Upon the dismantling of his Nachtigall battalion in 1941, he had been appointed deputy commander of a German-controlled, Ukrainian militia unit assigned the Germans' *Schmutzarbeit* (dirty work) – killing Jews and Communists. Shukhevych boasted that his battalion 'was conducting frequent punitive operations, not only against Soviet partisans, but also against the civilian population of Belorussia'. A member of his unit later testified that Shukhevych, who had a violent temper, maintained discipline among his soldiers by force, including physical abuse, reflecting his 'sadistic inclinations since his childhood'. He enjoyed friendly relations with his German counterparts. On one occasion he met SS-Obergruppenführer Erich von dem Bach-Zelewski, *Bevollmächtiger für Bandenbekämpfung*, senior officer responsible for anti-partisan warfare on the eastern front (who was also responsible for war crimes, including massacres of Jews). Bach-Zelewski was delighted with Shukhevych: he accorded him the ultimate Nazi compliment, pronouncing him 'entirely of Germanic type'.[67]

The admiration was not altogether mutual. Shukhevych and his comrades became increasingly disillusioned with the Nazis, disappointed that they were not treated with the respect due to allies. Hence the decision to form the underground UPA. Thousands of fighters eventually joined the force. Among them were at least seventeen young men and one woman from Krakowiec. The UPA had a camp in the forest between Jaworów and Krakowiec, and the danger posed to Leon Scher's group and any other Jews hiding in the vicinity was therefore close at hand.

Most of the Jews of eastern Galicia having been slaughtered by mid-1943, Shukhevych's adherents turned their attention to Poles. Mykola Lebed, a fellow UPA commander (he had been one of the terrorists arrested in 1934, together with Bandera and Shukhevych, for the murder of the Polish interior minister), declared the necessity 'to cleanse the entire revolutionary territory of the Polish population'.[68] On 25 February 1944 Shukhevych ordered: 'In view of the success of the Soviet forces it is necessary to speed up the liquidation of the Poles; they must be totally wiped out, their villages burned ... only the Polish population must be destroyed.'[69] Tens of thousands of Poles were killed by Shukhevych's ethnic cleansers and thousands of Ukrainians were victims of Polish retaliatory attacks.

Unable to look for protection to the German occupation regime, Poles organized their own resistance. The underground Polish Home Army (AK), loyal to the government-in-exile in London, had an estimated thirty thousand members in eastern Galicia at the end of 1943. It established a branch in Krakowiec, headed by Roman Tworzydło. But it was under observation by enemies. The AK chief in Krakowiec said that 'strangers' had been seen in town, staying with Ukrainians. 'In the evenings they go somewhere and for sure they are these Ukrainians ... Presumably they are gathering somewhere.' There were similar reports from neighbouring villages. One young AK member, sent to Krakowiec in October 1943 with money for a bereaved Polish family, was waylaid, shot in the head, and buried. The money was taken. A Polish rescue party was arrested by the Germans and imprisoned at Jaworów. Later the AK found out that local Ukrainians were following them and betraying them to the Germans.[70]

By early 1944 a complex war of all against all was being waged in which the UPA, the Polish Home Army, German security forces and Soviet partisans all battled for supremacy. The German police in Lwów estimated that in Galicia alone the UPA had eighty thousand men under arms.[71] Another German report gave details of large-scale Soviet partisan activity throughout the area around Krakowiec, involving, in some cases, groups of several hundred men of various nationalities.[72]

In the spring of 1944 a ferocious battle broke out between Poles and Ukrainians in a village near Krakowiec. The Roman Catholic parish priest of Krakowiec, Adolf Łabno, pleaded with a German officer to intervene to protect the Poles. He refused, saying he had no such orders. Just in time, a twenty-strong AK unit under Tworzydło arrived from Krakowiec. The 'Banderovtsy' withdrew, leaving five Poles dead. Łabno survived but died of natural causes a few months later. However, a Greek Catholic priest who had denounced the killing of Poles was killed by his co-religionists together with his wife and daughter.[73]

According to Polish underground reports, the entire Ukrainian police force of Jaworów deserted on 3 April, bolting fully armed into the forest. Directly afterwards they began massive attacks on Polish villages. Dozens of Poles were killed and their houses burned down. Those who remained alive were forcibly concentrated in Jaworów, Wielkie Oczy and Krakowiec. From these places they were expelled westwards.[74]

On 5 May the Red Army crossed the old (pre-1939) Soviet–Polish border into eastern Galicia. As Soviet forces advanced, civilians fled. The UPA intensified its attacks and burned buildings abandoned by Poles. On 23 July the Russians reached Jaworów. Leon Scher and his companions emerged alive from their bunker. Four days later the Red Army captured Lwów. The pre-war Jewish population of the city had been 104,700. The Soviets registered 1,689 survivors.[75] In Krakowiec one Jew, who had hidden in the town, emerged alive. His name is unknown.[76]

*

Berl Wasserstein, Czarna and Lotte had not been among the Jews killed in the Jaworów ghetto. They managed to elude the transportations from Krakowiec in December 1942. For more than a year they were sheltered in a hut near the edge of the town by a local Ukrainian, Mikola Mikhailovich Olanek, a carter and odd-job man, aged twenty-one in 1943. His motives are uncertain. They probably did not include Christian charity or neighbourliness (my reasons for reaching this conclusion will emerge later). Olanek most likely hid Berl and his family in return for money – or perhaps the promise of future reward.

What were Berl's thoughts during the long winter months of 1943–44? Did he despair? A faithful Jew, did he find succour in prayer? Did he reflect on the past or plan hopefully for the future? He left no record of his life in hiding so we are reduced to conjecture. We can make some reasonable assumptions. Like most people in such situations, considerations of food, warmth and shelter must have been paramount. For all these the family were dependent on the uncertain favour of their protector. As for warmth, it is unlikely they had any form of heating. The average January temperature in Krakowiec in January is minus 5°C (23°F) and that winter was bitterly cold. Unlike Anne Frank in the 'secret annex' on the Prinsengracht in Amsterdam, Berl in his wretched shack in Krakowiec almost certainly had no access to a radio or other source of news. Even if he had learned of the German capitulation at Stalingrad in February 1943, he probably did not know of the slow advance of the Red Army that ensued. Like the Franks, he no doubt speculated as to how long the war would last. In the meantime, he and his family could not venture into the open air in the small town where they were certainly recognizable by everyone, and where Wolf and his dog were on the prowl.

Confined in their small, miserable space for months on end, cut off from other human contact, with no possibility of medical help in the event of illness, they could only wait with diminishing hope. To Czarna's normal concern as a mother for her teenage daughter was added the anguish of watching her suffer without being able to offer her much help. Now eighteen years old, Lotte had spent half her life under Nazi rule, treated as a pariah, thrown out of her native country, unable to complete her education and now hunted like an animal. For all three, the predominant moods must have been never-ending fear, compounded by boredom, loneliness and yearning for a normal human existence.

In April 1944, three months before the liberation of Krakowiec, Berl and his family were betrayed to the Nazis. It seems they were forced to dig their own graves near the lake and then shot dead. The betrayer was the same Olanek who had sheltered them over the previous year.[77]

Naturally, I have often wondered what were Berl's last thoughts. I have no doubt that he tried to comfort his wife and daughter with words of tenderness. Did he also think of his son and wonder what had become of him? Did he intone the affirmation that pious Jews are supposed to utter at the point of death: '*Shema yisrael adonai eloheinu adonai ehad*' (Hear, O Israel, the Lord our God, the Lord is one)? Or did he, like Kafka's Joseph K., cry out, 'Like a dog!', in protest against the final humiliation? There are no answers to these disturbing questions which linger in the mind.

Another question troubled me: why would a rescuer turn into a betrayer? Did Berl's money or credit with Olanek run out? Rewards were available for turning Jews in to the Germans but in general these were not great: 'no more than some quarts of vodka, several pounds of sugar or salt, cigarettes, or occasionally small sums of money'.[78] Was Olanek, who served as a volunteer policeman, inspired by nationalist ideology? The historian John-Paul Himka has noted that 'the impression created by the German documentation is that the extreme Ukrainian nationalists were so indifferent to the fate of the Jews that they would either kill them or help them, however best suited their political goals.'[79] But there is no evidence that Olanek had any 'political goals' – or that any such objective might be served by protecting Jews and then turning them in to the Germans. So the baffling question remained: what was going on inside the man's head?

The first glimmer of an answer dawned on me unexpectedly in the course of an interview in Lakewood, New Jersey in 1996. The psychologies of rescuer and betrayer, I began to realize, are not necessarily far apart. Both may be understood as forms of dominance, each affording a measure of gratification and self-justification.

Berl Lax, a retired kosher butcher, one of the handful of Jewish survivors of Krakowiec, had moved to the United States after the war.

At the time I met him he was close to death and knew it. The interview acquired, on that account, a macabre quality, akin to a deathbed confession. Lax had spent much of the war in Krakowiec, though he eventually ran away and joined partisans in the forest. He related to me that in Krakowiec he had had a protector, a Ukrainian former schoolmate who had joined the collaborationist Ukrainian police. He volunteered his protector's name: it was Mikola Mikhailovich Olanek. Mikola had been his best friend. His mother had sometimes worked as a *shabbes goya* for the Lax family: she lit the oven, milked the cow and so forth, activities forbidden to pious Jews on the Sabbath. Mikola even spoke some Yiddish.

One day in 1942, before the transportations to Jaworów, the two men met in the street in the little Jewish ghetto area of Krakowiec and engaged in conversation. 'Watch this', Olanek said, as he took out his gun and shot at random at a passing Jew. The man dropped dead. Horrified, Lax said, 'What are you doing? Are you going to shoot me next?' To which Olanek replied, as if by way of reassurance, unconsciously echoing the phrase used by Joseph Roth's Count Chojnicki, 'Don't worry. *You* have nothing to worry about. *You* are one of *my* Jews.'[80]

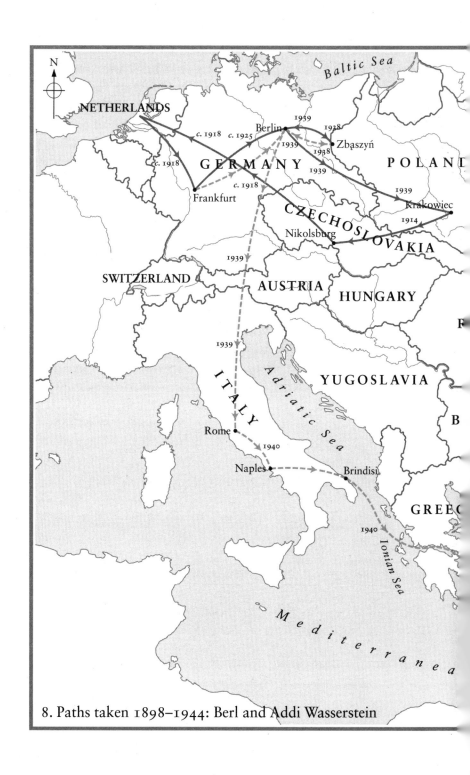

8. Paths taken 1898–1944: Berl and Addi Wasserstein

II

'A little place – you won't have heard of it'

Stuck in Berlin in the summer of 1939 after the departure of his parents and sister, Addi was near the end of his tether. The experience of several months' enforced internment in no-man's-land had had a profound effect on him. The successive shocks of sudden transition from ordinary city life to the overcrowded encampment of Zbąszyń and then back again were traumatic. He was a half grown-up, bookish, intellectually ambitious teenager who was inspired by Rainer Maria Rilke to dream of becoming a poet. Now he was forced to fend for himself in a hostile and threatening environment.

In Zbąszyń, after his father's departure, Addi had stopped observing the strict daily rituals of Jewish orthodox life such as 'laying *tefillin*' (donning phylacteries while saying morning prayers). He also began for the first time to eat non-kosher food. His predominant feeling at the time was an overwhelming desire to return to Berlin – to a Germany that he still regarded as home.

But Addi no longer had a home in Berlin and upon his return he found there was not much for him to do there. He had a little money but otherwise he was thrown on his own resources. Lodging with friends of the family, he tried desperately to find a way out of Germany. His phony South American papers were useless for this purpose. Meanwhile, his permitted residence period in Berlin expired and his continued presence there became illegal. With nowhere to go, he became, in effect, an outlaw.

Following his father's guidance, his first thought was to complete his education. His record at the Adass Jisroel school had been good and his father was insistent that he must obtain the *Abitur* (leaving certificate). There was a longstanding plan for him to go to England.

Some time earlier he had been admitted to St Christopher's School at Letchworth, near London. Founded by Theosophists, this was an eccentric, independent boarding school with a Quaker headmaster. It might seem an odd choice for orthodox Jewish parents. Possibly it was chosen because it served pupils a vegetarian (therefore kosher) diet. Or maybe it was the only school willing to accept Addi. Admission, however, was only half the battle. In order to attend, he would need a visa to enter the UK. That did not materialize. He might perhaps have qualified for entry with the so-called 'Kindertransport' ('Children's Movement'), which brought nearly ten thousand children from Germany to Britain in 1938–39. This was restricted to those under the age of eighteen. Addi was still seventeen but in February 1939 the upper age limit had been lowered to sixteen, so that he no longer qualified.

The Polish government, which had barred Addi and others like him from returning to Poland, appealed to the British to admit the remaining Zbąszyń refugees to Palestine. Or if not to Palestine then to a colonial territory such as British Guiana, which, improbable though it might seem, the British government was actively investigating as a possible refuge for Jews.[1] But the fantasy of Jewish settlement in this jungle area came to nothing.[2]

As for Palestine, the British government had a few weeks earlier issued a White Paper (policy document), severely restricting immigration to the 'Jewish National Home' over the next five years. The British hoped thereby to curb Arab nationalist hostility and solidify their position in the Middle East in the event of war. Addi visited the Zionist Organization office in Berlin but he, like others in the crowd of supplicants, was informed that there was no hope of his securing one of the few available certificates to enter Palestine. It was theoretically possible to go there outside the normal immigration quota as a 'capitalist' upon showing possession of a thousand pounds. This was a considerable amount in those days (equivalent to around $95,000 in 2022). Addi had no way of raising such a sum. By now war was clearly imminent and Addi understood that time was very short.

Armed with a list of addresses of all the foreign consulates in Berlin, he spent his days tramping from one to another in the vain search for an entry visa. He made no progress at the British embassy. He even tried the embassies and legations of such improbable destinations as Iran, Iraq and Afghanistan, all with the same result.

One day, while walking down the street in the diplomatic quarter on his way from one foreign mission to another, he happened to pass a travel agency opposite the opera house on the Unter den Linden. This grand avenue had been declared off limits to Jews. As yet, however, Jews were not required to wear the humiliating 'yellow star', so presumably enforcement of the ban was difficult. A sign in the window invited potential tourists to '*COME TO SUNNY ITALY!*' Addi went inside and cautiously made inquiries. He was told that all he needed was a railway ticket. When he asked whether a visa was necessary, he was told that it was not. After all, Germany and Italy were allies! Hitler had signed his 'Pact of Steel' with the Italian dictator, Benito Mussolini, just a few weeks earlier. Addi had a Polish passport but he was assured that 'no formalities' were required for entry to Italy. All that was required was a small sum of money to be lodged in a bank account in Rome to assure his support. He therefore cabled his relatives in South Africa who wired the requisite amount to Addi's credit at the Banca Commerciale Italiana in Rome. His father, writing from Krakowiec on 30 July, approved the plan, adding 'you can be happy that you don't have to land up here.'[3]

Addi travelled by train from Berlin through the Brenner Pass into Italy on 8 August 1939 without interference from either German or Italian border guards. He was lucky to get out of Germany when he did. On 19 August Italy suspended all tourist visas. The German invasion of Poland on 1 September was quickly followed by a so-called 'second *Polenaktion*': on 8 September, 750 Polish Jews were rounded up in Berlin and over three thousand more elsewhere. This time they were not sent to the border. They were consigned to a concentration camp, where they were brutally handled. Most did not survive the war.[4]

It was Addi's first journey outside Germany, apart from a school trip to Paris and his visits, voluntary and involuntary, to Poland. When he arrived in Rome he lodged in a *pensione* not far from the Villa Borghese. Among his fellow *pensionari* were one or two other Jewish refugees, so he was not lonely. He found more friends almost immediately. With just enough money to survive, he ate a dish of pasta every day. He did not hear much from Krakowiec, apart from a couple of telegrams from his father (delayed several weeks 'for inquiries') assuring him that all was well.

Soon after arriving in Rome, Addi went to the Polish consulate, which continued to function in Rome until June 1940. As required by law, he presented himself for military service in the Polish armed forces, at that time regrouping in France. He was laughed out of the building by officials who made it plain that his services were not required.

Although he was no longer strictly observant, Addi went to synagogue occasionally and attended Talmud classes given by the Chief Rabbi of Rome, Israel Zolli, in the Tempio Maggiore (Great Synagogue) on the bank of the Tiber. Born Israel Anton Zoller in Brody, Galicia, Zolli had served as rabbi of Trieste and taken Italian citizenship. A gifted scholar with broad interests in philosophy and theology, including the New Testament, he helped Addi find his feet in Italy.

Hebrew lessons, however, would not solve the problem of Addi's lack of the *Abitur*. The precipitate end of Addi's education in Germany had left him one year short of completing his secondary schooling. Now that the plan to go to England had fallen through, he hoped to enter a good school in Rome. For that he would need certification of his educational record in Germany. He therefore wrote to Dr Nachman Schlesinger, the director of the Adass Jisroel school which he had attended in Berlin. Schlesinger had been arrested after the Kristallnacht but had recently been released from a concentration camp. Although Addi suspected that Schlesinger 'did not much like *Ostjuden*', he readily provided the required document.

Under the 'racial laws', enacted a few months before Addi's arrival in Rome, Jews were forbidden to attend public schools in Italy. With the help of Schlesinger's testimonial, Addi was admitted to a Jewish *liceo classico*. The atmosphere there was very different from his old school in Berlin. Unlike the Adass Jisroel, this school taught no Jewish subjects at all; it was Jewish in its patronage and student body, not in educational philosophy. The school had been started only in response to the racial laws. The pupils came mainly from wealthy, highly assimilated families – at least so it appeared to Addi, although some were also drawn from the poor inhabitants of the Rome ghetto. Addi was the only German Jew in his class. He learned Italian fast and did quite well. He even seemed to find Dante easier than some of the Italian boys – perhaps because many of the archaic words were recognizable to him from Latin.

Addi enjoyed his sojourn in Italy. In spite of the fascist government, official anti-Semitism, and Mussolini's diplomatic alignment with Hitler, Jews there felt little discomfort at this time. Addi's *permesso di soggiorno* was inscribed, 'The holder of this permit is of the Hebrew race.'[5] As a result he fell under the authority of the racial laws but apart from such formalities he never encountered anti-Semitism directly in Italy. He told the story of a conversation with the director of the *liceo*, a lazy but agreeable man who had been installed in this sinecure as a political appointee by the Fascist Party. He asked Addi, 'Why are you not a member of GUF (Gioventù Universitaria Fascista, the fascist student organization)?' Addi pointed out that he was not yet a university student but apparently this was not a satisfactory let-out, since final-year schoolboys were permitted to join. 'But I am Jewish', he then said. The response was 'Don't be silly, that has nothing to do with it!' Many Italian Jews had, after all, been enthusiastic supporters of Fascism until the passage of the anti-Jewish laws in the autumn of 1938. Prudently, Addi avoided joining.

This Roman interlude was cut short as a result of Hitler's offensive against the Low Countries and France in May 1940. By the end of the month the British had withdrawn from Dunkirk and France stared defeat in the face. Rumours began to spread that Italy would soon enter the war. Addi's friends advised him to leave the country as soon as possible, since departure would probably become much more difficult if Italy became a belligerent. Once again, he began to cast around for some country that might take him in. He resorted to the now familiar round of consulates but had no luck. Palestine seemed out of the question because of the still rigorous controls on Jewish immigration. The only two places said to be open to Jewish refugees were Tangier and Turkey.

Under a treaty signed in 1923, the international zone of Tangier in Morocco was one of the few places on earth where no entry visa was required in May 1940. Like Casablanca in the 1942 film, it was seen by refugees as a possible jumping-off point towards the western hemisphere. But how to get there? Perhaps it was fortunate that Addi did not even try: on 14 June 1940, the day the Germans entered Paris, Tangier was occupied by Spanish forces loyal to the fascist regime of General Francisco Franco. The town thereupon lost its international status. Jewish refugees already there were not harmed but no more were admitted for the duration of the war. Addi had already written to his father in late February mentioning that he was thinking of going to Tel Aviv or Tangier. His father replied urging him to remain in Rome as long as possible, at least until he had completed his *Abitur*. After that, Berl suggested, it would be better to go to Switzerland.[6]

The Swiss, however, were no more eager than other nations to admit Jewish refugees. Immediately after the *Anschluss* in March 1938, the country's Federal Council had decided: 'If we do not want to create a basis for an anti-Semitic movement that would be unworthy of our country, we must defend ourselves with all our strength and, if need be, with ruthlessness against the immigration of foreign Jews, mostly those from the east.'[7] It was at the request of the Swiss that the Germans, shortly afterwards, began stamping the passports of German Jews with a large red letter 'J'. That would enable officials, as a Swiss report put it, 'to check at the border whether the carrier of the passport was Aryan or not Aryan'.[8] Swiss consular officers in Italy were reprimanded for disregarding the rules about Jewish immigration.[9] After the outbreak of war, Switzerland was concerned above all to preserve its neutrality. Its government lived in constant fear of a German invasion. In the first few days of June 1940 tension rose after engagements between German and Swiss planes near the French border: eleven German and two Swiss aircraft were shot down. The German defeat of France resulted in a surge of refugees seeking admission to Switzerland. In response, the Swiss strengthened border controls and considered subjecting refugees to internment or *refoulement* (deportation whence they came).[10] So Switzerland was not a realistic option.

Although Turkey held no greater attraction than Tangier, Addi thought it might be a way-station to Palestine. The overland route across Syria, a French mandated territory, was still open. The Turks, who were neutral and at that time seemed inclined to remain so, agreed to a British request to admit Polish nationals from Italy. Word about this arrangement quickly spread among the refugee community in Rome.

Addi's inquiries about entry to Turkey were encouraging. All he would require was a valid passport. Under the law of 1938, Addi's Polish passport would require a further endorsement of validity. He therefore returned to the Polish consulate and asked for the requisite 'chop'. Again, however, he was rudely rebuffed.

At this juncture an almost miraculous occurrence supervened. It so happened that an acquaintance of Addi, Reni, a Christian 'non-Aryan' refugee, a painter, was working on the restoration of paintings at the headquarters of the Society of Jesus. Reni, who had free access to the building, offered to introduce Addi to the Superior General (*Prepositus Generalis*) of the Jesuit order, Father Włodzimierz Ledóchowski. The holder of this eminent office was (and still is) popularly known as the 'black pope' – so-called on account of the colour of his habit and alleged mastery of the black arts of intrigue and chicanery often attributed to the Jesuits by their enemies.

The Ledóchowskis, an aristocratic family of Galician origin, had achieved distinction both as military men and in the Roman Catholic Church. Włodzimierz's grandfather, the one-legged General Ignacy Ledóchowski, was a hero of the Polish revolt against Russia in 1831. Count Mieczysław Ledóchowski, a cousin of Włodzimierz's father, was Archbishop of Gniezno-Posen in Prussian Poland and primate of the Polish church. He led the struggle against Bismarck's *Kulturkampf* in the 1870s. His refusal to accede to the imperial German government's insistence that all instruction in Catholic schools in Posen must be in German rather than Polish led to his imprisonment. While behind bars, he was elevated to the College of Cardinals. One of Włodzimierz's sisters, Maria Teresa, founded the Missionary Sisters of St Paul Claver and was beatified by Pope Paul VI in 1975. Another sister, Julia, worked for Polish war victims during the First World War. Adopting the name Ursula, she founded the sisterhood of the Agonizing Heart of Jesus (the 'Gray Ursulines'). She was beatified by the Polish Pope, John Paul II, in 1983 and canonized in 2003.

As with the rest of his family, the twin themes of deep piety and Polish patriotism characterized the life of Włodzimierz. Born at Loosdorf in Lower Austria in 1866, he entered the Society of Jesus in 1889. In 1915 he was elected its head. Profoundly conservative in his attitude towards all theological questions and in his administration of the Society, he was a close adviser to successive popes.

Addi had never before heard of Ledóchowski or his family. But thinking he had nothing to lose, he went with his friend to visit the prelate in his office on the Borgo Santo Spirito, just off St Peter's Square. Ushered into Ledóchowski's presence, Addi confronted an imposing figure, 'a man of middle height with unusually intelligent eyes, the wrinkled and moulded features of the savant, and the certainty of manner of a born aristocrat'.[11] Addi addressed him in German – his only Polish consisted of a few swear words he had picked up in the camp at Zbąszyń, hardly suitable for discourse with a senior ecclesiastic. Outlining his predicament, Addi explained that, being a Polish citizen, he sought an endorsement on his passport from the Polish consul. Ledóchowski listened and then inquired how it came about, if he was really Polish, that he could not speak a word of the language? Addi explained that although he had been born in Germany, his family hailed from Poland.

'Where in Poland?'

'A small town near Lwów.'

'What is the name of the place?'

'It's a little place. You won't have heard of it.'

'The name of the place?' Ledóchowski insisted.

'Krakowiec.'

This short exchange was the most consequential conversation of Addi's life.

Ledóchowski said not another word but pondered a moment and then motioned to his secretary, a young priest. The latter immediately escorted Addi out. He could not be sure whether he was being summarily dismissed but the priest accompanied him straight to the Polish consulate. By this time Addi must have been a well-known figure there. Yet instead of being booted out, as on his previous visits, he was now received, he later recalled, 'as if I were myself a prince of the Church'. The Father-General's imprimatur evidently counted, in the eyes of the consular officials, as something close to the word of God. The necessary rubber stamp was immediately produced and Addi's passport endorsed. As a result he quickly obtained the precious entry permit for Turkey. He left Italy a few days later. In 1943–4, thousands of Jews in German-occupied areas of Italy, including Rome, were rounded up and deported to death camps. But for Ledóchowski's intervention, Addi would most likely have been among them.

What led Ledóchowski to intervene in this way?

The Jesuits, after all, were not noted at this period for philo-semitism. Recalling a conversation with Ledóchowski in 1938, at the time of the introduction of Mussolini's anti-Jewish laws, an Italian diplomat wrote: 'He did not hide from me his implacable loathing for the Jews, who he believes are the origin of all the ills that afflict Europe.'[12] Ledóchowski has been credited with – or rather accused of – delaying and eventually suppressing the so-called 'hidden encyclical', *Humani Generis Unitas*, of Pope Pius XI. In that document, the pontiff, shortly before his death in February 1939, had intended to denounce racism. The evidence for this charge against Ledóchowski remains inconclusive.[13] Nevertheless, there can be no doubt that he was deeply imbued with traditional Catholic anti-Semitism.

Why did a man with that sort of outlook lift a finger on behalf of a Jewish refugee who had gained entry to his office by dubious means? In this case, we should certainly not discount the element of straightforward Christian charity. Other clerics who exhibited hostility to Jews in general, for example Metropolitan Sheptytsky in Lwów, nevertheless offered a helping hand to individual Jews threatened by the Nazis.

But there was something else. Only long afterwards did Addi discover that Ledóchowski's readiness to help was coloured by a personal aspect. We have already met the Jesuit's brother, General Ignacy Ledóchowski, and recorded his flight, with his wife Paulina, from their home near Krakowiec in September 1939. Paulina was the daughter of Jadwiga Łubieńska, owner of the Krakowiec estate. Jadwiga had inherited from her father the family seat at Wólka Rosnowska, an estate a few miles east of Krakowiec on the road to Jaworów. Later Jadwiga presented the Wólka Rosnowska manor house and estate to her daughter. The Ledóchowskis and Łubieńskis were therefore neighbours and closely related by marriage.

With other members of his family, Włodzimierz had spent childhood summer holidays in the district. The name Krakowiec conjured up for the Jesuit distant memories of an earlier, sunnier time. 'Kra-kowiec' therefore operated as a kind of shibboleth – in the biblical sense of the term: Addi had only to utter it, pronouncing it correctly *Krah-KOV-yets*, notwithstanding his lack of Polish, to be recognized as a *Landsmann*.

Addi left Italy at the start of June aboard a small steamer, the *Città di Bari*, sailing through the Corinth Canal and calling briefly at Piraeus. He landed in Istanbul on 5 June.[14] Once again he was just in time. Three days later the *Città di Bari* was requisitioned by the Italian navy.[15] On 10 June Mussolini declared war on Britain and France. On 15 June the Italian Ministry of the Interior ordered the arrest and internment of all German, Polish, Czechoslovak and stateless Jews between the ages of eighteen and sixty. Refugees henceforth found it almost impossible to leave the country. Many of them were subsequently murdered by the Nazis.

Upon disembarking in Istanbul, Addi was immediately accosted by seedy-looking touts, like the 'agent' later memorably portrayed by Peter Ustinov in the film *Topkapi*. One of these offered him a free taxi ride to the 'Turing Palas' Hotel. After a couple of days in this down-at-heel establishment, he moved into lodgings with a Jewish family. One of his first calls was at the Polish consulate where he once again volunteered for military service and again was summarily dismissed.

At this time it was still possible to communicate by mail with Krakowiec. Letters from Rome and later from Turkey reached Soviet-occupied eastern Galicia, albeit with considerable delay. From time to time, Addi received replies. Probably because of strict censorship in this Soviet frontier area, they contained little hard information other than that the family was in good health. The constant, almost obsessive theme of Berl's letters, perhaps recalling the disruptive effect of the previous world war on his own education, was that Addi should finish the last year of his schooling and obtain the *Abitur*.

Addi had left Italy before his final examinations at the *liceo*. He therefore still did not possess that dearly desired certificate but was armed merely with a letter stating that he had attended the final year of school. In order to complete his much-interrupted education, he tried to secure admission to Robert College, the famous English-language school in Istanbul. Unfortunately his English was not quite up to scratch. Although he had read quite a lot, he had never spoken the language. At the interview he was asked, 'Do you know English?' In his excitement, he blurted out, 'Oh yes, I have written many English books' – of course, he meant *read*. Not surprisingly, he was rejected. There was no other school in the city where it seemed useful to apply, so he spent the next few months at a loose end, unsure where to go or what to do.

Turkish attitudes to refugees were correct but chilly. The foreigners in Istanbul tended to keep to themselves. Addi's friends were refugees and local Jews. Travel to other parts of Turkey was forbidden to foreigners. Since there was not much else to do, he spent most of his time reading, mainly English and classical literature.

For some time he had contemplated trying to get to Krakowiec. There, after all, he would at least be with his family, from whom he had been so abruptly separated. Soviet-Turkish relations at that time were uneasy but he thought it might be possible for him to cross into Soviet Ukraine. His father was aghast when he heard of the idea. In a letter dated 3 February 1940, when Addi was still in Rome, Berl advised him to put it entirely out of his head. Probably intending to convey to him the awfulness of conditions in Krakowiec without arousing intervention by the Soviet postal censor, he told Addi that 'it was better in Zbąszyń.' In another postcard, in January 1941, he underlined: 'You must absolutely not come here.' And he repeated that in a postcard dated 25 March 1941.[16] In this he also approved Addi's latest plan: to go to Palestine.

Hitherto Addi had been at most a lukewarm Zionist. His involvement in Zionist youth movements in Germany had been prompted more by social than ideological motives. In Istanbul, however, his attitude began to change. Soon after he arrived, several new parties of refugees reached the city. One included young people who had been with him at Zbąszyń. They mainly came via Vilna and Kaunas, an area that had been taken over by the Russians in 1940. The British mandatory administration decided to allow a trickle of refugees, within the limited official quota, to enter Palestine. The Jewish Agency (the British-recognized body closely linked to the Zionist Organization) arranged for them to leave for Palestine via Istanbul. There was certainly no long-term future for Addi in Turkey so he decided to seek permission to follow his friends to Palestine. After a long wait, he received the coveted certificate authorizing entry to Palestine.

Addi left Istanbul on 22 June 1941. On his way by train to the southern Turkish port of Mersin he heard the momentous news that the Germans had invaded the Soviet Union early that morning. At that stage, he did not, of course, know the terrible implications that that would have for his family in Krakowiec.

When Addi arrived in Haifa, he was interrogated by a Polish security officer, as were all arriving Polish citizens. By chance, he had already encountered this large, overbearing and unhelpful man in the course of his multiple visits to Polish consulates in Rome and Istanbul. The officer, too, recognized Addi as the youth he had earlier thrown out of his office. On inspecting his luggage he came across a volume of the writings of Karl Marx in German that Addi had purchased in Rome. He confiscated the book but, in the absence of anything more incriminating, Addi was allowed to move on.

After the German attack on the Soviet Union, communication with Krakowiec, now in what the British regarded as enemy-occupied territory, ceased almost completely. For a while, Krakowiec Jews in South Africa managed to maintain contact with relatives back home via an intermediary in Argentina but that link was soon cut. Messages between Krakowiec and Palestine could henceforth be sent only via the International Red Cross and took several weeks to arrive. They were 'not to exceed 25 words' and might contain only 'family news of strictly personal character'. A message that Addi dispatched, reporting his safe arrival in Palestine, reached his father in Krakowiec. Berl managed to send a brief handwritten reply on 17 March 1942, again assuring Addi that the family were all well and signed 'Berl Wasserstein'.[17] After that, there was only silence.

12

One fish

Shortly after the recapture of Krakowiec from the Nazis at the end of July 1944, the re-established Soviet administration set up an inquiry into human and material losses during the German occupation. A district committee was appointed under the aegis of the nationwide Extraordinary State Commission for the Establishment and Investigation of the Crimes of the German-Fascist Invaders and Their Accomplices and of the Damage They Caused to Citizens, Collective Farms, Public Organizations, State Enterprises, and Institutions of the USSR. This body had been set up on Stalin's orders in 1943. Its lengthy handle was notable for the omission of one word: 'Jew'.[1] The seven members of the Krakowiec committee comprised three Ukrainians, three surviving Jews, and the local head of the NKVD.

After questioning residents and examining documents, the committee reported in February 1945 that, of the 190 Jewish families known to have lived in the district before the Germans arrived, at least 168 had perished.[2] The committee stated that it was impossible to ascertain the names of the remaining twenty-two families. Altogether at least 787 persons were said to have been killed, a total that included residents of villages in the area. In spite of the committee's attempt at precision, the figure can be regarded only as an approximation. The report gives the names only of heads of families and the numbers of family members. A few of those listed as killed are known to have survived: for example, Nochim Majer Pompius, the town's 'Communist commissar'; he returned to Poland from the USSR at the end of the war and later moved to the United States. Others who are listed as victims are known to have died before the arrival of the Nazis, for example, Berl's father, Jacob Wasserstein.

The commission also conducted a painstaking examination of property losses, listing, in each case, the exact measurements of every building destroyed or damaged, as well as the value of crops, trees, gardens, livestock and requisitioned stores. One hundred homes and sixty barns or storehouses in Krakowiec had been destroyed. Eighty cows and sixty horses had been confiscated. The total value of property losses in the town was calculated at 13,880,750 roubles.[3] At the official exchange rate in 1945, that amounted to $2,619,009. Of course, the official exchange rate was a fiction. But we need not attempt a more realistic valuation since we know exactly what the Jews lost: everything.

The findings of the committee were fed into regional and national data that were boiled down into published reports. These were carefully doctored in order to comply with Soviet propaganda requirements. For example, where documents described the mass murder of the Jews in a given area, this was automatically corrected to 'Soviet citizens.'[4] A final, posthumous indignity was thus inflicted on the victims: deprivation of their core identity.

The post-war border between Poland and the USSR essentially followed the line agreed between the Nazis and Soviets in 1939 (*see map on p. 206*). The issue had been discussed by Stalin with Roosevelt and Churchill at the Tehran Conference in December 1943. Stalin demanded that the new frontier conform to the Curzon Line of 1920. But there was some dispute over its correct delineation. According to the Soviet version, it ran west of Lwów, according to the British, east of the city. If the British view were accepted, Lwów, and with it, Krakowiec, would remain Polish; if Stalin's, both would fall under Soviet rule. The wrangling continued at the subsequent great-power conferences at Yalta and Potsdam in 1945. The British Foreign Secretary, Anthony Eden, made a half-hearted effort to save Lwów for the Poles. But Churchill and Roosevelt were inclined to give way to Stalin. The Communist regime in Warsaw was in no position to argue against the *diktat* from Moscow. The ghost-like, anti-Communist Polish government-in-exile in London looked for diplomatic support to its hosts. But the British had long made it clear that their guarantee of 1939, on the basis of which they had gone to war with Germany, was an assurance of support for Polish independence but not for Poland's claim to sovereignty over its eastern territories. The London Poles registered their objection to the loss of what they regarded, with some justification, as a historic Polish city. Deprived even of British and American support, however, they were whistling in the chill wind from the east. Stalin was adamant and in the end the Soviets, as the power in possession, got their way: the frontier was established a little to the east of the San River. The new border cut through what had once been the Cetner/Lubomirski/Łubieński lands. Krakovets (this was now its official name) was to remain under Soviet rule.

Ukrainian–Polish fighting continued long after the arrival of the Red Army in 1944. In the final months of the Second World War Polish and Ukrainian nationalist militias engaged in fierce clashes and mutual atrocities. According to an NKVD report, a thirty-strong unit of Polish militiamen shot eight Ukrainian villagers and robbed ten farms near Krakovets on 10 February 1945. A few days later in another village in the district two hundred Polish soldiers and fifty militiamen were said to have perpetrated a 'pogrom' against Ukrainians.[5]

The UPA's campaign against Polish peasants in eastern Galicia, amounting in places to ethnic cleansing, was little noticed by the outside world. The barbarity of the UPA *Banderovtsi* recalled the ruthlessness of the *Haidamaky* Cossacks in their slaughter of Polish gentry and Jews during their rebellions in the eighteenth century, as depicted by Taras Shevchenko.

> In villages the beasts that feed
> On human corpses howl. The Poles
> Were left unburied, food for wolves,
> Until the heavy winter snows
> Concealed their bones . . .[6]

The UPA killers targeted not only Poles and Jews but also fellow Ukrainians. Some of these were political rivals. Others were victims of a fanatical extension of ethnic cleansing – members of families, among them several in Krakovets, of mixed Greek and Roman Catholic marriages. Were they 'Polonized' Ukrainians or 'Ukrainized' Poles? They knew not which way to turn. Their plight recalled the horror of the eighteenth-century Cossack chief Gonta, depicted by Shevchenko, who, in the frenzy of his oath-driven slaughter of Poles, raised his 'sanctified sabre' and murdered his own two sons by a Roman Catholic mother.

The objective of both Polish and Ukrainian nationalists, as in the aftermath of the previous war, was to carve out territory for sovereign states. But they were at the same time engaged in no less bitter civil wars against Communists who enjoyed one overwhelming advantage: the presence of the Red Army.

For several years after the Soviet reoccupation of eastern Galicia, both the Soviet and the Polish Communist authorities did their utmost to obliterate the UPA, which remained active in the border region with some covert support from the CIA. The conflict was on a massive scale. In the seventeen months ending in June 1945, according to NKVD reports, Soviet forces killed 91,615 Ukrainian nationalist 'bandits' in the region; a further 96,444 were captured and 41,858 surrendered. Tens of thousands more were killed, captured, or deported over the next few years.[7] Nikita Khrushchev, still at the time head of the Ukrainian Communist Party, set the tone on a visit to the region in January 1945, when he declared: 'We just won't be respected if we don't take measures; we must arrest every single one of the participants, whom we must then judge, perhaps hang, and then exile the rest of them; that way we will take a hundred for one . . . They must hear our vengeance.'[8] In order to deter potential UPA recruits or supporters, public executions were organized in front of thousands of spectators.[9]

Krakovets was at the epicentre of this conflict. According to the exile arm of the UPA, between July 1944 and July 1947 Soviet security forces launched 462 raids on villages in the Krakovets district and a further 222 in woods and forests. A total of 1,074 people were arrested: of these 139 were executed and 149 were sent to Siberia and the Donbas region as convict labourers. Many more were arrested but held only for short periods. In addition, 1,448 persons were 'mobilized by force into the Red Army, of whom 394 perished.'[10] Of course, anti-Communists had an interest in magnifying such episodes – but this report conforms with the general outline of what is known from other sources about the scale of repression in the area at the time.

The UPA responded with thousands of killings, ferocious atrocities and terror tactics. Death squads wreaked savage vengeance against Ukrainians suspected of collaboration with the Soviets. The rebels 'murdered my wife and two young children. They burned my house and ruined my whole farm,' related a grieving peasant in the Krakovets district.[11] Hoping to combine terror with propaganda, the UPA distributed leaflets in and around the town.[12]

Ultimately the guerrillas were no match for the Soviet forces that steadily ground them down. In May 1949 the MGB (the new shorthand for the Soviet secret police) reported an encounter at Lubienie, near Krakovets, with Semen Matviev (*nom de guerre* 'Chomyn'), leader of a 'regiment' of forty Ukrainian 'bandits'. Semen was shot and killed but others with him eluded pursuers with dogs.[13] A few days later two Ukrainian flags were raised in Krakovets.[14] A captured UPA document in 1950 recorded further UPA losses in the district, including that of Tadaj Vengerak (*nom de guerre* 'Zahirny') who had been born in Krakovets in 1923 and was killed there. He was said to have been involved in 'education of youth' during the German occupation and had earned a medal for bravery.[15]

Roman Shukhevych and his surviving adherents pursued their struggle doggedly to the end. The UPA commander hid out in the forests near his birthplace for nearly five years after the end of the war. The climax came in a shoot-out with the Soviet secret police in a suburb of Lwów on 5 March 1950: Shukhevych was killed (according to one account, he shot himself).[16] The head of the unit responsible for his liquidation crowed that with his death 'the organized guerrilla resistance in Western Ukraine collapsed.'[17] This was not quite the case: Shukhevych's successor at the head of the UPA, Vasyl Kuk (whom we met earlier as chief of the militia unit that arrived in Krakowiec in June 1941) carried on the campaign until his capture and imprisonment in 1954. Released after six years, he lived long enough to see the rebirth of an independent Ukraine in 1991. He died, aged ninety, in Kiev in 2007.

The most far-reaching consequence of the Polish–Ukrainian struggle was the large-scale, two-way transfer of population that took place between Poland and Soviet Ukraine in the immediate post-war years.

Like other such episodes in modern history (for example, the mutual expulsion of populations between Greece and Turkey in the 1920s), this was euphemistically described as a voluntary exchange; it is more correctly understood as a ruthless process of two-way ethnic cleansing. The historian Timothy Snyder has plausibly suggested that 'the "repatriation" of Poles from Soviet Ukraine is best seen as an unofficially cooperative effort of the NKVD and the UPA.'[18] An estimated 1.3 million Poles moved or were removed from what had become Ukraine to Poland. Around half a million Ukrainians and Lemkos, a small Slavic people related to Ukrainians, moved in the other direction. In addition, large numbers of Ukrainians from south-east Poland were resettled in the territories newly acquired by Poland from Germany. From the Lviv oblast alone, 200,000 Poles and some remaining Jews were relocated to Poland, while sixty thousand Ukrainians from Poland moved to Ukraine. The migrants often settled in the empty former homes of people who had gone in the other direction – or of Jews who were no longer alive.

Demographic transformation of eastern Galicia, henceforth called western Ukraine, was accompanied by a cultural and socio-economic revolution. The Greek Catholic church, to which most Ukrainians in Galicia adhered, was forced to cancel the Brest Union of 1596 and 'fuse' with the state-controlled Russian Orthodox church. Many of its bishops were arrested. Iosif Slepoi, who had been elevated to lead the Greek Catholic church upon the death of Andrey Sheptytsky in 1944, spent eighteen years in a Soviet prison. In Lubienie at Christmas 1950, the Greek Catholic priest was forbidden to sing carols.[19]

Collectivization of agriculture, which effectively took away rights that peasants had enjoyed since the abolition of serfdom in 1848, was greeted with consternation by the bulk of the rural population. In one kolkhoz in the Krakovets district peasants had the temerity to lodge a complaint with the secretary of the Lviv Obkom (Communist Party committee), Ivan Grushetski. They said they couldn't pay their taxes – actually, requisitions in kind – and asked that they be lowered. Arriving to deal with the matter, accompanied by a security guard of two armoured cars with secret policemen, Grushetski gave them short shrift.[20]

Hard on the heels of collectivization came another calamity:

famine. The main cause was the worst drought in the region in living memory. It affected the whole of Ukraine. A local official reported to Khrushchev after a visit to a woman worker in a kolkhoz who had been driven mad by hunger:

> I found a scene of horror. The woman had the corpse of her own child on the table and was cutting it up. She was chattering away as she worked. 'We've already eaten Manechka [Little Maria]. Now we'll salt down Vanechka [Little Ivan]. This will keep us for some time.'[21]

Given the burdens of his office, we may doubt that Khrushchev had found time to read Jonathan Swift's *A Modest Proposal* (1729), with its bitingly satirical suggestion for the breeding and consumption of children as a cure for Irish peasant poverty. The Ukrainian leader had little reason to exaggerate, since the alleged incident had taken place on his watch. What he later recounted was probably true.

Soviet propaganda nevertheless puffed up the supposed achievements of the new order. In November 1956, at a 'solemn gathering' in Krakovets to commemorate the thirty-ninth anniversary of the 1917 revolution, a local woman was reported to have undertaken to 'extract 2,100 litres of milk from each cow in 1957' in response to the imperialist aggression in Egypt and Hungary [*sic*]. She called upon all collective farmers to follow her example.[22] Reported average milk production in Soviet kolkhozes in 1957 was 1,650 litres per cow; the comparable figure for the USA was 2,714 litres.[23] Unfortunately I was not able to ascertain data for Krakovets in that year.

What were the fates of people we have encountered in the later period of this history?

The two senior German officials most directly involved in the 'Polenaktion' of 28 October 1938, Ernst von Weizsäcker, State Secretary of the Foreign Ministry and Werner Best of the security apparatus, were both canny survivors. Weizsäcker has been called 'the Devil's Diplomat'.[24] After the war he presented himself as a supporter of the German resistance. Tried nevertheless at Nuremberg for war crimes, he was sentenced to seven years' imprisonment but served only eighteen months. In an excoriating review of Weizsäcker's self-exculpatory memoirs, Namier called him 'crafty and naïve'.[25] Weizsäcker died shortly after his release from prison.

As a Wehrmacht officer in 1943, Weizsäcker's son Richard learned of the atrocities committed by the Nazis in occupied eastern Europe. After the war, as a law student, Richard participated in his father's legal defence team at Nuremberg. On 8 May 1985, the thirtieth anniversary of VE Day, Richard, by then President of the Federal Republic, delivered a speech calling on his fellow-countrymen to

> have the strength to look truth straight in the eye . . . The perpetration of this crime was in the hands of a few people . . . There is no such thing as the guilt or innocence of an entire nation. Guilt is, like innocence, not collective, but personal . . . The vast majority of today's population were either children then or had not been born. They cannot profess a guilt of their own for crimes that they did not commit. No discerning person can expect them to wear a penitential robe simply because they are Germans. But their forefathers have left them a hard legacy.

It was a thoughtful and influential statement. Yet there was a mote in Richard Weizsäcker's eye: the case of his own father. He persisted in his view that the verdict on his father had been 'historically and morally unjust'.[26]

Best served the Nazis faithfully from before the start of their regime until long after the finish. As early as 1930 he wrote of 'exterminating' the nation's enemies. An exponent of what he termed 'heroic realism', he has been called 'two-faced and oddly equivocal'.[27] He supervised the deportation to their deaths of Jews from France. It was later claimed that, as 'Reich Plenipotentiary' in occupied Denmark in 1943, he had given the 'tip-off' that enabled most Danish Jews to escape to neutral Sweden, thereby avoiding transportation to the death camps. In 1948 he was nevertheless sentenced to death for war crimes by a Danish court; but the sentence was commuted and he was released in 1951. Thereafter, he pursued a successful legal-political career in West Germany in association with the Free Democratic Party. He became a central coordinator of the defence of ex-Nazis against accusations of war crimes.[28] He died shortly before the fall of the Berlin Wall in 1989.

Both these men were white-collar criminals who craved respectability. They were not among the authors of the genocidal grand design for the New Order in Europe – Hitler and his immediate associates. Nor can they be classified with executioners, the uniformed thugs whose excuse was that they were obeying orders. Both were among the critically important, middle-level decision-makers who made the Nazi system work.

Hans Frank, head of the General Gouvernement in Poland, was captured by US troops in May 1945. He was placed on trial at Nuremberg and told the court, 'I am possessed by a deep sense of guilt.' He maintained, however, that he had had nothing to do with concentration camps and that the SS had operated independently of his administration. As for the Jews, he told the court, 'I myself have never installed an extermination camp for Jews, or promoted the existence of such camps; but if Adolf Hitler personally has laid that dreadful responsibility on his people, then it is mine too.' He protested that he had merely heard 'rumours' about the mass murder of Jews. He was found guilty of war crimes and crimes against humanity, sentenced to death, and executed in October 1946.[29]

The British lawyer-historian Philippe Sands has recently investigated the post-war escape from justice of Frank's subordinate, Otto von Wächter. Sands relates how Wächter hid in Austria for three years and, after crossing the Alps on foot, made his way to Rome. He stayed there under the protection of the Rector of the Collegio Teutonico, Bishop Alois Hudal. Wächter hoped to escape to Argentina with the assistance of the so-called Vatican 'Ratline', which aided Nazi fugitives from justice. Before he could leave Italy, however, he died in mysterious circumstances in 1949.[30]

Like Wächter, Friedrich Katzmann, SS and Police Leader in Galicia, never faced trial. This was in spite of the fact that the United Nations War Crimes Commission had placed him on a list of known criminals and that his self-incriminating 1943 'final report on the solution to the Jewish problem in Galicia' was entered into evidence at the Nuremberg tribunal. Little effort seems to have been made to track him down. He lived quietly in West Germany after the war under an assumed name and died in his bed in Darmstadt in 1957. He was buried, however, under his correct identity.

Theodor Oberländer, who had been the Abwehr's liaison officer with Roman Shukhevych's 'Nachtigall' battalion, served under Chancellor Konrad Adenauer as Minister for Expellees, Refugees and War Injured in West Germany from 1953 to 1960. Denounced as the 'butcher of Lemberg', accused of responsibility for the mass murder of Jews and others in Lwów in 1941, he was tried in absentia in East Berlin and sentenced to life imprisonment. The sentence could not, however, be enforced in West Germany. He was forced to resign as a minister but remained a free man and a member of the Bundestag. The 1960 verdict was overturned by a Berlin court in 1993 as 'rechtsstaatswidrig' (contrary to the rule of law). In 1996 the public prosecutor in Cologne re-examined the case and opened new proceedings against Oberländer. These, however, had not led to any court decision by the time of his death, aged 93, in 1998.

The German historian Dieter Pohl has analysed the post-war judicial reckoning with other perpetrators of genocide and their collaborators in east Galicia.[31] The most energetic effort in this direction was made by the region's Communist rulers after the arrival of the Red Army in 1944–45. The Soviet secret police arrested no fewer than 17,300 people in Lwów alone in just six days, 3 to 8 January 1945. Many of these were tried before secret police courts that barely observed judicial forms. The accused included members of the wartime Ukrainian police as well as other Nazi collaborators, a number of whom were denounced to the Soviet investigating commission in Krakowiec in 1944.[32] Soviet war crimes policy, however, had a distinctly political complexion. A historian who examined Soviet court records reports that 'from several trials against Ukrainian nationalists we get the impression that, in the understanding of the Soviet authorities, it was worse to be a Ukrainian nationalist than to participate in the murder of hundreds of Jews.'[33] Trials of alleged war criminals continued in the USSR for several decades. After 1947, however, none was sentenced to death.

The western powers showed little interest in pursuing war criminals after the Nuremberg trials wound down in 1949. Large numbers of Ukrainians and others with dubious war records were admitted as immigrants to the United States and Britain as refugees from Communism. Canada welcomed several thousand veterans of the

Waffen-SS Division 'Galizien'. After many years, the matter became a subject of public debate and there were fierce recriminations between Ukrainian and Jewish Canadians. A Commission of Enquiry under Justice Jules Deschênes in 1986 cleared the division of collective involvement in war crimes. *Prima facie* evidence of war crimes by individuals was found in twenty cases.[34] Three prosecutions ended without securing convictions. A cenotaph honouring those members of the division who died in action (against an allied coalition of which Canada was a member) was erected in the St Volodymyr Ukrainian cemetery in Oakville, near Toronto. The cemetery is the resting-place of 270 former soldiers of the division. In June 2020 the memorial was spray-painted with the words 'Nazi war monument'. The local police announced that they would investigate the incident as a 'hate crime'; later a clarification was issued, announcing that it was being investigated as vandalism.[35]

Many Germans and others responsible for war crimes in east Galicia settled down in West Germany without suffering legal consequences for their actions. The few trials for wartime murders in the region that took place in the 1950s resulted in what were sometimes risibly brief prison sentences. A Central Office for the Investigation of National Socialist Crimes (Zentral Stelle), based in Ludwigsburg, was established only in 1958. It gathered evidence and pressed for the prosecution of war criminals, including some responsible for killings in east Galicia. As a result, more trials took place in the 1960s. Pohl concluded soberly that the overall judicial results of criminal investigation of the murder of more than half a million Jews of east Galicia were quite limited.

The headmaster of the Adass Jisroel school in Berlin, Nachman Schlesinger, might have found it possible, like more than half the Jews in Germany, to leave before the outbreak of war. He insisted, however, on remaining, with his wife and children, 'as long as there is a single Jewish child here who needs a Jewish education'. He carried on teaching until 1942, when he fell ill. In December that year he was removed from the Jewish hospital of Berlin on a stretcher and deported to Auschwitz with his family. They were all murdered there. The greater part of Addi's classmates in the school, however, survived. They scattered to Britain, Israel and the United States. In later decades, they held occasional reunions, like alumni of any old school.

Stanisław Maczek, who commanded the vigorous but doomed stand by the Polish army in Krakowiec in September 1939, managed to escape from Poland with some of his officers. In 1944 he commanded the First Polish Armoured Division, which participated in the invasion of Normandy. His 'Black Devils' later entered Breda, the first city to be liberated in the Netherlands. For this he was awarded honorary Dutch citizenship. But the post-war Polish Communist government stripped him of his Polish passport as well as his military pension. He was reduced to working as a bartender in Scotland. Maczek died in Edinburgh in 1994, aged 102.

Chief Rabbi Zolli survived the German occupation of Rome in 1943–4 in hiding. On 27 September 1944, four months after the liberation of the city, he caused a scandal in the Jewish community: while officiating in the Great Synagogue on Yom Kippur (the Day of Atonement, the holiest day of the Jewish year), he beheld a vision of Jesus in a meadow. He gave up his rabbinical position and converted to Christianity. At his baptism, he took the Christian names of Pope Pius XII, 'Eugenio Maria'. Zolli's apostasy gave rise to many interpretations. One had it that he had converted out of gratitude for the help given to Rome Jews by the Vatican during the war. Another maintained that Zolli had learned in advance that a German roundup of Jews was about to take place and, instead of standing by the community, as some rabbis elsewhere did, sought to save his own skin by going into hiding. According to this version, his behaviour gave rise to angry accusations after the war, as a result of which he fell out with his congregation and in a pique abandoned the faith. He disputed that accusation. Zolli was appointed to a position at the Pontifical Biblical Institute and wrote and lectured widely on his new-found faith.[36] Shortly before Zolli's death in 1956, Addi, back in Rome on a research trip, encountered his old teacher by chance in the Vatican Library. Addi avoided talking to him. He could not overcome a visceral abhorrence of apostates – or I should say rather of *this* apostate, since he seemed to have no such problem regarding some other converts from Judaism who became his friends.

The head of the Jesuit order, Włodzimierz Ledóchowski, died in

Rome in December 1942. In a dispatch to the Foreign Office reporting his death, the British envoy to the Holy See wrote: 'As a patriotic
Pole – and he was noted for his devotion to his own country – the
crucifixion of Poland by the Nazis filled him with grief, and there can
be little doubt that he deplored the attitude of extreme caution
adopted by the Holy See in the face of the German crimes there and
elsewhere.'[37] His death was widely regretted and there was talk of
beatification. Some historians, however, have been less commenda-
tory and in recent years Ledóchowski has been heavily criticized for
his alleged role in blocking publication of the so-called 'hidden
encyclical'.

In 1978, on a visit to relatives in Johannesburg, Addi once again
encountered a Włodzimierz Ledóchowski. This one, it turned out, was
the son of General Ignacy Ledóchowski and therefore a nephew of the
Jesuit. While his parents endured Nazi occupation, the younger
Włodzimierz had served in the Polish army, acting as a courier between
Poland and the country's armed forces in exile. On a clandestine visit
to Poland, Włodzimierz had had one last meeting with his parents. In
1944 Ignacy was arrested by the Germans and charged with participation in the underground Home Army. He died in March 1945 in
Dora-Mittelbau, a German concentration camp.

After the end of the war, when the family lost their estates in Poland
and what had now become part of Soviet Ukraine, Włodzimierz emigrated to South Africa. The common tie with Krakowiec brought him
into contact with Addi's uncles in Johannesburg. Thus were tables
turned: in 1940 a Ledóchowski intervened to help Addi, an action
that probably saved his life; a few years later, another Ledóchowski,
now himself a refugee, was befriended by Addi's family who helped
him to establish himself in business in Africa. Włodzimierz
Ledóchowski returned to Poland in 1984 and died there three years
later. He never revisited Krakowiec.[38]

The anxiety of Włodzimierz's mother, Paulina, about the fate of her
mother, left behind in Krakowiec, proved sadly justified. In September
1941 the dowager Countess Jadwiga Łubieńska, by now in her late
eighties, was forced to move out of what remained of the manor
house. She found refuge in the cottage of a poor old Jew, 'Yedidya',
said to have been aged 104. One of her daughters came to visit her.

She found her seated at a table, writing down time after time the words of the national anthem, composed by her great-grandfather, 'Jeszcze Polska nie zginęła,' 'Poland has not yet perished', as if to ensure that they would not be forgotten. Jadwiga died a few months later.[39] It was a melancholy end to the last human link with Krakowiec in the *belle époque*.

I was particularly interested in ascertaining what had become of the brutish Wolf, who, with his dog, terrorized wartime Krakowiec. In 1994 the Director of the Zentral Stelle in Luwigsburg, Wilhelm Dreßen, sent me an informative letter about the legal pursuit of war criminals in east Galicia. He reported that he could find next to no data on Wolf, save that he had been born in about 1891 and had been mentioned in passing in a trial as a participant in the liquidation of the Jaworów ghetto in 1943. I also inquired at the Berlin Document Center, an archive that was under American control until 1994. It held massive personnel records of the Nazi party, the SS and related institutions. The director, David Marwell, kindly undertook a search with a view to identifying Wolf. There were many records of persons with this surname. Without a forename, it was impossible to pin the man down. It was not until 2019 that I was informed by a local historian in Lviv, Eugen Lunio, that he had heard that Wolf had been shot dead by a Ukrainian in 1943 or 1944, while hunting with another German in the Krakovets forest.

A handful of Krakowiec Jews survived the war one way or another. These did not include the unidentified man who had emerged from hiding in the town at the liberation: he was recruited into the Red Army and killed in action before the end of the war.[40]

A young girl, Sala Ohringer, had fled just before the removal of Jews from Krakowiec to Jaworów in December 1942. She hid for a day or two with a teacher in a village adjacent to Krakowiec and then with another teacher. After that, she went to stay in Lwów with an uncle who had 'Aryan papers'. Pretending to be Christian, she found work as a maid for a family of Rumanian itinerants, and travelled with them to Warsaw and, in mid-1944, to Vilna. She managed to obtain identity papers from the Rumanian consul there before continuing to Bratislava in Slovakia. At the liberation she returned briefly

16. Addi Wasserstein (*centre*), aged seventeen, with fellow internees, Zbąszyń, 1939.

17. Addi Wasserstein, aged eighteen, Rome, 1940.

18. General Stanisław Maczek, commander of the Polish Tenth Mechanized Cavalry Brigade, which made a doomed stand against the Germans at Krakowiec in September 1939. He is shown here in the turret of a Cromwell tank in July 1944. Shortly afterwards, his Polish First Armoured Division was transferred to Normandy where it played a critical role in the Battle of the Falaise Pocket.

9. Father Włodzimierz Ledóchowski, *repositus Generalis* of the Jesuit order and close adviser to successive popes. Addi's utterance of the shibboleth 'Krakowiec' led the cleric to intervene on his behalf, thereby saving his life.

20. General Ignacy Ledóchowski, brother of the Jesuit. His wife Paulina recorded their flight from Krakowiec in 1941: 'the whole sky was burning and above Lwów was a sea of fire.'

21. Soviet war memorial in Krakovets, photographed in 1993.

22. Krakowiec-born Ukrainian nationalist Roman Shukhevych in uniform as commander of the Nachtigall (Nightingale) Battalion that entered Lwów with the German army in 1941 and participated in a pogrom that left 4,000 Jews dead.

23. Protector and betrayer: Mikola Mikhailovich Olanek.

24. Ukrainian postage stamp honouring Roman Shukhevych, 2007: in that year he was accorded the posthumous title of 'hero of Ukraine' by President Viktor Yushchenko.

25. Roman Shukhevych monument in the main square of Krakovets, 2019: site of annual gathering of UPA veterans.

לזכר היהודים
שנרצחו בידי
הנאצים ב'אבו
רוב בקרקוביץ
בסנדובה-וישניא
בוילקוטש'
בשנים 1941-1944

В ПАМ'ЯТЬ ЕВРЕЇВ
ЯВОРІВЩИНИ РОЗ-
СТРІЛЯНИХ ФАШИСТ
СЬКИМИ КАТАМИ
1941 1944 рр

16. Memorial in the Porudenko forest 'in memory of the Jews who were murdered by the Nazis in Jaworów, Krakowiec, Sądowa Wisznia, and Wielkie Oczy in the years 1941–1944'. Barely visible on the photograph, taken in 2019, is a small swastika that has been incised near the bottom right of the tablet.

27. Old and new Greek Catholic churches, Krakovets, 2019: the old church, on the left, has been lovingly restored since the fall of communism. The new, grander-looking edifice, under construction next door, is an empty shell; completion has stalled for lack of money.

28. Ukrainian refugees passing through Krakovets, one of the main crossing-points into Poland. By November 2022, nine months after the Russian invasion, nearly eight million Ukrainians had fled the country.

to Krakowiec and then moved to Cracow. Later she emigrated to Israel, where I met her in 1995.

Leon Scher and his comrades, who hid out in the forest near Krakowiec, were discovered by Russian soldiers in July 1944. They took the Jews on board their tanks and delivered them to Jaworów. Leon was drafted into the Red Army, serving in Poland and Germany. After the war he spent three years with his wife in a displaced persons' camp at Bad Reichenhall in Bavaria. With help from relatives in America, they secured permission to emigrate to the USA in 1949. Leon worked in a shoe factory. Later he opened a restaurant in Paterson, New Jersey, and then another, bigger one, not far away, in Plainfield. But the 'long hot summer' of 1967 brought race riots to the town and the business collapsed. Left with nothing, Leon had to start all over again and opened a diner. He died in 2008 in Century Village, a retirement community in Pembroke Pines, Florida. His extraordinary testimony of wartime survival is in the Visual History Archive, established by Steven Spielberg at the University of Southern California.

Mala Abend, daughter of a Jewish shopkeeper in Krakowiec, fled from the Jaworów ghetto just before it was liquidated. She had been able to buy forged 'Aryan papers'. In Lwów she happened to meet a Polish woman from Krakowiec, a former customer of her father's, who took pity on her and sheltered her in the city. When Mala returned to Krakowiec shortly after the liberation, she met a fellow Krakowitzer, Herzl Gottlieb, who had survived in hiding in the forest. They married shortly afterwards and emigrated to Australia.

Among those who saved their lives by fleeing to the Soviet Union in June 1941 was Sonia Berg (Regina Laub's cousin). She worked in a cotton factory in Tashkent and, like other Polish citizens in the USSR, was permitted to leave for Poland at the end of the war. From there she emigrated to Israel. Gifted with a remarkably precise memory, she shared her recollections with me in an interview in Ramat Gan in 1994. The Krakowiec doctor, Henryk Berger, also returned to Poland from Russia, taking up residence in Cracow.

The Glick and Silberman families were among those who had been deported to the east by the Soviets before the German invasion. Wolf Silberman died in Siberia. But Elimelech Glick served in the Soviet navy and survived. When he returned to Krakowiec, he could barely recognize it. Most of the houses had been looted and destroyed. The headstones in the old Jewish graveyard had been used to pave sidewalks. The synagogue had been set on fire: the stone walls remained but the wooden roof and the interior were destroyed. Glick's family home was still standing: unlike most of the other houses it had been built of stone rather than wood. He discovered that it was serving as the local office of the NKVD. Boldly, he went along to the local procurator and declared that, as a returning Soviet serviceman, he had been promised by Stalin that he would get his home back. The procurator replied circumspectly: 'There's a problem. My advice would be to take the house just opposite instead.' Glick pointed out that he would have to give that up if the owner returned. The procurator told him that if he insisted on reclaiming his own house his only recourse would be to go to law. It would have been a tall order to test the independence of the Soviet legal system by suing the secret police. Prudently, Glick decided to let the matter go. Shortly afterwards he left for Poland; later he emigrated to Israel where I interviewed him in 1994.

Three other survivors were less fortunate. Shloime Wassner, a horse dealer, served on the Soviet district committee for investigation of war crimes. Such service did not make him popular among local residents. Possibly for this reason, or perhaps just as a criminal act to steal his horses, he was killed not long after the liberation on the road to Jaworów.[41] Wolf Pfefferkorn, who had lived in Ruda Krakowiecka, also returned after service in the Red Army. He came back to search for valuables that his family had hidden in their former home. He found what he was looking for but was caught in the act by local people who seized the loot and killed him.[42] Shmuel Nacht, the son of a butcher, had been deported to the east by the Soviets before the German invasion. He too survived the war and returned to Krakowiec only to be murdered there.[43]

Addi met my mother, Maca (Margaret), in Palestine and married her there in November 1942. She had arrived in Palestine as an illegal immigrant from Hungary in November 1939. At first, she was threatened by the British authorities with deportation to her homeland. Fortunately, they found it impossible to carry out this threat, since the

Hungarian government made it clear that it would bar any such re-patriations. She was merely interned for a few weeks, then released and allowed to remain in the country. Maca was fortunate to survive: her parents and sister were murdered at Auschwitz.

After the war, Addi and Maca moved to Britain so that my father could pursue university studies there. Their three children were all born in the UK. Meanwhile, Addi embarked on an academic career in Britain. But they had always dreamed of returning to Israel. In 1969 Addi was appointed professor of classics at the Hebrew University of Jerusalem. They became Israeli citizens and, for the rest of their lives, their home was in Jerusalem.

For many years after the war, Addi tried to regain possession of his family's two apartment blocks in Berlin. During the war the German state had seized them. They had been damaged in wartime bombing but continued to be occupied by tenants. The buildings were situated in what became, after 1945, the Russian occupation sector of Berlin, later the capital of the Communist-ruled German Democratic Republic. Although Addi's title to the properties was recognized, the GDR would not allow him to exercise effective rights of ownership, nor collect the rents. Even after the fall of the Berlin wall in 1989 and the reunification of Germany, many years of legal proceedings ensued before the properties were returned. The restoration was not, how-ever, to Addi but to his estate, as he had died in Jerusalem in 1995.

Under Soviet rule, Krakovets fell into a deep slumber. It was literally at the end of the road, up against the border with Poland. Behind the scenes it remained a strategic point of interest to the great powers. In April 1962, during a dangerous phase of the Cold War, the CIA sus-pected that the Soviets had set up a medium-range ballistic missile launch site near Krakovets. At this time the United States had no aer-ial reconnaissance capability in the area: overflights of the USSR by US spy planes had been halted since 1960 when the Soviets had shot down an American U-2 over Soviet territory. In June 1962, however, photographs from a US space satellite revealed no evidence of such a missile site in the Krakovets area.[44] The CIA continued to keep its cameras focused on the Soviet border and in 1973 it noticed construc-tion of army barracks near the Krakovets waste disposal plant.[45] In

1981, at the height of an internal political crisis in Poland, when the Solidarity movement endangered Communist rule in the country, the Russians held the threat of invasion over the head of the Polish government 'as a deterrent to counter-revolution'.[46] The CIA reported that Krakovets was earmarked in Soviet military planning as a 'transit highway' for a potential advance against NATO on the 'Carpathian front'.[47] On 2 December Soviet forces actually crossed the border into Poland from Krakovets in what was officially termed a 'military exercise'.[48] Within days the Polish government succumbed to Soviet pressure, declared martial law, and suppressed Solidarity. The crisis was over and Krakovets relapsed into obscurity.

Like most towns in the region, Krakovets had been transformed. What remained of the lord's palace had been demolished. The surrounding estate gardens were empty fields. The 'privileges' that had been granted to the town by Polish kings were long forgotten. There was a hospital, a 'house of culture', a park – and not much else. The Roman Catholic church was repurposed as a tractor repair workshop, then as a bakery, later as a collective farm office. The synagogue became a cinema. The Greek Catholic church remained open but under Orthodox control. The market that for centuries had given the town its primary economic *raison d'être* had vanished. Apart from its function as a Soviet military outpost, Krakovets seemed to have little remaining purpose in existing. The population dwindled to barely a thousand. The Jews had been murdered, the Poles expelled. What had for several centuries been a multi-ethnic community was now almost entirely Ukrainian. The three fishes had been reduced to one.

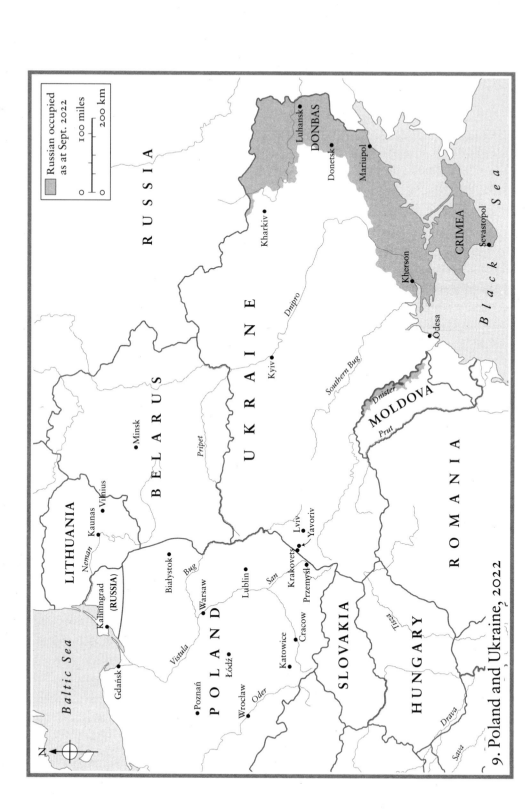

9. Poland and Ukraine, 2022

13
Return to Krakowiec

I remember the first time my father spoke to me directly about the deaths of my grandparents. It was on 25 August 1958. I was ten years old. We were on holiday in the south of France, our first overseas trip as a family. Addi was driving his much-treasured, elegant but elephantine Humber Hawk (at that period he would not think of buying anything but a British car) up a narrow, winding hill road to the mountain village of La Garde-Freinet where we were staying. He persisted in driving on the left-hand side of the road, not because he thought he was still in Britain but because he feared toppling over the steep slope on the other side. Every so often a speed merchant hurtling downhill in the other direction in a sports car would miraculously avoid smashing into us. Perhaps to calm himself down, my father switched on the car radio. An announcer reported the death the previous day of J. G. Strijdom, prime minister of South Africa. The news ignited a sudden explosion of wrath in my father. Surprised by this uncharacteristic eruption, I asked him to explain. He told me angrily that Strijdom was one of the architects of *apartheid* and that his party treated black people abominably. More than that, they had sympathized with the Nazis and it was their sort of outlook that had contributed to the murder of my grandparents during the war.

My reaction was one of shock. I had already been told my grandparents' story in outline by my mother, but my father had never before referred to it. Now it suddenly burst out unpremeditatedly as he rounded a hairpin bend on the wrong side of the road. I am sure he had not meant to tell me then or in that rough way. Under the extreme tension of driving conditions, the announcement of Strijdom's death must have triggered the memory of his mother's fruitless visit to South Africa in 1935 and of her honourable but tragic rejection of the idea of living there because of the racism of its white rulers. After that, he rarely spoke of his parents' fate again until I was an adult. He preferred to bury the traumatic events of the Nazi period in a grim, silent area of his consciousness.

Addi never received an official confirmation of his parents' and sister's deaths. The closest he ever got was a letter in Ukrainian from M. Kartashov, 'secretary of the district committee of workers' representatives', dispatched from Krakovets on 18 August 1945. This stated that Berl, Czarna and Lotte Wasserstein as well as Czarna's brother, Samuel Laub, his wife, Esther, and his daughter Regina, 'who lived in Krakovets in 1942/3, together with the entire Jewish population, were transported to the town of Jaworów. It is unknown to us what happened to them there.'[1] This served as a formal death notice, although, as we have seen, it was deficient both as a statement of what actually happened to Berl and his family and in its transparent attempt to shuffle off any responsibility for such dangerous knowledge.

For many years after the war, Addi refused to set foot in Germany. In the mid-1970s he overcame his repugnance sufficiently to spend an academic year in Heidelberg. Somewhat to his own surprise, he enjoyed it and came to respect much in the new (West) Germany, in particular the readiness, at any rate of many of the younger generation, to face the past unflinchingly.

In 1988 we met in Berlin and, together with my brother, strolled through some of my father's childhood haunts in Berlin Mitte, in what was then the Communist-controlled part of the city. That district had been so heavily bombed by the Allies that he found little that was recognizable. The house where he had lived as a child was gone: the entire street had been obliterated by Allied bombing.

Addi never evinced the slightest interest in revisiting the place where his parents were born and where they died. In July 1993, however, my brother and I returned to Krakovets. We returned, that is, to a place we had never been before. My father did not encourage us to embark on this expedition but he did not discourage it either. I think he understood that we could learn something, if only self-knowledge, by going there.

We went to Krakovets at almost the earliest moment that it was possible for us to do so. From the end of the Second World War until December 1991 Krakovets had been on the border between the Soviet Union and Poland. During the Cold War Soviet frontier areas were closed military zones into which foreign visitors could not normally enter. With the disintegration of the USSR, the town returned to a Ukrainian sovereignty that it had known only for a brief period in its modern history, after the First World War. Post-Communist Ukraine opened its borders to foreign visitors, particularly those carrying hard currency. Upon payment of the exorbitant visa fee of $113 each, our passports were stamped and we were told that, apart from the Sevastopol naval base in Crimea, we could go anywhere in the country that we pleased.

Why did we go? We did not do so, in the manner of some wanderers in the old world, in search of our roots. Those, at any rate the ones in Krakovets, had all been torn up. Our only intention, initially at any rate, was to say Kaddish, the memorial prayer for the dead – or so we told ourselves. Beforehand, we wrestled with the question of whether to go at all. The precise location of our grandparents' graves was unknown. The Kaddish could, in any case, be recited just as properly in Boston (my then home) or Jerusalem (my brother's) as at a graveside. Moreover, neither of us is deeply religious: the recitation of the prayer would be more an act of historical consciousness and familial homage than an expression of faith. Yet we sensed somehow that we had unfinished business in a place that had hovered at the edge of our awareness since our youth.

We set out for Krakovets by car from Lviv at 6 a.m. on a dreary, wet morning. Our journey took us past the decayed but still handsome neo-classical and Secession-style buildings of the Habsburg period in the city centre, past the statue of Taras Shevchenko and the opera house (a replica of the old Paris Opéra Garnier). In the suburbs the road paving turned to cobblestones, with many potholes. We drove past huge, concrete Soviet-era housing estates, already degenerating into grubby slums. The countryside beyond the city was dotted with cottages with corrugated tin roofs as well as further occasional blocks of apartments that seemed to have been dumped haphazardly in the middle of fields without any amenities.

Our first stop was at Jaworów, now Yavoriv, where we parked in what had been the market square. This was now a large, open space. Nazism had killed the Jewish traders; Communism had abolished the market. In spite of the fall of the Soviet Union, there was little sign of a revival of trading. In a covered area, a handful of peasant women squatted in front of small piles of fly-ridden fruit and vegetables. No buyers were in sight. Possibly the reason for inactivity was that it was a Greek Catholic holy day. Near the square we saw the town's largest church. It was immediately identifiable as Uniate by its distinctive golden onion-dome. Since 1989 the Greek Catholic church had re-emerged from its enforced union with Russian Orthodoxy, albeit with a new name: the Ukrainian Catholic Church of the Byzantine Rite. We saw many people in holiday clothing walking towards the church. Inside the recently restored building was a crowd of worshippers, their faces glowing with faith and illumined by hundreds of candles.

There was no trace of the former ghetto or synagogue.

We asked a bystander whether he knew where the forest of Porudenko was. That was the place to which Jews from the Jaworów ghetto, including former residents of Krakowiec, had been taken in April 1943 and shot. We were told that Porudenko was a village nearby and were given directions. In order to reach it, we had to turn off the main road on to what was little more than a dirt track. After a couple of miles of bumping along, we reached a few houses. An old woman approached, also apparently on her way to church. I enquired whether she knew the location of a large Jewish grave in a nearby forest. She immediately told us that it was at a place called in Ukrainian 'Six Hills', near the end of the road. We drove on, past shabby cottages, until we arrived at what was clearly the less favoured side of the village. Three peasant women came out of a tumbledown dwelling. It was drizzling but the oldest woman was walking barefoot in the mud, oblivious to the dirt. The women readily directed us to 'Six Hills' but seemed reluctant to accompany us there; perhaps they felt dread about approaching the place. A passer-by, a man in his mid-sixties, agreed to show us the way. We came to a small clearing in the forest. There was not much to see. The man told us he had lived in the vicinity all his life and that he remembered, as a boy, seeing 'the earth heave' at the spot after the massacre in April 1943.

We proceeded to Krakovets. Our first glimpse of the town was from the edge of the lake, a romantic view similar to that depicted in a lithograph published in the mid-nineteenth century (*see plate* 2). On closer inspection, however, the town was in a decrepit state. As in Yavoriv, the market square was empty – or rather it seemed to have returned to nature, since it was heavily overgrown with weeds, shrubs and trees. Not many people were around. A goose waddled over to a puddle. We identified the locations of some former landmarks such as the school and the old mill that had been leased from Countess Łubieńska by Lazar Kampel. That was now an empty space; we were told it had been demolished several years earlier.

The handsome façade of the Roman Catholic church was still standing, though minus its decorative portico. The building had been badly damaged in the war but was partly renovated. We found that the Communist authorities had committed an act of architectural vandalism: they attached the church to a plastics factory that they constructed immediately next door. The juxtaposition of the delicate classical frontage and the brutalist, concrete slabs of the factory was worse than incongruous: it seemed to compound the appalling act of sacrilege. A small chapel in the church had, however, been restored. We were told that about thirty people, mainly elderly Polish women married to Ukrainian men, gathered for mass every so often.

We asked some townsfolk whether the Jewish cemetery had survived. No, we were told, it had been destroyed by the Nazis. The tombstones had later been used to pave roads. A few had survived and had been kept nearby. We found them where they had been left, dumped in a pile in the corner of a field. It was a pathetic sight. Many were broken, some were half-buried. A handful were intact and we deciphered their Hebrew inscriptions, which ranged back to the early nineteenth century.

The former synagogue building still stood – after a fashion. It was now being used as a bakery with no sign of its former function. We asked to go in. The woman in charge at first resisted but eventually relented and allowed us to enter. She even inquired whether we would like to buy the business. I did not find the idea of re-establishing my great-grandfather Jacob's enterprise an enticing investment prospect.

By this time our presence had aroused the curious interest of some townsfolk. We were invited to the town hall, which consisted of two rooms above a bank. When we explained that we were descendants of former residents, we were ushered into the larger of the rooms. It was dominated by a Ukrainian flag and an oil painting of a man in uniform. This, we were told, was the Krakovets-born, Ukrainian freedom fighter Roman Shukhevych. I had not previously heard of him and learned only later of his record as a Nazi collaborator, anti-Soviet guerrilla leader and ethnic cleanser of Poles and Jews. We were greeted by the *vuit* (a kind of mayor) and offered cake.

After we left the municipal office, an elderly man showed us round the town and, with his help and that of old maps, we quickly identified the sites of our Laub and Wasserstein ancestors' homes. Neither existed any more in its original form (the houses on the square had suffered badly during wartime fighting). On ground abutting the main square, in front of where Jacob Wasserstein's house had once stood, was a small sign in Ukrainian: 'Here will be erected a statue to General Roman Shukhevych'.

At the town hall, a secretary had, at my request, recited to us a list of names of current inhabitants of the town. One of the names was Olanek – not Mikola Mikhailovich Olanek, who, we were informed, had died a year earlier, but his widow. In a way I was relieved. I am not at all sure what I would have done if the betrayer of my grandparents had still been alive. Would I have confronted him, interrogated him, or preferred not to encounter him at all?

For some reason the *vuit* seemed keen for us to visit the widow Olanek. So we called on her pitiable, tin-roofed cottage. She was the second wife of the late Mikola, having married him after the death of his previous spouse in 1961. As we arrived, she said, 'I have the feeling you have brought bad news.' I saw no reason to upset her by relating what we knew about her late husband, so I gave her no 'news' at all. We asked her some questions about Mikola's life history but she didn't know much about the period before they married. For reasons I cannot fathom, perhaps because I was the only person who had ever expressed much interest in her husband, she insisted on presenting me with a photograph of him. I was not sure whether to publish it in this book. Is there something to be learned from the facial features of such a man? I doubt it. But in the end, I decided to include it (*see plate 23*).

As we were standing in the street outside the town hall, one of the locals who had attached himself to us said, 'Here's a Jewish woman to talk to you.' An old lady appeared and addressed us excitedly in a mixture of Yiddish and Ukrainian. We asked her name. Her maiden name, she said, had been 'Grynszpan'. No, she explained, she was no relation of the young man whose assassination of a German diplomat in Paris in 1938 had provided the pretext for the Kristallnacht pogrom. She was not a native of Krakovets but had come there after the war and married a Ukrainian who was now dead. Her daughter lived in another town so that she was the last Jew left in Krakovets. Pathetically, she had half-forgotten her native tongue. As she struggled to pour out her life story, each of her sentences began in Yiddish, then collapsed into Ukrainian. I had the impression we were the first fellow-Jews she had encountered for many years. In the end she burst into tears.

We said Kaddish near the edge of the lake at what might have been the resting place of Berl, Czarna and Lotte (we were told that Jews who had been shot in the town were buried there) and left.

I visited Krakovets for a second time in the spring of 2019. In the intervening quarter century much had changed. The town looked somewhat more prosperous, evidently profiting from trade, legal and otherwise, at what was now a major crossing point for freight between Poland and Ukraine. Two or three shops were open. Many of the houses had been fixed up and extended.

In the beautifully refurbished, little Greek Catholic church, a group of women was preparing vestments for a forthcoming festival. On a mound nearby, the shell of a huge new church was in a state of half-completion. A caretaker showed me round and explained that parishioners were building it themselves but had run short of funds necessary to finish the work. I offered a token donation but this was spurned: I could only speculate as to the reason for refusal. Was it too trivial an amount? Was such a gift from a Jew unwelcome?

The former synagogue was no longer occupied. The roof had fallen in and trees were growing up through what had become a dilapidated and dangerous ruin. There was no sign to indicate the original purpose of the structure.

The site of the former manor house was an empty field. At ground level there was no vestige of the Xanadu that Ignacy Cetner had created there. I nevertheless had an intuition that some relic of it might yet remain. Later I recalled the work of the pioneering historian W. G. Hoskins, who used aerial photography in his study of the evolution of the English landscape – for example, to help him identify the locations and characteristics of abandoned medieval villages in Leicestershire.[2] Upon scrutinizing aerial photographs of Krakovets on Google Earth, I discovered that one could still discern, as if through a telescope into the past, faint outlines of former buildings on the lord's estate and of paths in what had been the famous garden.

The local school that my grandfather Berl had attended was still there, though it had been greatly extended and renamed the Roman Shukhevych school. I heard a babble of voices within. Entering, I found that the school director, Miroslav Kropevnytsky, was delivering a speech in the gymnasium at the conclusion of a sports event. He was standing in front of a bust of Roman Shukhevych and handed the winning team a trophy named after Shukhevych.

Later he welcomed me into his office, a shrine to the memory of the school's eponymous hero, and presented me with a eulogistic biography of same. He related a lengthy, glamorized account of Shukhevych's career and showed me a wall plaque recording the names of 'fighters for Ukrainian freedom' who hailed from the town. In one corner of the hall was what looked like a niche or sanctuary devoted to the Virgin Mary: it was dedicated not to the Mother of God but to a secular saint – Roman Shukhevych.

En passant, Mr Kropevnytsky informed me that Natalya Berezynska, Shukhevych's wife, had, with her husband's approval, sheltered a Jewish girl from the Nazis during the war. This, incidentally, is a claim that has been voiced repeatedly by promoters of the Shukhevych cult in Ukraine – for example by Moisei Fishbein (1946–2020), a Jewish writer who was frequently wheeled out for propagandistic purposes by Ukrainian nationalists.[3] There are, of course, many cases of murderers who have chosen to spare potential victims, for whatever political or psychological reasons. How to assess this plea in extenuation of Shukhevych – if that is how it should be seen? One essential step, of course, is to establish the facts. The recognized authority for examining the evidence and evaluating such claims on behalf of purported wartime rescuers of Jews is Yad Vashem, the Israeli Holocaust memorial institution. As of 2021, Natalya Berezynska was not one of the 2,673 Ukrainians honoured by Yad Vashem as 'righteous among the nations'.

Mr Kropevnytsky escorted me outside to the main thoroughfare, now renamed Roman Shukhevych Street. The former market place had been cleared of the undergrowth that was almost overwhelming it on my previous visit. Paths had been laid out, edged in the blue and yellow national colours. Near the centre of the square stood a large statue of Shukhevych that had been erected in 1996. Above it, in addition to Ukrainian national flags, a banner of the UPA fluttered in the breeze.

I subsequently learned that a ceremony is held in the square every year, at which veterans of the UPA congregate to salute their former commander, deliver patriotic speeches and sing the old songs. Later I watched the 2017 commemoration on YouTube. On that occasion the encomium was delivered by UPA veteran Petro Vushko. The effort proved too much for the 91-year-old: he collapsed while speaking and was pronounced dead on the spot.[4]

The flame of Roman Shukhevych was kept alive by the Ukrainian exile community in countless books and newspaper articles.[5] The thirty-one-year-long imprisonment by the Soviets of Roman's son, Yuriy, provided a living martyr to burnish the memory of the dead one. In the aftermath of restored Ukrainian independence in 1991, a veritable cult of Shukhevych emerged.[6] His image appeared on postage stamps and commemorative coins. The house where he was killed was turned into a museum, 'a site of outright Shukhevych and UPA veneration'.[7] A film sanitizing his crimes and glorifying his exploits appeared in 2000.[8] In 2007 President Viktor Yushchenko of Ukraine, a pro-western politician who had been catapulted to power three years earlier by the 'orange revolution', accorded Shukhevych the posthumous title of 'hero of Ukraine'. This designation in the centenary year of Shukhevych's birth provoked outrage, especially among Jews. Yushchenko, however, refused to rescind the award. Instead he dug in his heels and later issued a further 'hero of Ukraine' award to the no less notorious Stepan Bandera. Both awards were annulled only after Yushchenko left office.

The fall of the Soviet Union and the re-emergence of an independent Ukraine led to the rehabilitation of former members of the UPA and its affiliates. In 1993 a thousand veterans gathered in a park in Lviv to mark the fiftieth anniversary of the foundation of the SS 'Galizien' Division. This 'world congress' was notable for one omission: it 'dropped all references to the SS and called itself merely the Galicia division'.[9]

What to make of this glorification of Shukhevych? His devotees are undoubtedly sincere believers. But as Oscar Wilde observed, 'A little sincerity is a dangerous thing, and a great deal of it is absolutely fatal.' The Shukhevych cult is not just old soldiers' nostalgia for what they recall as their glory days. Nor is it merely a mythic device instrumentalized by nationalists to mobilize support. It is those things but more. Undoubtedly it responds to a felt need among a part of Ukraine's population, including some current residents of Krakovets, for what is sometimes called a 'usable past'. That their imagined hero bears only a passing resemblance to the actual historical figure is beside the point. The same might, after all, be said of Robin Hood, Joan of Arc, or, to take a more directly relevant case, Bogdan Khmelnytsky. Such mythopoeia is part and parcel of many nationalisms. Some might dismiss it as harmless exuberance. My view is that collective identities based on falsification of history are inherently contaminated and potentially dangerous. I struggled to contain my feelings as I contemplated the effigy of the war criminal towering over the square where several generations of my family had lived – and from which the Jews of the town were transported to their deaths.

Shortly after the liberation of Krakovets in 1944, a few surviving Jews set up an improvised memorial to the victims of the Shoah. It is pictured in a *yizkorbukh* (remembrance volume) published many years later in Israel.[10] For unaccounted reasons, that monument disappeared.

Today there is no memorial to its former Jewish inhabitants in Krakovets, apart from a wooden signpost placed in an empty field to mark the location of the former Jewish cemetery. The absence thus exhibited calls to mind a disturbing phrase in the apocryphal book of Ecclesiasticus: *And some there be, which have no memorial; who are perished, as though they had never been; and are become as though they had never been born; and their children after them.*[11] As the last words suggest, memorials are for the living no less than for the dead. We are the ones to whom such monuments might convey some kind of meaning and, perhaps, a modicum of comfort.

In the autumn of 2019, I returned to Krakovets again, this time with a small group of members of my extended family. With some difficulty, we found the scene of the massacre in the forest near Porudenko, where I had first been taken in 1993. There we discovered a small plaque commemorating the Jews of Jaworów and Krakowiec. It had been erected by the *landsmanshaft* of Jaworów Jews in Israel and marked the execution ground and burial place of Jews from the Jaworów ghetto who died in the massacre of April 1943. We gazed at it sombrely for a while and then recited the Kaddish together.

Yet even this modest token of remembrance was apparently too much for some local people. Comparative, or rather competitive, martyrology is a depressingly common feature of relations among peoples in our world. A few feet away, we noticed another memorial, this one to Ukrainian 'soldiers' (i.e. members of Shukhevych's UPA) said to have been executed in the same place by the Soviets. A long-burning candle was alight in front of this latter monument, as if to assert that Ukrainians, not Jews, were the true victims of this history and would have the last word.

What kind of future can Krakovets look forward to? Much depends, of course, on whether Ukraine can carve out a sustainable independence, caught as it is between the NATO alliance and a resurgent Russia determined to reassert dominance over its 'near abroad'. The town has few natural resources. The current effort to fashion it as some kind of tourist attraction, based on a manufactured version of history, seems doomed to failure. Can it develop into anything more than a frontier post and motorway service station on the road from Cracow to Lviv? Could a luxury resort hotel be built next to the lake? Might some Ukrainian oligarch seek to emulate Ignacy Cetner and invest a fortune in regenerating the town? A more credible prognosis is that Krakovets will continue to plod along without much change either for better or worse.

In a few towns in eastern Europe, derelict synagogues have been painstakingly restored at the initiative of former Jewish residents or their descendants. In the absence of Jewish communities, such buildings serve no current spiritual purpose. They function primarily as magnets for a kind of heritage tourism. In larger cities, such as Cracow, this has developed into a significant dollar-earning industry. No such prospect beckons in Krakovets, where the synagogue is a crumbling ruin and the handful of Jewish Krakowitzers in exile manifest no nostalgic yearning to reconstruct it.

In a famous passage in his *Theses on the Philosophy of History*, written in 1940, shortly before he committed suicide while on the run from the Nazis, Walter Benjamin wrote about the 'angel of history' whose

> face is turned toward the past. Where we perceive a chain of events, he sees one single catastrophe which keeps piling wreckage upon wreckage and hurls it in front of his feet. The angel would like to stay, awaken the dead, and make whole what has been smashed. But a storm is blowing from Paradise; it . . . irresistibly propels him into the future to which his back is turned, while the pile of debris before him grows skyward. This storm is what we call progress.[12]

I have spent the whole of my professional life as a historian but have encountered this angel only once. It did not appear as a vision but took corporeal form. By serendipity, this happened in Krakovets.

In 1993, towards the end of our first expedition to the town, my brother and I were groping through the thickets that had proliferated in the former market square. As we pushed aside the foliage, we suddenly came upon the angel – not a spectre but a marble cherub, delicately balanced on its pedestal. According to the Bible, when God expelled Adam from the Garden of Eden, He placed cherubim at the east of the garden 'to guard the way to the tree of life.' (Gen. 3: 24). The guardian angel of Krakovets was, in all probability, the last survivor of the pleasure garden of Ignacy Cetner. It is still there, albeit overshadowed by the gigantic statue of Shukhevych. The two stand in uneasy juxtaposition, their faces turned towards the wreckage of a troubled past, propelled backwards into an uncertain future.

Postscript

Suddenly, as this book goes to press, Krakovets once again finds itself at the eye of the storm. The Russian invasion of eastern and northern Ukraine on 24 February 2022 stirred up a tsunami of refugees sweeping westwards across the whole country. The border post at Krakovets was assailed by thousands of desperate people fleeing into Poland. In late February I clicked my computer screen to the 24-hour webcam at the crossing point and watched with astonishment as the horde of cars, buses and pedestrians, all proceeding in one direction, built into a tailback that stretched for ten miles along the highway from Lviv.

At first, the adjacent frontier with a NATO member state seemed to protect Krakovets from the Russian onslaught. But on 13 March thirty Russian cruise missiles were launched against a Ukrainian military base just north of Yavoriv (Jaworów), not far from Krakovets. A resident reported that 'the sky turned red'. Thirty-five people were killed. Further attacks on Lviv and other places in the vicinity indicated that no part of Ukraine was immune from attack. As Russian fury grew at the supply of advanced weaponry to Ukraine by Poland and other NATO countries, the threat to transit points such as Krakovets increased.

The war produced an extraordinary reversal in Polish–Ukrainian relations. The violent hostility of earlier times was replaced by an outpouring of neighbourliness and hospitality from Poles as millions of Ukrainians sought refuge from Russian attacks on civilian targets. Krakovets, for so long a military outpost of the Austrians, the Nazis and the Soviets, now became a kissing point where families separated or were reunited and where Ukrainians and Poles embraced their European brotherhood.

I must confess that my own feelings were mixed. On the one hand, I fully shared the general abhorrence at Russian aggression and brutality. I was reminded of a key moment in my political education, on 20 August 1968, when Soviet forces, with east European allies, invaded Czechoslovakia, snuffing out the 'Prague spring' and destroying the country's independence for the next two decades.

On the other hand, I also recalled one of the first political events of which I had been conscious. As a child in November 1956, I became aware that my mother's homeland, Hungary, was being subjected to Soviet military occupation. Massive sympathy for Hungarian resistance erupted in the west. Britain and other countries opened their doors to refugees. But when they arrived, some told unexpected stories: we learned that they were not only fleeing from the Russians. Jewish relatives recalled how anti-Semitic slogans of the old, nationalist, far right had reappeared, daubed on walls in Budapest. They feared that if the revolutionaries won and communism were overthrown, they would be plunged back into a terrible past. Their anxieties may have been exaggerated; but they were real and understandable. As we contemplate Viktor Orbán's regime in Hungary today, with its authoritarian, xenophobic outlook, tinged with anti-Semitism, we might conclude that they were not all that mistaken.

Of course, Russian claims about 'Nazis' in Ukraine are outrageous black propaganda. Ukraine today is a democracy, albeit a fragile one, beset by corruption and not much less kleptocratic than Russia. Ultra-nationalist forces, such as those recruited into the famous 'Azov Battalion' that, as I write, is making a final stand in Mariupol, represent only a small fraction of society. But it looks ominously as if this war will persist for a long time. As the Russians continue to pummel homes, schools, railway stations and hospitals across the country, and as the west bolsters Ukrainian resistance with an inexhaustible supply of arms and other support, a natural consequence must be to boost nationalist feeling in both Russia and Ukraine. If Putin prevails, we may look forward to a victory parade in Red Square. If Ukraine overcomes the invader, may we expect a procession past the garlanded statue of Roman Shukhevych in Krakovets? Such a prospect is quite conceivable and fills me with unease.

In 2023 Krakovets will mark six centuries since its foundation. For much of that time it was a peaceful backwater, barely ruffled by out-side influences. At other periods, as now, it was assaulted by tumultuous, uncontainable forces that aroused hatred and bloodlust and wreaked devastating havoc.

I pray that the people of Ukraine will surmount this terrible ordeal. Resistance against a hostile invader must be a common cause for all who share humane values. My ancestors' home is not my home; yet immersed as I have been for so long in its history, Krakovets has a special place in my consciousness. Will it suffer the fate of Mariupol and other towns that have been almost obliterated by the invaders? The auguries are grim and I am fearful as to what I might find if I ever visit Krakovets again. At any rate, my task is now discharged: I have unveiled the history of the town, its people, and its intimate, tortured relationship with my family. It has taken this book and this crisis to enable me finally to come to terms with the shrouded references in my childhood to that 'little place you've never heard of'.

Amsterdam

May 2022

Sources

FAMILY PAPERS

ARCHIVES

American Jewish Joint Distribution Committee archives, New York and Jerusalem
Archiwum Akt Nowych, Warsaw
Archiwum Główne Akt Dawnych, Warsaw
Archiwum Głowne Urszulanek SJK, Pniewy
Archiwum Państwowe w Krakowie
Archiwum Państwowe w Przemyślu
Bundesarchiv, Koblenz/Berlin/Freiburg
Central Archives for the History of the Jewish People, Jerusalem
Central Zionist Archives, Jerusalem
Derzhavnyi arkhiv L'vivs'koi oblasti
Entschädigungsamt, Berlin
Haluzevyy derzhavnyy arkhiv SB Ukrayiny
Harvard Law School Library
Hoover Institution Archives, Stanford, California
International Tracing Service Archive, Arolsen
Israel State Archives, Jerusalem
Jagiellonian University Library manuscript dept., Cracow
Jewish Historical Institute archive, Warsaw
Landesarchiv Berlin
Leo Baeck Institute Archive, New York
Library of Congress, Washington DC
Lvivska natsionalna naukova biblioteka imeni V. Stefanyka
Österreichisches Staatsarchiv, Vienna
Polish Institute and Sikorski Museum archive, London
Rossiiskii gosudarstvennyi voennyi arkhiv

Polish Underground Movement Study Trust, London
State Archive of the Russian Federation, Moscow
State Historical Archive of Ukraine, Lviv
UK National Archives, Kew
United States Holocaust Memorial Museum Archive, Washington DC
United States National Archives, Washington DC
Wiener Library archive, London
Yad Vashem Archives, Jerusalem
YIVO archive, New York

INTERVIEWS

(a) Interviews conducted by the author

Aharon Berg, Kibbutz Mishmar Hasharon, 1994
Yisrael and Dov Berg, Tel Aviv, 1995
Israel Getzler, London, 1993
Elimelech Glick, Rishon le-Tsiyyon, 1995
Mala Gottlieb, Jerusalem, 1995
(forename unclear) Grynszpan, Krakovets, 1993
Anna Kozak, Krakovets, 1993
Miroslav Kropevnytsky, Krakovets, 2019
Berl Lax, Lakewood, N.J., 1996
Hela Laub, Jerusalem, 1996
Sonia Levensolt, Ramat Gan, 1994
Frejde Nacht, Gan Yavne, 1995
Shmuel Nacht, Rishon le-Tsiyyon, 1995
Eli Silberman, Brooklyn, N.Y, 1996
Volodymir Shkondra, Krakovets, 1993
Oksana Ivanivna Strus, Krakovets, 2019
Sara Tenenbojm, Netanya, 1995
Abraham Wasserstein, Oxford/London, 1993

(b) Other interviews

Klara Bielec (*née* Bogen), USC Shoah Foundation, Wrocław, 1997
Shalom Bierman, USC Shoah Foundation, Berlin, 1996
Leah Binstock, USC Shoah Foundation, Cleveland, 1996
Frieda Blum, USC Shoah Foundation, Givatayim, 1995

Rafal Dominic, USC Shoah Foundation, Toronto, 1995
Mark Geller, USC Shoah Foundation, Montreal, 2013
Yehuda Goldman, Yad Vashem, Jerusalem, 4 August 1948
Herzl and Mala Gottlieb (interviewer: Jane Grossberg), Melbourne, 1993
Jonas Kampel (interviewer: David J. Wasserstein), Jerusalem, 1993
Stefania Kupfer, USC Shoah Foundation, Paris, 1996
Leon Scher, USC Shoah Foundation, La Cañada, Calif., 1996
Jacob Schreiber, USC Shoah Foundation, Albany, NY, 1997
Esther Sperling-Mayden, USC Shoah Foundation, Boca Raton, 1996
Ben Steltzer, USC Shoah Foundation, Lincolnwood, Ill., 1995
Zelda Susser (interviewer: David J. Wasserstein), 1994/5
Sabina Sweidan (interviewer: Barbara Meyerowitz), USC Shoah Foundation, 1996

WRITTEN TESTIMONIES

Jonas Beer and Włodzimierz Hochberg (no date given), Jewish Historical Institute, Warsaw
Antoni Budzianowski (Hoover Institution Archives, Poland, Min. Inf. Box 138, Folder 2)
Tslila Harari, Haifa, 24 August 1995 (letter to author)
Jonas Kampel, unpublished memoir, undated, Johannesburg
Jack Baruch Keil, Leo Baeck Institute, New York, no date given
Ahron Klahr, Mościska, 12 January 1948, Yad Vashem archive, Jerusalem
Julius Kühl recollections, Los Angeles Museum of the Holocaust
David Majus, 12 January 2002 (communication to author)
Israel (Ignacy) Manber, Jewish Historical Institute, Warsaw, 12 July 1946
Juda Metzler, Jewish Historical Institute, Warsaw, Chorzów, no date given
Mira Ringel (Lichtenholtz), Yad Vashem, Jerusalem, 2 March 1948
Miriam Rosenblum, Yad Vashem, Jerusalem, August 1974

WEBSITES

https://www.cia.gov/readingroom/
The Ledóchowski family: http://www.ledochowski.eu/rodzina/index.html
'Return to Krakowiec' (Laub family video): https://www.youtube.com/watch?v=wo5NRMZhQhI (no longer available)

DISSERTATIONS

Bacon, Ewa Katherine, 'Austrian Economic Policy in Galicia 1772–1790', University of Chicago PhD, 1975

Dunagan, Curt, 'The Lost World of Przemyśl: Interethnic Dynamics in a Galician Center, 1868–1921', Brandeis University PhD, 2009

Ostapchuk, Matthew R., '"Glory to Ukraine! Glory to the heroes!" The Portrayal of the Organization of Ukrainian Nationalists (OUN) in the Museums of Lviv', University of Alberta MA, 2015

Sorokowski, Andrew Dennis, 'The Greek Catholic Parish Clergy in Galicia, 1900–1939', School of Slavonic and East European Studies, London University PhD, 1991

Wojnowski, Zbigniew, 'Patriotism and the Soviet Empire: Ukraine Views the Socialist States of Eastern Europe, 1956–1985', University College London PhD, 2011

PRINCIPAL PUBLISHED SOURCES
Official Publications

Austria

Glaise-Horstenau, Edmund, et al., eds., *Österreich-Ungarns letzter Krieg, 1914–1918*, vols. 1 & 2 (Vienna, 1930–31)

Österreichische Statistik (Vienna, 1882–1916)

Sprawozdanie Stenograficzne z Rozpraw Galicyjskiego Sejmu Krajowego (Lwów, 1861–1914)

Great Britain

Documents on British Foreign Policy 1919–1939

Report by Sir Stuart Samuel on his Mission to Poland (Cmd. 674, London, 1920)

USA

Foreign Relations of the United States

Vatican

Blet, Pierre, et al., eds., *Actes et documents du Saint Siège relatifs à la seconde guerre mondiale*, 11 vols., (Vatican, 1965–81)

Books and Articles

Anon. [Alphons Heinrich Traunpaur, Chevalier d'Orphanie], *Dreyßig Briefe über Galizien oder Beobachtungen eines unpartheyischen Mannes der sich mehr als nur ein paar Monate in diesem Königreiche umgesehen hat* (Berlin, 1990 [1st ed., Vienna, 1787])

Abramsky, Chimen, Jachimczyk, Maciej, and Polonsky, Antony, eds., *The Jews in Poland* (Oxford, 1986)

Abramson, Henry, *A Prayer for the Government: Ukrainians and Jews in Revolutionary Times, 1917–1920* (Cambridge, Mass., 1999)

Adamska, Barbara, 'Portret Anny z Cetnerów', *Skarby Podkarpackie* 36: 1 (2015), 30–2

Adlgasser, Franz, ed., *Die Aehrenthals: Eine Familie in ihrer Korrespondenz 1872-1911* (2 vols., Vienna, 2002)

Aftanazy, Roman, *Dzieje rezydencji na dawnych kresach Rzeczypospolitej* (2nd rev. ed., 11 vols., Wrocław, 1991–97), vol. 8: entry on Krakowiec, 53–63

Aly, Götz, et al., eds., *Die Verfolgung und Ermordung der europäischen Juden durch das nationalsozialistische Deutschland, 1933–1945* (16 vols., Munich, 2008), 21

Amar, Tarik Cyril, *The Paradox of Ukrainian Lviv: A Borderland City between Stalinists, Nazis, and Nationalists* (Ithaca, NY, 2015)

Anderson, Truman O., 'Germans, Ukrainians and Jews: Ethnic Politics in *Heeresgebiet Süd*, June–December 1941', *War in History*, 7: 3 (2000), 325–51

Ansky, S., *The Enemy at his Pleasure: A Journey Through the Jewish Pale of Settlement During World War I* (*Khurbn Galitsye*, ed. and trans. Joachim Neugroschel, New York, 2002)

Anusik, Zbigniew, 'Krótkie życie i niespodziewana śmierć młodego magnata. Janusz Paweł ks. Ostrogski i jego testament z 6 sierpnia 1619 roku', *Przegląd Nauk Historycznych*, 19: 1 (2020), 215–39

Arad, Yitzhak, Gutman, Israel, and Margaliot, Abraham, eds., *Documents on the Holocaust* (8th ed., Lincoln, Neb., 1999)

Armstrong, John A., *Ukrainian Nationalism 1939–1945* (3rd ed., Englewood, Col., 1990)

Arneth, Alfred Ritter von, ed., *Maria Theresia und Joseph II: Ihre Correspondenz sammt Briefen Joseph's an seinen Bruder Leopold*, Bd. II 1773–Juli 1778 (Vienna, 1867)

Arski, Stefan, and Chudek, Józef, eds., *Galicyjska działalność wojskowa Piłsudskiego, 1906–1914: dokumenty* (Warsaw, 1967)

Aschheim, Steven E., *Brothers and Strangers: The East European Jew in German and German Jewish Consciousness, 1800–1923* (Madison, Wis., 1982)

Aster, Howard, and Potichnyj, Peter J., eds., *Ukrainian-Jewish Relations in Historical Perspective* (2nd ed., Edmonton, 1990, 3rd ed., Edmonton, 2010)

Auffenberg-Komarów, Moriz [*sic*] Freiherr von, *Aus Österreichs Höhe und Niedergang: eine Lebensschilderung* (Munich, 1921)

Baker, Mark, 'Lewis Namier and the Problem of Eastern Galicia', *Journal of Ukrainian Studies*, 23: 2 (1998), 59–104

Barkai, Avraham, *From Boycott to Annihilation: The Economic Struggle of German Jews 1933–1943* (Hanover, NH, 1989)

Bar-Lev, N., ed., *Matsevet zikaron le-kehilat yavorov ve-ha-sevivah* (Haifa, 1979)

Bartal, Israel, and Polonsky, Antony, eds., *Polin: Studies in Polish Jewry*, vol. 12 *Focusing on Galicia: Jews, Poles, and Ukrainians 1772–1918* (London, 1999)

Bartov, Omer, *Erased: Vanishing Traces of Jewish Galicia in Present-Day Ukraine* (Princeton, NJ, 2007)

_____, *Anatomy of a Genocide: The Life and Death of a Town Called Buczacz* (New York, 2018)

_____, and Weitz, Eric D., eds., *Shatterzone of Empires: Coexistence and Violence in the German, Habsburg, Russian, and Ottoman Borderlands* (Bloomington, Ind., 2013)

Bauer, Yehuda, *The Death of the Shtetl* (New Haven, 2009)

Beales, Derek, *Joseph II* (2 vols., Cambridge, 1987 & 2009)

Bedriy, Anatole W., 'An Exemplary Freedom-Fighter: On the 20th anniversary of the Death of Roman Shukhevych (Taras Chuprynka)', *Ukrainian Review*, 1 (1970), 6–18

Berkhoff, Karel C., and Carynnyk, Marco, 'The Organization of Ukrainian Nationalists and Its Attitude toward Germans and Jews: Iaroslav Stets'ko's 1941 *Zhyttiepys*', *Harvard Ukrainian Studies*, 23: 3/4 (1999), 149–84

Bernacki, Ludwik, 'Materiały do życiorysu i twórczości Ignacego Krasickiego' *Pamiętnik Literacki*, 26 (1929) & 28 (1931).

Bernard, Paul P., *From the Enlightenment to the Police State: The Public Life of Johann Anton Pergen* (Urbana, Ill., 1991)

Bertelsen, Olga, and Shkandrij, Myroslav, 'The Secret Police and the campaign against Galicians in Soviet Ukraine, 1929–1934', *Nationalities Papers: The Journal of Nationalism and Ethnicity*, 42: 1 (2014), 37–62

Betlej, A., 'Kościoł parafialny p. w. Św Jakuba Apostola (większego) w Krakowcu', in Ostrowski, J. K., ed., *Materiały do dziejów sztuki sakralnej na ziemiach wschodnich dawnej Rzeczypospolitej, pars I: Kościoły i klasztory rzymskokatolickie dawnego województwa ruskiego*, vol. 3 (Cracow, 1995), 95–108

Biale, David, et al., *Hasidism: A New History* (Princeton, 2018)

Binder, Harald, 'Making and Defending a Polish Town: "Lwów" (Lemberg) 1848–1918', *Austrian History Yearbook*, 34 (2003), 57–81

Blumenbach, Wenzel Carl Wolfgang, *Neuestes Gemälde der Oesterreichischen Monarchie*: vol. 3 (Vienna, 1833)

Bostel, Ferdynand, *Żydzi ziemi lwowskiej i powiatu żydaczowskiego w r. 1765* (Cracow, 1891)

Bothe, Alina, 'Forced over the Border: The Expulsion of Polish Jews from Germany in 1938/39', *Jahrbuch des Simon Dubnows Instituts*, vol. 16 (Leipzig, 2019), 267–88

Bourgoing, Jean de, ed., *Briefe Kaiser Franz Josephs an Frau Katharina Schratt* (Vienna, 1949)

Brawer, A. J., *Galizien wie es an Österreich kam: Eine historisch-statistische Studie über die inneren Verhältnisse des Landes im Jahre 1772* (Leipzig, 1910)

Bredetzky, Samuel, *Reisebemerkungen über Ungarn und Galizien*, vol. 2 (Vienna, 1809)

Brustin-Berenstein, Tatiana, 'Der protses fun farnikhtn di yidishe yishuvim oyfn shetakh fun azoy gerufenem "distrikt galitsyen"', *Bleter far geshikhte*, 6: 3 (1953), 45–153

_____, *Eksterminacja ludności żydowskiej w Dystrykcie Galicja (1941–1943)* (Warsaw, 1967)

_____, 'Jüdische Soziale Selbsthilfe' in Gruner, Wolf, ed., *Arbeitsmarkt und Sondererlass. Menschenverwertung, Rassenpolitik und Arbeitsamt* (Berlin, 1990), 156–74

Buchen, Tim, *Antisemitism in Galicia: Agitation, Politics, and Violence against Jews in the Late Habsburg Monarchy* (New York, 2020)

Budzyński, Zdzisław, *Ludność pogranicza polsko-ruskiego w drugiej połowie xviii wieku* (2 vols., Przemyśl, 1993)

_____, and Przyboś, Kazimierz, eds., *Rejestr poborowy ziemi przemyskie z 1628 r.*, (Rzeszów, 1997)

_____, *Rejestr poborowy ziemi przemyskie z 1651 r.* (Rzeszów, 1997)

Burds, Jeffrey, 'AGENTURA: Soviet Informants' Networks and the Ukrainian Underground in Galicia, 1944–48', *East European Politics and Societies*, 11: 1 (1997), 89–130

_____, 'Gender and Policing in Soviet West Ukraine, 1944–1948', *Cahiers du Monde russe*, 42: 2/3/4 (2001), 279–320

Butterwick, Richard, *Poland's Last King and English Culture: Stanisław August Poniatowski, 1732–1798* (Oxford, 1998)

Chasanowitch, L., ed., *Les Pogromes Anti-Juifs en Pologne et en Galicie en Novembre et Décembre 1918: Faits et Documents* (Stockholm, 1919)

Chernetsky, Vasyl, *Krakovets* (n. p., 1899)

Chłędowski, Kazimierz, *Pamiętniki*, vol. 1 *Galicja (1843–1880)* (Wrocław, 1957)

Churchill, Winston, *The Unknown War: The Eastern Front* (New York, 1931)

Ciolek, Gerard, *Gärten in Polen: I Teil: Inhalts- und Gestaltsentwicklung* (Warsaw, 1954)

Cohen, Israel, *Travels in Jewry* (London, 1952)

Cohn, Samuel K., *Epidemics: Hate and Compassion from the Plague of Athens to AIDS* (Oxford, 2018)

Conrad von Hötzendorf, Franz, *Aus meiner Dienstzeit 1906–1918* (5 vols., Vienna, 1921–25)

Coppa, Frank J., 'The Hidden Encyclical of Pius XI Against Racism and Anti-Semitism Uncovered – Once Again!', *Catholic Historical Review*, 84: 1 (1998), 63–72

Corrsin, Stephen C., 'Literacy Rates and Questions of Language, Faith and Ethnic Identity in Population Censuses in the Partitioned Polish Lands and Interwar Poland (1880s–1930s)', *Polish Review*, 43: 2 (1998), 131–60

Davies, Norman, *White Eagle, Red Star: The Polish–Soviet War 1919–20 and the 'Miracle on the Vistula'* (London, 1972)

_____, 'Great Britain and the Polish Jews, 1918–20', *Journal of Contemporary History*, 8: 2 (1973), 119–42

_____, *God's Playground: A History of Poland*, 2 vols. (New York, 1982)

_____, and Polonsky, Antony, eds., *Jews in Eastern Poland and the USSR, 1939–1946* (New York, 1991)

Dean, Martin, *Collaboration in the Holocaust: Crimes of the Local Police in Belorussia and Ukraine, 1941–1944* (New York, 2000)

Des Noyers, Pierre, *Lettres de Pierre Des Noyers secrétaire de la reine de Pologne Marie-Louise de Gonzague . . . pour servir à l'histoire de Pologne et de Suède de 1655 à 1659* (Berlin, 1859)

Döblin, Alfred, *Journey to Poland* (trans. Joachim Neugroschel, London, 1991)

Dobroszycki, Lucjan, and Gurock, Jeffrey S., eds., *The Holocaust in the Soviet Union: Studies and Sources on the Destruction of the Jews in the Nazi-Occupied Territories of the USSR, 1941–1945* (Armonk, NY, 1993)

Druk, S., *Yudenshtot yavorov: der umkum fun di yavorover yidn* (New York, 1950)

Edele, Mark, Fitzpatrick, Sheila, and Grossmann, Atina, eds., *Shelter from the Holocaust: Rethinking Jewish Survival in the Soviet Union* (Detroit, 2017)

Edwards, Robert, *Scouts Out: A History of German Armored Reconnaissance Units in World War II* (Mechanicsburg, Penn., 2013)

Eisenbach, Artur, *The Emancipation of the Jews in Poland, 1780–1870* (trans. Janina Dorosz, Oxford, 1991)

Engel, David, *In the Shadow of Auschwitz: The Polish Government-in-Exile and the Jews, 1939–1942* (Chapel Hill, 1987)

_____, 'Who is a Collaborator? The Trials of Michael Weichert', in Kapralsky, Sławomir, ed., *The Jews in Poland*, vol. II (Cracow, 1999), 339–70

Engel, Rudolf, *Geschichte des k. und k. Infanterieregiments Philipp Herzog von Württemberg Nr. 77, von der Errichtung 1860 bis 1906* (Przemyśl, 1906)

Feldman, Gerald D., *Allianz and the German Insurance Business, 1933–1945* (New York, 2001)

Finder, Gabriel N., and Prusin, Alexander V., 'Collaboration in Eastern Galicia: The Ukrainian Police and the Holocaust', *East European Jewish Affairs*, 34: 2 (2004), 95–118

Fischer, Rolf, *Verfolgung und Vernichtung: Die Dortmunder Opfer der Shoah* (Essen, 2015)

Fleischer, Rudolf, 'Rückzug nach Przemysl im Herbst 1914 (Erinnerungen eines Truppenoffiziers)', *Militärwissenschaftliche und technische Mitteilungen*, 55 (1924), 18–26 & 120–9

Friedländer, Saul, *Nazi Germany and the Jews* (2 vols., New York, 1997 & 2007)

Friedman, Philip, *Roads to Extinction: Essays on the Holocaust* (Philadelphia, 1980)

Fuks, Tania, *A vanderung iber okupirte gebitn* (Buenos Aires, 1947)

Gelber, N. M., 'The National Autonomy of Eastern-Galician Jewry in the West-Ukrainian Republic, 1918–1919' in Isaac Lewin and N. M. Gelber eds., *A History of Polish Jewry during the Revival of Poland* (New York, 1990)

Gengler, J., 'Ornithologische Beobachtungen aus Österreichisch-Schlesien, Ungarn, und Galizien', *Verhandlungen-Ornith-Ges-Bayern*, 12 (1914–1916), 215–37

Ginsberg, Ben-Tsiyon, 'Nito mit vos zikh tsu shehmen als galitsyaner', *Der Galitsyaner Yorbukh* (New York, 1939), 21–4

Glatz, Ludwig, *Galizien* (Vienna, 1864)

Goebbels, Joseph, *Die Tagebücher von Joseph Goebbels*, Part I, vol. 9 (ed. Elke Fröhlich, Munich, 1998)

Golczewski, Frank, 'Shades of Grey: Reflections on Jewish–Ukrainian and German–Ukrainian Relations in Galicia', in Ray Brandon and Wendy Lower eds., *The Shoah in Ukraine: History, Testimony, Memorialization* (Bloomington, Ind., 2008), 114–55

Gombin, Krzystof, 'Lwów w ceremoniale Trybunału Koronnego prowincji małopolskiej', *Annales UMCS, Artes* 8: 2 (2010), 27–41

Górska, Maria, *Gdybym mniej kochała: dziennik lat 1889–1895* (Warsaw, 1996)

Gotfryd, Anatol, *Der Himmel in den Pfützen: Ein Leben zwischen Galizien und dem Kurfürstendamm* (Berlin, 2005)

Gottesfeld, Chone, *Mayn rayze iber galitsye* (New York, 1937)

Gross, Jan Tomasz, *Polish Society under German Occupation: The General-gouvernement, 1939–1944* (Princeton, 1979)

_____, *Revolution from Abroad: The Soviet Conquest of Poland's Western Ukraine and Western Belorussia* (Princeton, 2002)

Gutman, Yisrael, et al., eds., *The Jews in Poland Between Two World Wars* (Hanover, NH, 1989)

Hagen, William W., 'The Moral Economy of Popular Violence: The Pogrom in Lwów, November 1918', in Robert Blobaum ed., *Antisemitism and Its Opponents in Modern Poland* (Ithaca, NY, 2005), 124–47

_____ *Anti-Jewish Violence in Poland, 1914–1920* (Cambridge, 2018)

Hann, Christopher, and Magocsi, Paul Robert, *Galicia: A Multicultured Land* (Toronto, 2005)

Harasiewicz, Michael (Baron von Neustern), *Annales Ecclesiae Ruthenae gratiam et communionem cum s. Sede Romana habentis, ritumque Graeco-Slavicum observantis, cum singulari respectu ad dioeceses ruthenas Leopoliensem, Premisliensem et Chelmensem* (Stauropegion Institute, Lwów, 1862)

Harris, Bonnie M., 'From German Jews to Polish Refugees: Germany's Polenaktion and the Zbąszyń Deportations of October 1938', *Kwartalnik Historii Żydów*, 2: 230 (2009), 175–205

Hartglas, Maximilian Meir Apolinary, ed., *Shoat yehudei Polin* (Jerusalem, 1940)

Hauser, Zbigniew, 'Krakowiec', *Spotkania z Zabytkami*, 52/2002, 20–1

Hayton, D. W., *Conservative Revolutionary: The Lives of Lewis Namier* (Manchester, 2019)

Heller, Celia, *On the Edge of Destruction: Jews of Poland between the Two World Wars* (Detroit, 1994)

Herbert, Ulrich, *Best: Biographische Studien über Radikalismus, Weltanschauung und Vernunft 1903–1989* (Bonn 1996)

Hilberg, Raul, *Perpetrators, Victims, Bystanders: The Jewish Catastrophe 1933–1945* (London, 1993)

_____, *The Destruction of the European Jews* (3rd ed., 3 vols., New Haven, 2003)

Himka, John-Paul, 'Serfdom in Galicia', *Journal of Ukrainian Studies*, 9: 2 (1984), 3–28

_____, *Galicia and Bukovina: A Research Handbook About Western Ukraine, Late 19th and 20th Centuries* (Edmonton, Alberta, 1990)

_____, 'Western Ukraine between the Wars', *Canadian Slavonic Papers*, 34: 4 (1992), 391–412

_____, 'Ukrainian Collaboration in the Extermination of the Jews during World War II', *Studies in Contemporary Jewry*, vol. 13 (1997), 170–89

_____, 'The Lviv Pogrom of 1941: The Germans, Ukrainian Nationalists, and the Carnival Crowd', *Canadian Slavonic Papers*, 53: 2/4 (2011), 209–43

_____, 'Metropolitan Andrey Sheptytsky and the Holocaust', *Polin: Studies in Polish Jewry*, vol. 26 (2014), 337–59

_____, 'Former Ukrainian Policemen in the Ukrainian National Insurgency: Continuing the Holocaust Outside German Service', in Wendy Lower and Lauren Faulkner Rossi eds., *Lessons and Legacies XII: New Directions in Holocaust Research and Education* (Evanston, Ill., 2017), 141–63

_____, *Ukrainian Nationalists and the Holocaust: OUN and UPA's Participation in the Destruction of Ukrainian Jewry, 1941–1944* (Stuttgart, 2021)

Hoelzl, Karl, 'Botanische Beiträge aus Galizien', *Verhandlungen der k. k. zoologisch-botanische Gesellschaft in Wien*, 11 (1861), 149–60

Horn, Maurycy, *Żydzi na Rusi Czerwonej w XVI i perwszej połowie XVII w.* (Warsaw, 1975)

Hoszowski, Stanisław, *Ceny we Lwówie w latach 1701–1914* (Lwów, 1934)

Hryniuk, Stella, 'Peasant Agriculture in East Galicia in the Late Nineteenth Century', *Slavonic and East European Review*, 63: 2 (1985), 228–43

_____, 'Polish Lords and Ukrainian Peasants: Conflict, Deference and Accommodation in Eastern Galicia in the Late 19th Century', *Austrian History Yearbook*, 24 (1993), 119–32

Hundert, Gershon, *Jews in Poland-Lithuania in the Eighteenth Century: A Genealogy of Modernity* (Berkeley, 2004)

Iwańska, Katarzyna, 'Geneza rodu mjr. Aleksandra Iwańskiego, przebieg jego służby wojskowej i życie rodzinne', *Wadoviana. Przegląd historyczno-kulturalny*, 17 (2014), 52–86

Janeczek, Andrzej, 'Miasta prywatne na Rusi Koronnej do końca XV wieku', *Roczniki Dziejów Społecznych i Gospodarczych*, 77 (2016) 143–78

Janusz, Bohdan, *Zabytki przedhistoryczne Galicyi Wschodniej* (Lwów, 1918)

Jaworski, Franciszek, *Lwów: stary i wczorajszy: szkice i opowiadania* (Lwów, 1910)

Jonca, Karol, 'The Expulsion of Polish Jews from the Third Reich in 1938', *Polin: Studies in Polish Jewry*, vol. 8 (1994), 255–81

Judson, Peter, *The Habsburg Empire: A New History* (Cambridge, Mass., 2016)

Kagan, Berl, *Seyfer ha-prenumerantn: vegvayzer tsu prenumerirte hebreyishe sforim* (New York, 1975)

Kalik, Judith, *Scepter of Judah: The Jewish Autonomy in the Eighteenth-Century Crown Poland* (Leiden, 2009)

Karniel, Josef, 'Das Toleranzpatent Kaiser Josephs II fuer die Juden Galiziens und Lodomeriens', *Jahrbuch des Instituts fuer Deutsche Geschichte* (Tel Aviv University), 11 (1982), 55–89

Karpiński, Franciszek, *Pamiętniki* (Poznań, 1844)

Katz, Jacob, *With My Own Eyes: The Autobiography of a Historian* (Hanover, NH, 1995)

Keith, James Francis Edward, *A Fragment of a Memoir of Field-Marshal James Keith Written by Himself* (Edinburgh, 1843)

Kertzer, David I., *The Pope and Mussolini: The Secret History of Pius XI and the Rise of Fascism in Europe* (New York, 2014)

Kiebuzinski, Ksenya, and Motyl, Alexander, eds., *The Great West Ukrainian Prison Massacre of 1941* (Amsterdam, 2017)

Kiryk, Feliks, ed., *Żydzi w Małopolsce* (Przemyśl, 1991)

Klein-Pejšová, Rebekah, 'Beyond the "Infamous Concentration Camps of the Old Monarchy": Jewish Refugee Policy from Wartime Austria-Hungary to Interwar Czechoslovakia', *Austrian History Yearbook*, 45 (2014), 150–66

Knapp, Josef Armin, *Die bisher bekannten Pflanzen Galiziens und der Bukowina* (Vienna, 1872)

Komornicki, Stefan, *24 Pułk Ułanow: zarys historii 1920–1947* (London, 1976)

Konopczyński, Władysław, 'Ignacy Cetner', in *Polski Słownik Biograficzny*, vol. 3 (Cracow, 1937), 238–39

Kopstein, Jeffrey S., and Wittenberg, Jason, *Intimate Violence: Anti-Jewish Pogroms on the Eve of the Holocaust* (Ithaca, NY, 2018)

Korzec, Paweł, and Szurek, Jean-Charles, 'Jews and Poles under Soviet Occupation (1939–1941): Conflicting Interests', *Polin: Studies in Polish Jewry*, 4 (1989), 204–25

Koter, Marek, ' "Kresy" as a Specific Type of Borderland – Its Origin and Characteristics', *Geographica Slovenica*, 34: 1 (2001), 131–48

Krasicki, Ignacy, *Korespondencja Ignacego Krasickiego*, eds. Zbigniew Goliński et al. (2 vols., Wrocław, 1958)

Kravtsiv, Bohdan, *Liudyna i voiak: v druhu rychnytsiu smerty* sl. p. *Romana Shukhevycha-Chuprynky* (New York, 1952)

Krochmal, Jacek, 'Batei kneset u-batei almin yehudiim be-hevel Przemyśl be-emtsa ha-meah ha-18', *Gal-Ed*, 18 (2000), Hebrew section, 73–82

Kubijovyc, Volodymyr, *Ethnic Groups of the South-Western Ukraine (Halyčyna-Galicia)* (Wiesbaden, 1983)

Kuczyński, Stefan, ed., *Rocznik Polskiego Towarzystwa Heraldycznego*, n. s., vol. 3 (Warsaw, 1997)

Kudela, Jiří, 'Die Emigration Galizischer und Osteuropäischer Juden nach Böhmen und Prag zwischen 1914–1916/17', *Studia Rosenthaliana*, 23 (1989), 119–34

Kuk, Vasyl, 'Derzhavotvorcha diial´nist´ OUN u 1941 rotsi (akt vidnovlennia ukraïns´koï derzhavy vid 30 chervnia 1941 roku)', *Vizvol'nii shliakh*, 54: 7 (640) (July 2001), 36–55

'Kurcz, F. S.' [Franciszek Skibiński], *The Black Brigade* (Harrow, Middlesex, 1943)

Kuropatnicki, Ewaryst Andrzej, *Geografia albo dokładne opisanie królestw Galicyi i Lodomeryi* (Przemyśl, 1786)

Kuzmany, Börries, *Brody: A Galician Border City in the Long Nineteenth Century* (Boston, 2017)

Lane, Hugo, 'Szlachta Outside the Commonwealth. The Case of Polish Nobles in Galicia', *Zeitschrift für Ostmitteleuropa-Forschung*, 52: 4 (2003), 526–42

Langer, Jiří, *Nine Gates to the Chasidic Mysteries* (trans. Stephen Joly, Northvale, NJ, 1993)

Laub, Hela, *My Heritage* (Tel Aviv, 1987)

Ledóchowska, Julia, *Poland Ravaged and Bereaved* (London, 1916)

Ledóchowski, Włodzimierz, *Mój nierodzinny kraj* (Cracow, 1988)

_____, *Pamiętnik pozostawieny w Ankarze* (Warsaw, 1990)

Lehmann, Rosa, *Symbiosis and Ambivalence: Poles and Jews in a Small Galician Town* (New York, 2001)

Lev, Vasyl, and Barahura, Volodymyr, eds., *Iavorivshchyna i krakovechchyna: regional'nyi istorychno-memuarnyi zbirnyk* (New York, 1984)

Levin, Dov, *The Lesser of Two Evils: Eastern European Jewry Under Soviet Rule, 1939–1941* (Philadelphia, 1995)

Lewicki, Jan, *Ruch Rusinów w Galicji w pierwszej połowie wieku panowania Austrji, 1772–1820* (Lwów, 1879)

Lindman, Naum, and Koifman, Marcos, eds., *Galitsyaner yidn yoyvel-bukh* (Buenos Aires, 1966)

Liske, Xawery, *Cudzoziemcy w Polsce* (Lwów, 1876)

Łoziński, Władysław, *Prawem i lewem: obyczaje na Czerwonej Rusi w pierwszej połowie XVII wieku*, vol. 2 (Cracow, 1957)

Łubieński, Stanisław, *Stanislai Lubienski opera posthuma, historica, historico-politica, variique discursus, epistolae et aliquot orationes* (Antwerp, 1643)

Łukaszewicz, Józef, *Dzieje kościołów wyznania helweckiego w dawnej Małej Polsce* (Poznán, 1853)

Maczek, Stanisław, *Avec mes blindés: Pologne, France, Belgique, Hollande, Allemagne* (Paris, [1967])

Madajczyk, Czesław, *Die Okkupationspolitik Nazideutschlands in Polen 1939–1945* (Cologne, 1988)

Mahler, Raphael, *Hasidism and the Jewish Enlightenment: Their Confrontation in Galicia and Poland in the First Half of the Nineteenth Century* (Philadelphia, 1985)

_____, 'The Economic Background of Jewish Emigration from Galicia to the United States', in Deborah Dash Moore ed., *East European Jews in Two Worlds: Studies from the Yivo Annual* (Evanston, Ill., 1990), 125–37

Maleczyński, Karol, et al., *Lwów i Ziemia Czerwieńska* (Lwów, [1938])

Margoshes, Joseph, *A World Apart: A Memoir of Jewish Life in Nineteenth Century Galicia* (Boston, 2008)

Markovits, Andrei S., and Sysyn, Frank E., eds., *Nationbuilding and the Politics of Nationalism* (Cambridge, Mass., 1982)

Marrus, Michael R., 'The Strange Story of Herschel Grynszpan', *The American Scholar*, 57: 1 (1988), 69–79

_____, 'The Vatican on Racism and Antisemitism, 1938–39: A New Look at a Might-Have-Been', *Holocaust and Genocide Studies*, 11: 3 (1997), 378–95

Mazower, Mark, *Hitler's Empire: Nazi Rule in Occupied Europe* (London, 2009)

McCagg, William O., *A History of Habsburg Jews 1670–1918* (Bloomington, Ind., 1989)

Meir, Natan M., *Stepchildren of the Shtetl: The Destitute, Disabled, and Mad of Jewish Eastern Europe, 1800–1939* (Stanford, 2020)

Mendelsohn, Ezra, *Zionism in Poland: The Formative Years, 1915–1926* (New Haven, Conn., 1981)

Metternich, Klemens von, *Memoirs of Prince Metternich 1815–1829*, vol. 4 (New York, 1881)

Michalewicz, Jerzy, *Żydowskie okręgi metrykalne i żydowskie gminy wyznaniowe w Galicji* (Cracow, 1995)

Mick, Christoph, '"Only the Jews do not waver . . ." L'viv under Soviet Occupation', in Elazar Barkan et al. eds., *Shared History – Divided Memory: Jews and Others in Soviet-Occupied Poland, 1939–1941* (Leipzig, 2007)

———, 'Incompatible Experiences: Poles, Ukrainians and Jews in Lviv under Soviet and German Occupation, 1939–1944', *Journal of Contemporary History*, 46: 2 (2011), 336–63

———, *Lemberg, Lwów, L'viv, 1914–1947: Violence and Ethnicity in a Contested City* (West Lafayette, Ind., 2016)

Milton, Sybil, 'The Expulsion of Polish Jews from Germany October 1938 to July 1939: A Documentation', *Leo Baeck Institute Year Book*, 29 (London, 1984), 169–99

Mirchuk, Petro, *Against the Invaders: Taras Chuprynka (Roman Shukhevych), Commander-in-Chief of the UPA* (New York, 1997)

Mises, Ludwig von, *Die Entwicklung des gutsherrlich-bäuerlichen Verhältnisses in Galizien (1772–1848)* (Vienna, 1902)

Moskovich, Wolf, 'Galicia and Bukovina under Austrian Rule and after: Ethnic Problems and Interethnic Relations', in Wolf Moskovich ed., *Jews and Slavs*, vol. 9, *Festschrift Professor Jacob Allerhand: Judaeo-Slavica et Judaeo-Germanica* (Jerusalem, 2001), 222–60

Motylewicz, Jerzy, 'Uwagi o początkach Krakowca w związku z publikacją dokumentu przeniesienia miasta na prawo magdeburskie', *Przemyskie Zapiski Historyczne*, 4/5 (1987), 209–14

———, 'Żydzi w miastach ziemi przemyskiej i sanockiej w drugiej połowie XVII w XVIII wieku', in Feliks Kiryk ed., *Żydzi w Małopolsce* (Przemyśl, 1991), 113–36

Namier, Julia, *Lewis Namier: A Biography* (London, 1971)

Namier, L. B., '1848: The Revolution of the Intellectuals', *Proceedings of the British Academy*, 30 (1944), 161–282

Nathans, Eli, *The Politics of Citizenship in Germany: Ethnicity, Utility and Nationalism* (Oxford, 2004)

Nowicki, Maximilian Siła, *Enumeratio Lepidopterorum Haliciae Orientalis* (Lwów, 1860)

_____, 'Beitrag zur Lepidopterenfauna Galiziens', *Verhandlungen der kaiserlich-königlichen zoologisch-botanischen Gesellschaft in Wien*, 15 (1865), 175–92

Orłowicz, Mieczysław, *Ilustrowany Przewodnik po Przemyślu i okolicy* (Lwów, 1917)

Palej, Emil, 'Notatki z mego życia', *Quod Libet* (Cracow), nos. 73, 75, 79, 80, 81, & 83 (2011–2013)

Passelecq, Georges, and Suchecky, Bernard, *L'Encyclique cachée de Pie XI: Une occasion manquée de l'Eglise face à l'antisémitisme* (Paris, 1995)

Penter, Tanja, 'Collaboration on Trial: New Source Material on Soviet Postwar Trials against Collaborators', *Slavic Review*, 64: 4 (2005), 782–90

Peszke, Alfred B., 'The Bomber Brigade of the Polish Air Force in September 1939', *Polish Review*, 13: 4 (1968), 80–100

Piekarz, Mendel, *Sifrut ha-edut al ha-shoah ke-makor histori: ve-shalosh hasidiyot be-artsot ha-shoah* (Jerusalem, 2003)

Pinchuk, Ben-Cion, *Shtetl Jews under Soviet Rule: Eastern Poland on the Eve of the Holocaust* (Oxford, 1990)

Pinkas ha-kehilot: Polin: entsiklopedyah shel ha-yishuvim ha-yehudiyim le-min hivasdam ve-ad le-ahar shoat milhemet ha-olam ha-sheniyah (Jerusalem, 1976–2005), vols. 2 & 3: Galicia

Plokhy, Serhii, *The Gates of Europe: A History of Ukraine* (London, 2015)

Pohl, Dieter, *Nationalsozialistische Judenverfolgung in Ostgalizien 1941–1944: Organisation und Durchführung eines staatlichen Massenverbrechens* (Munich, 1997)

Polonsky, Antony, 'The German Occupation of Poland during the First and Second World Wars: A Comparison', in Roy A. Prete and A. Hamish Ion eds., *Armies of Occupation* (Waterloo, Ontario, 1984), 97–142

_____, 'The Revolutionary Crisis of 1846–1849 and Its Place in the Development of Nineteenth-Century Galicia', *Harvard Ukrainian Studies*, 22 (1998), 443–69

_____, *The Jews in Poland and Russia* (3 vols., Oxford, 2010–2012)

Popiński, Krzysztof, Kokurin, Aleksandr, and Gurjanow, Aleksandr, *Drogi śmierci: ewakuacja więzień sowieckich z Kresów Wschodnich II Rzeczpospolitej w czerwcu i lipcu 1941* (Warsaw, 1995)

Präg, Werner, and Jacobmeyer, Wolfgang, eds., *Das Diensttagebuch des deutschen Generalgouverneurs in Polen 1939–1945* (Stuttgart, 1975)

Prager, Moshe, *Hatsalat ha-rabi mi-belz mi-ge ha-harigah be-Polin: mesupar mi-pi 'ede re'iyah* (Jerusalem, 2000)

Prüller, Wilhelm, *Diary of a German Soldier* (eds. and trans. H. C. Robbins Landon and Sebastian Leitner, London, 1963)

Prusin, Alexander V., *Nationalizing a Borderland: War, Ethnicity, and Anti Jewish Violence in East Galicia, 1914–1920* (Tuscaloosa, Al., 2005)

Purchla, Jacek, et al. eds., *The Myth of Galicia* (Cracow, 2014)

Radwański, Feliks, *Wiersz na akt weselny jaśnie wielmoznego jmci pana Kaietana Potockiego starosty dimirskiego [. . .] z j.o. xiężną Anną jeymoscią z Cetnerow pierwszym związkiem Sanguszkową marszałkową W. X. Litt. a powtórnym Sapiezyną generałową srtyl. litt. od nayżyczliwszego* (privately printed, n. p.,1790)

Rady, Martin, *The Habsburgs* (London, 2020)

Radziejowski, Janusz, *The Communist Party of Western Ukraine 1919–1929* (Edmonton, Alberta, 1983)

Rakhmanny, Roman, *In Defense of the Ukrainian Cause* (North Quincy, Mass., 1979)

Rauchensteiner, Manfried, *The First World War and the End of the Habsburg Monarchy* (Vienna, 2014)

Rauscher, Anton, ed., *Wider den Rassismus: Entwurf einer nicht erschienenen Enzyklika (1938): Texte aus dem Nachlass von Gustav Gundlach SJ* (Padeborn, 2001)

Redlich, Shimon, *Together and Apart in Brzezany: Poles, Jews, and Ukrainians, 1919–1945* (Bloomington, Ind., 2002)

_____, 'Metropolitan Andrei Sheptyts'kyi, Ukrainians and Jews during and after the Holocaust', *Holocaust and Genocide Studies*, 5: 1 (1990) 39–51

Ringelblum, Emanuel, 'Zbąszyń (der letster reportazh ongeshribn in 1939)', *Bleter far geshikhte*, 19 (1980), 27–30

Rodal, Alti, 'A Village Massacre: The Particular and the Context', in Simon Geissbühler ed., *Romania and the Holocaust: Events – Contexts – Aftermath* (Stuttgart, 2016), 59–88

Roja, Bolesław, *Legendy i fakty* (Warsaw, 1931)

Rosman, Murray Jay, *The Lord's Jews: Magnate–Jewish Relations in the Polish-Lithuanian Commonwealth in the Eighteenth Century* (Cambridge, Mass., 1990)

Rossino, Alexander B., *Hitler Strikes Poland: Blitzkrieg, Ideology, and Atrocity* (Lawrence, Kans., 2003)

Rossoliński-Liebe, Grzegorz, *Stepan Bandera: The Life and Afterlife of a Ukrainian Nationalist: Fascism, Genocide, and Cult* (Stuttgart, 2014)

Rudling, Per Anders, 'Theory and Practice: Historical Representation of the Wartime Accounts of the Activities of the OUN-UPA (Organization of Ukrainian Nationalists–Ukrainian Insurgent Army)', *East European Jewish Affairs*, 36: 2 (2006), 163–89

_____, 'The Cult of Roman Shukhevych in Ukraine: Myth Making with Complications', *Fascism*, 5: 1 (2016), 26–65

_____, 'Rehearsal for Volhynia: Schutzmannschaft Battalion 201 and Hauptmann Roman Shukhevych in Occupied Belorussia, 1942', *East European Politics and Societies and Cultures*, 34: 1 (2020) 158–93

_____, 'Survivor Testimonies and the Coming to Terms with the Holocaust in Volhynia and Eastern Galicia: The Case of the Ukrainian Nationalists', *East European Politics and Societies and Cultures*, 34: 1 (2020), 221–40

Rudnytsky, Ivan L. 'The Ukrainians in Galicia under Austrian Rule', *Austrian History Yearbook*, 3: 2 (1967), 394–429

Rusin, Bartłomiej, 'Lewis Namier, the Curzon Line, and the shaping of Poland's eastern frontier after World War I', *Studies in the History of Russia and Central-Eastern Europe*, 48 (2010), 5–26

Sale, Giovanni, *Hitler, Santa Sede e gli ebrei* (Milan, 2004)

Sandkühler, Thomas, *"Endlösung" in Galizien: Die Judenmord in Ostpolen und die Rettungsinitiativen von Berthold Beitz 1941–1944* (Bonn, 1996).

Sands, Philippe, *East West Street: On the Origins of Genocide and Crimes Against Humanity* (London, 2016)

_____, *The Ratline: Love, Lies and Justice on the Trail of a Nazi Fugitive* (London, 2021)

Schelcher, Raimund, 'Ornithologische Beobachtungen in Galizien', *Verhandlungen der Ornithologischen Gesellschaft in Bayern*, 14: 1 (1919), 3–36

Schenk, Dieter, *Der Lemberger Professorenmord und der Holocaust in Ostgalizien* (Bonn, 2007)

Schindler, John, 'Steamrollered in Galicia: The Austro-Hungarian Army and the Brusilov Offensive, 1916', *War in History*, 10: 1 (January 2003), 27–59

_____, *Fall of the Double Eagle: The Battle for Galicia and the Demise of Austria-Hungary* (Lincoln, Neb., 2015)

Schneid, Yechiel, 'A kapitele galitsye', *Yivo Bleter*, 40 (1956), 175–84

Schoenfeld, Joachim, *Shtetl Memoirs: Jewish Life under the Austro-Hungarian Empire and in the Reborn Poland, 1898–1939* (Hoboken, NJ, 1985)

Schölzel, Christian, 'Fritz Rathenau (1875–1949). On Antisemitism, Acculturation and Slavophobia: An Attempted Reconstruction', *Leo Baeck Institute Year Book*, 48 (2003), 135–62

Schultes, Joseph August, 'Lettres sur la Galitzie', *Annales des Voyages, de la Géographie et de l'Histoire*, vol. 15 (Paris, 1811), 1–86

Shakh, Stepan, and Vas'kovych, Hryhoriï , *Heneral Roman Shukhevych (dvi dopovidi)* (Munich, 1966)

Shanes, Joshua, *Diaspora Nationalism and Jewish Identity in Habsburg Galicia* (Cambridge, 2012)

Siemann, Wolfram, *Metternich: Strategist and Visionary* (Cambridge, Mass., 2019)

Simons, Thomas W., 'The Peasant Revolt of 1846 in Galicia: Recent Polish Historiography', *Slavic Review*, 30: 4 (1971), 795–817

Sirka, Ann, *The Nationality Question in Austrian Education: The Case of Ukrainians in Galicia 1867–1914* (Frankfurt, 1979)

Skrzypek, Stanisław, *The Problem of Eastern Galicia* (London, 1948)

Slobodian, Vasyl', et al., *Synahohy Ukraïny* (Lviv, 1998)

Słomka, Jan, *From Serfdom to Self-Government: Memoirs of a Polish Village Mayor, 1842–1927* (London, 1941)

Snyder, Timothy, ' "To Resolve the Ukrainian Problem Once and for All": The Ethnic Cleansing of Ukrainians in Poland, 1943–1947', *Journal of Cold War Studies*, 1: 2 (1999), 86–120

_____, 'The Causes of Ukrainian-Polish Ethnic Cleansing, 1943', *Past and Present*, 179 (2003), 197–234

_____, *The Reconstruction of Nations: Poland, Ukraine, Lithuania, Belarus, 1569–1999* (New Haven, 2003)

_____, *Bloodlands: Europe between Hitler and Stalin* (New York, 2010)

_____, *Black Earth: The Holocaust as History and Warning* (London, 2015)

Solchanyk, Roman, 'The Foundation of the Communist Movement in Eastern Galicia, 1919–1921', *Slavic Review*, 30: 4 (1971), 774–94

Sorokina, Marina, 'People and Procedures: Toward a History of the Investigation of Nazi Crimes in the USSR', *Kritika: Explorations in Russian and Eurasian History* 6: 4 (2005), 797–831

Stampfer, Shaul, 'What Actually Happened to the Jews of Ukraine in 1648?', *Jewish History* 17: 2 (2003), 207–27

_____, 'Jewish Population Losses in the Course of the Khmelnytsky Uprising', *Judaica Ucrainica*, 4 (2015), 36–52

Stanislawski, Michael, *A Murder in Lemberg* (Princeton, 2007)

Stargardt, Nicholas, *The German War: A Nation Under Arms, 1939–1945* (London, 2015)

Stauter-Halsted, Keely, *The Nation in the Village: The Genesis of Peasant National Identity in Austrian Poland, 1848–1914* (Ithaca, NY, 2001)

Stęczyński, M. B., *Okolice Galicyi* (Lwów, 1847)

Steglich, Ulrike, and Kratz, Peter, *Das falsche Scheunenviertel* (Berlin, 1994)

Stopnicka-Rosenthal (Heller), Celia, 'Deviation and Social Change in the Jewish Community of a Small Polish Town', *American Journal of Sociology*, 60: 2 (1954), 177–81

Struve, Kai, 'Peasant Emancipation and National Integration: Agrarian Circles, Village Reading Rooms, and Cooperatives in Galicia', in Torsten Lorenz ed., *Cooperatives in Ethnic Conflicts: Eastern Europe in the 19th and Early 20th Century* (Berlin, 2006), 229–50.

_____, 'Rites of Violence? The Pogroms of Summer 1941', *Polin: Studies in Polish Jewry*, vol. 24 (2011), 257–74

_____, *Deutsche Herrschaft, ukrainischer Nationalismus, antijüdische Gewalt. Der Sommer 1941 in der Westukraine* (Munich, 2015)

Stupnicki, Hipolit, *Das Königreich Galizien und Lodomerien* (Berlin, 1989; 1st ed. Lwów, 1853)

Sulimierski, Filip, Chlebowski, Bronisław, and Walewski, Władisław, *Słownik geograficzny Królestwa Polskiego i innych krajów słowiańskich* (vol. 4, Warsaw, 1883), 605–7: article on Krakowiec)

Sworakowsky, Witold, 'An Error regarding Eastern Galicia in Curzon's Note to the Soviet Government of July 11, 1920', *Journal of Central European Affairs*, 4: 1 (1944), 1–26

Sword, Keith, ed., *The Soviet Takeover of the Polish Eastern Provinces, 1939–41* (New York, 1991)

Szubański, Rajmund, *Polska broń pancerna w 1939 roku* (Warsaw, 1982)

Tartakower, Aryeh, 'The Migrations of Polish Jews in Recent Times', *American Federation of Polish Jews Yearbook*, I (New York, 1964), 5–46

Tăslăuanu, Octavian C., *With the Austrian Army in Galicia* (London, [1918])

Tatarkiewicz, Władisław, *O sztuce polskiej XVII i XVIII wieku: architektura rzeźba* (Warsaw, 1966)

Taubman, William, *Khrushchev: The Man and His Era* (London, 2004)

Tcherikower, Elias, *Di ukrainer pogromen in yor 1919* (New York, 1965)

Tenenbaum, Joseph, *Galitsye, mein alte haym* (Buenos Aires, 1952)

Ther, Philipp, 'War Versus Peace: Interethnic Relations in Lviv during the First Half of the Twentieth Century', *Harvard Ukrainian Studies*, 24: 4 (2000), 251–84

Thies, Klaus-Jürgen, *Der Polenfeldzug: Eine Lageatlas der Operationsabteilung des Generalstabs des Heeres* (Osnabrück, 1989)

Tokarski, Sławomir, *Ethnic Conflict and Economic Development: Jews in Galician Agriculture 1868–1914* (Warsaw, 2003)

Tomaszewski, Jerzy, 'Lwów, 22 listopada 1918', *Przegląd Historyczny*, 75 (1984), 279–85

_____, 'Letters from Zbaszyn', *Yad Vashem Studies*, 19 (1988), 289–315

_____, 'Polish Diplomats and the Fate of Polish Jews in Nazi Germany', *Acta Poloniae Historica*, 61 (1990), 183–204

_____, *Preludium zagłady: wygnanie Żydów polskich z Niemiec w 1938 r.* (Warsaw, 1998)

Tretiak, Józef, *Historja wojny chocimskiej (1621)*, (Cracow, 1921)

Trillenberg, Wilfried, *Galizien: Teilungen und Vereinungen in Mittelosteuropa in den politischen Umbrüchen seit dem 18. Jarhrhundert* (Berlin, 2010)

Tronko, Petro, *Istoriia mist i sil Ukrains'koi RSR: v dvadtsiaty shesty tomakh*, vol. XIV, *Lvivska oblast* (Kiev, [1968]): entry on Krakovets, 927–8

Trunk, Isaiah, *Judenrat: The Jewish Councils in Eastern Europe Under Nazi Occupation* (New York, 1972)

Tsuker, Nehemyah, ed., *Pinkes galitsye* (Buenos Aires, 1945)

_____, ed., *Gedenkbuch galitsye* (Buenos Aires, 1964)

United Ukrainian Organizations of the United States, *Polish Atrocities in Ukraine* (New York, 1931)

Unowsky, Daniel, *The Pomp and Politics of Patriotism: Imperial Celebrations in Habsburg Austria, 1848–1916* (West Lafayette, Ind., 2005)

_____, *The Plunder: The 1898 Anti-Jewish Riots in Habsburg Galicia* (Stanford, 2018)

Veidlinger, Jeffrey, *In the Midst of Civilized Europe: The Pogroms of 1918–1921 and the Onset of the Holocaust* (New York, 2021)

Veryha, Wasyl, ed., *The Correspondence of the Ukrainian Central Committee in Cracow and Lviv with the German Authorities, 1939–1944*, (2 vols., Edmonton, Alberta, 2000)

Vigée-Le Brun, Louise-Elisabeth, *Souvenirs de Madame Vigée Le Brun* (2 vols., Paris, 1869)

Vushko, Iryna, *The Politics of Cultural Retreat: Imperial Bureaucracy in Austrian Galicia, 1772–1867* (New Haven, 2015)

Wandycz, Piotr S., *The Lands of Partitioned Poland 1795–1918* (Seattle, 1974)

Wargelin, Clifford F., 'A High Price for Bread: The First Treaty of Brest-Litovsk and the Break-up of Austria-Hungary, 1917–1918', *International History Review*, 19: 4 (1997), 757–88

Wasserstein, Bernard, *Britain and the Jews of Europe 1939–1945* (2nd ed., London, 1999)

Wątroba, Przemysław, 'Le Palais d'Ignacy Cetner à Krakowiec et son architecte Pierre Ricaud de Tirregaille: Nouvelles constatations et hypothèses', in A. Betlej et al. eds., *Velis quod possis: studia z historii sztuki ofiarowane profesorowi Janowi Ostrowskiemu* (Cracow, 2016), 67–73 & 644

Watson, Alexander, *Ring of Steel: Germany and Austria-Hungary at War, 1914–1918* (London, 2015)

_____, *The Fortress: The Great Siege of Przemyśl* (London, 2019)

Weh, Albert, *Übersicht über das Recht des Distrikts Galizien* (Cracow, 1943)

Weinryb, Bernard D., 'Polish Jews under Soviet Rule', in Peter Meyer et al., *The Jews in the Soviet Satellites* (Syracuse, NY, 1953), 327–69

Wertheimer, Jack, *Unwelcome Strangers: East European Jews in Imperial Germany* (New York, 1987)

Wierzbieniec, Wacław, 'The Processes of Jewish Emancipation and Assimilation in the Multi-ethnic City of Lviv during the Nineteenth and Twentieth Centuries', *Harvard Ukrainian Studies*, 24 (2000), 223–50

_____, *Żydzi w województwie lwowskim w okresie międzywojennym: Zagadnienia demograficzne i społeczne* (Rzeszów, 2003)

Winstone, Martin, *The Dark Heart of Hitler's Europe: Nazi Rule in Poland under the General Government* (London, 2014)

Wolff, Larry, *The Idea of Galicia: History and Fantasy in Habsburg Political Culture* (Stanford, 2010)

Wołoszczak, Eustach, 'Zur Flora von Jaworów in Galizien', *Verhandlungen der kaiserlich-königlichen zoologisch-botanischen Gesellschaft in Wien*, 24 (1874), 529–538

Wróbel, Piotr, 'The Jews of Galicia under Austrian-Polish Rule, 1869–1918', *Austrian History Yearbook*, 25 (1994), 97–138

_____, 'The Seeds of Violence: The Brutalization of an East European Region, 1917–1921', *Journal of Modern European History*, 1: 1 (2004), 125–49

Wunder, Meir, *Me'orei Galitsia: entsiklopedia le-ḥokhmei Galitsia* (4 vols., Jerusalem, 1978–2005)

Wylegała, Anna, 'About "Jewish things": Jewish Property in Eastern Galicia during World War II', *Yad Vashem Studies*, 44 (2016), 83–119

Zeynek, Theodor Ritter von, *Ein Offizier im Generalstabskorps erinnert sich* (Vienna, 2009)

WORKS OF IMAGINATIVE LITERATURE REFERRED TO IN TEXT

Agnon, S. Y., *A Simple Story* (*Sipur pashut*, first pub. in Hebrew, Berlin, 1935; trans. Hillel Halkin, New York, 1985)

Babel, Nathalie, ed., *The Complete Works of Isaac Babel* (trans. Peter Constantine, New York, 2002)

Barash, Asher, *Pictures from a Brewery*, (*Temunot mi-bet mivshal ha-shekhar*, first pub. in Hebrew, Jerusalem, 1929; trans. Katie Kaplan, London, 1972)

F. B. [Feliks Boznański], *Ostatnie marzenia starego Huzara* (Lwów, 1848)

Franko, Ivan, *Boa Constrictor and other Stories* (*Boa konstriktor*, first pub. in Ukrainian, 1878; trans. Fainna Solasko, Moscow, n.d. [1957])

_____, *Faces of Hardship* (anthology of stories first pub. in Ukrainian; trans. Maria Igorevna Kuroshchepova, Hendersonville, NC, 2016)

'Jan z Kiian', *Fraszki sowirzała nowego* (Cracow, 1614)

Kafka, Franz, *The Trial* (*Der Prozess*, first pub. in German, Berlin, 1925; trans. Willa and Edwin Muir, London, 1935)

Pol, Wincenty, *Poezyje Wincentego Pola* (4 vols., Vienna, 1857)

Roth, Joseph, *The Radetzky March* (*Radetzkymarsch*, first pub. in German, Berlin, 1932; trans. Eva Tucker, Woodstock, NY, 1983)

_____, *The Emperor's Tomb* (*Die Kapuzinergruft*, first pub. in German, Bilthoven, 1938; trans. John Hoare, Woodstock, NY, 1984)

_____, *Hotel Savoy and Other Stories* (trans. John Hoare, Woodstock, NY, 1986)

Shevchenko, Taras, *Poetry of Taras Shevchenko* (first pub. in Ukrainian; anthology, trans. [North Charleston, SC], 2015)

Sienkiewicz, Henryk, *With Fire and Sword* (*Ogniem i mieczem*, first pub. in Polish, Warsaw, 1884, trans. W. S. Kuniczak, New York, 1993)

Stryjkowski, Julian, *The Inn* (*Austeria*, first pub. in Polish, Warsaw, 1966; trans. Celina Wieniewska, New York, 1972)

Notes

ABBREVIATIONS USED IN NOTES

AAN	Archiwum Akt Nowych, Warsaw
APK	Archiwum Państwowe w Krakowie
APP	Archiwum Państwowe w Przemyślu
BA	Bundesarchiv, Koblenz/Berlin/Freiburg
CZA	Central Zionist Archives, Jerusalem
DALO	Derzhavnyi arkhiv L'vivs'koi oblasti (State Archive of Lviv Oblast)
DBFP	*Documents on British Foreign Policy*
FRUS	*Foreign Relations of the United States*
GARF	Gosudarstvennyi Arkhiv Rossiiskoi Federatsii (State Archive of the Russian Federation, Moscow)
HDA SBU	Haluzevyy derzhavnyy arkhiv Sluzhby bezpeky Ukrayiny (State Security Archive of Ukraine)
HIA	Hoover Institution Archives, Stanford
JDC	American Jewish Joint Distribution Committee archives, New York and Jerusalem
NAN	Lvivska natsionalna naukova biblioteka imeni V. Stefanyka (Lviv National Scientific Library of Ukraine)
ÖStA	Österreichisches Staatsarchiv, Vienna
TsDIAL	Tsentralnyi derzhavnyi istorychnyi arkhiv, m. Lviv (State Historical Archive of Ukraine, Lviv)
TNA	The National Archives, Kew
USNA	United States National Archives, Washington D.C.
YIVO	YIVO archive, Center for Jewish History, New York
YV	Yad Vashem Archives, Jerusalem

PREFACE

1. *Times Literary Supplement*, 10 September 2021.

CHAPTER I

1. Copy of letter to Abraham Wasserstein, 28 October 1938, archive of Entschädigungsamt, Berlin, file 277819.

2. Article 80 of the Peace Treaty of St Germain between the Allies and Austria in 1919 provided that 'Persons possessing rights of citizenship in territory forming part of the former Austro-Hungarian Monarchy, and differing in race and language from the majority of the population of such territory' could exercise a right of option to citizenship of 'Austria, Italy, Poland, Roumania, the Serb-Croat-Slovene State, or the Czecho-Slovak State, if the majority of the population of the State selected is of the same race and language as the person exercising the right to opt.' German-speaking Galician Jews such as Berl might, therefore, have been able to choose Austrian rather than Polish citizenship. But as Peter M. Judson points out (*The Habsburg Empire: A New History* [Cambridge, Mass., 2016], 445), 'Austria's Supreme Court and Interior Ministry ruled that they could not be considered "racially" German.'

3. Steven E. Aschheim, *Brothers and Strangers: The East European Jew in German and German Jewish Consciousness, 1800–1923* (Madison, Wisconsin, 1982), 43; Eli Nathans, *The Politics of Citizenship in Germany: Ethnicity, Utility and Nationalism* (Oxford, 2004), 111 ff.

4. Letter to Wilhelm Schwaner, 18 August 1916, in Walther Rathenau, *Briefe*, vol. 1 (Berlin, 1926), 220. Rathenau was echoing the historian Theodor Mommsen's *Auch ein Wort über unser Judenthum* (Berlin, 1880), 4–5.

5. Ben-Tsiyon Ginsberg, 'Nito mit vos zikh tsu shehmen als galitsyaner', *Der Galitsyaner Yorbukh* (New York, 1939), 21–4.

6. Christian Schölzel, 'Fritz Rathenau (1875–1949). On Antisemitism, Acculturation and Slavophobia: An Attempted Reconstruction', *Leo Baeck Institute Year Book*, 48 (Oxford, 2003), 149.

7. Copy of communiqué enclosed with Sir H. Kennard (Warsaw) to Lord Halifax, 31 March 1938, TNA FO 371/21808.

8. Memorandum dated 9 April 1938, Landesarchiv Berlin Pr. Br. Rep. 57/368.

9. Extract from Berlin consular report for month of June 1938, TNA FO 371/21635.

10. Kennard (Warsaw) to Halifax, 28 March 1938, TNA FO 371/21808.

11. Circular dated 26 October 1938, Landesarchiv Berlin Pr. Br. Rep. 57/369.

12. Ulrich Herbert, *Best: Biographische Studien über Radikalismus, Weltan-schauung und Vernunft 1903–1989* (Bonn, 1996), 216.

13. Telegraphed report dated 28 October 1938 in records of Reichssicher-heitshauptamt, in former Osobyi Archive (now held by Rossiiskii gosudarstvennyi voennyi arkhiv, Moscow) 500/1/88.

14. Jerzy Tomaszewski, *Preludium zagłady: wygnanie Żydów polskich z Niemiec w 1938 r.* (Warsaw, 1998), 109 ff.; Kennard (Warsaw) to Foreign Office, 29 October 1938, reporting statement by head of Western Division of Polish Ministry of Foreign Affairs, TNA FO 371/21808.

15. German translation of report by Polish border police commandant, 2 November 1938, in Rolf Fischer, *Verfolgung und Vernichtung: Die Dort-munder Opfer der Shoah* (Essen, 2015), 132–3. A somewhat different translation into English is in Karol Jonca, 'The Expulsion of Polish Jews from the Third Reich in 1938', *Polin: Studies in Polish Jewry*, vol. 8 (London, 1994), 279–80.

16. Kennard (Warsaw) to Foreign Office, 1 November 1938, TNA FO 371/21808.

17. A. J. Drexel Biddle Jr. to Secretary of State, 5 November 1938, USNA State Dept. CDF 862.4016/1824.

18. Text in Sir G. Ogilvie-Forbes (Berlin) to Foreign Office, 31 October 1938, TNA FO 371/21808.

19. M. C. Troper to J. C. Hyman (both were officials of the American Jewish Joint Distribution Committee), 1 December 1938, in Sybil Milton, 'The Expulsion of Polish Jews from Germany October 1938 to July 1939: A Documentation', *Leo Baeck Institute Year Book*, 29 (London, 1984), 191–2.

20. Michael Marrus, 'The Strange Story of Herschel Grynszpan', *The Ameri-can Scholar*, 57: 1 (1988), 79.

21. Ringelblum to Raphael Mahler, 6 December 1938, in Milton, 'The Expulsion', 191.

22. Message to the author, 12 June 1993.

23. Tomaszewski, *Preludium*, 200.

24. Weizsäcker to Foreign Minister, 8 November 1938, USNA RG 238, Nuremberg document NG 2799.

25. Tomaszewski, *Preludium*, 147–52.

26. Minutes of meeting, USNA RG 238, Nuremberg document 1816-PS.

CHAPTER 2

1. Bohdan Janusz, *Zabytki przedhistoryczne Galicyi Wschodniej* (Lwów, 1918), 153.

2. Vasyl Chernetsky, *Krakovets* (n.p., 1899), 4.

3. Isaak Walton, *The Compleat Angler or, The Contemplative Man's Recreation Being a Discourse on Fish and Fishing, not Unworthy the Perusal of Most Anglers* (London, 1653), 168–9.

4. Report by Tadeusz Nałęcz Bukojemski in *Okólnik. Organ Krajowego Towarzystwa Rybackiego w Krakowie*, no. 49, October 1900, 19. Bukojemski calls the first type he encountered at Krakowiec 'golden' carp but he probably meant the common carp.

5. Ulryk Werdum, writing in 1670–72, text in Xawery Liske, *Cudzoziemcy w Polsce* (Lwów, 1876), 112.

6. Maximilian Siła Nowicki, *Enumeratio Lepidopterorum Haliciae Orientalis* (Lwów, 1860); and idem, 'Beitrag zur Lepidopterenfauna Galiziens', *Verhandlungen der k. k. zoologisch-botanischen Gesellschaft in Wien*, 15 (1865), 175–92.

7. Karl Hoelzl, 'Botanische Beiträge aus Galizien', *loc. cit.*, 11 (1861), 149–60; Josef Armin Knapp, *Die bisher bekannten Pflanzen Galiziens und der Bukowina* (Vienna, 1872), 73–131.

8. Ivan Franko, *Faces of Hardship* (trans. Maria Igorevna Kuroshchepova, Hendersonville, NC, 2016), 95.

9. Jerzy Motylewicz, 'Uwagi o początkach Krakowca w związku z publikacją dokumentu przeniesienia miasta na prawo magdeburskie', *Przemyskie Zapiski Historyczne*, 4: 5 (1987), 209–14.

10. Document dated 18 May 1425, TsDIAL 134/1/91.

11. Stefan Kuczyński ed., *Rocznik Polskiego Towarzystwa Heraldycznego*, n. s., vol. 3 (Warsaw, 1997), 78–88.

12. Andrzej Janeczek, 'Miasta prywatne na Rusi Koronnej do końca XV wieku', *Roczniki Dziejów Społecznych i Gospodarczych*, 77 (2016), 166.

13. Chernetsky, *Krakovets*, 8.

14. Stanisław Łubieński, 'Vita et Obitus Matthiae de Buzenin Pstrokonski, Episcopi primum Praemisliensis' in *Stanislai Lubienski opera posthuma, historica, historico-politica, variique discursus, epistolae et aliquot orationes* (Antwerp, 1643), 432.

15. 'Cech Krakowiecki' in 'Jan z Kiian', *Fraszki sowizrzała nowego* (Cracow, 1614). I am grateful to Kinga Kosmala for the English translation on which this version is based.

16. Laura Silver, *Knish: In Search of the Jewish Soul Food* (Waltham, Mass., 2014), 132.

17. Mauricy Horn, *Żydzi na Rusi Czerwonej w XVI i pierwszej połowie XVII w.* (Warsaw, 1975).

18. Inventory of Gnojnica estate, 1620, Ossolineum, Wrocław, 3669/II.

19. Andrzej Maksymilian Fredro, *Scriptorum seu togae et belli notationum fragmenta*, quoted in Ludwig von Mises, *Die Entwicklung des gutsherrlich-bäuerlichen Verhältnisses in Galizien (1772–1848)* (Vienna, 1902), 16.

20. Mises, *Die Entwicklung*, 14.

21. An Israeli historian has concluded, after analysing the evidence, that Jewish population losses in the course of the Khmelnytsky rebellion were lower than commonly suggested, probably no more than twenty thousand. Even this, of course, was a large number. Shaul Stampfer, 'What Actually Happened to the Jews of Ukraine in 1648?', *Jewish History*, 17: 2 (2003), 207–27; and idem, 'Jewish Population Losses in the Course of the Khmelnytsky Uprising', *Judaica Ucrainica*, 4 (2015), 36–52.

22. Władysław Łoziński, *Prawem i lewem: obyczaje na Czerwonej Rusi w pierwszej połowie XVII wieku*, vol. 2 (Cracow, 1957), 28–31.

23. Michael Harasiewicz (Baron von Neustern), *Annales Ecclesiae Ruthenae gratiam et communionem cum s. Sede Romana habentis, ritumque Graeco-Slavicum observantis, cum singulari respectu ad dioeceses ruthenas Leopoliensem, Premisliensem et Chelmensem* (Stauropegion Institute, Lwów, 1862), 419.

24. Letter dated 18 March 1656 in *Lettres de Pierre Des Noyers secrétaire de la reine de Pologne Marie-Louise de Gonzague ... pour servir à l'histoire de Pologne et de Suède de 1655 à 1659* (Berlin, 1859), 107–9.

25. TsDIAL 113/1/1/4 and 113/1/1/5.

26. TsDIAL 113/1/13.

27. Jerzy Motylewicz, 'Żydzi w miastach ziemi przemyskiej i sanockiej w drugiej połowie XVII w XVIII wieku', in Feliks Kiryk ed., *Żydzi w Małopolsce* (Przemyśl, 1991), 113–36.

CHAPTER 3

1. Franciszek Jaworski, *Lwów: stary i wczorajszy: szkice i opowiadania* (Lwów, 1910), 394.

2. Peter Pulzer (echoing J. R. Seeley's famous remark about the British empire) in *Journal of Modern History*, 64: 1 (1992), 172.

3. Tim Blanning, *Frederick the Great: King of Prussia* (London, 2016), 294.

4. Derek Beales, *Joseph II*: vol. 2, *Against the World 1780-1790* (Cambridge, 2009), 247.

5. Joseph August Schultes, *Lettres sur la Galitzie* in *Annales des Voyages, de la Géographie et de l'Histoire*, vol. 15 (Paris, 1811), 13. This passage was written before the enactment of Joseph II's agrarian reforms.

6. Ibid., 23.

7. Hugo Lane, 'Szlachta Outside the Commonwealth. The Case of Polish Nobles in Galicia', *Zeitschrift für Ostmitteleuropa-Forschung*, 52: 4 (2003), 526–42.

8. Ignacy Krasicki to Antoni Krasicki, 25 May 1781, *Korespondencja Ignacego Krasickiego*, eds. Zbigniew Goliński et al. (Wrocław, 1958), vol. 2, 45–6.

9. Joseph II to his brother Leopold, 1 August 1773, in Alfred Ritter von Arneth ed., *Maria Theresia und Joseph II: Ihre Correspondenz sammt Briefen Joseph's an seinen Bruder Leopold*, vol. II 1773–Juli 1778 (Vienna, 1867), 16.

10. Agreement dated 1 June 1782, NAN 5/6351/109-114.

11. Declaration signed by Cetner, 12 August 1782, NAN 5/6351/115.

12. Władysław Konopczyński, 'Ignacy Cetner', in *Polski Słownik Biograficzny*, vol. 3 (Cracow, 1937), 238–9.

13. Ibid.

14. Jaworski, *Lwów*, 396.

15. Krasicki to Jacek Ogrodszki, 1 May 1765, in Goliński et al. eds., *Korespondencja Ignacego Krasickiego*, vol. 1, 100–2.

16. Samuel Bredetzky, *Reisebemerkungen über Ungarn und Galizien*, vol. 2 (Vienna, 1809), 221–2.

17. Przemysław Wątroba, 'Le Palais d'Ignacy Cetner à Krakowiec et son architecte Pierre Ricaud de Tirregaille: Nouvelles constatations et hypothèses', in A. Betlej et al. eds., *Velis quod possis: studia z historii sztuki ofiarowane profesorowi Janowi Ostrowskiemu* (Cracow, 2016), pp. 67–73 & 644.

18. Inventory in TsDIAL 134/2/402; see also Roman Aftanazy, *Dzieje rezydencji na dawnych kresach Rzeczypospolitej* (2nd rev. ed., 11 vols., Wrocław, 1991–7), vol. 8, 53–63.

19. Unfortunately the library has been unable to trace the titles of the books bequeathed from the Cetner collection (communication to author from Grzegorz Fulara, Jagiellonian University Library, 15 March 2021).

20. Ewaryst Andrzej Kuropatnicki, *Geografia albo dokładne opisanie królestw Galicyi i Lodomeryi* (Przemyśl, 1786), 67; Filip Sulimierski et al., *Słownik Geograficzny Królestwa Polskiego i Innych Krajów Słowiańskich*, vol. 4 (Warsaw, 1883), 606; Vasyl Lev and Volodymyr Barahura eds., *Iavorivshchyna i krakovechchyna: regional'nyi istorychno-memuarnyi zbirnyk*

(New York, 1984), 149–51; Aftanazy, *Dzieje rezydencji*, vol. 8, 54–5; Konopczyński, 'Cetner'.

21. Aftanazy, *Dzieje rezydencji*, vol. 8, 62; Hipolit Stupnicki, *Das Königreich Galizien und Lodomerien* (Berlin, 1989, originally published 1853), 67; Gerard Ciolek, *Gärten in Polen: I Teil: Inhalts- und Gestaltsentwicklung* (Warsaw, 1954), 192–3; W. C. Blumenbach, *Neuestes Gemälde der Oesterreichischen Monarchie*, vol. 3 (Vienna, 1833), 148.

22. M. B. Stęczyński, *Okolice Galicyi* (Lwów, 1847), 53–4. This rendering is based on a translation by Kamil Kiedos. See also the poem of Dyzma Bończa-Tomaszewski, *Rolnictwo. Poema oryginalne w czterech pieśniach* (Lwów, [1801]) and the review in *Annalen der Österreichischen Literatur*, no. 6 (January 1802), cols. 41–4.

23. Stęczyński, *Okolice Galicyi*, 53–4.

24. Kuropatnicki, *Geografia*, 67.

25. Franciszek Karpiński, *Pamiętniki* (Poznań, 1844), 23–4.

26. See Richard Butterwick, *Poland's Last King and English Culture: Stanisław August Poniatowski, 1732–1798* (Oxford, 1998), 174, 178.

27. Ignacy Krasicki to Antoni Krasicki, 2 October 1798, in Krasicki, *Korespondencja*, vol. 2, 695–6.

28. Krzystof Gombin, 'Lwów w ceremoniale Trybunału Koronnego prowincji małopolskiej', *Annales UMCS, Artes*, 8: 2 (2010), 27–41.

29. Karol Maleczyński et al., *Lwów i Ziemia Czerwieńska* (Lwów, [1938]), 206.

30. Aftanazy, *Dzieje rezydencjii*, vol. 8, 62.

31. Władysław Tatarkiewicz, *O sztuce polskiej XVII i XVIII wieku: architektura rzeźba* (Warsaw, 1966), 286.

32. Aftanazy, *Dzieje rezydencji*, vol. 8, 62–3.

33. Antoni Krasicki to Ignacy Krasicki, 22 February & 9 March 1782, Krasicki, *Korespondencja*, vol. 2, 102 ff.

34. *Wiersz na akt weselny jaśnie wielmoznego jmci pana Kaietana Potockiego starosty dimirskiego [. . .] z j.o. xięzną Anną jeymoscią z Cetnerow pierwszym związkiem Sanguszkową marszałkową W. X. Litt. a powtórnym Sapiezyną generałową srtyl. litt. od nayżyczliwszego* (privately printed, 1790).

35. Barbara Adamska, 'Portret Anny z Cetnerów', *Skarby Podkarpackie*, 36: 1 (2015), 30–32.

36. *Souvenirs de Madame Vigée Le Brun* (Paris, 1869), vol. 1, 161.

37. Decree of Krakowiec court, 1 May 1783, NAN 6350/7-8.

38. Decree of Krakowiec court, 1 May 1783, NAN 6350/17-18.

39. Death record of Ioannes Pagazij, Krakowiec Roman Catholic death register, 1 January 1794, AGAD 1/437/0/-/24.

40. *Poezyje Wincentego Pola*, vol. 1 (Vienna, 1857), 3–4. This rendering is based on a translation by Kinga Kosmala.

41. Marek Koter, '"Kresy" as a Specific Type of Borderland - Its Origin and Characteristics', *Geographica Slovenica*, 34: 1 (2001), 131–48.

42. Cetner's death date is wrongly given as 1800 in the standard Polish biographical encyclopedia: Konopczyński, 'Cetner', 238–9. The Krakowiec Roman Catholic death register, in the Polish National Archive (AGAD 1/437/0/-/24), records that he died on 2 (or 9) January 1809.

43. Stęczyński, *Okolice Galicyi*, 53–4.

CHAPTER 4

1. Jacek Krochmal, 'Batei kneset u-batei almin yehudiim be-hevel Przemyśl be-emtsa ha-meah ha-18', *Gal-Ed*, vol. 18 (2000), Hebrew section 76.

2. Motylewicz, 'Żydzi w miastach ziemi przemyskiej', 113–136.

3. Ferdynand Bostel, *Żydzi ziemi lwowskiej i powiatu żydaczowskiego w r. 1765* (Cracow, 1891), 15; price tables for Lwów in Stanisław Hoszowski, *Ceny we Lwówie w latach 1701–1914* (Lwów, 1934), esp. table 18; Judith Kalik, *Scepter of Judah: The Jewish Autonomy in the Eighteenth-Century Crown Poland* (Leiden, 2009), 277–84 (table 11).

4. Copy (28 January 1786) of document dated 10 October 1771, APK TS 792; and other credit notes dated 1755 and 1760, ibid.

5. Derek Beales, *Joseph II* : vol. 1, *In the Shadow of Maria Theresa 1741–1780* (Cambridge, 1987), 363.

6. William O. McCagg Jr., *A History of Habsburg Jews 1670-1918* (Bloomington, 1989), 19.

7. Anon. [Alphons Heinrich Traunpaur, Chevalier d'Orphanie], *Dreyßig Briefe über Galizien oder Beobachtungen eines unpartheyischen Mannes der sich mehr als nur ein paar Monate in diesem Königreiche umgesehen hat* (Berlin, 1990 [first published Vienna, 1787]), 94 ff.

8. Ewa Katherine Bacon, 'Austrian Economic Policy in Galicia 1772–1790', U. of Chicago PhD diss., 1975, 103–4.

9. Decree issued by the court of the *oekonom* (estate manager) of Krakowiec, 13 August 1782, NAN 6350/6.

10. 'Totalausweis über den Fortgang der jüdischen Ansiedlung in Ostgalizien bis Ende October 1805', APK TS 1798 (microform copy in Brandeis University Library DS135.P62 G374). Aron was very likely an ancestor of Chaim-Yitzhak Laub, father of my grandmother Czarna Wasserstein (*née*

Laub). Unfortunately, gaps in the surviving Jewish birth and death records for Krakowiec preclude definite establishment of the connection.

11. Thirteen named Jews of Krakowiec to Anna Lotaryńska, undated petition, TsDIAL 166/1/1732, leaves 169–70. The petition was 'inscriptum', i.e. formally recorded in the town records, in 1818, but it must have originated at some point between the death of Ignacy Cetner in 1809 and that of his daughter in 1814.

12. Bredetzky, *Reisebemerkungen*, 197–8.

13. *Memoirs of Prince Metternich 1815–1829*, vol. 4 (New York, 1881), 16–24: letters dated 23 & 29 September, 17 & 30 October 1823.

14. Wolfram Siemann, *Metternich: Strategist and Visionary* (Cambridge, Mass., 2019), 644.

15. Joseph Margoshes, *A World Apart: A Memoir of Jewish Life in Nineteenth Century Galicia* (Boston 2005), 17.

16. Jiří Langer, *Nine Gates to the Chasidic Mysteries* (trans. Stephen Joly, Northvale, NJ, 1993), 12.

17. Raphael Mahler, *Hasidism and the Jewish Enlightenment: Their Confrontation in Galicia and Poland in the First Half of the Nineteenth Century* (Philadelphia, 1985), 100–1.

18. Berl Kagan, *Seyfer ha-prenumerantn: vegvayzer tsu prenumerirte hebreyishe sforim* (New York, 1975). Three of the works are of special interest: *Ma'aseh Rokeah*, a discussion of the composition of the Mishnah, first published in Amsterdam in 1740. The author, Eleazar ben reb Shmuel Shmelke, was born in Cracow and served as Ashkenazi rabbi of Amsterdam from 1735 until 1740, when he moved to the Holy Land. Our edition was issued in Lwów in 1892. Its popularity in Krakowiec no doubt derived from the fact that its author was an ancestor of the founder of the Belz Hasidic dynasty. Secondly, *Sefer 'Amudei ha-shiv'ah: derushim gedolim ve-nifla'im* by Bezalel ben reb Shim'on mi-Kobrin (1640–1691), first published Lublin, 1766; our edition, Lwów, 1888. The third is *Sefer ha-Temunah*, apparently written in early thirteenth-century Spain (first surviving printed edition, Korets [north-west Ukraine], 1784; our edition, Lemberg, 1892). All three of these were kabbalistic works. Gershom Scholem, calls *Sefer ha-Temunah* 'the most outstanding example of . . . speculative or virtual "spiritualism" to be found in Kabbalistic literature' and notes that it greatly influenced the Sabbateans: Gershom Scholem, *The Messianic Idea in Judaism* (London, 1971), 111. However, four of the twelve Krakowiec subscribers to *Sefer ha-Temunah* were also subscribers to the *Ma'aseh Rokeah*, whose author was a fierce opponent of the Sabbateans.

19. 'Urkunde', 6 June 1788, APK TS 792.

20. Weekly supplement to *Gazeta Lwowska*, 11 June 1853.

21. For the problems in assessing census findings on literacy in Galicia, see Stephen C. Corssin, 'Literacy Rates and Questions of Language, Faith and Ethnic Identity in Population Censuses in the Partitioned Polish Lands and Interwar Poland (1880s-1930s)', *Polish Review*, 43: 2 (1998), 131–60.

22. *Gazeta Lwowska*, 8 April 1867.

23. *Kurjer Lwowski*, 11 February 1897.

24. Ivan Franko, *Boa Constrictor and other Stories* (trans. Fainna Solasko, Moscow, n.d. [1957]), 207–8.

25. Natan M. Meir, *Stepchildren of the Shtetl: The Destitute, Disabled, and Mad of Jewish Eastern Europe, 1800–1939* (Stanford, 2020), 109, citing the Austro-Galician rabbi and folklorist Samuel Rappoport.

26. Hela Laub, *My Heritage* (Tel Aviv, 1987), 37.

CHAPTER 5

1. Aftanazy, *Dzieje rezydencji*, vol. 8, 54–5.

2. Sale contract, 12 July 1845, in NAN MS f.141/582 E/357/362, leaves 387–90.

3. Order by Casimir Ritter von Milbacher, 22 February 1846, quoted in L. B. Namier, '1848: The Revolution of the Intellectuals', *Proceedings of the British Academy*, 30 (1944), 174.

4. Larry Wolff, *The Idea of Galicia: History and Fantasy in Habsburg Political Culture* (Stanford, 2010), 8.

5. F.B. [Felix Boznański, *c.* 1793–*c.* 1860], *Ostatnie marzenia starego Huzara* (Lwów, 1848), 89. This rendering is based on translations by Kinga Kosmala and Kamil Kiedos.

6. Daniel Unowsky, *The Pomp and Politics of Patriotism: Imperial Celebrations in Habsburg Austria, 1848–1916* (West Lafayette, Ind., 2005), 25.

7. Wolff, *The Idea of Galicia*, 256.

8. Raphael Mahler, 'The Economic Background of Jewish Emigration from Galicia to the United States', in Deborah Dash Moore ed., *East European Jews in Two Worlds: Studies from the YIVO Annual* (Evanston, Ill., 1990), 127.

9. Stella Hryniuk, 'Peasant Agriculture in East Galicia in the late Nineteenth Century', *Slavonic and East European Review*, 63: 2 (1985), 228–43.

10. *Gazeta Lwowska*, 7 September 1889. Translated from the Polish by Kamil Kiedos.

11. Joseph Roth, *The Radetzky March* (*Radetzkymarsch*, Berlin, 1932; trans. Eva Tucker, Woodstock, NY, 1983), 214–16.

12. Franz Joseph to Ludwig Windisch-Graetz, 6 September 1889, in Rudolf Engel, *Geschichte des k. und k. Infanterieregiments Philipp Herzog von Württemberg Nr. 77, von der Errichtung 1860 bis 1906* (Przemyśl, 1906), 286–7.

13. Jean de Bourgoing ed., *Briefe Kaiser Franz Josephs an Frau Katharina Schratt* (Vienna, 1949), 143: letter dated 7 September 1889.

14. *Gazeta Lwowska*, 10 September 1889.

15. *Loc. cit.*, 24 September 1889.

16. *Loc. cit.*, 7 September 1893.

17. *Einzelfeuer: Zweite Folge von "Habt acht!": 255 militärische Anekdoten und Witze* (Vienna, 1912), 104.

18. Mahler, 'The Economic Background of Jewish Emigration', 127.

19. *Wschód*, 16 August 1901.

20. *Teka Konserwatorska: rocznik Kola c. k. Konserwatorow Starożytnych Pomników Galicyi Wschodniej. 1892*, 160, recording meeting on 18 December 1891.

21. Hoszowski, *Ceny we Lwówie*.

22. *Gazeta Lwowska*, 9, 10 March 1852 and 16 April 1911; *Kurjer Lwowski*, 8 November 1895; *Gazeta Narodowa*, 12 February 1899.

23. *Słowo Polskie*, 25 August 1900.

24. Eustach Wołoszczak, 'Zur Flora von Jaworów in Galizien', *Verhandlungen der kaiserlich-königlichen zoologisch-botanischen Gesellschaft in Wien*, 24 (1874), 530.

25. Sławomir Tokarski, *Ethnic Conflict and Economic Development: Jews in Galician Agriculture 1868–1914* (Warsaw, 2003), 212.

26. Ivan L. Rudnytsky, 'The Ukrainians in Galicia under Austrian Rule', *Austrian History Yearbook*, 3 (1967), 397.

27. Andrew Dennis Sorokowski, 'The Greek Catholic Parish Clergy in Galicia, 1900-1939', University of London School of Slavonic and East European Studies Ph.D. diss., 1991, 43.

28. See reports on Prosvita in Krakowiec and surrounding district, 1908–1938, TsDIAL 348/1/3133, 3134, 3137, & 3138.

29. *Przewodnik Oświatowy: organ Towarzystwa Szkoły Ludowej, poświęcony sprawom oświaty pozaszkolnej i narodowego wychowania ludu polskiego*, vol. VII (Cracow, 1907), 98; Kai Struve, 'Peasant Emancipation and National Integration: Agrarian Circles, Village Reading Rooms, and Cooperatives in Galicia', in Torsten Lorenz ed., *Cooperatives in Ethnic*

Conflicts: Eastern Europe in the 19th and Early 20th Century (Berlin, 2006), 229–50.

30. *Słowo Polskie*, 17 September 1907.
31. Lev and Barahura eds., *Iavorivshchyna i krakovechchyna*, 178.
32. Ibid., 166 & 175 ff.
33. Quoted in Kerstin S. Jobst, 'Compromise and Confrontation: The So-Called National Question in Galicia', in Jacek Purchla and Wolfgang Kos et al. eds., *The Myth of Galicia* (Cracow, 2014), 166.
34. Roman Lekhniuk, 'Assassination of the Galician Governor and the Trial of His Murderer', Center for Urban History of East-Central Europe, Lviv, 2020, https://lia.lvivcenter.org/en/events/potocki-assassination/
35. McCagg Jr., *A History of Habsburg Jews*, 183.
36. Wolff, *The Idea of Galicia*, 283.
37. *Neues Fremden Blatt*, 21 March 1869.
38. Rachel Manekin, *The Rebellion of the Daughters: Jewish Women Runaways in Habsburg Galicia* (Princeton, 2020); David I. Kertzer, *The Kidnapping of Edgardo Mortara* (New York, 1997).
39. 'Inventar', 10 March 1849, APK TS 792.
40. *Gazeta Lwowska*, 18 October 1882. Memorandum, *c.* 1871, APK TS 792.
41. District Council, Jaworów, to provincial government, Lwów, 13 March 1877, TsDIAL 165.4a.14, 44–5.
42. *Österreichische Statistik, III Statistik des Sanitätswesens der im Reichsrathe vertretenen Königreiche und Länder für das Jahr 1880* (Vienna, 1883), 20–21.
43. Kazimierz Chłędowski, *Pamiętniki*, vol. 1 *Galicja (1843–1880)* (Wrocław, 1957), 275.
44. Petition submitted, 8 July 1880 *[Kadencja IV, sesja III, pos. 16] Sprawozdanie Stenograficzne z Rozpraw Galicyjskiego Sejmu Krajowego. 16. Posiedzenie 3. Sesyi IV. Peryodu Sejmu Galicyskiego*, 447.
45. Report to assembly by government commissioner Filip Zaleski, 16 October 1882 *[Kadencja IV, sesja V, pos. 27], loc. cit. 27. Posiedzenie 5. Sesyi IV. Peryodu Sejmu Galicyjskiego*, 574.
46. Beschwerde der Bezirksvertretung von Jaworów in Händen des Obmannes Johan Grafen Szeptycki gegen die Entscheidung des k. k. Ministeriums des Innern vom 2. März 1893, TsDIAL 165/4a/14.
47. Text of decision no. 7891, 9 May 1894, in Adam Freiherr von Budwiński ed., *Erkentnisse des k. k. Verwaltungsgerichtshofes*, vol. 18 (Vienna, 1894), 484–7.
48. Government report, 21 May 1894, TsDIAL 165/7/141/65.

49. *Allgemeine Israelitische Wochenschrift* (Berlin), 2 July 1897.

50. Report dated 7 October 1896, TsDIAL 165/7/141/27.

51. *Gazeta Narodowa*, 22 June 1897.

52. *Batkivshchyna*, 1 October 1879, quoted in John-Paul Himka, 'Ukrainian–Jewish Antagonism in the Galician Countryside During the Late Nineteenth Century', in Howard Aster and Peter J. Potichnyj eds., *Ukrainian–Jewish Relations in Historical Perspective* (2nd ed., Edmonton, 1990), 112.

53. Yaroslav Hrytsak, 'A Strange Case of Antisemitism: Ivan Franko and the Jewish Issue', in Omer Bartov and Eric D. Weitz eds., *Shatterzone of Empires* (Bloomington, Ind., 2013), 228–42.

54. Daniel Unowsky, *The Plunder: The 1898 Anti-Jewish Riots in Habsburg Galicia* (Stanford, 2018), 112.

55. Ibid., 14.

56. *Kurjer Lwowski*, 22 February 1902.

57. Tim Buchen, *Antisemitism in Galicia: Agitation, Politics, and Violence against Jews in the late Habsburg Monarchy* (New York, 2020), chapters 1 & 2.

58. Joseph Roth, *The Emperor's Tomb* (trans. John Hoare, Woodstock, NY, 1984), 29.

59. Joseph Roth, 'The Bust of the Emperor', in *Hotel Savoy and Other Stories* (trans. John Hoare, Woodstock, NY, 1986), 160.

60. Quoted in Jobst, 'Compromise and Confrontation', 167. Unfortunately Dr Jobst has been unable to provide me with a source for this quotation.

61. Asher Barash, *Pictures from a Brewery* (*Temunot mi-bet mivshal ha-shekhar*, Jerusalem, 1929; trans. Katie Kaplan, London, 1972).

CHAPTER 6

1. Report from Cracow, 13 August 1914, in Stefan Arski and Józef Chudek eds., *Galicyjska działalność wojskowa Piłsudskiego, 1906–1914: dokumenty* (Warsaw, 1967), 375–81.

2. John R. Schindler, *Fall of the Double Eagle: The Battle for Galicia and the Demise of Austria-Hungary* (Lincoln, Neb., 2015), 49.

3. Alexander Watson, *Ring of Steel: Germany and Austria-Hungary at War, 1914–1918* (London, 2015), 154.

4. Stanisław Maciszewski, quoted in Adam Kożuchowski, 'A Tentative Dissolution of Austria-Hungary: The 1914–15 Russian Occupation of Lviv in Polish Memory', *Austrian History Yearbook*, 52 (2021), 169.

5. Gerhard Oberkofler and Eduard Rabofsky, 'Tiroler Kaiserjäger in Galizien', in Sabine Weiss et al. eds., *Historische Blickpunkte: Festschrift für Johann Rainer* (Innsbruck, 1988), 505.

6. Report from Cracow, 13 August 1914, in Arski and Chudek eds., *Galicyjska działalność wojskowa Piłsudskiego*, 375–81.

7. See e.g. Jan Słomka, *From serfdom to self-government: memoirs of a Polish village mayor, 1842–1927* (London, 1941), 210, 213.

8. Manfried Rauchensteiner, *The First World War and the End of the Habsburg Monarchy* (Vienna, 2014), 193.

9. Theodor Ritter von Zeynek, *Ein Offizier im Generalstabskorps erinnert sich* (ed. Peter Broucek, Vienna, 2009), 189.

10. *Freie Stimmen* (Klagenfurt), 26 July 1928.

11. Moriz [sic] Freiherr von Auffenberg-Komarów, *Aus Österreichs Höhe und Niedergang: eine Lebensschilderung* (Munich, 1921), 364.

12. Diary entry dated 18 September 1914 in Octavian C. Tăslăuanu, *With the Austrian Army in Galicia* (London, [1918]), 85.

13. Ibid., 64.

14. *Słowo Polskie*, 15/28 November 1914.

15. Watson, *Ring of Steel*, 199–201; Rebekah Klein-Pejšová, 'Beyond the "Infamous Concentration Camps of the Old Monarchy": Jewish Refugee Policy from Wartime Austria-Hungary to Interwar Czechoslovakia', *Austrian History Yearbook*, 45 (2014), 150–66; Jiří Kudela, 'Die Emigration Galizischer und Osteuropäischer Juden nach Böhmen und Prag zwischen 1914–1916/17', *Studia Rosenthaliana*, 23 (1989), 119–34.

16. Winston Churchill, *The Unknown War: The Eastern Front* (New York, 1931), 231.

17. Alexander Watson, *The Fortress: The Great Siege of Przemyśl* (London, 2019); Edmund Glaise-Horstenau et al. eds., *Österreich-Ungarns letzter Krieg, 1914–1918*, vol. 1 (Vienna, 1930), esp. 318–19; Franz Graf Conrad von Hötzendorf, *Aus meiner Dienstzeit 1906–1918* (5 vols., Vienna, 1921–5), vol. 4, 726–80 & vol. 5, 118–19.

18. Quoted in William W. Hagen, *Anti-Jewish Violence in Poland, 1914–1920* (Cambridge, 2018), 66.

19. Julian Stryjkowski, *The Inn* (*Austeria*, Warsaw, 1966; trans. Celina Wieniewska, New York, 1972), 12, 20–1. The novel was the basis for an impressive film directed by Jerzy Kawalerowicz (1982).

20. Alexander Victor Prusin, *Nationalizing a Borderland: War, Ethnicity, and Anti-Jewish Violence in East Galicia, 1914–1920* (Tuscaloosa, Al., 2005), 13–14.

21. Christoph Mick, *Lemberg, Lwów, L'viv: Violence and Ethnicity in a Contested City* (West Lafayette, Ind., 2016), 41.

22. Prusin, *Nationalizing a Borderland*, 40.

23. Aftanazy, *Dzieje rezydencji*, vol. 8, 60.

24. *Wiener Medizinische Wochenschrift*, 24 July 1915.

25. Julia Ledóchowska, *Poland ravaged and bereaved* (London, 1916), 14.

26. Foreword by František Langer to Jiří Langer, *Nine Gates*, xxii.

27. Jacob Katz, *With My Own Eyes: The Autobiography of a Historian* (Hanover, NH, 1995), 21.

28. Arendt to Karl Jaspers, 13 April 1961, in Lotte Kohler and Hans Saner eds., *Hannah Arendt Karl Jaspers Correspondence 1926–1969* (trans. Robert and Rita Kimber, San Diego, 1993), 434. A better rendering of the German *unsympathisch* might be 'disagreeable' or 'uncongenial'.

29. Katz, *With My Own Eyes*, 20.

30. *New York Times*, 19 June 1915.

31. Glaise-Horstenau et al. eds., *Österreich-Ungarns letzter Krieg*, vol. 2 (Vienna, 1931), 474–5.

32. S. Ansky, *The Enemy at his Pleasure: A Journey Through the Jewish Pale of Settlement During World War I* (ed. and trans. Joachim Neugroschel, New York, 2002), 139–40.

33. *Jüdische Nachrichten für die deutschösterr. Provinz*, 24 September 1919.

34. L. Chasanowitch ed., *Les Pogromes Anti-Juifs en Pologne et en Galicie en Novembre et Décembre 1918: Faits et Documents* (Stockholm, 1918), 7.

35. John Schindler, 'Steamrollered in Galicia: The Austro-Hungarian Army and the Brusilov Offensive, 1916', *War in History*, 10: 1 (2003), 43.

36. *Bulletin of the Joint Distribution Committee*, 2: 6 (February 1918), 87–8.

37. Schedule of applications for compensation for war damage in Krakowiec, February–March 1917, TsDIAL 146/48/135.

38. Clifford F. Wargelin, 'A High Price for Bread: The First Treaty of Brest-Litovsk and the Break-up of Austria-Hungary, 1917–1918', *International History Review*, 19: 4 (1997), 757.

39. Rauchensteiner, *The First World War*, 818.

40. K. u. k. Armeeoberkommando Bericht über Zustände in Galizien an k. k. Ministerium d. Innern, Wien, Standort am 2. Juni 1918, ÖStA Ministerium des Innern Präsidiale 22.1877 Galizien 1918.

41. Watson, *Ring of Steel*, 502.

42. Full text of report by the Delegacy of the Polish Ministry of Foreign Affairs, 17 December 1918, in Jerzy Tomaszewski, 'Lwów, 22 listopada 1918', *Przegląd Historyczny*, 75 (1984), pp. 279–85.

43. Hagen, *Anti-Jewish Violence*, 148.
44. Mick, *Lemberg, Lwów, L'viv*, 164.
45. Chasanowitch ed., *Les Pogromes*, 23 & 41–5.
46. Mordechai Kaufman, 'Opgerisene zikhroynes funem idishn galitsye', in N. Tsuker ed., *Pinkes galitsye* (Buenos Aires, 1945), 89–102; *The Times*, 8 February & 27 June 1919; Israel Cohen, 'The Lemberg Pogrom', in *Travels in Jewry* (London, 1952), 82–93; Chasanowitch ed., *Les Pogromes*, 47–73; *Report by Sir Stuart Samuel on his Mission to Poland* (Cmd. 674, London, 1920); William W. Hagen, 'The Moral Economy of Popular Violence: The Pogrom in Lwów, November 1918', in Robert Blobaum ed., *Antisemitism and Its Opponents in Modern Poland* (Ithaca, NY, 2005), 124–47; Prusin, *Nationalizing a Borderland*, ch. 5.
47. Prusin, *Nationalizing a Borderland*, 95.
48. Laub, *My Heritage*, 42–3.
49. Lev and Barahura eds., *Iavorivshchyna i krakovechchyna*, 166–74; Bolesław Roja, *Legendy i fakty* (Warsaw, 1931), 294.
50. Ievhen Petrushevych, President of National Council of Provisional Government of Halycz to President Wilson, November 1918, *FRUS: The Paris Peace Conference 1919*, vol. 2 (Washington DC, 1942), 195–6.
51. Delegates of State Secretariat of West Ukraine to President of Polish-Ukrainian Armistice Commission, 24 May 1919, *DBFP*, First Series, vol. 3 (London, 1949), 322–3.
52. Stenographic report of meeting, 5 June 1919, *FRUS: The Paris Peace Conference 1919*, vol. 6 (Washington DC, 1946), 194–5, 198.
53. Namier, '1848', 224.
54. D. W. Hayton, *Conservative Revolutionary: The Lives of Lewis Namier* (Manchester, 2019), 113–14.
55. Extract from stenographic report of meeting in Paris on 5 June 1919, *DBFP*, First Series, vol. 3, 348–55.
56. Coolidge (Vienna) to Commission to Negotiate Peace, 9 January 1919, *FRUS: The Paris Peace Conference, 1919*, vol. 2, 227.
57. Rapport de la Commission des Affaires polonaises au Conseil Suprême, 20 November 1919, *DBFP*, First Series, vol. 2 (London, 1948), 372 ff.
58. Christopher Coker, 'Global locals', *Times Literary Supplement*, 5 December 2008.
59. Memorandum by Namier, June/July 1919, quoted in Julia Namier, *Lewis Namier: A Biography* (London, 1971), 144.
60. Ukrainian Diplomatic Mission in London to Foreign Office, 8 August 1919, TNA FO 371/3907.

61. Nathalie Babel ed., *The Complete Works of Isaac Babel* (trans. Peter Constantine, New York, 2002), 401.

62. Bartłomiej Rusin, 'Lewis Namier, the Curzon Line, and the shaping of Poland's eastern frontier after World War I', *Studies in the History of Russia and Central-Eastern Europe*, 48 (2010), 5–26.

63. Namier, '1848', 189.

64. Quoted in Mark Baker, 'Lewis Namier and the Problem of Eastern Galicia', *Journal of Ukrainian Studies*, 23: 2 (1998), 101.

65. Roman Solchanyk, 'The Foundation of the Communist Movement in Eastern Galicia, 1919-1921', *Slavic Review*, 30: 4 (1971), 774–94; 'Communist Party of Western Ukraine,' and 'Vasylkiv, Osyp,' in *Encyclopedia of Ukraine*, vols. 1 & 5 (Toronto, 1993); *Ukrainian Weekly*, 19 July 1998; Janusz Radziejowski, *The Communist Party of Western Ukraine 1919–1929* (Edmonton, 1983); Tarik Cyril Amar, *The Paradox of Ukrainian Lviv: A Borderland City between Stalinists, Nazis, and Nationalists* (Ithaca, NY, 2015), ch. 8; Olga Bertelsen and Myroslav Shkandrij, 'The Secret Police and the Campaign against Galicians in Soviet Ukraine, 1929–1934', *Nationalities Papers: The Journal of Nationalism and Ethnicity*, 42: 1 (2014), 37–62; Wojciech Roszkowski and Jan Kofman eds., *Biographical Dictionary of Central and Eastern Europe in the Twentieth Century* (Abingdon, 2015), 519–20.

66. Lev and Barahura eds., *Iavorivshchyna i Krakovechchyna*, 169.

67. Alfred Döblin, *Journey to Poland* (London, 1991), 145 & 152.

CHAPTER 7

1. *Gazeta Lwowska*, 26 June and 8 July 1903.

2. *Kurjer Lwowski*, 29 January 1900.

3. *Kurjer Lwowski* and *Gazeta Lwowska*, 21 May 1902.

4. Krakowiec Jewish death register, 16 June 1907, AGAD 1/300/0/-/3167.

5. Kudela, 'Die Emigration Galizischer und Osteuropäischer Juden', 19–134.

6. *Neues Wiener Tagblatt*, 12 December 1914.

7. Ulrike Steglich and Peter Kratz, *Das Falsche Scheunenviertel* (Berlin, 1994), 173.

8. David H. Weinberg, *A Community on Trial: The Jews of Paris in the 1930s* (Chicago, 1974), 21.

9. *Chwila* (Lwów), 3 April 1933.

10. Gideon Shimoni, *Jews and Zionism: The South African Experience 1910–1967* (Oxford, 1980), 144.

CHAPTER 8

1. Library of Congress, LCmss36483.
2. *Chwila* (Lwów), 24 July 1927.
3. *Der Morgen* (Lwów), 19 July 1928.
4. *Folksfreynd*, 27 July 1928.
5. *Forverts*, 27 January 1929.
6. Hamish Fraser, *The Coming of the Mass Market 1850–1914* (Hamden, Conn., 1981), 32.
7. Jonathan Lynn, 'Finally Getting Somewhere', *Times Literary Supplement*, 13 December 2019.
8. Lady Antonia Fraser, *My History: A Memoir of Growing Up* (London, 2015), 106.
9. Memoir by Jack Baruch Keil, Archive of Leo Baeck Institute, New York, ME 1516.
10. S. Y. Agnon, *A Simple Story* (*Sipur pashut*, Berlin, 1935; trans. Hillel Halkin, New York, 1985), 111.
11. Correspondence and proposed statute, August–November 1932, DALO 1/53/1572.
12. *Pinkas ha-kehilot: Polin: entsiklopedyah shel ha-yishuvim ha-yehudiyim le-min hivasdam ve-ad le-ahar shoat milhemet ha-olam ha-sheniyah* (Jerusalem, 1976–99), vol. 2 [East Galicia], 492.
13. Correspondence, 6 & 8 May, & 12 August 1935, CZA microfilm CM448.
14. Extract from report by Lieut. R. C. Foster (Warsaw), 9 January 1919 in Prof. A. C. Coolidge (Vienna) to Commission to Negotiate Peace, 11 January 1919, *FRUS: The Paris Peace Conference 1919*, vol. 2, 230.
15. Jan Tomasz Gross, *Polish Society under German Occupation: The Generalgouvernement, 1939–1944* (Princeton, 1979), 15–16.
16. *Nowy Dziennik*, 20 November 1937; Emil Palej, 'Notatki z mego życia', *Quod Libet*, 73 (2011), 15–19.
17. Petro Tronko, *Istoriia mist i sil Ukrains'koi RSR: v dvadtsiaty shesty tomakh*, vol. XIV, *Lvivska oblast* (Kiev, [1968]), 927–8.
18. Gross, *Polish Society*, 19.
19. TsDIAL 348/1/3138.
20. Response dated 27 April 1931 to questionnaire for Greek Catholic schematism, APP Archiwum Greckatolickiego Biskupstwa w Przemyślu, 6607/810.
21. Frank Golczewski, 'Shades of grey: Reflections on Jewish–Ukrainian and German–Ukrainian Relations in Galicia', in Ray Brandon and Wendy

Lower eds., *The Shoah in Ukraine: History, Testimony, Memorialization* (Bloomington, Ind., 2008), 124.

22. Quoted in Timothy Snyder, *The Reconstruction of Nations: Poland, Ukraine, Lithuania, Belarus, 1569–1999* (New Haven, 2003), 143.

23. *Narod i Wojsko*, 14 November 1937.

24. *Polish Atrocities in Ukraine* (United Ukrainian Organizations of the United States: New York, 1931), 320–1. Petition to League of Nations by Ukrainian parliamentarians, 31 December 1930; other petitions, Observations of the Polish Government, 6 April 1931, League of Nations Document C.741.1931.I.

25. Anatole W. Bedriy, 'An Exemplary Freedom-Fighter: On the 20th anniversary of the Death of Roman Shukhevych (Taras Chuprynka)', *Ukrainian Review*, 17: 1 (1970), 9 & 11.

26. Lev and Barahura eds., *Iavorivshchyna i Krakovechchyna*, 170.

27. Parliamentary question to Minister of Justice by Stefan Nawrocki, 23 January 1939, AAN Praesidium of Council of Ministers Ref. 3A-15, 68-70, AS. Kol.-T76/0036/01-03.

28. Mick, *Lemberg, Lwów, L'viv*, 259.

29. Interviews with Aharon Berg, 1994, and Elimelech Glick, 1995.

30. *Głos Jaworowski*, October–November 1938.

31. Chone Gottesfeld, *Mayn rayze iber galitsye* (New York, 1937), 31.

32. M. Rettig, 'A rirender brif fun galitsye', *Der Galitsyaner* (New York, 1939), 7.

33. M. Ohringer et al. to 'Krakovyetser landslayt in Amerike', 5 March 1939, YIVO 335.7/202.

34. British Embassy, Warsaw, to Foreign Office, 13 December 1938, TNA FO 371/21639.

35. Sir H. Kennard (Warsaw) to Viscount Halifax, 20 November 1938, TNA FO 371/21638.

36. Family papers.

CHAPTER 9

1. Postcard, 30 July 1939, family papers.

2. BA AOK 14 Ia, RH 20-14/2.

3. Stanisław Maczek, *Avec mes blindés: Pologne, France, Belgique, Hollande, Allemagne* (Paris, [1967]), 75.

4. F. S. Kurcz [Franciszek Skibiński], *The Black Brigade* (Harrow, Middlesex, 1943), 82.

5. Robert Edwards, *Scouts Out: A History of German Armored Reconnaissance Units in World War II* (Mechanicsburg, Penn., 2013), 337–9. The context of the battle from the Polish side is described in operational reports and memoranda in Polish Institute and Sikorski Museum, London, B1 58A-D; compte-rendu by François Skibiński, ibid. Also Stefan Komornicki, *Pułk Ułanow: zarys historii 1920-1947* (London, 1976), 121, 137, & 161; and Rajmund Szubański, *Polska broń pancerna w 1939 roku* (Warsaw, 1982), 209–10.

6. Alfred B. Peszke, 'The Bomber Brigade of the Polish Air Force in September 1939', *Polish Review*, 13: 4 (1968), 94.

7. Maczek, *Avec mes blindés*, 81.

8. Klaus-Jürgen Thies, *Der Polenfeldzug: Eine Lageatlas der Operationsabteilung des Generalstabs des Heeres* (Osnabrück, 1989), maps 11–16.

9. Interview with Dov and Yisrael Berg, Tel Aviv, 9 January 1995.

10. S. Druk, *Yudenshtot yavorov: der umkum fun di yavorover yidn* (New York, 1950), 3–5, 20; Kai Struve, *Deutsche Herrschaft, ukrainischer Nationalismus, antijüdischer Gewalt: Der Sommer 1941 in der Westukraine* (Oldenbourg, 2015), 62–4; Klara Bielec (*née* Bogen), interviewed by Joanna Wiszniewicz for USC Shoah Foundation, Wrocław, 1 March 1997.

11. *Soldaten Zeitung*, 16 and 18 September 1939.

12. Interview with Frejde Nacht, Gan Yavne, Israel, 9 April 1995. Ms Nacht did not name the priest. He may have been Father Vasyl (Basilius) Matkivskyi.

13. Interview with Sonia Levensolt, Ramat Gan, 19 December 1994.

14. Interview with Dov and Yisrael Berg, Tel Aviv, 9 January 1995.

15. Wilhelm Prüller, *Diary of a German Soldier* (London, 1953), 27.

16. John Erickson, 'The Red Army's March into Poland, September 1939', in Keith Sword ed. *The Soviet Takeover of the Polish Eastern Provinces, 1939–1941* (London, 1991), 15–16.

17. William Taubman, *Khrushchev: The Man and His Era* (London, 2004), 138–9.

18. Lev and Barahura eds., *Iavorivshchyna i krakovechchyna*, 364.

19. Diary/memoir, probably written in 1944, manuscript in Archiwum Głowne Urszulanek SJK, Pniewy.

20. Operational report of Polish Sixth Army, 8.00 pm, 30 September 1939, in Czesław Grzelak et al. eds., *Agresja sowiecka na Polskę w świetle dokumentów – 17 września 1939* (3 vols., Warsaw, 1994–5), vol. 2, part 3, 216–17.

21. Alexander B. Rossino, *Hitler Strikes Poland: Blitzkrieg, Ideology, and Atrocity* (Lawrence, Kans., 2003), 97.

22. Announcement dated 22 September 1939, Royal Institute of International Affairs *Bulletin of International News*, 16: 20 (7 October 1939), 1060.

23. Thies, *Der Polenfeldzug*, maps 17 ff.

24. Interview with Sonia Levensolt, Ramat Gan, 19 December 1994.

25. Dov Levin, *The Lesser of Two Evils: Eastern European Jewry under Soviet Rule, 1939–1941* (Philadelphia, 1995), 35.

26. Struve, *Deutsche Herrschaft*, 152.

27. Mick, *Lemberg, Lwów, L'viv*, 271.

28. Taubman, *Khrushchev*, 137.

29. Statement by 'U.M.' (possibly Maria Urbaniec), HIA Polish Ministry of Information papers, box 132, folder 5, # 4745.

30. Aharon Weiss, 'Some Economic and Social Problems of the Jews of Eastern Galicia in the Period of Soviet Rule (1939-41)', in Norman Davies and Antony Polonsky eds., *Jews in Eastern Poland and the USSR, 1939–1946* (New York, 1991), 77–109.

31. Translated transcript in Sword ed., *The Soviet Takeover*, 295–300.

32. Statement by 'U.M.' (possibly Maria Urbaniek), HIA Polish Ministry of Information papers, box 132, folder 5, # 4745.

33. Testimony of Antoni Budzianowski, HIA Polish Ministry of Information, Box 138, folder 2.

34. Sheptytsky to Cardinal Tisserant, 26 December 1939, in Pierre Blet et al. eds., *Actes et Documents du Saint Siège relatifs à la Seconde Guerre Mondiale*, vol. 3, part one (Vatican City, 1967), 168–73.

35. Mala Gottlieb interviewed by Jane Grossberg, Melbourne, 16 October 1993.

36. Interview with Eli Silberman, Brooklyn, 24 September 1996.

37. 'Krakowiec', 1940, DALO 335/1/16.

38. A reconstruction of population statistics conducted after the war by a Ukrainian exile, Volodymyr Kubijovyc, estimated the population of Krakowiec in January 1939 as 1,840 of whom 770 were Jews, 640 Ukrainians, 350 Poles, and 80 'Latynnyky'. The latter were described as a transitional group, Ukrainian in ethnic background but Roman Catholic by religion, and at this period mainly Polish-speaking. (Volodymyr Kubijovyc, *Ethnic Groups of the South-Western Ukraine (Halyčyna-Galicia)* (Wiesbaden, 1983), 30.) The apparent doubling of the town's Jewish population since 1931 is surprising and calls for comment. Kubijovyc, an ardent Ukrainian nationalist and Nazi collaborator, had no

reason to exaggerate the size of the Jewish population and does not appear to have done so in his estimates for other towns in Galicia. Part of the explanation may be that the 1931 census, carried out by the Polish authorities, under-counted Jews. But their number in the town had probably increased significantly by 1939. A rough Jewish estimate in April 1939 put the Jewish population at 600 out of 1,600 inhabitants (I. Giterman, Joint Distribution Committee, Warsaw, to Joint Distribution Committee, Paris, 12 April 1939, YIVO 335.7/202). Some Jews may have come to Krakowiec from outlying villages. The further increase by 1940 is probably explained by the arrival of Jewish refugees from Nazi-held territory west of the San.

39. Ben-Cion Pinchuk, *Shtetl Jews under Soviet Rule: Eastern Poland on the Eve of the Holocaust* (Oxford, 1990), 60.

40. 'Vi azoy men lebt itst in sovetisher galitsye', *Forverts* (New York), 9 March 1940.

41. Levin, *The Lesser of Two Evils*, 312, n. 26.

42. Pinchuk, *Shtetl Jews*, 114. The story is considered authentic by Pinchuk, who cites the memoirs of Moyshe Grossman, *In Farkishuftn land fun legendern Dzugashvili: mayne zibn yorn lebn in ratnfarband* (Paris, 1949), 94. Grossman did not, however, witness the episode himself; he says he heard about it from someone else. Still, even if apocryphal, it is *ben trovato*.

43. Christoph Mick, '"Only the Jews do not waver ..." L'viv under Soviet Occupation', in Elazar Barkan et al. eds., *Shared History – Divided Memory. Jews and Others in Soviet-Occupied Poland, 1939–1941* (Leipzig, 2007), 252.

44. See notations in Krakowiec birth register entries, AGAD 1/300/0/-/504, for Ryfka Adler (b. 7 September 1889), Michuel Dawid Feld (b. 5 October 1887), Gittel Scher (b. 15 June 1888), and Golda Wasserstein (b. 7 November 1889). These registers performed the function of a population register; hence the notations. Whether these persons actually left Krakowiec is unclear: in the case of Gittel Scher, she appears to have remained in Krakowiec until the German invasion of the Soviet Union in June 1941, whereupon she fled *east*.

45. Antony Polonsky, *The Jews in Poland and Russia*, vol. III, *1914–2008* (Oxford, 2012), 398.

46. The numbers are disputed. NKVD records yield a total of at least 453,000 deportees and persons resettled from border areas. At least 20 per cent of these were Jews. See Polonsky, *The Jews in Poland and Russia*, vol. III,

381–4; Mark Edele, Sheila Fitzpatrick, and Atina Grossmann eds., *Shelter from the Holocaust: Rethinking Jewish Survival in the Soviet Union* (Detroit, 2017), 95–131; Z. S. Siemaszko, 'The Mass Deportations of the Polish Population to the USSR', in Sword ed., *The Soviet Takeover*, 224–5; Pinchuk, *Shtetl Jews*, 10–11, 38–9; Levin, *The Lesser of Two Evils*, 194–7; and Mick, *Lemberg, Lwów, L'viv*, 273.

47. Pinchuk, *Shtetl Jews*, 110–11.

CHAPTER 10

1. Feinddarstellung vom 22.6-27.6.1941, BA RH 24-49/159.
2. Recollection of John Partyka (Sr.), as reported by his son John Partyka (Jr.) in a communication to the author, 4 February 2009.
3. Morgenmeldung 26.6.41, BA RH 24-49/162.
4. Account given by Majus to Abraham Wasserstein after the war; interview with Frejde Guttman (*née* Nacht), Gan Yavne, 1995.
5. SS operational situation reports, 30 June and 1 July 1941, BA R58/214 leaves 39ff. Einsatzgruppe B was later designated Einsatzgruppe C.
6. Truman O. Anderson, 'Germans, Ukrainians and Jews: Ethnic Politics in *Heeresgebiet Süd*, June–December1941', *War in History*, 7: 3 (2000), 325–51.
7. Albert Speer, *Spandau: The Secret Diaries* (London, 1976), 49.
8. Regierungssitzung des Generalgouvernements, 11 March 1942, quoted in Amar, *The Paradox of Ukrainian Lviv*, 92.
9. Text of report, 16 July 1941 in Bert Hoppe and Hildrun Glass eds., *Die Verfolgung und Ermordung der europäischen Juden durch das nationalsozialistische Deutschland 1933–1945*, vol. 7 (Munich, 2011), 174–82.
10. Kai Struve, 'Rites of Violence? The Pogroms of Summer 1941', *Polin: Studies in Polish Jewry*, vol. 24 (2011), 260.
11. Vasyl Kuk, 'Derzhavotvorcha diial'nist' OUN u 1941 rotsi (akt vidnovlennia ukraïns'koï derzhavy vid 30 chervnia 1941 roku)', *Vizvol'nii shliakh*, 54: 7 (640) (July 2001), 43.
12. John-Paul Himka, 'The Lviv Pogrom of 1941: The Germans, Ukrainian Nationalists, and the Carnival Crowd', *Canadian Slavonic Papers*, 53: 2/4 (2011), 227; Kai Struve, *Deutsche Herrschaft*, 264–8.
13. John-Paul Himka, *Ukrainian Nationalists and the Holocaust: OUN and UPA's Participation in the Destruction of Ukrainian Jewry, 1941–1944* (Stuttgart, 2021), 222.

14. Ksenya Kiebuzinski and Alexander Motyl eds., *The Great West Ukrainian Prison Massacre of 1941* (Amsterdam, 2017).

15. Article by Joseph Hansen in *Vestfold Presse*, 10 January 1942, German translation in Katja Happe et al. eds., *Die Verfolgung und Ermordung der europäischen Juden durch das nationalsozialistische Deutschland 1933–1945*, vol. 5 (Munich, 2012), 120–1.

16. Krzystof Popiński, Aleksandr Kokurin, and Aleksandr Gurjanow, *Drogi Śmierci: Ewakuacja więzień sowieckich z Kresów Wschodnich II Rzeczpospolitej w czerwcu i lipcu 1941* (Warsaw, 1995), citing an Einsatzgruppe report dated 16 July 1941.

17. Mick, *Lemberg, Lwów, L'viv*, 292.

18. Nicholas Stargardt, *The German War: A Nation under Arms, 1939–1945* (London, 2015), 164.

19. Mick, *Lemberg, Lwów, L'viv*, 292.

20. Elke Fröhlich ed., *Die Tagebücher von Joseph Goebbels*, part I, vol. 9, 433 (Munich, 1998): entry for 8 July 1941.

21. Eleonora Narvselius and Igor Pietraszewski, 'Academics Executed on the Wulecki Hills in L'viv: From a Local Wartime Crime to a Translocal Memory Event', *Slavic Review*, 79: 1 (2020), 139–62.

22. Himka, 'The Lviv Pogrom', 227.

23. Gabriel N. Finder and Alexander V. Prusin, 'Collaboration in Eastern Galicia: The Ukrainian Police and the Holocaust', *East European Jewish Affairs*, 34: 2 (2004), 102; Karel C. Berkhoff and Marco Carynnyk, 'The Organization of Ukrainian Nationalists and Its Attitude toward Germans and Jews: Iaroslav Stets'ko's 1941 *Zhyttiepys*', *Harvard Ukrainian Studies*, 23: 3/4 (1999), 149–84.

24. Finder and Prusin, 'Collaboration in Eastern Galicia', 108.

25. John A. Armstrong, *Ukrainian Nationalism* (3rd ed., Englewood, Col., 1990), 57–8.

26. Struve, *Deutsche Herrschaft*, 289.

27. John-Paul Himka, 'Metropolitan Andrey Sheptytsky and the Holocaust', *Polin: Studies in Polish Jewry*, vol. 26 (2014), 337–59; Blet et al. eds., *Actes et Documents du Saint Siège*, vol. 3, part 2 (Vatican City, 1967), 625–9.

28. Gross, *Polish Society*, 184.

29. Karl von Roques, quoted in Anderson, 'Germans, Ukrainians and Jews,' 337.

30. Mark Mazower, *Hitler's Empire: Nazi Rule in Occupied Europe* (London, 2009), 4.

31. Gross, *Polish Society*, 59 ff.

32. Extract from speech in Yitzhak Arad, Israel Gutman and Abraham Margaliot eds., *Documents on the Holocaust* (8th ed., Lincoln, Neb., 1999), 246.

33. Philippe Sands, *East West Street: On the Origins of Genocide and Crimes Against Humanity* (London, 2016), 224–6.

34. The most authoritative account of the genocide of the Jews of Galicia is Dieter Pohl, *Nationalsozialistische Judenverfolgung in Ostgalizien 1941–1944: Organisation und Durchführung eines staatlichen Massenverbrechens* (Munich, 1997).

35. Stargardt, *The German War*, 291–2.

36. Omer Bartov, *Anatomy of a Genocide: The Life and Death of a Town Called Buczacz* (New York, 2018), 220.

37. David Biale et al., *Hasidism: A New History* (Princeton, 2018), 655.

38. Mendel Piekarz, *Sifrut ha-'edut al ha-shoah ke-makor histori: ve-shalosh hasidiyot be-artsot ha-shoah* (Jerusalem, 2003), 145–77; Moshe Prager, *Hatsalat ha-rabi mi-belz mi-ge ha-harigah be-Polin: mesupar mi-pi 'ede re'iyah* (Jerusalem, 2000); N. Shemen, 'Malkus Belz' in Naum Lindman and Marcos Koifman eds., *Galitsyaner yidn yoyvel-bukh* (Buenos Aires, 1966), 180–2; article by Menashe Unger in *Der Tog/Morgen-Zhurnal* (New York), 24 December 1961; Tamir Granot, 'The Rebbe of Belz and Rav Teichtal on the Holocaust': https://www.etzion.org.il/en/ philosophy/issues-jewish-thought/issues-mussar-and-faith/ rebbe-belz-and-rav-teichtal-holocaust

39. Orders signed by Lembergland Kreishauptmann Dr Werner Becker, DALO 24/1/392.

40. Landkommissar, Gródek, to Becker, 12 June 1942, DALO 24/1/123.

41. Dr Leib Landau (JSS, Lemberg) to Abteilung Devisen u. Aussenwirtschaft in der Regierung des Generalgouvernments, Krakau, 21 April 1942, YV microfilm 99.2693-4/1672-4 (original in DALO).

42. JSS, Cracow, to Gedaliah Wasserstein, Krakowiec, 20 May 1942, JDC, Jerusalem, microfilm box LII.

43. JSS, Cracow, to Delegatura, Krakowiec, 3 July 1942, JDC, Jerusalem, microfilm box LI, reel 5/21.

44. Circular dated 15 July 1942, DALO 24/1/261.

45. YV microfilm 99.2693-4 /1567-73; 2693-4 /1273-1282.

46. Landkommisssar, Gródek, to Becker, 12 June 1942, YV microfilm 99. 2693-4/903-4 (original in DALO).

47. List in DALO 24/1/252.

48. Testimony of Israel (Ignacy) Manber, 12 July 1946, Jewish Historical Institute archive, Warsaw.

49. Lev and Barahura eds., *Iavorivshchyna i Krakovechchyna*, 367; interview with Shalom Bierman, Berlin, 10 April 1996, USC Shoah Foundation; testimony of G. I. Pryishlyak, September 1944, GARF 7021/67/82; interview with Berl Lax, Lakewood, NJ, 3 May 1996.

50. Interviews with Oksana Ivanivna Strus, Krakovets, 10 March & 16 September 2019.

51. Interview with Elimelech Glick, Rishon le-Tsiyyon, 17 December 1994, reporting what he learned from a witness in 1945.

52. Herzl Gottlieb interview with Jane Grossberg, Melbourne, 16 October 1993.

53. Interviews with Mala Abend, Jerusalem, 14 February 1995, and Berl Lax, Lakewood, NJ, 3 May 1996.

54. Written record dated 13 January 1943, YV film 99.2693-4/1273-1282/11 (original in DALO).

55. Post-war testimony by Jonas Beer and Włodzimierz Hochberg, Jewish Historical Institute archive, Warsaw.

56. *British Medical Journal*, 14 January 1939.

57. Tatiana Brustin-Berenstein, 'Der protses fun farnikhtn di yidishe yishuvim oyfn shetakh fun azoy gerufenem "distrikt galitsyen"', *Bleter far geshikhte*, 6: 3 (1953), 80.

58. Interview with Shalom Bierman, Berlin, 10 April 1996, USC Shoah Foundation.

59. Postwar testimony by Jonas Beer and Włodimierz Hochberg, Jewish Historical Institute, Warsaw.

60. Emil Palej, 'Notatki z mego życia', *Quod Libet*, 79 (2012), 10–12.

61. AK report, December 1942, quoted in Mick, *Lemberg, Lwów, L'viv*, 317–18.

62. 'Verbliebene Wäsche nach den Juden in Jaworow' (signature unclear), 4 May 1943, DALO 24/2/9.

63. The classic account is Victor Klemperer, *The Language of the Third Reich: LTI, Lingua Tertii Imperii: a philologist's notebook* (originally published 1947; trans. Martin Brady, London, 2000).

64. Nuremberg Trials Document L18: copy in Harvard Law School Library.

65. Leon Scher interview, La Cañada, Calif., 16 October 1996, USC Shoah Foundation.

66. Roman Rakhmanny, *In Defense of the Ukrainian Cause* (North Quincy, Mass., 1979), 44.

67. Per Anders Rudling, 'Theory and Practice: Historical representation of the wartime accounts of the activities of the OUN-UPA (Organization of Ukrainian Nationalists–Ukrainian Insurgent Army)', *East European*

Jewish Affairs, 36: 2 (2006), 171–4. See also Per Anders Rudling, 'Rehearsal for Volhynia: Schutzmannschaft Battalion 201 and Hauptmann Roman Shukhevych in Occupied Belorussia, 1942', *East European Politics and Societies and Cultures*, 34: 1 (2020) 158–93.

68. Timothy Snyder, 'The Causes of Ukrainian-Polish Ethnic Cleansing 1943', *Past and Present*, 179 (2003), 202.

69. Rudling, 'Theory and Practice', 172.

70. Emil Palej, 'Notatki z mego życia', *Quod Libet*, 80 (2012), 13–15.

71. Philip Friedman, *Roads to Extinction: Essays on the Holocaust* (New York, 1980), 196.

72. Landkommissar, Sądowa-Wisznia, to Kreishauptmann Lemberg-Land, 3 March 1944, DALO 24/2/110.

73. Emil Palej, 'Notatki z mego życia', *Quod Libet*, 81 (2012), 10–12.

74. AK reports dated 29 April and 29 May 1944, in Serhij Bohunow et al. eds., *Polacy i ukraińcy pomiędzy dwoma systemami totalitarnymi 1942– 1945*, vol. 4 (Warsaw, 2005), 1061–7.

75. Pohl, *Nationalsozialistische Judenverfolgung in Ostgalizien*, 385.

76. Interview with Berl Lax, Lakewood, NJ, 3 May 1996. Unfortunately Lax did not name this survivor.

77. For this reconstruction of the last months in Krakowiec of Berl, Czarna, and Lotte, I am dependent on accounts given to my father by a cousin, Zelda Laub, and by Pinkas Majus. Neither was in Krakowiec in 1943–44; their reports were based on what they learned after the liberation. They must therefore be treated with appropriate caution. I also derived some corroborative information from interviews with Jewish survivors and elderly inhabitants of the town in and after 1993.

78. Friedman, *Roads to Extinction*, 200.

79. John-Paul Himka, 'Ukrainian Collaboration in the Extermination of the Jews During the Second World War: Sorting Out the Long-Term and Conjunctural Factors', *Studies in Contemporary Jewry*, 13 (1997), 180.

80. Interview with Berl Lax, Lakewood, NJ, 3 May 1996.

CHAPTER 11

1. Polish Ministry of Foreign Affairs to Ambassador in London, 1 June 1939, HIA Polish Embassy in London papers, box 60, folder 4.

2. See my *Britain and the Jews of Europe 1939–1945* (2nd ed., London, 1999), 25.

3. Postcard, family papers.

4. Alina Bothe, 'Forced over the Border: The Expulsion of Polish Jews from Germany in 1938/39', *Jahrbuch des Simon Dubnows Instituts*, 16 (Leipzig, 2019), 285–6.

5. Family papers.

6. Postcard dated 16 March 1940, family papers.

7. Quoted in Saul Friedländer, *Nazi Germany and the Jews*, vol. 1 (New York, 1997), 264.

8. Ibid.

9. Friedländer, *Nazi Germany and the Jews*, vol. 2 (New York, 2007), 192.

10. *Documents Diplomatiques Suisses 1848–1945*, vol. 13 (Berne, 1991), 692–731.

11. Prince Bernhard von Bülow's characterization, quoted in David I. Kertzer, *The Pope and Mussolini: The Secret History of Pius XI and the Rise of Fascism in Europe* (New York, 2014), 234.

12. Count Bonifacio Pignatti, quoted in Kertzer, *The Pope and Mussolini*, 300.

13. Kertzer, *The Pope and Mussolini*; Georges Passelecq and Bernard Suchecky, *L'encyclique cachée de Pie XI: Une occasion manquée de l'Église face à l'antisémitisme* (Paris, 1995); Anton Rauscher ed., *Wider den Rassismus: Entwurf einer nicht erschienen Enzyklika (1938): Texte aus dem Nachlass von Gustav Gundlach SJ* (Paderborn, 2001); Giovanni Sale, *Hitler, la Santa Sede e gli ebrei* (Milan, 2004); Michael R. Marrus, 'The Vatican on Racism and Antisemitism, 1938-39: A New Look at a Might-Have-Been', *Holocaust and Genocide Studies*, 11: 3 (1997), 378–95; Frank J. Coppa, 'The Hidden Encyclical of Pius XI Against Racism and Anti-Semitism Uncovered – Once Again!', *Catholic Historical Review*, 84: 1 (1998), 63–72.

14. According to *Lloyd's List* (my thanks to Stawell Heard of the Library of the National Maritime Museum, Greenwich).

15. Copy of requisition order supplied to the author by l'Ufficio Storico della Marina Militare, Rome.

16. Letter dated 3 February 1940, copy in Landesarchiv Berlin, WGA 2104/65. Postcards dated 20 September 1940, 2 January 1941 & 25 March 1941, family papers.

17. Family papers.

CHAPTER 12

1. See Marina Sorokina, 'People and Procedures: Towards a History of the Investigation of Nazi Crimes in the USSR', *Kritika: Explorations in Russian and Eurasian History*, 6: 4 (2005), 797–831.

2. Report dated 24 February 1945, GARF 7021/67/108.

3. Ibid., GARF 7021/67/37, 82, & 108.

4. Sorokina, 'People and Procedures', 830.

5. NKVD report to Lavrenti Beria, before 14 April 1945, GARF 9478/1/375.

6. Taras Shevchenko, 'Haidamaki' (1841; trans. John Weir, *Poetry of Taras Shevchenko* [North Charleston, S. C.], 2015), 65.

7. Jeffrey Burds, 'AGENTURA: Soviet Informants' Networks and the Ukrainian Underground in Galicia, 1944–48', *East European Politics and Societies*, 11: 1 (1997), 97.

8. Iurii Shapoval, 'The Ukrainian Years, 1894–1949', in William Taubman et al. eds., *Nikita Khrushchev* (New Haven, 2000), 38.

9. Mick, *Lemberg, Lwów, L'viv*, 334.

10. *Ukrainian Weekly*, 12 March 1951 & 29 December 1952.

11. Jeffrey Burds, 'Gender and Policing in Soviet West Ukraine, 1944–1948', *Cahiers du Monde russe*, 42: 2/3/4 (2001), 304.

12. See captured UPA report, July–December 1949, HDA SBU 13/376/73.

13. Extract from operational report of military operation in Krakovets district, 10 May 1949, HDA SBU 13/372/49.

14. Report by 'Zenon' on propaganda for April–June 1949 covering Yavoriv and Krakovets districts, HDA SBU 13/376/73.

15. Undated report by 'Zenon', 1950, HDA SBU 13/376/47.

16. Grzegorz Rossoliński-Liebe, *Stepan Bandera: The Life and Afterlife of a Ukrainian Nationalist: Fascism, Genocide, and Cult* (Stuttgart, 2014), 306.

17. Burds, 'AGENTURA', 121. See also captured UPA reports, 1949–50, HDA SBU 13/372/49 & 13/376/47.

18. Snyder, *The Reconstruction of Nations*, 188.

19. UPA report, 31 December 1950, HDA SBU 13/376/78.

20. UPA report, 1947, HDA SBU 13/376/78.

21. Strobe Talbott ed. and trans., *Khrushchev Remembers* (Boston, 1970), 235.

22. Zbigniew Wojnowski, 'Patriotism and the Soviet Empire: Ukraine Views the Socialist States of Eastern Europe, 1956–1985' (University College, London PhD diss., 2011), 81.

23. Roger W. Opdahl, 'Soviet Agriculture since 1953', *Political Science Quarterly*, 75: 1 (1960), 60; US Department of Agriculture Agricultural Marketing Service, *Milk Production on Farms and Statistics of Dairy Plant Products 1957* (Washington DC, 1958), 3.

24. Christoph Gunkel in *Der Spiegel*, 17 March 2010.

25. 'A German Diplomatist', *Times Literary Supplement*, 1 June 1951.

26. https://www.kas.de/en/web/geschichte-der-cdu/biogram-detail/-/content/richard-von-weizsaecker-2

27. Ian Buruma, *Guardian*, 13 March 2014.

28. Herbert, *Best*, 454 ff.

29. https://famous-trials.com/nuremberg/1929-franktestimony

30. Philippe Sands, *The Ratline: Love, Lies and Justice on the Trail of a Nazi Fugitive* (London, 2020).

31. Pohl, *Nationalsozialistische Judenverfolgung in Ostgalizien*, 385–96 & 411–23.

32. Their names and details are listed in GARF 7021/67/37 & 82.

33. Tanja Penter, 'Collaboration on Trial: New Source Material on Soviet Postwar Trials against Collaborators', *Slavic Review*, 64: 4 (2005), 787.

34. https://publications.gc.ca/Collection-R/LoPBdP/CIR/873-e.htm (web page no longer available).

35. *Now* magazine (Toronto), 25 July 2020.

36. Louis Newman, *A 'Chief Rabbi' of Rome becomes a Catholic: a study in fright and spite* (New York, 1945); Shalom Goldman, 'The apostasy of Rabbi Zolli', *Tablet* online magazine, 4 March 2016: https://www.tabletmag.com/sections/community/articles/the-apostasy-of-rabbi-zolli

37. F. D'A. G. Osborne to Anthony Eden, 21 December 1942, TNA FO 371/37540.

38. For details of Ledóchowski family history, including spirited accounts by Jan Ledóchowski of the lives of his father, Włodzimierz, and his Jesuit great-uncle, see the Ledóchowski family website: http://www.ledochowski.eu/index.html. In a book published after his death (*Pamiętnik pozostawiony w Ankarze*, Warsaw, 1990) the younger Włodzimierz expressed some dissatisfaction concerning his financial relations with the Laub family. There were also other disagreements: see Laub, *My Heritage*, 48–9. The friendship nevertheless endured.

39. Information from Jan Ledóchowski, Eli Silberman, and Sonia Levensolt.

40. Interview with Berl Lax, Lakewood, NJ, 3 May 1996.

41. Interviews with Mala Gottlieb, Jerusalem, 14 February 1995, Eli Silberman, Brooklyn, 24 September 1996, and Berl Lax, Lakewood, NJ, 3 May 1996.

42. Interview with Elimelech Glick, Rishon le-Tsiyyon, 17 December 1994; interview with Sala Tenenbojm, Netanya, 2 April 1995.

43. Interview with Eli Silberman, Brooklyn, NY, 24 September 1996.

44. Committee on Overhead Reconnaissance reports, 18-20 April and 23-26 June 1962, CIA-RDP78B04560A000200010007-9, page 14, https://www.cia.gov/readingroom/document/cia-rdp78b04560a000200010007-9; and CIA-RDP78B04560A000200010050-1, page 5, https://www.cia.gov/readingroom/document/cia-rdp78b04560a000200010050-1.

45. Report dated 24 March 1973, CIA-RDP78T04752A000700010008-2, page 65, https://www.cia.gov/readingroom/document/cia-rdp78t04752 a000700010008-2; and report dated 11 August 1973, CIA-RDP78T 04752A000900010007-1, page 107, https://www.cia.gov/readingroom/ document/cia-rdp78t04752a000900010007-1.

46. Report to Soviet Politburo by K. Chernenko, Y. Andropov, D. Ustinov et al., 16 April 1981, *Cold War International History Project Bulletin*, 5 (1995), 130–1.

47. CIA Intelligence Information Report, 'Warsaw Pact Fronts Within the Western Theater of Military Operations', 'late 1981', page 5, https:// www.cia.gov/readingroom/document/5166d4f999326091c6a60966.

48. *Moscow News*, 12 April 1992.

CHAPTER 13

1. Copy in archive of Entschädigungsamt, Berlin, 79847.

2. W. G. Hoskins, *Essays in Leicestershire History* (Liverpool, 1950), 67–107.

3. See text of his speech at the Ukrainian Ministry of Foreign Affairs, 3 November 2008: http://khpg.org/en/1225920831. Fishbein, who was dubbed a 'Ukrainian Messiah' and 'blessed by God', was awarded the Order of Prince Yaroslav the Wise (5th class). For an adulatory remembrance of Fishbein by an Israeli journalist, see https://ukrainian-jewishencounter.org/en/intertwined-worlds-in-memory-of-a-poet/. See also Yohanan Petrovsky-Shtern, *Anti-Imperial Choice: The Making of the Ukrainian Jew* (New Haven, 2005), chapter 5.

4. https://www.wykop.pl/link/3823441/banderowiec-umarl-w-trakcie-przemowienia-gloryfikujacego/strona/34/.

5. For example, Bohdan Kravtsiv, *Liudyna i voiak: v druhu rychnitsiu smerty Sl. Romana Shukhevycha-Chuprynky* (New York, 1952); and Stepan Shakh and Hryhoriï Vas'kovych, *Heneral Roman Shukhevych (dvi dopovidi)* (Munich, 1966).

6. Per Anders Rudling, 'The Cult of Roman Shukhevych in Ukraine: Myth Making with Complications', *Fascism*, 5: 1 (2016), 26–65.

7. Matthew R. Ostapchuk, '"Glory to Ukraine! Glory to the heroes!" The Portrayal of the Organization of Ukrainian Nationalists (OUN) in the Museums of Lviv', MA thesis, University of Alberta, 2015, 49.

8. 'Neskornyy' (The Undefeated), dir. Oles Yanchuk.

9. *Boston Globe*, 15 August 1993.

10. N. Bar-Lev ed., *Matsevet zikaron li-kehilat yavorov ve-ha-sevivah* (Haifa, 1979).

11. Ecclesiasticus (Wisdom of Ben Sira) 44: 9.

12. Walter Benjamin, *Illuminations* (ed. Hannah Arendt, trans. Harry Zohn, London, 1973), 259–60.

Index

Abend, Mala 201
Abwehr 121, 151, 153
Adass Jisroel Realgymnasium
    105–6, 175, 178, 197–8
Adenauer, Konrad 196
Agnon (Czaczkes), Shmuel Yosef
    118
Akhva 119
Alexandrowicz, Wilhelm 9
American Jewish Joint Distribution
    Committee 9, 89
anti-Semitism 23, 74–5, 112, 124,
    179, 183
Arendt, Hannah 86
Argentina 186
Armia Krajowa, (AK, Polish Home
    Army) 154, 162–3, 167
Auffenberg, Moritz von 81, 83
Augustus II, King 24
Auschwitz 157, 197, 203
Ausgleich (1867) 59
Australia 201
Austria 24, 28–9, 112, 155, 180
Austria-Hungary 59, 79–91

Babel, Isaac 96–7
Bach-Zelewski, Erich von dem
    166–7
Bad Reichenhall 201

Bandera, Stepan 151, 153, 167, 215
Bar, Confederation of 28
Barash, Asher 76–7
Bartmański, Oswald 72
Basel 74
Beck, Józef 10
Belcredi, Richard 73
Belz 28, 47, 86, 157
Bełżec 156
Benjamin, Walter 218
Bentele, Ferdinand 133
Bereza Kartuska 123
Berg (Levensolt), Sonia 136, 201
Berger, Henryk 114, 118, 143, 150,
    201
Berlin 1–6, 104, 110, 155, 208
Berlin Document Center 200
Berliner Tageblatt 109
Best, Werner 4–6, 193–5
Betar 118
Biała Podlaska 146
Bilczewski, Józef 91–2
Bismarck, Otto von 2
Bnei Akiva 118
Bochnia 157
Bolesław 'the Pious', Duke 20
Bolsheviks 95–8
Borysław-Drohobycz region 139
Boy-Żeleński, Tadeusz 153

Brafman, Jakob 75
'Bread Peace' (1918) 90
Breda 198
Brest, Synod of 17, 192
Brest-Litovsk 90
Britain 203
British Guiana 176
Brody 62, 178
Brown, Craig xii
Brusilov, Aleksei 89
Buczacz 118
Buczyński, Commandant 98
Budapest 64, 157, 220
Budyonny, Semyon Mikhailovich
    96–7
Bund 9, 145

Cambon, Jules 95
Canada 196–7
Carpathian mountains 131
Catherine II, Empress 28–9
Central Intelligence Agency (CIA)
    203–4
Central Office for the Investigation
    of National Socialist Crimes
    197, 200
Cetner, Anna 31–2, 35–6, 45, 52,
    57, 71, 133
Cetner, Ignacy 27–36, 38–9, 57,
    133, 218
Cetner, Józef 24
Cetner, Ludwika 31
Chaimowicz, Oszor 44
Charles XII, King 23–4
Charles-Eugène de Lorraine 35, 57
Cholm (Chelm) 90
Choma, Grzegorz 64
Chruszcz, Leopold 142
Churchill, Winston 83, 188
Chwila 115

Communism 9
Communist Party of Eastern
    Galicia 98
Conrad von Hötzendorf, Franz
    80–83, 103
Coolidge, A. C. 95
Cossacks 22–4, 83–4, 88
Council of Ambassadors 98
Cracow 32, 201
Curzon line 95–7, 188
Czarniecki, Stefan 23
Czechoslovakia 220

Dąbrowski march 60
Dachau 4
Danysh, Bogdan 124
Darmstadt 195
Defenders of the Homeland 121–2
Denmark 194
Deschênes, Jules 197
Dmowski, Roman 74, 79
Döblin, Alfred 99
Dora-Mittelbau concentration
    camp 199
Douglas, Robert 23
Draczakiewicz, Daniel 37
Dreßen, Wilhelm 200

Eden, Anthony 188
Edinburgh 198
Eichmann, Adolf 86
Einsatzgruppen 134–5, 139, 150–1,
    153
Eliot, George (Mary Ann Evans) x
Eliyahu ben Shlomo Zalman (Gaon
    of Vilna) 47

First World War 79–91
Fishbein, Moisei 214, 277 n. 3
Forwerts 115

France 194
Franco, Francisco 180
Frank, Anne 169
Frank, Brigitte 155
Frank, Hans 150–1, 155, 195
Frank, Jacob 46–7
Frankfurt am Main 104
Frankfurter Zeitung 109
Franko, Ivan 15, 52, 74
Franz Joseph, Emperor 59,
  61–3, 83
Fraser, Lady Antonia 117
Frederick II, King 28
Fredro, Andrzej Maksymilian 21
Fredro (Krakowiecki), Franciszek 16
Fredro (Krakowiecki),
  Stanisław 18

Galicia
  as *Kriegsschauplatz* 60–61
  demography 63–4
  Diet 69, 72, 74
  education in 50–51
  eastern 39, 47, 74, 79–80, 85,
    90–98, 120–22, 131, 151, 154,
    164, 167, 184, 189–92
  elections 59, 68–9
  emigration 59, 64
  German occupation (1941–44)
    149–71
  in First World War 79–91
  Jews of 20, 22–5, 28–9, 43–6, 58,
    69, 84–5, 156, 163–4
  Josephine reforms 43–5
  peasantry 28–9
  Polish nationalism in 67
  poverty 28–9, 59, 64
  refugees (First World War) 82, 89
  revolt (1846) 58
  revolution (1848) 58

Soviet occupation (1920) 97,
  (1939–41) 139ff.
Toleranzpatent (1782) 44
Ukrainian nationalism in 67,
  74, 98
Galician Soviet Socialist Republic
  (1920) 96–7
galitsyaner 86
'Galizien', Waffen-SS Division 154,
  196–7, 216
Gawrońska, 'worthy widow' 36–7
Gazeta Lwowska 63
Gazeta Narodowa 73–4
Germany
  attack on USSR (1941) 149ff.,
    186
  Deutsche Demokratische Partei
    109
  Federal Republic 194–5, 197
  Free Democrat Party 194
  German Democratic Republic
    203
  Jews in 1–5, 8, 11–12, 109, 110
  Polenaktion (1938) 1, 6–8 (1939)
    177
  Weimar 3, 107
Gerstler, Elias 64
Gioventù Universitaria Fascista 179
Glick, Elimelech 201–2
Gnojnica 16, 20, 72, 81, 86, 133
Goebbels, Joseph 152–3
Gołąb 23
Gold, Steven 117
Gołuchowski, Agenor 51
Gonta, Ivan 189–90
Goremykin, Ivan 84
Göring, Hermann 11–12
Gorlice 86
Gottesmann, Jacob 158
Gottlieb, Herzl 201

Gracko, Józef 68
Great Northern War 23–4
Greek Catholics 17, 67, 69, 142–3, 192
Grushetski, Ivan 192
Grynszpan (forename unknown) 213
Grynszpan, Herschel 10
Guibaut, Pierre-Denis 34

Habonim 109
Hahn, Ludwig 134
Haifa 186
Haller, Józef 93
Halwaz, Jan 37
Hashomer Hatsair 110, 118
Hasidim 46–50
haskalah 47, 49
Hausner, Gideon 86
Hebrew language 102, 106, 118
Hebrew University of Jerusalem, The 203
Heidelberg 208
Heidereutergasse Synagogue 106–7
Herrmann, Günther 150
Hertzog, J. B. M. 112
Herzl, Theodor 74
Hessen-Homburg, Ludwig von 24
Heydrich, Reinhard 6, 11, 151
Himka, John-Paul 170
Himmler, Heinrich 154–5
Hirsch, Baron Maurice de 101–2
Hitler, Adolf 4, 11, 28, 109, 150, 152–3, 177, 195
Hitler-Stalin pact (1939) 137, 139
Horodenko 83
Hoskins, W. G. 214
Hubicki, Alfred von 132–4
Hudal, Alois 195
Hungary 28, 60, 85–6, 157, 202–3, 220

Innitzer, Theodor 4
International Red Cross 158, 186
Israel 201–3
Istanbul 184–6
Italy 177–84

Jahr, Saul 135
'Jan of Kijany' 19
Janowska labour camp 162
Jarosław 95, 131
Jaworów (Yavoriv) 22, 24, 51, 63, 72–3, 86–8, 92–3
and Curzon line 95
in Second World War 138, 149, 152, 168
Jews in 135, 160–65
peasant protests 120
post-Communist 210
Russian missile attack (2022) 219
Jędrziowska, Mrs 37
Jerusalem 86, 118, 203
Jesuit order 181–2
Jewish Agency 185
Johannesburg 112, 199
John Casimir, King 23
John Paul II, Pope 181
Joseph II, Emperor 28–30, 73
Joseph Ferdinand, Grand Duke of Tuscany 81, 89
Jüdische Rundschau 109–10
Jüdische Soziale Selbsthilfe (JSS) 158–9

Kabbalah 49, 255 n. 18
Kafka, Franz 1, 48, 170
Kagan, Berl 49–50
Kahane, Debora 65
Kamchatka 85
Kampel (Laub), Hela 52
Kampel, Lazar 114, 211

Karaczay regiment 38
Karpiński, Franciszek 34
Kartashov, M. 208
Katz, Jacob 86
Katzmann, Friedrich 149, 163–4, 195
Kauffman, Angelica 36
Kaunas 185
Kazimierz III, King 20
Keith, James 24
Khmelnytsky, 'Bogdan' 22
Khrushchev, Nikita 137–8, 140, 149, 190, 193
Kiev 90
Kindertransport 176
Kirponos, Mikhail Petrovich 149
Kleist, Ewald von 131
Klüger, Meir 110, 160
Klüger, Meshulam 116
Komsomol 145
Kowalyk, Iwan 102
Krakowiec (Krakovets): 12–3
   agreement with Ignacy Cetner (1782) 29–30
   AK unit in 167–8
   and Curzon line 95
   author's visits 209ff.
   castle 18, 30
   cholera 52–3, 85
   collectivization of agriculture 141, 192–3
   courts 36–8, 44, 121
   effects of Russian invasion (2022) 219
   egg trade 116–18
   elections 113, 141
   epidemics 85, 102, 156
   fires 24, 63, 88, 102, 114–16
   flora and fauna 13–15
   future prospects 217–18, 221

garden 32–3
Greek Catholic church 121, 204, 213
Greek Catholics 17, 30, 210
Hasidism in 49
Hebrew school 118
hospital 52, 71–3, 143
in First World War 79–83, 86–90
in Khmelnitsky revolt 22–3
in memory ix – xiii
in German-Polish war (1939) 131–9
isolation of 66
Jews of 13, 17, 19, 41–5, 49–53, 62, 64, 69–73, 88–9, 113–15, 144–5, 158ff., 187–8
Judenrat 158
joke 63
lake 13, 132
Magdeburg privileges 16
markets and marketplace 16, 116, 136, 144, 204, 211, 215–16, 218
memorial to Jews of 216–17
mill 114, 132, 211
Matrikelbücher 44, 159
name xxi, 16
palace/manor house 31–2, 57, 60, 62–3, 85, 97, 132–3, 213
peasant protest 120
Polish-Ukrainian conflict in 68, 92–3, 189–91
population xi, 17, 113, 159
pre-historic 13
prosperity in Cetner period 36
Prosvita society 67–8, 121, 123
public health 51–2, 72
Roman Catholic church 18, 22, 24, 34–5, 42–3, 133, 204, 211
Roman Catholics 17

Krakowiec – *cont'd.*
  school 22, 36, 50–51, 101–2, 113,
    125–6, 214
  socio-economic conditions 102,
    113–14, 126, 144–5
  synagogue 65, 114, 201, 204,
    211, 213, 218
  under German occupation
    (1941–44) 149–71
  under Soviet rule (1939–41)
    139ff., 144–5; (1944–91)
    187ff., 203–4
  volunteers from in UPA 167
  yizkorbukh 216
  Zionism in 118–19
Krakovitser Kranken Untershtitsing
  Verein 65
Krasicki, Ignacy 27, 29, 31, 34–5
Krasnaya Zvezda (Red Star) 142
Krawiec, Fedek 102
Krilyk (Vasylkiv), Iosip 98, 143
Kristallnacht (1938) 11
Kropevnytsky, Miroslav 214–15
Krug, Chaje 64
Krug, Moses 65
Krug, Rosa 64
Krug, Tomas 64
Krug, Willy 64
Krüger, Friedrich Wilhelm 155
Kubijovyc, Volodymyr 150–1
Kuk, Vasyl 151, 191
Kuropatnicki, Ewaryst Andrzej
  32–4
Kvas, Vasyl 93

Łabno, Adolf 114, 168
Labruzzi, Pietro 35–6
Łahodowski, Andrzej 21–3
Lakewood, N. J. 170
Lambrani, Maciej 37

Langer, František 85
Langer, Jiří 48
Lasch, Karl 155
Laub, Aron 45
Laub, Chaim-Yitzhak 89, 115, 128
Laub, Chana-Gittel 89–90, 116
Laub, Esther 208
Laub, Regina 136, 140, 208
Laub, Samuel (Beinish) 107, 109,
  136, 208
Lax, Berl 170–71
Lazarus, Maurycy 73
League of Nations 96, 111, 122, 125
Lebed, Mykola 167
Ledóchowski, Ignacy (early 19th
  century) 181
Ledóchowski, Ignacy (early 20th
  century) 96, 114, 138,
  183, 199
Ledóchowska, Julia (Ursula) 181
Ledóchowska, Maria Teresa 181
Ledóchowski, Mieczysław 181
Ledóchowska, Paulina 97, 138–9,
  183, 199
Ledóchowski, Włodzimierz (Jesuit)
  181–4, 198–9
Ledóchowski, Włodzimierz (Polish
  resister) 199
Lemberger Togblat 115
Lemkos 192
Lipnica 138
Lisiewicz, Thomas Antoni 133
List, Wilhelm 131, 134
Livadia 57
Lloyd George, David 94–5
Loosdorf 181
Łosie 16
Luba, Augustin 44
Lubienie 191–2
Łubieński, Alfred 61–2

Łubieńska, Jadwiga 60, 97, 114, 138, 183, 199–200, 211
Łubieński, Kazimierz 60
Lubomirski, Adam 57–9, 71
Lubomirski, Hieronym 60
Lunio, Eugen 200
Lwów (Lviv): 13, 17
  and Curzon line 95, 188–9
  Brygidki prison 142
  Cetnerówka park 34
  Communists in 98
  exchange of population with Poland 192
  in First World War 80, 84, 88, 91
  in Second World War 131ff., 144ff., 196
  Jewish hospital 73
  name xxi
  pogroms (1914) 84; (1918) 91–2; (1941) 152–3
  post-Communist 209
  revolution (1848) 58
  riots (1908) 69
  royal tribunal 34
  Soviet arrests (1945) 196
  Ukrainian nationalism in 66, 92, 99, 124, 150
  Zionist Organization in 119
Lynn, Jonathan 117

Maczek, Stanisław 131–4, 198
Majus, Naftali 114, 158
Majus, Pinkas ix, 136, 147, 150
Manchester Guardian 126
Maria Theresa, Empress 28–30, 43
Marie-Antoinette, Queen 36
Marie-Louise, Queen 23
Mariupol 221
Marwell, David 200

Marx, Karl 186
Meir Julius 49
Melnyk, Andrii 151
Mendele Moykher Sforim (S. Y. Abramovich) 50
Mendelssohn, Moses 43
Merlini, Domenico 34
Mersin 186
Metella, Seweryn 67
Metternich, Klemens von 46
MGB 190
Mick, Christoph 152
Minkiewicz, Henryk 93
misnagdim
Młyny 132, 152
Modena regiment 38
Morańce 122
Moravia 46, 82, 85, 103
Mortara, Edgardo 71
Mościska 66, 95
Moszczany 70
Munkács 86
Mussolini, Benito 177, 179, 184

Nacht, Shmuel 202
Nachtigall battalion 153, 166, 196
Namier, Lewis x – xi, 94, 96–7, 194
Netherlands, The 103, 198
Neue Freie Presse 73–4
New York 64–5, 126
New York Times 86–7
Niemirów 81
Nicholas II, Emperor 83
Nikolsburg (Mikulov) 82, 103
NKVD 98, 137, 142–3, 152, 189–90, 192, 202
Nuremberg laws (1935) 110
Nuremberg trials 193–6
Nusskern, Reisel 64

Oberländer, Theodor 151, 153, 196
Ohringer, Sala 200–201
Olanek, Maria Ivanivna 212
Olanek, Mikola Mikhailovich
    169–71, 212
Onufrik, Ivan 143
Orbán, Viktor 220
Organization of Ukrainian
    Nationalists (OUN) 121–4,
    151–4, 166
Ostjuden 2–3, 26–7, 104, 106–7,
    133, 178
Ostrogski, Aleksander 18
Ostrogska, Anna 18
Ostrogski, Konstantyn 18
Oświęcim (see also Auschwitz) 82

'Pact of Steel' (1939) 177
Paderewski, Ignacy 92, 94
Palestine 64, 111, 119, 157, 176,
    179, 185–6
Palmerston, Lord 93–4
Paris 10, 124, 180
Passover (1898) 101, (1938) 112,
    (1943) 161
Paul VI, Pope 181
Peace Conference (1919) 93–6
Peter 'the Great', Emperor 24
Petliura, Symon 124–5
Pfefferkorn, Wolf 202
Pieracki, Bronisław 123
Pilkowicz, Jan 16
Piłsudski, Józef 79, 98, 125
Pius XI, Pope 183
Pius XII, Pope 198
Plattdeutsch 103–4
Plehve, Pavel Wenzel von 81
Pohl, Dieter 196–7
Pol, Wincenty 38–9
Poland:

anti-Semitism in 125, 154
border police 7
citizenship law (1938) 4–6
Council of Four Lands 41–2
General Gouvernement 150, 155
government in exile 167, 188
in Second World War 131ff.
Jews in 9–10, 20, 22, 41–2, 46,
    110, 127
landowners' attitudes 119–20
peasants 120
Minorities Treaty (1919) 93, 125
National Democrat party
    ('Endeks') 74, 79
partitions 24, 28, 38
population exchange with
    Ukraine (1945–7) 191–2
post-1945 border with USSR
    188–9
'propination' laws 20
Sejm 28, 124
Polish language 107, 115, 182
Polish-Lithuanian Commonwealth
    16–17, 39
Poltava 24
Pompius, Nochim Majer 143, 187
Pona, Dmitri 63
Pona, Rózia 62–3
Poniatowski, Stanisław August,
    King 28, 34, 42
Porudenko 132, 210, 217
Potocki, Andrzej 69
Potocki Kajetan 35
Potocki, Leon 57, 71
Potsdam Conference (1945) 188
Prague 48
prenumerantn 49–50, 255 n.18
Presser, Jacques xii
Protocols of the Elders of Zion 75
Prüller, Wilhelm 137

Prussia 2, 24, 59
Przedborze 16
Przemyślany 157
Przytyk 125
Przemyśl 17, 20, 70–71
  and Curzon line 95
  anti-Jewish riots (1898) 74;
    (1918) 92
  fortress 61, 80
  in First World War 83–4, 86
  in Second World War 131, 134,
    138–9, 149
  Jews of 41, 84, 134
  purchased by Ignacy Cetner 30
Przyborz, Marcin 36–7
Pstrokoński, Maciej 18–19

Radwański, Feliks 35
Radymno 101
Raków 18
Ransome, Arthur 96
Rappoport, Shloyme Zanvel
    (S. Ansky) 87–8
Rath, Ernst vom 10–11
Rathenau, Walther 3
Reni (painter) 181
Reuter, Fritz 104
Ricaud de Tirregaille, Pierre 32
Riga, Treaty of (1921) 97–8
Rilke, Rainer Maria 175
Ringelblum, Emanuel 9
Robert College, Istanbul 184–5
Rockefeller Foundation 85
Rohatyn 23
Rokeach, Aharon
    (fourth Belzer rebbe) 157
Rokeach, Issachar Dov (third Belzer
    rebbe) 48, 86
Rokeach, Shalom
    (first Belzer rebbe) 47

Rome 35–6, 177–84, 195, 198
Roosevelt, Franklin Delano 57, 188
Roth, Joseph 62, 75–6, 171
Ruda Krakowiecka 72, 202
Rudky 80
Rumania 137
Rundstedt, Gerd von 131, 149
Russia (see also Union of Soviet
    Socialist Republics) 24, 60, 90,
    94, 96–7, 217, 219–20
Ruthenians (see also Ukrainians) 17,
    21–3, 60, 66–9, 102

Sabbatai Tsvi 46
Sacher-Masoch, Leopold von 49
Safed 118
St Christopher's School 176
San, River 13, 23, 61, 81, 83, 131–2,
    138–9, 149, 189
Sandhaus, Chaim 158
Sands, Philippe 195
Sanguszko, Józef 35
Sapieha, Jan 27
Sapieha, Kazimierz Nestor 35
Scher, Leon 164–5, 167, 201
Schlesinger, Nachman 178, 197
Schleswig-Holstein question 93–4
Schratt, Katharina 62
Schröger (Szreger), Efraim 34
Schutzstaffel (SS) 151–2, 156,
    159–60, 163–4, 166–7, 195,
    200
Schwarzbard, Sholem 124–5
Semen, Matviev ('Chomyn') 191
serfdom 21, 28–30
Shakhinsky, Andri 93
'Shalom Aleichem' (Shalom
    Rabinovitz) 66
Sheptytsky (Szeptycki), Andrey 69,
    142–3, 154, 183, 192

Shevchenko, Taras 66,
    189–90, 209
Shevchenko Scientific Society 66, 68
Shukhevych (Berezynska), Natalya
    214–15
Shukhevych, Osip 68–9, 80, 123
Shukhevych, Roman 68, 122–3, 153,
    166–7, 191, 212, 214–18, 220
Shukhevych, Stepan 123
Shukhevych, Volodymyr 122
Shukhevych, Yevhenia 68
Shukhevych, Yuriy 215
Sich Riflemen 92, 123
Sichynskyi, Myroslav 69
Sienkiewicz, Henryk 22
Silberman, Israel 126–7
Silberman, Wolf 201
Slepoi, Iosif 192
Słowo Polskie 68
Snyder, Timothy 192
Sobieski, Jan 22–3
Sobiński, Stanisław 123
Socinians 18
Sohor, Lev 152
Sonnenthal (flautist) 68
South Africa 111–12, 128, 145, 186,
    207–8
Spielberg, Steven 201
Stalin, Joseph 140–2, 146–7, 187–8
Stalingrad 169
Stanisławów 156
Stargardt, Nicholas 156
Starzava 82
Stetsko, Yaroslav 153
Strijdom, J. G. 112, 207
Stryjkowski, Julian (Pesach Stark)
    83–4
Stülpnagel, Carl Heinrich von 149
Sub-Carpathian Ruthenia 86, 132
Sweden 23, 194

Świdnica 122
Swift, Jonathan 140, 193
Switzerland 180
Syria 180
Szamyło, Michał 37
Szczepek, Jan 67
Szeptycki, Jan Kanty 72–3
Szeptycki, Stanisław 72–3
Szkło stream 17, 81
Szowdrak, Fedor 37

Tangier 179–80
Tarnawa 16
Tarnopol 96
Tarnów 9, 101
Tascher, Joachim François 57
Tashkent 201
Tatars 18, 22–3
Tehran Conference (1943) 188
Thalerhof 80
Tolstoy, Leo xii
Toronto 197
Turkey 22–3, 179–81, 184–6
Tworzydło, Roman 167–8

Ukraine 191–2, 209, 215–16,
    219–21
Ukrainian militias 92–3, 135,
    151–4, 166, 189
Ukrainian language 124
Ukrainian Central Committee 151
Ukrainian Communist Party 190
Ukrainian Insurgent Army
    (UPA) 166–8, 189–92, 215–17
Ukrainian National Democratic
    Alliance (UNDO) 121
Ukrainian National Republic 124
Ukrainian Rada (Council) 90
Ukrainian Soviet Socialist Republic
    140

Ukrainians (*see also* Ruthenians)
120–21
Uniates: *see* Greek Catholics
Union of Soviet Socialist Republics
9, 22, 96–7, 146–7, 149ff.,
187–8, 196
United Nations War Crimes
Commission 195
United States of America 64,
110–11, 127–8, 158, 196
Unowsky, Daniel 74

Vatican 195, 198
Vengerak, Tadaj ('Zahirny') 191
Vienna 64, 73, 82, 85, 103, 137
Vigée-Le Brun, Elisabeth-Louise 36
Vilna 185
Visual History Archive 201
Volhynia 166
Voroshilov, Kliment Efremovich
96–7
Vushko, Peter 215

Wächter, Otto Gustav von 155–6,
195
Walton, Izaak 14
War of the Polish Succession 24
Wasserstein, Abraham (Addi) ix,
xii – xiii, 207–8
Berlin properties 203
birth and childhood 104–9
deportation to Zbąszyń 1–2, 6–9,
12, 175, 182
in Britain 203
in Istanbul 184–6
in Palestine 186, 202
in Rome 177–84, 198
last days in Berlin 129,
175–7
return to Germany 208

return to Israel 203
visits to Krakowiec 113–14,
116–17
Wasserstein (Stein), Abraham 65
Wasserstein, Alte Perl 64
Wasserstein, Bernhard (Berl) xii
birth and childhood 101–3
confirmation of death 208
deportation to Zbąszyń
(1938–9) 1–3, 6–7, 9,
12, 127–8
in Berlin 104–12, 128
in Krakowiec (1939–44) 136–7,
145, 147–8, 169–70, 178,
184–6
marriage 103
possible burial place 213
Wasserstein, Charlotte (Lotte) 2, 12,
104, 128, 131, 136, 148,
169–70, 208
Wasserstein (Laub), Czarna 2, 12,
103–8, 111–12, 128, 131, 136,
148, 169–70, 208
Wasserstein, Gedaliah 119, 158
Wasserstein, Hannah 101
Wasserstein, Jacob 101, 115–16,
128, 187, 211–12
Wasserstein (Ecker), Margaret
(Maca) ix, 202–3
Wasserstein, Noe 102–3
Wassner, Shloime 202
Watson, Alexander 91
Weichert, Michael 158
Weizmann, Chaim 118
Weizsäcker, Ernst von 10,
193–5
Weizsäcker, Richard 194
Weltsch, Robert 109–10
West Ukrainian People's Republic 91
Wielkie Oczy 63, 132, 158–9, 168

Wilde, Oscar 216
Wilson, Woodrow 92, 95
Windisch-Graetz, Ludwig zu 62
Witte, Sergei 84
Władisław II Jagiełło, King 16
Wolf (German police officer) 159,
    162, 169, 200
Wolff, Larry, 69
Wólka Rosnowska 97, 138, 183
Wołoch, Mikołaj and Stefan
    (Steczko) 16
Wurm, Mathilde 3
Wybicki, Józef 60

Yad Vashem 215
Yalta Conference (1945) 57, 188
Yanushkevich, Nikolai 87
Yedidya ('poor old Jew') 199
Yiddish 102, 107, 115, 147, 213
Yushchenko, Viktor 215

Zakopane 153
Zbąszyń 6–10, 12, 126–7, 176
Zionism 9, 74, 145, 185–6
Zionist Organization 111,
    118–19, 176
Zolli (Zoller), Israel 178, 198